Politics, Media, and Modern Democracy

Politics, Media, and Modern Democracy

An International Study of Innovations in Electoral Campaigning and Their Consequences

Edited by David L. Swanson and Paolo Mancini

Praeger Series in Political Communication

Westport, Connecticut
London

Library of Congress Cataloging-in-Publication Data

Politics, media, and modern democracy : an international study of
   innovations in electoral campaigning and their consequences / edited
   by David L. Swanson and Paolo Mancini.
      p. cm. — (Praeger series in political communication, ISSN 1062–5623)
   Includes bibliographical references and index.
   ISBN 0–275–95182–0 (alk. paper). — ISBN 0–275–95183–9 (pbk. :
alk. paper)
   1. Campaign management. 2. Electioneering. 3. Comparative
government. I. Swanson, David L. II. Mancini, Paolo.
III. Series.
JF2112.C3C55   1996
324.7—dc20   95–43773

British Library Cataloguing in Publication Data is available.

Library of Congress Catalog Card Number: 95–43773
ISBN: 0–275–95182–0
      0–275–95183–9 (pbk.)

First published in 1996

Praeger Publishers, 88 Post Road West, Westport, CT 06881
An imprint of Greenwood Publishing Group, Inc.

Printed in the United States of America

The paper used in this book complies with the
Permanent Paper Standard issued by the National
Information Standards Organization (Z39.48–1984).

10   9   8   7   6   5   4   3   2   1

[] • [] • [] • [] • []

Contents

[] • [] • [] • [] • []

Tables

[] • [] • [] • [] • []

Series Foreword

Those of us from the discipline of communication studies have long believed that communication is more important than all other fields of inquiry. In several other forums, I have argued that the essence of politics is "talk" or human interaction.[1] Such interaction may be formal or informal, verbal or nonverbal, public or private, but it is always persuasive, forcing us consciously or subconsciously to interpret, to evaluate, and to act. Communication is the vehicle for human action.

From this perspective, it is not surprising that Aristotle recognized the natural kinship of politics and communication in his writings *Politics* and *Rhetoric*. In the former, he establishes that humans are "political beings [who] alone of the animals [are] furnished with the faculty of language."[2] And in the latter, he begins his systematic analysis of discourse by proclaiming that "rhetorical study, in its strict sense, is concerned with the modes of persuasion."[3] Thus, it was recognized over 2,300 years ago that politics and communication go hand in hand because they are essential parts of human nature.

Back in 1981, Dan Nimmo and Keith Sanders proclaimed that political communication was an emerging field.[4] Although its origin, as noted, dates back centuries, a "self-consciously cross-disciplinary" focus began in the late 1950s. Thousands of books and articles later, colleges and universities offer a variety of graduate and undergraduate coursework in the area in such diverse departments as communication, mass communication, journalism, political science, and sociology.[5] In Nimmo and Sanders' early assessment, the "key areas of inquiry" included rhetorical analysis, propaganda analysis, attitude change studies, voting studies, government and the news media, functional and systems analyses, technological changes, media technologies, campaign techniques, and research techniques.[6] In a survey of the state of the field in 1983, the same authors and Lynda Kaid found additional, more specific areas of concerns such as the presidency, political polls, public opinion, debates, and advertising to name a few.[7] Since the first study, they also noted a shift away from the rather strict behavioral approach.

A decade later, Dan Nimmo and David Swanson argued that "political communication has developed some identity as a more or less distinct domain of scholarly work."[8] The scópe and concerns of the area have further expanded to include critical theories and cultural studies. While there is no precise definition, method, or disciplinary home of the area of inquiry, its primary domain is the role, processes, and effects of communication within the context of politics broadly defined.

In 1985, the editors of *Political Communication Yearbook: 1984* noted that "more things are happening in the study, teaching, and practice of political communication than can be captured within the space limitations of the relatively few publications available."[9] In addition, they argued that the backgrounds of "those involved in the field [are] so varied and pluralist in outlook and approach . . . it [is] a mistake to adhere slavishly to any set format in shaping the content."[10] And more recently, Nimmo and Swanson called for "ways of overcoming the unhappy consequences of fragmentation within a framework that respects, encourages, and benefits from diverse scholarly commitments, agendas, and approaches."[11]

In agreement with these assessments of the area and with gentle encouragement, Praeger established the Praeger Series in Political Communication. The series is open to all qualitative and quantitative methodologies as well as contemporary and historical studies. The key to characterizing the studies in the series is the focus on communication variables or activities within a political context or dimension. As of this writing, nearly forty volumes have been published and there are numerous impressive works forthcoming. Scholars from the disciplines of communication, history, journalism, political science, and sociology have participated in the series.

Robert E. Denton, Jr.

NOTES

1. See Robert E. Denton, Jr., *The Symbolic Dimensions of the American Presidency* (Prospect Heights, Ill.: Waveland Press, 1982); Robert E. Denton, Jr., and Gary Woodward, *Political Communication in America* (New York: Praeger, 1985; 2nd ed., 1990); Robert E. Denton, Jr., and Dan Han, *Presidential Communication* (New York: Praeger, 1986); and Robert E. Denton, Jr., *The Primetime Presidency of Ronald Reagan* (New York: Praeger, 1988).

2. Aristotle, *The Politics of Aristotle*, trans. Ernest Barker (New York: Oxford University Press, 1970), p. 5.

3. Aristotle, *Rhetoric*, trans. Rhys Roberts (New York: The Modern Library, 1954), p. 22.

4. Dan Nimmo and Keith Sanders, "Introduction: The Emergence of Political Communication as a Field," in *Handbook of Political Communication*, ed. Dan Nimmo and Keith Sanders (Beverly Hills, Calif.: Sage, 1981), pp. 11–36.

5. Ibid., p. 15.

6. Ibid., pp. 17–27.

7. Keith Sanders, Lynda Kaid, and Dan Nimmo, eds., *Political Communication Yearbook: 1984* (Carbondale: Southern Illinois University, 1985), pp. 283–308.

8. Dan Nimmo and David Swanson, "The Field of Political Communication: Beyond the Voter Persuasion Paradigm," in *New Directions in Political Communication*, ed. David Swanson and Dan Nimmo (Beverly Hills, Calif.: Sage, 1990), p. 8.

9. Sanders, Kaid, and Nimmo, *Political Communication Yearbook: 1984*, p. xiv.

10. Ibid.

11. Nimmo and Swanson, "The Field of Political Communication," p. 11.

Politics, Media, and
Modern Democracy

Chapter One

Politics, Media, and Modern Democracy: Introduction

Paolo Mancini and David L. Swanson

Election campaigns are critical periods in the lives of democracies. They select decision makers, shape policy, distribute power, and provide venues for debate and socially approved expressions of conflict about factional grievances and issues, national problems and directions, and international agendas and activities. Elections can accomplish each of these goals in different measure in relation to the particular form of government and political party system existing in a given country at a given point in time.[1] Symbolically, campaigns legitimate democratic government and political leaders, uniting voters and candidates in displays of civic piety and rituals of national renewal. The shared values, history, and aspirations celebrated in election campaigns are perhaps the clearest expression of a democracy's continually evolving mythology and perception of its own essential character. Both the practical outcomes and symbolic meaning of campaigns are important to the health of democracies; if practical outcomes seem to contradict symbolic commitments, or if symbolic commitments ring hollow, the usual result is public cynicism and disaffection with government. In both pragmatic and symbolic terms, campaigns are a microcosm that reflects and shapes a nation's social, economic, cultural, and, of course, political life.

The manner in which democracies conduct their election campaigns is in some ways as important as the results of the voting. The concept of democracy rests, after all, on a view of appropriate procedures for selecting representatives and making political decisions. Governments are regarded as democratic not because their rhetoric describes them as such, but because their manner of choosing decision makers is consistent with some recognizable conception of democracy. In addition, campaign practices are important because of their influence on the conduct, responsiveness, and effectiveness of government. Among other things, the way in which a democracy conducts its election campaigns can empower or silence particular segments of the electorate, achieve or disrupt a balance of power among institutions of government, support or undercut the strength of political parties, and foster public support or alienation from government.

In recent years, campaign practices have been changing rapidly in many democracies. These changes have often been the subject of intense scrutiny and debate in the countries in which they have occurred. However, the broader question of whether there are patterns and common implications in the changes taking place simultaneously in different countries has received less attention. Scholars have been hard pressed to catalogue the rapid changes in campaigning in various countries, although a modest comparative literature on the subject is beginning to emerge (e.g., Butler & Ranney, 1992b). Growing out of this young literature is what might appear to be a curious phenomenon: Around the world, many of the recent changes in election campaigning share common themes despite great differences in the political cultures, histories, and institutions of the countries in which they have occurred. Increasingly, we find such common practices as political commercials, candidates selected in part for the appealing image they project on television, technical experts advising candidates on strategies and voters' sentiments, media professionals hired to produce compelling campaign materials, mounting campaign expenses, and mass media moving to center stage in campaigns.

The rapid pace of change in how democracies conduct their elections and the apparent similarities in the kinds of changes taking place raise important questions about the nature and future of modern democracy. In countries that have the longest experience with them, the campaign practices mentioned previously have been cited by some as leading to very significant and not always anticipated changes in political institutions, the effectiveness of government, and government's relation to the people. In the United States, for example, such innovations have been linked by some analysts to ineffectual political parties, unresponsive government, failure to address serious national problems, and other ills (e.g., Bennett, 1992a; Jamieson, 1992). Will adoption of these innovations lead to similar concerns in countries that are only now beginning to implement them fully? Or can such innovations be adapted to complement and support the host country's indigenous political culture and institutions? Does the pattern of apparent similarities between countries suggest that, around the world, democracies are developing along a common path? What influences might cause such seeming convergence in widely dissimilar contexts? Or are the similarities more apparent than real? Do superficial similarities mask profound national differences? In short, what can these developments tell us about the practice and path of modern democracy as, caught up in rapidly accelerating changes, democratic government in all its variations alternately strides and lurches into the post–Cold War era?

Our aims in this volume are to explore recent changes taking place in how democracies conduct their election campaigns, to test how well the appearance of similarity holds up under close examination of developments in different countries, and to gauge what the apparent similarities may reveal about common influences and processes shaping the evolution of democracies around the world. We endeavor to place these changes within a framework that explains why apparently similar developments may occur in otherwise quite different national contexts. We attempt to identify the general pattern of change and the possibilities for variation within that pattern. Throughout the analysis, we hope to locate the causes of changing campaign practices in more general social, economic, cultural, political, and technological developments. It is in the context of these developments, we believe, that new practices can best be understood, their significance and likely consequences assayed, and questions about national similarities and differences pursued most fruitfully. In undertaking this analysis, we are keenly aware of the risk of self-fulfilling hypotheses that might lead us to overlook the special structures and elements characterizing the mass media and political systems of each country and to attribute unwarranted significance to superficial similarities (Gurevitch & Blumler, 1990). We shall therefore be cautious in pointing out common characteristics, and in every case shall try to be attentive to how similar practices find different applications in each context.

In a larger sense, beyond our specific subject matter, this book is about democracy and change. It appears at a time when those two terms seem welded together. Around the world, we see new democracies struggling to take root, as in the countries of the former Soviet Union, and older democracies that have returned to life after limited periods of authoritarian rule, such as Brazil and Chile. When hopeful new democrats look to the established democracies, they find not only inspiration and guidance, but also manifestations of ferment and calls for reform: declining confidence in political institutions and leaders in most of the major Western democracies, voters overturning the long-standing political order in countries such as Japan and Spain, the traditional system of proportional representation being challenged and restricted in some Western European countries, concern about whether government is capable of acting effectively to address trenchant problems in the United States, and so on. Democracy always has been a system of government that is keyed to fostering and managing change. Democracy as practiced in the United States in the 1990s is dramatically different in many ways from American democracy in the 1950s, and the same could be said for other established democracies. During the last few years, however, change has occurred so rapidly on so many fronts that it is difficult to have much confidence that we understand very well what is going on and where it is leading. Can close examination of changing election campaign practices in many different countries shed light on broader issues of change and transformation? As we examine developments and their implications on the smaller stage of election campaigning, many themes of the larger drama of modern democracy will necessarily come into play.

OUR APPROACH TO THE SUBJECT

Election campaigns are complicated subjects to study. What happens within them reflects, in each campaign, a singular coming together of history, opportunity, circumstance, tradition, personality, political culture, and other things. No campaign is exactly like any other. Certainly, no nation's election campaigns are exactly like those of any other nation. And the methods and practices used in election campaigns are changing constantly. How might one begin, then, to come to grips with this complex and continually changing subject, and do so in a comparative manner that looks beyond national boundaries without overlooking national differences in the process?

"Americanization" and "Modernization" as Working Hypotheses

In order to provide a starting point for comparing campaign practices in different countries, we believe the "Americanization" hypothesis is useful. In brief, the hypothesis holds that campaigning in democracies around the world is becoming more and more Americanized as candidates, political parties, and news media take cues from their counterparts in the United States. Many campaign methods and practices that have been adopted by other countries developed first in the United States, so Americanization suggests itself as an easy characterization of this pattern of innovation (e.g., Elebash, 1984). The appropriateness of the term is contested, however, by some who argue that surface similarities obscure important national adaptions and variations (e.g., Waisbord, 1993). And, of course, not all recent changes in campaigning in every country of interest represent adoption of methods and practices that emerged first in the United States. We regard the matter as an open question, and offer Americanization not as a conclusion, but as a reference point and a working hypothesis with which to begin the analysis. We believe the concept will be useful for comparing common elements in electoral change, as long as care is taken not to overlook national variations, adaptations, and deviations from the general pattern, as Schou (1992) recommends in a related context concerning Americanization as a more general cultural phenomenon.

Despite its flaws, our use of the term Americanization reflects some important facts that are relevant to recent changes in election campaigns around the world. The results of U.S. elections may have important consequences for many countries, which creates in those countries great interest in following U.S. campaigns. However, it often happens that, as persons in other countries follow the progress of a U.S. campaign, their attention shifts from the candidates' goals and policies which can have serious effects abroad to the way in which the election campaign itself is conducted. Seen from the perspective of other countries, U.S. campaigns are in many ways striking, curious, and strange. Such spectacles of the 1992 U.S. presidential campaign as billionaire businessman Ross Perot's on-again, off-again candidacy unconnected to any political party and the journalistic attention given to candidate Bill Clinton's marital fidelity do not easily find parallels in many other countries.

Because of widespread interest in them, U.S. campaigns receive extensive news coverage around the world, nearly equivalent to the coverage given to domestic stories (Gurevitch & Blumler, 1990). Information about U.S. campaigns received from news coverage has been supplemented by popular cultural materials. Popular films about U.S. political campaigning are now part of everybody's imagination: *The Candidate, Nashville,* and *Power* have all helped to create the myth of the figures and professions associated with the U.S. political campaign.

Knowledge of new campaign practices developed in the United States has also been spread to other countries through wide dissemination of technical information. Great numbers of politicians, public-relations personnel, and other interested persons from many countries have visited the United States to study and report firsthand on election campaigns.[2] In addition, the publication of books and manuals on the subject has helped to spread U.S. campaign methods and expertise to other countries.[3] These works have helped especially to support the professionalization of political campaigning in many countries along U.S. lines, in which technical experts in mass media, opinion polling, fund-raising, and campaign strategy are regarded as essential to effective campaigning. Professionalization has been further supported by the frequent involvement of U.S. political consultants in electoral campaigns in other countries.[4] The export of new campaign practices to other countries also reflects the more general, central role the United States has played in development and diffusion of mass-media communication. The United States occupies a pivotal position in today's interlinked, global networks of mass communication and information (see Fisher, 1987; Friedland, 1992; Wallis & Baran, 1990). The United States has long been the pacesetter for innovations in mass communication and campaign practices around the world, inventing new media, strategies, models, and structures. This is particularly clear in the case of the internationalization of U.S. advertising firms (Anderson, 1984; Kaynak, 1989). In 1988, foreign billings exceeded domestic billings of U.S. advertising agencies for the first time (Frazer, 1990). Acting within a field very close to that of election campaigns, the increasingly global reach of the U.S. advertising firms has served as a vehicle for spreading adoption and adaptation of U.S. practices in other countries.

One effect of the dissemination of information about U.S. campaign techniques, both through popular sources (news, popular culture) and technical sources (campaign manuals, firsthand observation of U.S. methods), has been to create a mythology of the great power of U.S. election campaign practices. Naturally, many politicians and political operatives in other countries have sought to take advantage of new, powerful-seeming U.S. campaign practices by importing them for use in their own countries, as in the early case of political advertising.

The term "Americanization" will be useful as our initial reference point, provided it is understood in a particular, restricted sense. Readers may have encountered the term, most often in debates about cultural imperialism and whether the United States exerts undue cultural influence over other countries. Although the question of cultural influence is an important aspect of our subject, the question is a very complex one that concerns topics far beyond campaign practices; accordingly, we shall not consider here the question of cultural imperialism per se.[5] Rather, we use the term Americanization to refer descriptively to particular types and elements of election campaigns and professional activities connected with them that were first developed in the United States and are now being applied and adapted in various ways in other countries. Hence, spread of these elements has naturally been described as Americanizing political campaigns in other countries. In conceiving of Americanization, we do not mean to imply that these processes have taken place everywhere or always in the same ways with the same consequences or the same intensity; indeed, one of our major concerns will be to understand and account for differences between countries in the extent and ways the techniques we are interested in have been adopted. Nor do we mean to suggest in any way that Americanization is necessarily a desirable model for electioneering in democracies (indeed, this model is more deplored than celebrated in the United States) or that it accurately describes the course of transformations that have occurred in other countries. The latter issue is, in fact, the question we investigate in this volume.

Our concerns in this volume are not limited to the use of particular campaign techniques. Rather, we believe that campaign practices are worth examining, in part as an entry point to considering fundamental changes that may be occurring in democracies around the world. We hypothesize that adoption of Americanized campaign methods may reflect a wider, more general process that is producing changes in many societies, changes which are difficult to attribute to a single cause and which go far beyond politics and communication. Following several theoretical hypotheses (Giddens, 1990; Murdock, 1993; Tomlinson, 1994), we call this more general process "modernization."[6]

Thus, we are interested in Americanization, the export and local adaptation of particular campaign techniques, and in modernization, the more general and fundamental process of change that we hypothesize leads to adoption of these techniques in different national contexts. Most especially, we are interested in the relationship between Americanization and modernization. In that relationship, we believe, lie the keys to understanding the causes, significance, and implications of changing campaign methods and practices.

Innovations in election campaigns over the last few years that resemble practices developed first in the United States result fundamentally, we believe, from transformations in the social structure and form of democracy in countries where the innovations have taken place. These transformations are part of the modernization process: The more advanced is the process of modernization in a country, the more likely we are to find innovations in campaigning being adopted and adapted. We cannot discuss modernization in detail here; that would require another volume, no doubt a very long one. Nevertheless, we believe it is important to point out those elements of the modernization process which are most closely related to election campaigning.

National Data and Comparative Analysis

Our approach focuses on detailed analyses of electoral changes that have occurred in a diverse group of countries. The countries that will be examined are Argentina, Germany, Israel, Italy, Poland, Russia, Spain, Sweden, the United Kingdom, the United States, and Venezuela. These countries were selected to present vivid contrasts along a number of dimensions that we hope will reveal the advance and variety of campaign innovations, and their adaptations and consequences in différing contexts. The sample includes countries with long traditions of ideologically based voting and countries where ideology has been less important. Both parliamentary and presidential systems are represented. Within parliamentary systems, the sample includes genuine multiparty systems and systems where only two or three dominant parties compete for power. Some of the youngest and oldest democracies are included, along with a mix of more traditional and more modernized societies. Some of the countries to be studied are found at the leading edge of campaign innovations, others at the trailing edge. The world's most technologically advanced national media systems are represented, as are less advanced systems, and various patterns of media structure and ownership are found in the sample. Also found are countries that closely regulate campaign techniques and countries that do less to control campaign practices. By maximizing variation along dimensions such as these, we hope to get a comprehensive picture of patterns of electoral change and their causes and consequences in various contexts.

The volume will progress through a series of chapters that each examine, in detail, the particular experiences of a single country concerning electoral change. In this way, the analysis of each country will give due attention to the unique aspects of that country's situation and campaign practices. These chapters provide the rich data stressing national differences which any comparative analysis must take into account. The explicit comparative analysis will be offered in a concluding chapter that, among other things, assesses the merits and limitations of the unitary Americanization hypothesis in light of the practices and unique aspects of electoral campaigning in the countries that have been examined. Within the comparative analysis, we also hope to gauge how Americanized practices have been mingled with and superimposed over previous practices and models, leading to new adaptations and combinations that differ in important ways from the U.S. model. Finally, the comparative analysis will offer more general conclusions concerning common experiences and directions in modern democracy.

The remainder of this introductory chapter outlines an analytical framework that sets the stage for the detailed analyses of individual countries that follow. The framework is general and abstract, as it precedes the chapters that present intensive analyses of individual countries. We will return to this framework in the concluding chapter, where it will be tested against data provided in the analyses of particular countries. For now, we outline the framework in order to define some of the major topics and issues that make up our subject.

DEMOCRACY AND THE MODERNIZATION PROCESS

Modernization and Social Complexity

The most basic and far-reaching attribute of the modernization process is steadily increasing social complexity. The concept of social complexity is not easy to define. According to a simplified interpretation, it could be reduced to the high number of subjects that interact in today's society and to the mul-

tiplicity of their interactions. Several authors have dealt with the problem of
social complexity from various perspectives. The German sociologist, Niklas
Luhmann (1975), has relied on systems theory to develop an interpretative
hypothesis that has proved useful in understanding such phenomena as public
opinion (Noelle-Neumann, 1993) and can be of some help in our effort. According to Luhmann, social complexity is tied to the functional differentiation of society and the development of specialized competing and overlapping
systems.

Following Luhmann, social complexity can be said to be articulated in two
major dimensions: a formal or structural dimension and a symbolic dimension. The first dimension refers to increasing functional differentiation within
society, in which growing numbers of subsystems develop that become more
and more specialized to satisfy the increasing demands of particular sectors
of society and groups of citizens. Interactions between these subsystems become more and more complex, with each subsystem acting to protect its own
area of autonomy and public or constituency.

Development of specialized and competing subsystems undermines or ren-
ders irrelevant the traditional, aggregative structures of socialization, authority, and community, replacing them with more narrowly defined and fluid
structures of identification and interest. While traditional structures are based
on inclusion and aggregation of interests, specialized systems in more differentiated societies are based on fragmentation and exclusion. Among the specialized systems that develop in the modernization process are both
microaggregations of all kinds and larger interest-based organizations of citizens which have autonomous symbolic structures and powers and operate
in a wide and varied sphere of problems and interests. The latter organizations sometimes are able to intervene in questions of public policy (even when
their focal concerns center on the private interests of the individual or family,
as in the case of organizations based on religion or avocational interests) and
influence the development of opinions and the process of public decision
making. Such aggregations partly replace earlier structures of interpersonal
exchange such as is seen, in some European countries, in the weakening of
the traditional role of the parish in socialization, political socialization, education, and even entertainment and village governance.

The newer, more specialized aggregations that develop in modernization
often have a lower level of institutionalization and hierarchy as compared to
the parish, for example, and are able to form networks with each other using
opportunities provided by new information technologies such as computer
networks, desktop publishing, and low-cost computer support for creating
mailing lists and compiling information. In the United States, for instance,
these technologies have been used to good effect by very large numbers of
loosely organized and highly specialized groups that have developed around
particular issues and interests of all kinds.

The symbolic dimension of the concept of social complexity underscores
how increasing social differentiation is accompanied by the fracturing of citizens' identities. Old aggregative anchors of identity and allegiance in traditional social structures, such as church and political party, are replaced by
overlapping and constantly shifting identifications with microstructures that

themselves are always entering into changing patterns of alliances with other structures in search of more effective ways of advancing interests. In order to achieve and maintain their viability, the new microstructures create their own symbolic realities; their own symbolic templates of heroes and villains, honored values and aspirations, histories, mythologies, and self-definition. Each such symbolic reality reflects the particular interests and viewpoint of the given microstructure and its public. As a result, microstructures tend to produce symbolic realities that conflict with and may contradict those produced by other microstructures representing other interests.

In modern societies, as Luhmann points out, citizens typically affiliate with or operate with reference to multiple microstructures, each of which offers a particular symbolic reality. Accordingly, the citizen's task in imposing order upon experience becomes increasingly difficult as his or her identity is framed in terms of the contending symbolic realities propounded by multiple microstructures, each of which is embedded in its own spatial and temporal dimensions (Giddens, 1990; Luhmann, 1975; Meyrowitz, 1985; Tomlinson, 1994). In general terms, then, modernization fragments social organization, interests, and identity, creating a complicated landscape of competing structures and conflicting symbolic realities which citizens must navigate.

Increasing Complexity and the Political Process

Increasing social complexity leads to a series of radical social changes, including, in particular, changes in the forms and practices of democratic government. Contemporary democracies are marked by ever-growing numbers of groups and organizations that participate to advance their interests and their increasingly bitter competition for public resources and social capital. This takes the form of establishing increasing numbers of structures that act as intermediaries between citizens and the political system, structures to which citizens entrust responsibility for advancing their private interests. As a result, more powers compete with each other for political influence and are in conflict than in previous forms of society. At the same time, direct participation by citizens in the political process may decline as citizens deputize intermediary organizations and structures to act as their agents in influencing the political system. The form of democracy that arises in this situation has been described by Dahl (1956, 1971) as "polyarchy,"[7] an arena within which different groups, not of a strictly political nature (e.g., interest groups, conglomerates, media organizations), confront and struggle with each other. In this arena, the mass media system undertakes socialization functions which previously were performed by the political parties.

Social differentiation also implies a change in the form of political parties, as more specialized groups of various kinds (e.g., economic, social, cultural, and issue-centered groups) coexist and act within the same party organization. The needs of the new forms of organizations for representation seem to be answered by what Kirchheimer (1966) defines as "catch-all parties." These political parties are segmented and pluralistic organizations that have weak or inconsistent ideological bases, well exemplified, on some accounts, in U.S. political parties. Catch-all parties allow assimilation and representation of

diverse, even sometimes conflicting, interests and demands of different groups
and may embrace ideologically contradictory policy alternatives. This form
of organization has not been possible within the monolithic structure of "mass
parties" of the traditional European kind, whose strong ideological mold requires more precise choices about political representation and stronger links
with specific groups of people and social interests. Catch-all parties are close
to what other political scientists call "electoral parties," that is, organizational structures whose main goal is that of raising consensus at the election
moment. Their organization structure becomes weaker and weaker, and co-
exists with a strong capacity by individual politicians for aggregating consensus, mainly at election time, and in the absence of strong ideological ties
with the voters. For this reason, other observers have described this type of
structure as the "opinion party" (Parisi & Pasquino, 1977): Its constituency is
inherently unstable, being dependent on the appeal of a constantly changing
cast of individual politicians, a constantly shifting pattern of group alliances,
and on the mass media to present appealing politicians in a favorable light.
In the view of these observers, the opinion party is taking the place of the
ideological party, which was so widespread in Europe and other continents
until just a few years ago. Thus, one result of the advance of modernization is
to question the future of mass parties.

As has been implied, another political effect of modernization is to empower individual political figures at the expense of the authority of the political parties within which the figures operate, as the diverse social groups
which act within the polyarchy tend to aggregate around single political leaders. This has occurred in the last few years in Europe, where the role of stable
internal factions within political parties has been declining, while the capacity of individual politicians to aggregate the support of diverse groups has
been expanding, especially at voting time. The growing tendency to aggregate around individual politicians produces a personalization of politics reflecting the atomization of power, which breaks up into many competing
centers that conflict and cooperate with each other and seek a political authority, exercised and personified by a single individual, with which to identify. These changes all are part of a circular process in which power flows
from the party structure, the traditional intermediary of political consensus,
to individual politicians, resulting in a lessening of the ability of parties to
manage political institutions and, in turn, a decline of the institutions' ability
to act effectively.

The establishment of a relationship of personal trust between the citizen
and his or her chosen representative in the state administration can be different from charismatic leadership. The latter, according to Max Weber's interpretation, concerns a few figures who, through natural talents and qualities,
rise to the highest office within political organizations and the state. Thus,
following Weber, Duverger (1991) distinguishes between personalization as
the exercise of power on a reduced scale in small groups, and the creation of
charismatic leadership exercised in large communities. Both personalization
and charismatic leadership are connected to mass media, "which have established by means of the television screen personal contact between political

leaders and their voters" (Duverger, 1991, p. 261). Both are important trends in the new campaign models, but in this volume we shall be concerned primarily with personalization, because it represents the more general, pervasive, and fundamental element in the process of change of election campaigns.

Modernization and Media Power

Duverger's analysis brings us to the theme of mass media in modernization. No longer merely a means by which other subsystems, such as political parties, can spread their own messages, mass media emerge in modern polyarchies as an autonomous power center in reciprocal competition with other power centers. As Butler and Ranney note, "the role of the media has . . . moved increasingly from being merely a channel of communication to being a major actor in the campaigning process, as it selects the persons and issues to be covered and as it shapes its portrayal of leaders" (1992a, p. 283). In Europe and elsewhere, the decline of party-controlled media and the rise of independent, privately owned commercial media have transformed mass communication into a force that operates in a situation of mutual material and symbolic exchange with other power centers. As an independent power center, mass communication operates autonomously, according to its own economic and symbolic logics.[8]

The emergence of mass media as an autonomous power center has had important consequences for modern politics. Media institutions and practices become indissolubly linked to "the institutions and practices of democratic politics" (Garnham, 1992, p. 362), as campaigning for office and governing are increasingly tailored to the needs and interests of mass media. In a growing number of countries, television and other media have begun to self-consciously advance their own agendas in covering politics (see, for example, Semetko, Blumler, Gurevitch, & Weaver, 1991). In countries having technologically advanced media systems, media collaboration and competition with politicians and government in "the modern publicity process" (Blumler, 1990) is now at the very heart of modern democracy.

Mass media also play a very important role in accentuating the process of personalization. Here, television is key. Television is the medium through which voters typically encounter political candidates and officials, and it is through television that the attachments are formed that link citizens to their representatives. Thus, skillful use of television to cultivate personal support is regarded as essential to political success in every democracy that is well along in the modernization process.

In countries that allow political advertising, television has had the further effect of greatly increasing the cost of political campaigns. Candidates and parties that are better able than their opponents to finance expensive media campaigns are thereby thought to be advantaged in the ongoing effort to lure the fickle voters of modern democracy. Moreover, the need to raise larger amounts of money to pay for media campaigns has made candidates and parties more dependent than before on the interests that provide large financial contributions. As Bennett (1992a) has pointed out with reference to the

United States, dependence on contributors can enmesh political parties and officeholders in a web of countervailing loyalties that leaves them powerless to act effectively.

On a number of levels, then, increasing social complexity in the modernization process is associated with a transformation in the role of mass media, with important results for campaigning, governing, and political institutions following in train.

Modernization and Redistribution of Political Functions

Increasing social complexity and its associated transformations in politics and government and in the status of mass media produce what amounts to an epochal change in all spheres of community life that formerly performed political functions. The political parties, as traditionally formed, lose their preeminence as producers of political culture and, instead, must compete with multiple structures that now play roles in producing political culture. As political parties change from grassroots organizations of volunteers who campaign locally for candidates to centralized structures of executives and managers, as has happened in the United States (Salmore & Salmore, 1985), the elaborate networks of interpersonal communication within the party, which previously were main sites of political socialization and channels for disseminating political information, are disappearing, depriving the party not only of channels of communication but also of the volunteers and activists who represented its main organizational structure in years past.

In countries where modernization is most advanced, the formerly vast number of publications controlled or managed by political parties have almost disappeared. The exemplary case is party newspapers, that previously were the main if not only source of journalistic information for party activists and sympathizers. Their circulation has declined, while rising costs have nearly put them out of business completely.

As political parties lose their channels of communication and thereby their control over the production of political culture, new, more specialized groups arise, creating competing sites for political socialization and producing political culture. Commercial interests, groups focused on a single political issue (such as abortion in the United States, immigration in Germany, and regional autonomy in Spain), avocational groups, professional associations, and other structures of all kinds tend to take on more narrowly drawn versions of the parties' former aggregative, affiliative, representative, and cultural functions.

In this situation, the mass media of communication play especially important roles. The development of mass media has occurred comparatively rapidly and largely without control, producing what appear, in many countries, to be very powerful institutions that quickly have overwhelmed other institutions and assumed functions and tasks formerly carried on by other structures and by interpersonal communication networks, including especially the functions that formerly were managed by the party apparatus. The process is one of quantitative and qualitative homologation, as the structure of the mass communication systems that develop in different countries tends to conform, over time, to a single production model; to a format and content which are becoming more and more alike. This is a process of media "globalization," referring not just to the international spread of media contents and forms, but also to structures of relationship and ownership that increasingly are assimilating the systems of mass communication found in different countries (Cohen, Adoni, & Bantz, 1990; Gurevitch & Blumler, 1990; Gurevitch, Levy, & Roeh, 1991; Wakeman, 1988). This process is one of the "universals" that determines how election campaigns are conducted in all countries and has been claimed to be "a fundamental cause of the widespread 'Americanization' of electioneering" (Butler & Ranney, 1992a, p. 280).

For present purposes, the most important aspects of the changing roles of mass media in modernization have to do with developments concerning the values, formats, and culture of commercial television. What took place in Europe in the 1980s is symptomatic: The monopoly long held by the national public broadcasting services was progressively reduced by the development of commercial media. The "commercial deluge" (Blumler, 1992b) has completely transformed and reshaped the medium along lines that increasingly resemble the U.S. model of a media system driven by commercial interests and dominated by television as the public's major source of information and entertainment. In particular, the development of commercial television has radically changed the character of election campaigns. It has even changed the nature and role of election coverage provided by the public broadcasting services, introducing new opportunities and new formats.[9]

The televised political advertisement is the best example of this change and of its more general implications. Typically, ads create and disseminate images of individual candidates, and thus increase the personalization of politics. In general, the format of television favors personalization for formal and structural reasons. Formally, the medium favors representation of human figures over complex institutions such as political parties, while structurally the medium's commercial logic favors offering access to all candidates who can pay the cost of advertising, passing over the parties. Commercial television often has been identified as an important contributor to the crisis of political parties (e.g., Agranoff, 1972). As the technical experts tell us, themes developed in political advertising are most effective when they are repeated and reinforced in other forms of communication—speeches, posters, meetings, and statements of all kinds. The United States offers a clear example of how advertising tends, in this way, to influence the entire content of political campaigns, and how the requirements of effective advertising can become constraints that shape all forms of political discourse (Jamieson, 1992).

Even in countries where political advertising is prohibited, advertising techniques are being incorporated more and more frequently into the longer television programs that political parties are allowed to present. Brazil, France, and the United Kingdom are good examples of this latter way in which advertising is injected into the political dialogue (see Angell, Kinzo, & Urbaneja, 1992; Gerstlé, 1992; Scammel & Karan, 1992).

To accurately understand the epochal change associated with television, it is important to appreciate, but not exaggerate, television's influence. The processes of change in political systems and democratic forms are taking place in parallel with the continuing evolution of traditional means of communication. As a result, traditional forms persist and continue to develop in the changing context, sometimes taking on new functions. As a matter of fact, the fragmentation of social interests and identities and growing aggregation of citizens into small and medium-sized groups have caused a return to the popularity of microcircuits of communication and interpersonal forms of communication which television had, in many cases, debased if not destroyed altogether. It turns out, then, that modern communication technology exerts both centrifugal and centripetal influences in society. Thus, we are witnessing the coexistence of elements of the old and the new in ways congruent with transformations in the fabric of society and responsive to developing communication needs. The modernization process that gives rise to changes in campaign practices brings new structures of socialization and aggregation which affect the political domain and lead to the transformation and adaptation of preexistent forms.

THE ELEMENTS OF MODERN CAMPAIGNING

Thus far, we have theorized that a general process of modernization, proceeding at different rates in different countries, leads to profound changes in the political and other domains of national life. These changes, in turn, are reflected in and spurred by alterations in how election campaigns are conducted. Our preliminary working description of the pattern of alteration in campaign methods and practices is Americanization. In this section, we sketch more explicitly some of the major elements associated with modernized or Americanized campaigning.

Personalization of Politics

In thoroughly modernized campaigns, as we have noted, the voter's choice depends increasingly upon the voter's relationship with the individual candidate. This relationship replaces traditional ideological and fiduciary bonds between voters and the party apparatus. As a result, the party is weakened as a symbolic aggregation and as an organizing structure. Candidates run on their own, with personal organizations and personally obtained financing. At the same time, charismatic figures of leaders built up by the mass media system replace the symbolic links previously assured by the political parties.

"Scientificization" of Politics

We are adopting here the term Habermas used to indicate the transformations he observed in the 1960s, when he wrote of the "scientificization" of politics. He pointed to the ever more frequent use of experts, technicians, and scientists in the political field, leading to control by specialists of the production, possession, and comprehension of information thought necessary to sound decision making (Habermas, 1978). In the field of election campaigns, we have observed the increasing roles of technical experts, supplying expertise and making decisions that formerly were made within the party apparatus. Some specialists in public relations began to make forays into election campaigning as early as the 1930s, but it was not until the 1960s and 1970s that technical experts came into full flower as standard features of modern campaign teams, often with decision-making responsibilities in campaign strategy, media use, and other key matters (Nimmo, 1970; Sabato, 1981).

The expanding role of technical experts in campaigns reflects, on the one hand, the sophisticated methods and skills that are thought necessary to effective campaigning in the modern political and media environment (including skills associated with opinion polling and other methods for monitoring voters' sentiments, creating compelling television advertising, winning frequent and favorable media coverage for the candidate, and raising campaign funds) and, on the other hand, the weakening of the role of the parties, which are not able to supply the needed funds and competencies. Moreover, candidates frequently run in competition with others within the same party, as in the U.S. primary elections and the growing number of "first past the post" or other direct election systems elsewhere. Intraparty competition has led candidates to assemble their own staffs of technical experts to provide support that cannot be claimed from their party, resulting in campaigns that are candidate centered rather than party centered (Agranoff, 1972; Sabato, 1981).

The goal of the scientificization process is simply the electoral victory, not finding useful public-policy alternatives. This goal seems to result inescapably from the weakening of party organizations and the changes we have seen in political systems.

Detachment of Parties from Citizens

In modern societies, increasing functional differentiation and social fragmentation make it more difficult than in traditional societies for political leaders and parties to know the concerns, viewpoints, and life situations of voters. At the same time that the task of knowing the voters' situations has become more challenging, political parties' ability to perform the task has declined, because their broad-based interpersonal communication networks have shrunk, as we noted earlier. These far-flung networks of long-standing supporters and activists formerly served as conduits of information that kept the parties in touch with the needs, moods, and interests of citizens. The loss of this traditional point of contact is especially important as parties move from ideological bases to opinion bases. The parties' modern substitute for interpersonal contact is the opinion poll, an objectified statistical construction that, especially in periods of instability and rapid change, may leave the parties at a loss to understand voters' sentiments, grievances, and desires (see Herbst, 1993, esp. pp. 153–175).

Autonomous Structures of Communication

As we have stressed, one feature of modernization is the development of powerful, autonomous mass media of communication whose far-reaching influence places them at the center of social, political, economic, and cultural life. Modern media are more powerful, more independent, and more determined to pursue their own interests through a professional culture of their own making. They tend to take on political functions formerly performed by party organizations and party-controlled media, such as political socialization and providing information to the public about politics and government. At the same time, modernization makes politicians more dependent on media and produces the professionalization of political and government communication as officials and political leaders devote increasing resources and expertise to trying to manipulate autonomous media (see Semetko, Blumler, Gurevitch, & Weaver, 1991). One result is the potential for struggle between officials and journalists for control of the agenda and for the power to frame or interpret the important events and issues of the day. With the proliferation of powerful, privately owned media devoted to commercial interests, politicians and officials no longer can demand preferential and favorable treatment, but instead must adapt to the priorities and conventions of the media. Similarly, news media must have a regulatory environment in which they can prosper, and free access to politicians and officials in order to do their job, yet at the same time must be seen to stand apart from politics in order to legitimate their institutional role in modern society.

The relationship between media and politics as autonomous power centers engaged in both competition and cooperation affects campaigning and governing in many ways. In these days of more volatile and fragmented electorates whose sentiments are more swayed by media images, political power does not rest on the secure and enduring base of generations of party loyalty anchored in group and class interests. Public approval gained through effective media campaigns can be lost as quickly as it was won, when media images turn sour and officials seem unable to control events. Public approval must be cultivated constantly if it is to be maintained. In some countries, the result has been the creation of what amounts to a never-ending election campaign, in which government is obligated to attempt to court public favor continuously in order to remain in power. The need to use autonomous media to maintain voters' support becomes a daily, unrelenting priority of government, and the technical experts and strategists who can provide guidance concerning media may become ever more powerful in political parties and government.[10]

From Citizenship to Spectatorship

As the modernization process advances, the essential form of citizens' participation in election campaigns changes from direct personal involvement to spectatorship. That is, campaigns are conducted primarily through mass media, and citizens participate in them as members of the media audience. "Political spectacle" as described by Edelman (1988) emerges as an approach to politics that mediates between the conflicting interests and demands of the multiple structures competing for power in the polyarchy. As a form of political action, "spectacle" concentrates more on respecting the symbolic commitments and serving the practical interests of many contending constituencies than on accurately diagnosing and solving real problems. Hence, in political spectacle, the test of government programs is not so much whether they accomplish actual results, as whether they serve the competing desires and ambitions of the many parties that have interests in the programs (Edelman, 1988).[11] Spectatorship also reflects the fact that citizens in modern society tend to delegate to a complex network of intermediary structures responsibility for representing the citizens' interests to the political system. Some of these intermediary structures are created expressly for the purpose of influencing the outcomes of elections, as in the case of political action committees in the United States (in various forms, similar practices are beginning in several other countries). Other intermediary structures have permanent existence and devote their energies primarily to influencing day-to-day activities of government on issues that relate to the structures' particular interests. This is the case with professional associations, political activities of trade unions, and associations representing a wide variety of interests, such as religious convictions, single-issue concerns, and even hobbies and leisure interests. With intermediaries deputized to advance his or her various interests, the voter can relate to media-centered campaigns more as spectacle than as political action. Instead of speaking of spectatorship, Murdock, in relation to the conditions of modernity, has proposed a distinction between the identities of consumers and that of citizens: "On the one side stood the crowd, emotional, seduced by dramatic images, acting in concert, bargaining by riot and demonstration. On the other side stood the citizen, rational, open to sequential argument, making considered personal choices and registering preferences soberly, in the solitude of the voting booth" (Murdock, 1993, p. 527).

CONTEXTUALIZATION OF MODERN CAMPAIGNING

The elements of modern campaigning described above outline an ideal type, a model of practice that grows organically out of the modernization process. In practice, however, these elements are being adapted and applied in different ways in particular national settings, producing many variations on the archetype. The elements of modern campaigning are proving highly malleable and are being contextualized in ways that reflect each county's election system, structure of party competition, regulation, political culture, and media system. Each of these contextual influences will be discussed briefly.

Election Systems

There are many different electoral systems around the world, and no doubt each offers a slightly different context that is more or less hospitable to the introduction of modern campaigning. To illustrate the point, we will call attention here only to the difference in this regard between majority and proportional electoral systems. Majority or "first past the post" systems allow voters to cast ballots for individual candidates, with the win going to the candidate who receives a plurality or majority of the votes cast. For reasons described earlier, majority systems privilege the role of the individual representative and thus foster personalization. Candidates may seek support from ideologically heterogenous groups of voters by stressing their personal appeal rather than party affiliation and political program. In proportional systems, in contrast, voters typically cast their ballots for party lists of candidates; seats in the assembly are then apportioned among the parties based on the percentage of votes each party list received. Party officials usually select the candidates who will appear on the lists, and proportional voting focuses attention more on the party with its ideological and political commitments than on individual candidates. Proportional systems thus appear to limit the influence of personalization in politics.

The advance of modernization seems to be favoring personalization, despite the nature of a nation's electoral system. As noted, many observers believe that the traditional ideological party that was so common in Europe and elsewhere until just a few years ago is being replaced by catch-all parties devoted to personalization. At the same time, proportional electoral systems are being modified to allow direct voting for individual candidates, as recently happened in Italy. Thus, the difference between majority and proportional electoral systems may turn out to be that personalization proceeds more rapidly in majority systems and more slowly in proportional systems, and that majority systems are focused more strongly on the role of television, which stresses the simplification of a choice between one party or the other.

The Structure of Party Competition

The structure of party competition is another contextual factor which can influence the development of the modern model of campaigning. Bipartisan competition (that is, systems dominated by just two or three viable, competitive parties) between catch-all parties favors the modern model, using sophisticated communication strategies to create volatile and temporary aggregations of interests within a fragmented society. The United States and the United Kingdom are good examples of bipartisan competition of this type. On the other hand, multiparty systems (that is, systems in which many parties are competitive with none dominating the electorate) require parties to differentiate themselves by establishing more well-defined relationships to particular social, economic, and interest groups, and thereby provide the grounds for more stable, organic political representation. Good examples of such systems are Italy, Israel, and Poland. As we will see, elements of the modern model can be found virtually everywhere, including the three countries listed as examples of multiparty systems. Thus, as with electoral systems, the difference between bipartisan and multiparty competition may turn out to affect the speed with which the modern model is adopted and the ways in which its elements are adapted to local circumstances more than it determines whether the modern model is adopted in some form.

Regulation of Campaigning

Democracies regulate campaign activities in various ways that can affect the development and adaptation of modern elements of campaigning. Regulations concerning campaign financing are common (Alexander, 1984; Debbasch, 1989). A restrictive system which limits private or public contributions obviously reduces recourse to commercial media, the use of experts outside the party apparatus, the frequency of polls, and other elements of the modern model. Also important are regulations that control use of communication media and methods, such as prohibitions of political advertising, restrictions on the length of the campaign period when campaign messages may be broadcast or distributed, restrictions on the amount of television time that can be provided or purchased for campaigning, and restrictions on the content of campaign programs. Such restrictions do not prevent the adoption of modern methods (as in the European countries, where the modern model was well advanced before the advent of commercial television and the possibility of political advertising), but they may limit the particular forms and adaptations of modern methods that can be used effectively.

National Political Culture

The methods and customs of election campaigning are deeply embedded in each nation's political culture. Various aspects of that culture affect the introduction and adaptation of innovations associated with modernization. Perhaps the most important aspects of national political culture that affect campaign practices concern political socialization and participation, structures of social aggregation and the development of consensus, and the roles and functions of primary and secondary groups and the effectiveness of their channels of communication. Crudely put, the relevance of these factors can be seen in a contrast between extremes of traditional and modern societies.

In the traditional archetype, election campaigns employ already existing structures of communication and socialization that are well entrenched in and define community life. This is the case in the so-called Mediterranean cultures of Spain, Italy, Portugal, and Greece, where traditional family, parish, and friendship networks become, at election time, the main channels of political information and the main sites for developing political consensus. In these countries, for example, politicians often are present at the both religious and civil ceremonies that characterize family life, such as baptisms and weddings. In these contexts, political communication uses preexisting channels of face-to-face interaction: Information about citizens' opinions and interests are provided to the parties through traditional networks, and mass media often are secondary in campaigns to interpersonal channels.

In the modern archetype, social fragmentation undermines and enfeebles traditional structures of socialization and community, so campaigns must construct their own structures in competition with the many other, rapidly shifting structures of micro- and macroaggregation. Campaigns must therefore compete for the voters' attention and interest and for access to channels of communication outside of primary groups. In these cases, the election campaign is carried out mainly through channels of mass communication with the weight of all accompanying requirements for professionalization, personalization, financing, and so on. Here, perhaps, the link between the modernization process and development of the individual elements of modern campaigning can most clearly be seen.

Other relevant aspects of political culture are the means and traditions it provides for citizens' involvement in political institutions, organizations, and efforts of all kinds, as well as the more general customs of a society and the levels at which it expresses and organizes itself outside the structure of formal institutions. In many countries, it is common for private citizens to support a wide range of different kinds of initiatives by volunteering their time and economic support, as in charitable efforts. In other countries, this practice is much rarer. The relevance of these aspects of political culture to election practices can be seen mostly clearly with reference to campaign financing. In Europe, party organizations and campaigns are financed mostly through state support and party membership. In the United States, in contrast, contributions to the individual candidate from individual citizens, organizations, and groups of all kinds are much more common and, taken together, exceed the public financing that presidential candidates receive. A political culture of voluntarism and private participation may facilitate the personalization process, as especially attractive candidates garner a disproportionate share of private support; a political culture that focuses more on formal institutions and public financing may prop up centralized political parties and party authority—at least for a while—against the advance of modernization.

National Media System

Adoption and adaptation of elements of the modern model of campaigning are influenced also by various attributes of each nation's media system. The degree to which the media system favors development of new models is influenced heavily by the structure of its ownership. As we have noted, the new election campaign models are closely tied to television and, in particular, to commercial television. This offers the individual candidate the possibility of reaching, by payment, millions of voters, while in public-service media systems access is offered more or less free to the party organization according to rules designed in one way or another to ensure impartiality and pluralism. In the former case, recourse to political ads favors the process of political personalization and requires the support of technical experts to gauge voters' sentiments, plan and produce the message, and buy airtime in the most productive locations and periods. Candidates can and do mount campaigns with little or no support or participation from their political party. The same teams of experts may be employed by political parties who receive free television time in public service systems, but in this case the focus of the campaign is designed to remain more on the party than on individual candidates.

More generally, an additional element that has important effects is the degree to which the media system is technologically advanced. Technologically advanced media systems provide voters easy access to multiple sources of information and entertainment, usually with television as the most important medium reaching the largest and most heterogenous audience. Less advanced media systems offer the public less access to fewer sources. When there is no genuine mass medium that can reach the entire population quickly and economically, as in countries where large numbers of people lack television receivers or cannot receive television signals, the development of media-centered modern campaigning is inhibited.

CONCLUSION

We have outlined an introductory framework for thinking about the nature and significance of changes going on around the world in how democracies conduct their elections. The following chapters present detailed analyses of campaign practices in a number of quite dissimilar countries. The introductory framework will be useful, we hope, in drawing attention to common processes and phenomena as the reader progresses through the individual country chapters. These countries were selected for examination because each presents a somewhat different picture of the origins and consequences of modern campaign innovations and, taken together, the countries vary along key dimensions that we believe shape how modern campaigning is contextualized in any given case (e.g., nature of the government and electoral systems, standing of the political parties, nature of the media system).

The country chapters are ordered on the basis of a single consideration: what we might describe as the stability of the democracy in each country. This is not an interpretative model; we do not attempt to judge the strength and quality of democracy in these countries. We simply mean to differentiate between countries in which the political system has remained unchanged, at least in its formal and substantial rules, from countries in which these rules have recently undergone significant modification or are currently facing revision. Conceived in this way, the country chapters represent three different levels of stability. First are countries that possess a strong and enduring political culture, diffuse and well-established networks of political socialization, and an electoral system that has remained stable in its essential details throughout recent years. These countries are the United States, the United Kingdom, Sweden, and Germany.

The second group consists of countries in which democracy has recently been restored after long periods of dictatorship: Russia, Poland, and Spain. Of course, there are deep differences between the histories and current situations of these countries, but they share some important similarities. Each made a relatively recent and quite abrupt transition to democracy, with new political parties and leaders emerging rapidly.

The third group of countries—consisting of Israel, Italy, Argentina, and Venezuela—is even more complex and varied. Each of these countries has a more or less long-standing democratic tradition, but has experienced pressures that have already or might well lead to political instability (such as, in Israel, large numbers of immigrants from nations with political cultures and systems that differ importantly from those of their new home, and the continuing tensions between Jews and Arabs, religious and nonreligious Jews, and other groups). Democracy has been threatened or recently restored in Argentina and Venezuela. All of the countries in this group have recently undergone very important social and political changes, often reflected in violent and bloody events. This third group of countries thus consists of established democracies in which the electoral process has been under pressure with high actual or potential instability.

The concluding chapter of the volume will revisit the general framework, and its usefulness will be tested against the data provided by the detailed examinations of the experience of each country. At that point, we will endeavor for frame grounded conclusions concerning the presence or absence of common influences that are shaping modern democracy and the long-term significance of changes that are now occurring so rapidly.

NOTES

1. For example, in coalitional political systems, elections distribute power among the political parties, while bipartisan systems allow voters to shape policy more directly.

2. In this regard, the activities of the United States Information Service and U.S. embassies around the world have been particularly important. On many occasions, they have invited politicians and professionals from advertising or public relations firms to visit the United States to observe the conduct of election campaigns. U.S. political parties have also played a role. In 1992, for example, Harvey Thomas, a British consultant, managed the Republican Party's "Leadership Program," in which persons from several countries were invited to the United States to observe the Republican National Convention in Houston, Texas.

3. American textbooks, commentaries, scholarly studies, and practical manuals concerning U.S. election campaigns have been translated into many other languages (for example, Patterson, 1980; White, 1961). A good example is Nimmo's *The Political Persuaders* (1970). With chapters devoted to professional campaign managers, opinion polling, and sophisticated use of media, this scholarly treatment of "the techniques of modern election campaigns" was translated into several languages, including Japanese (Nimmo, 1971), and quickly became a standard work for scholars, journalists, and others around the world who wished to understand U.S. campaign practices. Also, authors from Europe and elsewhere have written books on campaigning that draw heavily on U.S. practices (for example, Le Seach, 1975; Mancini, 1988; Noir, 1977).

4. Several U.S. political consultants have conducted election campaigns abroad. One of the most active has been Joseph Napolitan who, starting in 1969, has worked for political campaigns in various countries, including the Philippines and Venezuela. U.S. consultants John Deardourff and Patrick Caddell have also worked on Venezuelan campaigns. Other U.S. political consultants have been quite active in other South American countries, Great Britain, Israel, and elsewhere. Meetings of the International Association of Political Consultants provide regular occasions for consultants from the United States and other countries to share expertise and market their services (Sabato, 1981). The professionalization process has now advanced to the point where many countries have developed an indigenous campaign-consultant industry. Recently, French political consultant Jacques Seguela, who conducted the successful campaigns of French President Francois Mitterand, has exported his expertise to several countries in Eastern Europe which are in the early stages of developing democratic processes (Seguela, 1992). In 1993, Saatchi and Saatchi, the British public relations firm, was hired to manage one of the party campaigns in Poland's first Western-style election.

5. Scholars from a variety of fields have written at length about the theme of cultural imperialism, especially in relation to diffusion around the world of the means of mass communication. Within this literature, some of the most influential works that focus on television and journalism are Schiller's *Communication and Cultural Domination* (1976), Mattelart and Siegelaub's anthology, *Communication and Class Struggle* (1979), and Tunstall's *The Media Are American* (1977).

6. The issue of the influence of the U.S. experience on the evolution of political institutions and practices in Europe has received continuous attention from European scholars. Mostly, they have been interested in the evolution of the political party system, the process of leadership, and the issue of balancing power among the different branches of the state.

7. Dahl uses the term *polyarchy* rather than *democracy* to emphasize the actual or attainable character of the government of many *(polis)*, as distinguished from the abstract ideal of the government of the people *(demos)*.

8. While the concept of economic logic needs no explanation, the idea of symbolic logic refers to both the influence of mass media on the traditional circuits of communi-

cation and cultural socialization (Meyrowitz, 1985) and to the spreading of particular discourse formats (Altheide & Snow, 1979).

9. Discussions of how these structural changes have affected public television include Blumler (1992a, 1992b); Blumler, Gurevitch, and Nossiter (1995); Blumler and Hoffmann-Riem (1992); Jakubowicz (1992); Mancini (1992); Porter and Hasselbach (1991); Reyes-Matta (1992); and Wolton (1992).

10. This analysis is taken from Swanson (1993).

11. For a range of viewpoints on the role and significance of political spectacle in the United States, see Bennett (1992b), Gurevitch and Kavoori (1992), Sigelman (1992), Swanson (1992), and Zarefsky (1992). All appeared in a special issue of *Communication Monographs* (December 1992) concerned with the topic, "Are media news spectacles perverting our political processes?"

REFERENCES

Agranoff, R. (Ed.). (1972). *The new style in election campaigns*. Boston: Holbrook Press.

Alexander, H. E. (1984). *Financing politics: Money, elections, and political reform*. Washington, D.C.: CQ Press.

Altheide, D. L., & Snow, R. P. (1979). *Media logic*. London: Sage.

Angell, A., Kinzo, M. A., & Urbaneja, D. (1992). Latin America. In D. Butler & A. Ranney (Eds.), *Electioneering: A comparative study of continuity and change* (pp. 43–69). Oxford: Clarendon Press.

Anderson, M. H. (1984). *Madison Avenue in Asia*. Rutherford, N.J.: Associated University Presses.

Bennett, W. L. (1992a). *The governing crisis: Media, money, and marketing in American elections*. New York: St. Martin's Press.

Bennett, W. L. (1992b). White noise: The perils of mass mediated democracy. *Communication Monographs, 59*, 401–406.

Blumler, J. G. (1990). Elections, the media, and the modern publicity process. In M. Ferguson (Ed.), *Public communication—The new imperatives: Future directions for media research* (pp. 101–113). London: Sage.

Blumler, J. G. (1992a). News media in flux: An analytical afterword. *Journal of Communication, 42*(3), 100–107.

Blumler, J. G. (Ed.). (1992b). *Television and the public interest: Vulnerable values in Western European broadcasting*. Newbury Park, Calif.: Sage.

Blumler, J.G., Gurevitch, M., & Nossiter, T. J. (1995). Struggles for meaningful election communication: Television journalism at the BBC, 1992. In I. Crewe & B. Gosschalk (Eds.), *Political communications: The general election campaign of 1992* (pp. 65–84). Cambridge: Cambridge University Press.

Blumler, J. G., & Hoffmann-Riem, W. (1992). New roles for public television in Western Europe: Challenges and prospects. *Journal of Communication, 42*(1), 20–35.

Butler, D., & Ranney, A. (1992a). Conclusion. In D. Butler & A. Ranney (Eds.), *Electioneering: A comparative study of continuity and change* (pp. 278–286). Oxford: Clarendon Press.

Butler, D., & Ranney, A. (Eds.). (1992b). *Electioneering: A comparative study of continuity and change*. Oxford: Clarendon Press.

Cohen, A. A., Adoni, H., & Bantz, C. R. (1990). *Social conflict and television news*. Newbury Park, Calif.: Sage.

Dahl, R. A. (1956). *A preface to democratic theory*. Chicago: University of Chicago Press.

Dahl, R. A. (1971). *Polyarchy: Participation and opposition*. New Haven: Yale University Press.

Debbasch, C. (1989). *Campagnes électorales: Principe d'égalité et transparence financière* [Election campaigns: The equality principle and open financing]. Paris: Economica.

Duverger, M. (1991). Personalizzazione del potere o istituzionalizzazione del potere personale [Personalization of power or institutionalization of personal power]. In M. Vaudagna (Ed.), *Il partito politico americano e l'Europa* [The American political party and Europe] (pp. 259–268). Milan: Feltrinelli.

Edelman, M. (1988). *Constructing the political spectacle.* Chicago: University of Chicago Press.

Elebash, C. (1984). The Americanization of British political communications. *Journal of Advertising, 13*(3), 50–58.

Fisher, G. (1987). *American communication in a global society* (rev. ed.). Norwood, N.J.: Ablex.

Frazer, C. F. (1990). Issues and evidence in international advertising. *Current Issues & Research in Advertising, 12*, 75–90.

Friedland, L. A. (1992). *Covering the world: International television news services.* New York: Twentieth Century Fund Press.

Garnham, N. (1992). The media and the public sphere. In C. Calhoun (Ed.), *Habermas and the public sphere* (pp. 359–376). Cambridge: MIT Press.

Gerstlé, J. (1992, May). *The modernization of election campaigns in France.* Paper presented at the annual meeting of the International Communication Association, Miami, Fla.

Giddens, A. (1990). *The consequences of modernity.* Cambridge: Polity Press.

Gurevitch, M., & Blumler, J. G. (1990). Comparative research: The extending frontier. In D. L. Swanson & D. Nimmo (Eds.), *New directions in political communication* (pp. 305–325). Newbury Park, Calif.: Sage.

Gurevitch, M., & Kavoori, A. P. (1992). Television spectacles as politics. *Communication Monographs, 59*, 415-420.

Gurevitch, M., Levy, M. R., & Roeh, I. (1991). The global newsroom: Convergences and diversities in the globalization of television news. In P. Dahlgren & C. Sparks (Eds.), *Communication and citizenship: Journalism and the public sphere in the new media age* (pp. 195–219). London: Routledge.

Habermas, J. (1978). *Teoria e prassi della società tecnologica* [Theory and praxis in technological society]. Bari, Italy: Laterza.

Herbst, S. (1993). *Numbered voices: How opinion polling has shaped American politics.* Chicago: University of Chicago Press.

Jakubowicz, K. (1992). From party propaganda to corporate speech? Polish journalism in search of a new identity. *Journal of Communication, 42*(3), 64–73.

Jamieson, K. H. (1992). *Dirty politics: Deception, distraction, and democracy.* New York: Oxford University Press.

Kaynak, E. (1989). *The management of international advertising.* Westport, Conn.: Quorum Books.

Kirchheimer, O. (1966). The transformation of the Western European party systems. In J. La Palombara & M. Weiner (Eds.), *Political parties and political development* (pp. 177–200). Princeton: Princeton University Press.

Luhmann, N. (1975). *Macht* [Power]. Stuttgart: Enke Verlag.

Mancini, P. (1988). *Come vincere le elezioni* [How to win elections]. Bologna: Il Mulino.

Mancini, P. (1992). Old and new contradictions in Italian journalism. *Journal of Communication, 42*(3), 42–47.

Mattelart, A., & Siegelaub, S. (Eds.). (1979). *Communication and class struggle* (2 vols.). New York: International General.

Meyrowitz, J. (1985). *No sense of place: The impact of electronic media on social behavior.* New York: Oxford University Press.

Murdock, G. (1993). Communications and the constitution of modernity. *Media, Culture and Society, 15*, 521–539.

Nimmo, D. (1970). *The political persuaders: The techniques of modern election campaigns.* Englewood Cliffs, N.J.: Prentice-Hall.

Nimmo, D. (1971). *The political persuaders: The techniques of modern election campaigns* (Japanese edition). Tokyo: Seiji Koho Center. (Original work published 1970)

Noelle-Neumann, E. (1993). *The spiral of silence: Public opinion—Our social skin* (2nd ed.). Chicago: University of Chicago Press.

Noir, M. (1977). *Reussir une campagne electorale: Suivre l'exemple americaine* [Managing an election campaign: Following the American example]. Paris: Les Editions d'Organisation.

Parisi, A., & Pasquino, G. (1977). Relazioni partiti–elettori e tipi di voto [Party–electorate relations and types of voting]. In A. Parisi & G. Pasquino (Eds.), *Continuità e mutamento elettorale in Italia* [Electoral continuity and change in Italy] (pp. 215–250). Bologna: Il Mulino.

Patterson, T. E. (1980). *The mass media election: How Americans choose their president.* New York: Praeger.

Porter, V., & Hasselbach, S. (1991). Beyond balanced pluralism: Broadcasting in Germany. In P. Dahlgren & C. Sparks (Eds.), *Communication and citizenship: Journalism and the public sphere in the new media age* (pp. 94–115). London: Routledge.

Reyes-Matta, F. (1992). Journalism in Latin America in the '90s: The challenges of modernization. *Journal of Communication, 42*(3), 74–83.

Sabato, L. (1981). *The rise of political consultants: New ways of winning elections.* New York: Basic Books.

Salmore, S. A., & Salmore, B. G. (1985). *Candidates, parties, and campaigns: Electoral politics in America.* Washington, D.C.: CQ Press.

Scammel, M., & Karan, K. (1992, May). *Limits of American influence: A comparative assessment of political advertising in Britain and India.* Paper presented at the 9th Intercultural and International Communications Conference, Miami, Fla.

Schiller, H. I. (1976). *Communication and cultural domination.* White Plains, N.Y.: M. E. Sharpe.

Schou, S. (1992). Postwar Americanisation and the revitalisation of European culture. In M. Skovmand & K. C. Schrøder (Eds.), *Media cultures: Reappraising transnational media* (pp. 142–158). London: Routledge.

Le Seach, M. (1975). *L'État marketing: Comme vendre des idées et des hommes politiques* [Marketing the state: How to sell political ideas and politicians]. Paris: Alain Moreau.

Seguela, J. (1992). *Vote au-dessu d'un nid de cocos* [Voting beneath the coconuts]. Paris: Flammarion.

Semetko, H. A., Blumler, J. G., Gurevitch, M., & Weaver, D. H., with Barkin, S., & Wilhoit, G. C. (1991). *The formation of campaign agendas: A comparative analysis of party and media roles in recent American and British elections.* Hillsdale, N.J.: Erlbaum.

Sigelman, L. (1992). There you go again: The media and the debasement of American politics. *Communication Monographs, 59,* 407–410.

Swanson, D. L. (1992). The political-media complex. *Communication Monographs, 59,* 397–400.

Swanson, D. L. (1993, August). *Political institutions in media-centered democracy.* Lecture presented at the course on Parliament and Public Opinion sponsored by the Universidad Complutense de Madrid, El Escorial, Spain.

Tomlinson, J. (1994). A phenomenology of globalization? Giddens on global modernity. *European Journal of Communication, 9,* 149–173.

Tunstall, J. (1977). *The media are American.* London: Constable.

Waisbord, S. R. (1993). *Party lines: Political parties and mass media in Argentine election campaigns, 1983–1989.* Doctoral dissertation, University of California, San Diego.

Wakeman, F. (1988). Transnational and comparative research, *Item, 42*(4), 85–91.

Wallis, R., & Baran, S. J. (1990). *The known world of broadcast news: International news and the electronic media*. London: Routledge.

White, T. H. (1961). *The making of the president, 1960*. New York: Atheneum.

Wolton, D. (1992). Journalists: The Tarpeian rock is close to the capitol. *Journal of Communication, 42*(3), 26–41.

Zarefsky, D. (1992). Spectator politics and the revival of public argument. *Communication Monographs, 59*, 411–414.

PART I

Campaign Innovations in Established Democracies with Stable Political Cultures

Chapter Two

Politics, Media, and Modern Democracy: The United States

Dan Nimmo

In January 1994, the American Association of Political Consultants (AAPC) celebrated its 25th anniversary in its annual conclave in Las Vegas, Nevada. The venue was glittering: Bally's Casino Resort at the heart of the neon-hued, self-indulging Las Vegas Strip. Glittering, and also fitting. It seemed altogether appropriate that the profession that had done so much to advance campaign politics as Big Time Entertainment should offer its celebrated media consultants luxurious accommodations for congratulating one another between visits to glitzy stage productions, pollsters to discuss their probability samples and focus groups between visits to croupiers, and fund-raisers (no strangers to one-armed banditry) to ponder the odds of fortune while playing the gaming tables and slot machines. What a quarter of a century earlier had been but a convening of a mere fifty owners of cottage industries gathering in the Plaza Hotel in New York City, had become *the* only national association for political-consulting professionals.

In describing and analyzing the role and consequences of modern campaigning for the government and politics of democratic nations, it is appropriate to take note of the silver anniversary of the AAPC, and that of the IAPC (International Association of Political Consultants), that predated the AAPC's formation in 1969 by two weeks. Although the mix of campaign and media politics has been in a state of continuous flux throughout the twentieth century, producing a shift from partisan to merchandising and crusading campaigns (Jensen, 1980), the telepolitical era of casting, staging, orchestrating, and scripting of campaigns in the United States coincides neatly with the emergence of professional campaigning into young adulthood during the last quarter of a century (Nimmo, 1993).

This chapter explores that emergence and the changes it has wrought in the way Americans conduct their political affairs. First, the chapter adopts a view, or framework, for considering the principal elements of electoral campaigning in the United States. It then considers contemporary campaign practices within that framework and outlines the changes that brought about those conventions. Finally, the chapter explores the possible dehistoricizing, destructuring, and discarnate consequences of evolving campaign practices on the American polity.

ELECTORAL CAMPAIGNING IN THE UNITED STATES: THE RAMIFICATIONS OF PROLIFERATION

A quarter of a century ago, few students of American politics deigned to study electoral campaigns and their impact upon election outcomes, let alone their consequences for policy making or the long-range impact of changing campaign styles on the polity as a whole. Received wisdom, penned succinctly by Joseph Klapper (1960) in phrases that would ensnare students of communication for years to come, argued that mass communication worked within a context of mediating factors, largely reinforced rather than changed existing predispositions and conditions, were contributory not causal, and, hence, had marginal effects on voting. Although there were challenges to the "law of minimal consequences" (Lang & Lang, 1968, p. 4), for the most part, political scientists obeyed the sanction and concentrated not on the conduct of campaigns, but on the social and demographic backgrounds, social ties, and social psychological motivations voters took to those campaigns to explain electoral outcomes. As a result, theories of voting filled tomes and journals: economic (Downs, 1957), partisan (Campbell, Converse, Miller, & Stokes, 1960), issue oriented (Nie, Verba, & Petrocik, 1979), ideological (Maddox & Lilie, 1984), schema (Popkin, 1991), and rational choice (Bartels & Brady, 1993). By comparison, theories of campaigning (i.e., theories of electoral politics) were hard to find in the literature: Let the H. L. Menckens of the world fill the void with their impressionistic journalistic essays; certified scholars would find their insights under other lamp posts.

The contemporary recognition of the key role played by the mass media in elections is gradually shifting the scholarly focus away from voters (what media do *to* them and what they do *with* media) to campaign processes per se. Hence, there are several approaches for examining campaigns, varying widely in quality, that one may draw on in fashioning a framework useful in exploring the shifting relationships of politics, media, and democracy in the United States. To name but a few, there are functional schemes (Gronbeck, 1978; Trent & Friedenberg, 1991), rational choice models (Ferejohn & Noll, 1978), decision-making models (Lamb & Smith, 1968), marketing approaches (Mauser, 1983), temporal schemes (Kessel, 1988), heresthetical theories (Riker, 1986), and diagnostic/prescriptive analyses (Patterson, 1993).

Whatever the approach, there is a general agreement that campaign activity, as with any sociopolitical process, is extensional and durational, hence its major dimensions are aspectual and phasal (Bentley, 1908, 1935). Any shift in one or more aspects and/or phases yields consequences not only for general campaign processes, but for the workings of all politics. Such has been the case in the United States in the period since the AAPC/IAPC sought a professional identity for campaigners and their craft a quarter of a century ago.

The interlocking character of changes in campaign politics is particularly highlighted in Olson's (1967) probing of the structural dimensions of electoral politics. He offers a framework for integrating the key aspects and phases of modern campaigning and for speculating about the consequences of their shifting nature. Olson's focus on the "structure" of electoral politics is an attempt to adapt the concept from community-power studies, where structure refers to the distribution of power over community affairs to the campaign setting. In electoral politics, structure denotes a fourfold pattern of participation in elections: (1) scope of the election, (2) type of participants, (3) stages of the electoral cycle, and (4) factionalism. Olson's discussion offers a useful starting point for considering the recent evolution of campaign practices in the United States.

Scope of the Election

The scope of an election, and by extension of a campaign, refers to the number of offices filled by electoral politics, or policy choices made by initiative and/or referenda; the level of campaigns (national, state, local, district, etc.); the types of offices or policies at issue (executive, administrative, legislative, and judicial); and the character of the campaigns as partisan or nonpartisan. In the United States, there has historically been an ever-expanding electoral scope. In part, this has been a function of the long-term institutionalizing of the federal principle, with its division of authority among several levels of public jurisdictions. A plethora of campaigns result—for president, congress, governors, legislators, county courts, municipal officials, circuit judges, school districts, water districts, sewer authorities, and so on. No office is too trivial (or important?) to be ignored in the competition for office.

The expanding scope of U.S. elections, however, derives from sources other than the operation of the federal principle. As Schattschneider (1960), Crick (1962), Gilliatt (1987), and others have argued, at the heart of politics is the contagiousness of conflict. Be the argument between Alexander Hamilton and Thomas Jefferson, Abraham Lincoln and Stephen Douglas, or Beavis and Butthead, a fight consists of two elements: (1) the combatants at the center of the dispute, and (2) the audience attracted to the struggle. In politics, as Schattschneider notes, audience members are not mere spectators; as likely as not they determine the outcome of the fight by taking sides: "The number of people involved in any conflict determines what happens; every change in the number of participants, every increase or reduction in the number of participants affects the result" (Schattschneider, 1960, p. 2). Every time an audience member joins the fight, the balance of forces between the contenders shifts. That shift changes the tactics of the fight. The losing disputant has a vested interest in socializing the conflict, in recruiting allies to join in redressing the balance of forces; the winning side strives to privatize the dispute, thus containing the number of new entrants and maintaining an advantageous balance of power.

Consider the contagiousness, and expansion in scope, of conflict in the United States in recent decades. The conventional scope of bread, butter, and security issues that drove campaign politics in the New and Fair Deal eras (unemployment, living costs, and social security) expanded to include equally, and often more, contentious matters: civil rights, Vietnam, crime, urban blight, energy, the environment, sexual preference, abortion, health care, education, community development, transportation, technology, and so on. By the time he had assumed office in 1993, President Bill Clinton had specific policy recommendations for more than 250 major areas, ranging from timber sales to veterans' pensions, fusion-energy research to technology transfer, and cleaning up drinking water to taxing alcohol.

Few, if any, of these conflicts fail to influence the electoral arena, not merely as substantive issues, but as shapers of the *scope* of campaign politics. Many of the disputes have led to separate referenda elections, thus vastly expanding both the scope and the number of participants in campaign politics. There are innumerable single-issue groups active in local, state, and national politics: for and against gun control, for gay rights and against, for a local TV channel's airing of *NYPD Blue* and against, and others. Moreover, as the fortunes of contending sides have risen and fallen on various issues, there has been an expansion in the number of elections for public office. Disadvantaged contenders, eager to take their case to widened electorates, have called for electoral reform, especially of party nominating processes. The expansion of presidential primaries is but one case in point. In 1968, there were seventeen Democratic primaries to choose 37.5 percent of the delegates to the party's national convention and sixteen Republican primaries to select 34.3 percent of delegates; by 1992, the Democrats had expanded to thirty-seven primaries, electing two-thirds of delegates and Republicans to thirty-eight primaries, choosing more than three-fourths of delegates.

Political scientist Heinz Eulau designates this expansion of the scope of politics in America as a process of *proliferation*—the merging of a long-term trend toward social, economic, and political differentiation, with a post-1960s movement toward equalization, "evident in ever smaller social distances between highly diverse and differentiated social groups that increasingly share in or benefit from governance" (1981, p. 3). As a political process, proliferation "brings forth something that was not there before and replaces something else" (p. 4). Clearly, one aspect brought forth in contemporary campaign politics through the expansion of scope of issues, offices, and elections, one that has replaced older ways, is a key change in the second of Olson's elements of electoral structure: the type of participants.

Types of Participants

Prior to the onset of contemporary campaign practices in the United States, the types of campaign participants were both relatively limited in number and general in function, depending upon electoral level. The principal participant was the political party, operating either as an organization united behind a slate of candidates or, more frequently, a loose coalition of factional groupings vying for party control. In presidential politics, most of the nineteenth-century campaigns prior to the Civil War, then again following Reconstruction, were typified by competition between relatively consolidated parties. In the twentieth century, factional strife in presidential politics waxed and waned; intensifying, for example, in 1912 and 1948, but also apparent among Democrats in 1924 and 1928 and Republicans in 1916 and 1940. Below the presidential level, the reform politics of the 1930s stimulated broad factional strife, for example, in Minnesota between the forces of Floyd B. Olson and Ray P. Chase, in California in the 1934 contest between Frank F. Merriam and Upton Sinclair, and in New York City in 1933 in the three-way strife between Joseph V. McKee, Fiorello LaGuardia, and John P. O'Brien (Anderson, 1970).

In the era of party-driven campaigns there were other participant types as well: special interest groups protecting access to whatever party might win by limiting themselves to behind-the-scenes involvement in campaigns; electoral groups (now called Political Action Committees, or PACs) undertaking campaign financing and endorsements; caucus groups acting as nascent partisan participants in nonpartisan elections, such as the Boston caucus or Dallas Citizens Charter Association (Freeman, 1958); administrative agencies and public officials, usually acting informally; the contending candidates themselves; their "friends and neighbors" groups (Key, 1949) practicing the "politics of acquaintance" (Lee, 1960); the mass media (normally taken to mean newspapers) serving as a communication device for candidates via news and advertising and acting as sources of editorial endorsements; and, finally, the voters—partisan and independent, interested and indifferent, informed and ignorant.

In the spirit of Eulau's proliferation, contemporary campaign politics has witnessed an expansion in the sheer number of types of electoral participants and a differentiation in their character. Many of these new types previously existed, but are now highly specialized in what they do in campaigns. Others, in Eulau's phrase, were "not there before"; still others not there before now "replace something else." In any event, numerous campaign participants perform an ever more specialized set of campaign functions. And if one defines power as a relationship wherein power resides in an individual, group, or agency to the degree that others depend upon it for their own success or survival, then the new campaign participants ushered in with contemporary electoral practices are powerful. Candidates and voters alike find themselves increasingly dependent upon each of the following recruits to the new politics of campaigning.

The mass media were key participants even in the era of party-driven campaigns. In modern campaigning, however, the media have proliferated, almost to the point that "mass," in the sense of a single outlet reaching large, homogenous audiences with simultaneous messages, is a misnomer. First, network television news joined newspapers, newsmagazines, and radio as instruments (via free publicity and paid advertising) and reporters (via newscasts) of campaigning. Then, however, the differentiation genie escaped the

bottle and bestowed on candidates and voters cable and satellite communications that weakened the grasp of network television, helped redefine the
role of local TV news outlets infusing their political coverage with a national
scope rivaling network TV, and made possible publication and home deliv-
ery of leading metropolitan dailies, and *USA Today*, nationwide.

The quenchless thirst of cable channels for programming contributed to a
diversification of news formats. TV and radio talk shows, ranging from *Larry
King Live* to *Rush Limbaugh*, became around-the-clock options for viewers
and listeners. A "postmodern New News" full of glitz, gossip, and provoca-
tion supplemented and, for many Americans, replaced conventional "Old
News" broadcasts and documentaries (Campbell, 1993, p. 28). Presidential
candidates, officeholders, and spokespersons for sundry causes flocked to
MTV (Music Television), TNN (The Nashville Network), *Arsenio*, and *Donahue*
for cameo appearances as comics, saxophone players, and frugal gourmets.

Add to those shifts the technologies surrounding VCRs, direct mail,
telemarketing, desktop publishing, interactive media, computer networking,
electronic mail, fax machines, cellular phones, video telephony, 1-900 tele-
phoning, electronic books, and a seemingly endless array of other novelties
hawked by roadside stands along the information highway, and the possibilities for proliferating (and littering) the political media in campaigns prove
staggering. With the arrival of the digital world, never again would the phrase
"campaign media" (that once implied "one-way," "lowest common denomi-
nator," and "consumer") apply to the relationship of politics, media, and
modern democracy.

Even the most casual perusal of the fifteen volumes of *Campaigns & Elections*, the leading trade journal for campaign technicians that is now published bimonthly (and such rivals as *Campaign Industry News* or *Campaign*),
reveals that each new development in campaign media and attendant technologies has been accompanied by an emergence of campaign specialists offering skilled mastery in the use of each, either as professional advisers to
candidates or as vendors of the techniques themselves. These professionals
and vendors comprise an additional type of contemporary campaign participants—the campaign consultants. They cover all manner of specialties, most
of which were once the exclusive province of the political party: candidate
recruitment, campaign management, all phases of campaign media, fund-
raising, budgeting, scheduling, conforming to campaign laws, personnel recruitment and training, issue research, policy positioning, direct mail,
computer networking, voter research (polling, focus groups, in-depth analysis), voter segmentation, target marketing, speech writing, spin doctoring,
and hair styling.

Prior to the proliferation of types of electoral participation, electoral structures varied widely in the number of types participating and the relative
dominance of each. For example, in areas of tightly drawn party organizations (the infamous venues of party "machines" and "bosses" such as
Tammany Hall, the Daley machine in Chicago, or Boss Crump in Memphis),
the media, special interests, and even the candidate were supporting players
in the campaign drama. In contrast to this "party dominant" election struc-

ture, that of the "mixed type" involved a variety of participant categories, or an intermediate type might bring together a combination of parties and interest groups in an "omnipartisan" style (Olson, 1967, p. 362).

Proliferation, however, has worked several changes. One is particularly worthy of comment. As campaign media and campaign technicians "brought forth," in Eulau's phrase, by proliferation have replaced political parties as key participants, the variations in the character of electoral structures by participants' types has vanished. The shift began at the level of presidential politics and in key states, principally California (Kelley, 1956). In campaigns in those venues, campaign professionals and media specialists gradually displaced party stalwarts. The trend has now reached virtually *all* levels and *all* campaigns for *all* offices. Gone are dominant, mixed, and omnipartisan participatory patterns; they have been replaced by candidate-centered, consultant-based, and media-driven politics (Patterson, 1993; Wattenberg, 1992). A race for circuit judge in rural Sevier County, Tennessee, is no more immune from the triumph of Ellul's *la technique* than is the quest for the presidency of the United States (Ellul, 1964).

As electoral structures have become industrialized, specialized, and professionalized via proliferation, the costs of campaigning at all levels have increased substantially. Concerns that entire classes of citizens are denied access to the electoral arena have mounted, cases of campaign improprieties have multiplied, and cries for reform have become commonplace. As a result, a new category of participants has joined campaign and media technicians as major elements of the electoral structure. Campaigning is not only an industry, it is increasingly a regulated industry. Regulation at the national level with the establishment of the Federal Election Commission, and within a growing number of states having campaign ethics commissions, has spawned an ever-spiraling bureaucracy of regulators. The specialty of election law, scarcely recognized as such when the AAPC held its organizing session in 1969, now attracts aspiring young attorneys to its promises of profit.

The industrializing and professionalizing of campaign participants has added yet one other category of actors. In an era of party-centered elections, campaigners learned and honed their warrior skills by rising through the ranks of the party hierarchy. Those desiring entry into the industry today, however, take different routes. As the new politics came of age, many turned to readily available how-to-do-it guides with titles offering hope and fulfillment, for example, *The Selling of a Candidate: The Winning Formula* (Evry, 1971) or *The Campaign Manual: A Definitive Study of the Modern Political Campaign Process* (Guzzetta, 1981). An expanding number now look to classrooms and hands-on coursework in professional schools, along with consulting internships, to learn the trade. There they sit at the feet of media consultants, pollsters, statisticians, political scientists, communication researchers, and assorted gurus as they pursue advanced degrees in political management. The Graduate School of Political Management associated with George Washington University, for example, boasts a faculty of more than two dozen specialists teaching a curriculum including coursework in quantitative methods, statistical analysis of political data, data resources for political managers, the news media in politics, fundraising, fundamentals of lobbying, campaign advertising, campaign strategy, referendum politics, issue management, and election law.

One can but speculate about the manifold consequences that derive from this proliferation of electoral participants in the past quarter of a century or so. Most such speculation can be left until later. However, a single possibility intrudes at this point. As we have already seen, with the proliferation of electoral scope and participants, the campaign industry takes on a life of its own. The campaign no longer serves merely as a means to an end (i.e., as a means of achieving political office), but is an end in itself. The politician not only campaigns to hold office, but holds office to campaign. The imperative is for the campaign to propagate itself, prolong itself, and proliferate itself. Professional campaigners—be they candidates, consultants, journalists, regulators, educators, or anyone else—have a vested interest in The Campaign as more than a tool of democracy. For each category of participant, The Campaign is a vocation, an arena for flaunting professional legerdemain, and a source of pride; it may as well, perhaps, be a monster continuously to be fed, lest it devour its own.

The Electoral-Campaign Cycle

Students of election campaigns coin a variety of metaphors to distinguish the less publicized stages of electoral cycles from those phases that receive ample print and airtime from the media, such as primaries, conventions, and the general election. Hence, scholars speak of surfacing (Trent & Friedenberg, 1991); mist clearing (Kessel, 1988); and invisible stages (Binford, 1983). The metaphorical devices remind us that such activities as voter registration, candidate recruitment, securing financing, and media courting, although not always open to public scrutiny, are essential phases of the campaign pattern. And, as with the more widely publicized caucuses, primaries, conventions, and elections, these less noticeable phases vary with the scope of the election and the types of participants.

The same tendencies toward proliferation that have marked the expansion of the scope and participants of campaigns has influenced all phases of the electoral cycle as well. For example, the proliferation of electoral scope produces an increasing number of campaigns during any single calendar year. This has been particularly the case as states and local communities have multiplied substantially the use of popular referenda: sometimes placing them on the ballot to coincide with regularly scheduled national, state, or local elections; at others setting aside special elections at separate times. Scheduling aside, the mere proliferation of campaigns itself results in a complex overlap of electoral cycles. Granted that one may think in presidential contests along the simple lines of early days, initial contests, mist clearing, nominating conventions, and the general election (Kessel, 1988). But if one accepts the fact of electoral proliferation, then while the mist is clearing in the presidential season, a dense fog usually surrounds popular referenda and contests for lower offices for months to come. Hence, the electoral cycle has been pluralized in time and space (i.e., by overlapping time frames of specialized campaign activities at numerous electoral levels).

In an age of declining political party participation, no coordination of these manifold cycles exists. In Olson's framework, participant types differ depending upon electoral stages. "Continual participation of actors" consists of those "typically mobilized at all or most stages of the electoral cycle"; by contrast "segmental participation" involves campaigners who "typically confine themselves to one or only some stages" (1967, p. 363). The increasing specialization and division of labor among campaign professionals, however, produces a growing number of hybrids. These segmented–continuous types confine themselves to a single cycle phase, yet never stop campaigning, for they move from election to election across a single cycle. Hence, not only do professionals confine themselves to specialized functions—direct mail, 1-900 telebanks, TV time buying, and the like—they specialize temporally. Some hop between campaigns only during voter registration phases, others for caucus organizing, and yet others for exit polling.

The proliferation of electoral cycles adds to the trend toward the "permanent campaign," although in ways not originally intended in Blumenthal's (1982) coinage of the term. The permanence is akin to the vanishing "off season" in professional sports in America; for example, the championship of the National Basketball Association is scarcely decided on the court in mid-June before teams join in scouting combines, minicamps, and training camps prior to a round of exhibition games in September. Just as in the words of Nolan Ryan's Advil TV commercial, "there is no off season" anymore in baseball, there is none in campaigning. Somewhere on any given day one or more phases of election cycles are under way.

Consider also the development of a different type of campaign from the purely electoral contest—namely, the policy campaign. In an era of party-driven politics, for example, presidents and governors were elected, formulated policy proposals, then relied upon party leaders in congress and state legislatures to mobilize votes for passage. Today, paid consultants draft proposals (e.g., for educational reform or health-care reform) as part of their respective candidates' electoral-positioning strategies. Once elected, the victorious president or governor turns not to party leaders for legislative votes, but, again, to consultants to mount a campaign among the electorate and selected interest groups to bring pressure on legislative officials for support of such reforms. The professional consultant thus doubles in brass: first, as initiator of policy proposals that get candidates elected; second, as public lobbyist organizing post-election policy campaigns on behalf of the official the consultant elected to office.

Reinforcing cyclical proliferation of electoral and policy campaigns, and also contributing to campaign permanence, is media proliferation. News organizations, to be sure, chase ambulances, emergency vehicles, fire trucks, and police cruisers in pursuit of juicy breaking stories; however, they also thirst for developing, continuous stories with unfolding drama, turning points, and denouements. Tales of contest, conquest, and crises provide opportunities to build ever larger audiences to sell to advertisers. Electoral and policy campaigns offer promise of such a story of contest (Nimmo & Combs, 1990). News organizations at all audience levels, like campaign professionals astride constituency levels, have a vested interest in proliferating and elongating electoral and policy cycles. The more cycles there are and the more stages in each, the greater the opportunities for dramatizing the contest through an increased number of turning points.

Finally, technological innovations contribute to a changing temporal dimension of campaigns that is reflected in electoral cycles. One example will suffice. As modern post-World War II political campaigning was coming of age in the Eisenhower and Kennedy eras, news organizations were confined to a time-consuming task of sending crews to film campaign events, transporting the film back to the studio, editing, and anchor presentation on the now-nostalgic Six O'Clock News. The tedious newsgathering process limited the number of events reported in a day, week, month, or cycle stage. Today, minicams, videotape, satellite feeds, cellular telephones, and live and on-the-scene reporting in the absence of film and sound crews, editors, or anchors not only increases the quantity and variety of campaign stories; such news practices liberate candidates to campaign in more locales and over longer periods of time than ever before. Electronic wizardry elongates the campaign day by affording opportunities for candidates, freed from the Six O'Clock imperative, to make news anytime; it elongates the campaign season and proliferates its cycles by enhancing chances for candidates to build name recognition, establish a voter support base, and raise funds at a campaigner's pace, not in conformity with short- or long-term media scheduling.

Factionalism

Olson's model factionalism "measures the extent, types, and bases of cleavage and alignments among participants within an electoral structure," and applies to "any alignments among electoral participants," (1967, p. 363) not merely the subgroups within a political party. Throughout their existence, political parties have always been subject to factional strife. Pulling against the instrumental efforts of the party to cement collective benefits for all party subgroups, there have always been intraparty factions struggling to achieve ends of private benefit to members. And, although political parties in the American setting have not in themselves been synonymous with faction, the tendency persists for them to deteriorate "into something resembling faction," such that "factionalism is the ever-present temptation of a party arrangement and its ever-possible degeneration" (Sartori, 1976, p. 25).

However, in the time frame of this analysis of the relationship of politics, media, and democracy in the United States, it has not been principally the "ever-present temptation" of American parties to degenerate into factions that has proved the major threat to partisan domination of electoral structure. Rather, over approximately the last quarter of a century party degeneration has been sparked primarily from extra party alignments among electoral participants, of which Olson speaks. As suggested earlier, in discussing types of campaign participants, the proliferation of such factional alignments has taken several forms. Key among them are the single-issue groups active at all levels and stages of the electoral cycle in such matters as abortion, gun control, anti-smoking, drunk driving, environmental protection, the plight of the homeless, and the like.

Also key has been the proliferation of PACs. These organizations, through voluntary contributions of their members, play major roles in funding political campaigns at all electoral levels and through all stages of the electoral cycle. Like cockroaches, PACs multiplied with abandon. In the early 1970s, for example, there were fewer than one hundred corporate PACs; by the early 1980s there were more than a thousand. PACs of labor unions, environmental groups, professionals, civil rights groups, and so on—all mushroomed in numbers in the past two decades. So vital have PACs become to campaigning, that presidential candidates routinely organize their own political action committees, termed "nonconnected organizations," to defray expenses and fund activities in the period of the electoral cycle between the last election and the actual opening of the next presidential contest.

Although PACs can legally contribute money to party organizations (for example, to local and state parties for promoting voter turnouts on election day), a relatively small percentage of PAC funds assist party fortunes (Sorauf, 1988, 1992). A larger proportion of PAC money goes directly to political candidates. Yet, as an example, in presidential elections those contributions rarely exceed 3 percent of total money raised in a single year (Wayne, 1992). There are more than 4,700 PACs in the United States; less than a quarter of those contribute money to political candidates or causes. Only 2 percent (approximately 70) of PACs contribute $5,000 or more to candidates.

Where PACs acting as factions do loom large is in independent expenditures, often in a seeming nonpartisan guise, to educate, mobilize, and turn out voters. PAC independent expenditures on behalf of individual candidates have proliferated in recent decades. In 1987–1988 alone, PACs spent money on behalf of over 600 candidates for the U.S. House of Representatives and Senate (Wayne, 1992).

THE TWILIGHT ZONE OF U.S. CAMPAIGNS: THE DISCONTINUITIES OF TIME AND SPACE

The precise effects of contemporary campaign practices on voters' choices in individual contests is scarcely possible to determine; instead, one can but speculate about the more general features of the electoral structure that are emerging from trends of proliferation in electoral scope, participant types, electoral cycles, and factionalism. Others, too, have speculated about the diverse influences on contemporary politics: the impact of the decline of political parties on voting (Popkin, 1991), the growing power of the news media (Patterson, 1993), the mischievousness of PACs (Bennett, 1992), the emergence of a political marketing industry (Newman, 1994), and the decline of an alleged golden era of civil discourse (Jamieson, 1992). Their arguments are well known and, hence, require no needless repetition. Instead, we speculate about other matters.

The Dehistoricizing of Political Time

Contemporary campaign politics in the United States assumes a character outlined centuries ago in a letter written by Niccolo Machiavelli to Piero Soderini. In that correspondence, Machiavelli charted the "first law of politics," that is, the proneness to boredom: "As bitter things disturb the taste and sweet ones cloy it, so men get bored with good and complain of ill" (quoted in Minogue, 1972, p. 157). For Machiavelli, the task of the politician is to exploit that proneness to tire of things as they are ("There you go again," candidate Ronald Reagan scolded President Jimmy Carter in 1980). Whatever is in politics at any given time must be changed, or, more important, must *appear* to change.

The appearance of change recommended by Machiavelli to exploit the proneness to boredom he called *fantasia*, the engineering of imaginations (now called images). Governance by *fantasia* is necessarily a turning away from reason, logic, and fact, for reason and evidence impose limitations on imagination. Moreover, insofar as reason involves historical fact, *fantasia* contributes to a dehistoricizing of the polity: political thinking is "not the copying of an agreed belief on the ends of political order." Instead, "It is simply a *constantly changing concordance of the popular imagination*, and the business of politics is to maintain that concordance by any means available." For, while "reason is public, ordered, and predictable, *fantasia* . . . is private, chaotic, and unstable" (Minogue, 1972, p. 160; emphasis added).

There is a paradox. In one direction, the proliferation of politics has contributed, as already noted, to the elongation of campaigns; for example, producing the permanent campaign with no off season, or the campaign news day no longer geared to the Six O'Clock News but for around-the-clock coverage. Reason might dictate that with such a surfeit of campaign activities and news about them, Americans would be inundated with political information. That information, in turn, would provide opportunities for reasoned, logical, evidential analysis leading to, in Minogue's words, "public, ordered, and predictable" popular responses to campaign politics. Citizens would, in short, have an ever-deepening sense of an historical baseline against which to measure candidates.

The paradox, however, lies in the ahistorical and nonhistorical packaging of campaign information. As one package, for example, consider the sound bite. In 1960, the length of the average comment or commentary by a presidential candidate that appeared on TV newscasts was forty-five seconds; by 1992, that time was compressed to fifteen seconds. The "spot" ad is but another form of time compression: Once as long as five minutes in length, it now consists of thirty- and twenty-second snippets highlighting candidates' positions and personae. Moreover, factoids (pithy assertions of facts widely treated as true even though supporting evidence is not available) replace facts themselves (Pratkanis & Aronson, 1991). Visual factoids, the synthetic facts from news sources otherwise uninformed and uninterested, further dehistoricize; for example, the kindergarten child offers a snappy analysis of the candidate just shown visiting the class to underscore a concern with preschool education. Moreover, candidate debates packaged as joint news conferences preclude anything other than short, disjointed responses (Sproule, 1988).

But did not the 1992 presidential contest with Ross Perot's thirty-minute infomercials, Bill Clinton's plethora of town hall meetings, and popular participation in the staging of the second presidential debate reestablish a more ordered, reflective, and reasoned approach? Close scrutiny of such packaging suggests otherwise. Perhaps these alleged communication breakthroughs countered public boredom associated with the *gravitas* of sound bites, ads, and factoids; as novel *fantasia* they were scarcely the rich lode of political information that their promoters claimed. Nor were the opportunities for questions and answers between candidates and constituents any less time compressed or noncontextual than in conventional packaging; candidates' responses were contrived and rehearsed, the standardized fare Americans have come to expect in the finest campaign tradition (Nimmo, 1992).

One manifestation of the trend toward candidates and campaigns without histories has been the "new face" phenomenon, contributing to the arrival in U.S. politics of "flash candidacies" common in many parliamentary regimes. In the absence of party discipline, Americans have witnessed proliferating cameo appearances by new faces with the wherewithal to conduct background and tracking polls; voter targeting and direct mail; and grassroots and media campaigns in caucuses, primaries, and general elections: Eugene McCarthy in 1968, Jimmy Carter in 1976, John Anderson in 1980, Jesse Jackson and Pat Robertson in 1988, and Pat Buchanan and Ross Perot in 1992. Only Carter won a nomination or an election. Others, however, fight off the tendency of bored voters to ask, "Where are they now?"

The Destructuring of Political Space

In a democratic polity, the rationale for campaigning lies in mobilizing voters behind contending candidates or causes in free, impartial elections. To accomplish that mobilization, candidates and their supporters, both paid and voluntary, transmit sundry communication throughout and through the campaign. Campaigns are therefore not only communication events, their very raison d'être makes them communication media as well. If we entertain the possibility that Innis (1951) might have been correct in asserting that each medium has a time and space bias, then it is feasible that the dehistoricizing of campaigns that has been outlined derives from the time bias of contemporary campaigns, a seemingly contradictory bias of durational elongation and compression. Moreover, if Innis makes sense, then we might expect campaigns to work spatial changes as well.

In certain aspects, campaigns do so by reorganizing the spatial dimensions of elections, disaggregating participants, and, thereby, destructuring the electoral order. Scholars have long recognized that interest aggregation—the combining, accommodating, and regulating of competing claims and demands—is a principal function of politics. Interest aggregation occurs both through the formulation of general policies that take conflict into account and via the recruitment of political personnel, "more or less committed to a particular pattern of policy" (Almond & Coleman, 1960, p. 39). In framing the American polity, the constitutional founders from the outset rendered interest aggregation problematic. Describing the founders' elaborate efforts to make an "unjust combination of a majority of the whole very improbable, if not impracticable," James Madison in *The Federalist No. 51* called attention to the spatial advantages of "the extended republic" in securing the minority against a "coalition of the whole" (1937, pp. 339–341).

During the age of party-dominated elections, the biases against interest aggregation inherent in "the extended republic" were mitigated by political parties—decentralized in organization, to be sure, yet national in scope and symbolic appeal. Somewhere, Madison must be smiling, for the decline of parties as mobilizers of elections and of loyalties returns us to spatial disaggregation in political recruitment with a vengeance. For example, voting precincts and wards, once the basic units employed to aggregate interests through ever-larger county and statewide organizations within each party, have been replaced by TV ADIs (areas of dominant influence). ADIs mark the geographic boundaries of media markets—the county or counties where broadcasters in a city enjoy the greatest share of an audience. From the 7 million households that comprise the New York City ADI (the largest) to the 5,000 in Glendive, Montana (the smallest ADI), there are 212 ADIs in "the extended republic" of James Madison. Here are the geographic spaces where candidates buy advertising time (both over-the-air and cable), appear on newscasts, and target their appeals.

By tailoring their messages to ADI voters directly through electronic media and not through a party worker acting as mediator, candidates shift campaign space in another manner. Reaching the younger voter by MTV, the retired via video cassette targeted through AARP (American Association of Retired Persons) mailing lists, the crusader using the MADD (Mothers Against Drunk Driving) telephone bank, or the evangelical through the PTL (Praise the Lord) electronic ministry offers an illusion of intimate interpersonal space between candidates and voters, an illusion more powerful than that afforded by canvassing by a ward healer. Hence, the oft-cited aphorism of the electronic age: A TV set is like having the candidate, not just a precinct worker, in every home. The living room campaign serves as both medium and message.

Destructuring, disaggregation, and dealignment are manifested in policy making as well. Members of Congress, who in an age of party-driven political recruitment could always find a guide for how to vote on roll calls (and thereby a scapegoat if their voting stands were too much for constituents to stomach), now find themselves in a Hobbesian world of all against all; each to one's own salvation. They owe their election not to party, not to the president, not even to a clearly aligned aggregate of special interests. They arrive in office as a result of success at personalized media campaigns. But, once in Congress, they find that votes now *count*. Whether on deficit reduction, gun control, or health reform, there is no party line; only the disaggregated demands and claims of constituents—constituents mobilized by professional consultants in policy campaigns for and against presidential proposals. With no place to hide, yet buffeted by conflicting winds in policy campaigns, 435

Representatives and 100 Senators are just that, 535 self-interests in search of momentary aggregation, rather than an institutional embodiment of public regardingness.

A final area of destructuring warrants mention, one that follows from the professionalizing of campaign practices. As Jensen (1980) points out, presidential campaigns in the early decades of the twentieth century, especially those of Woodrow Wilson in 1912 and 1916, marked the movement away from party-driven to merchandising politics. Coincidentally, it was President Wilson who first begrudgingly turned to both policy and propaganda "experts" to aid his governance. Such experts emerged as a professionally trained infrastructure of technicians that Wilson thought should be "on tap, not on top." That, however, is not how it was to remain (Smith, 1991). It was not long until these technicians found routes to advance their careers that lay outside conventional party politics—private research organizations, reform associations, interest groups, foundations, universities, and the like.

A half century after Wilson departed office, professional campaign and policy technicians had proliferated as consultants to parties, politicians, candidates, and officials; to newspapers, radio, and TV organizations; and to a host of diverse specialized interest complexes, including health, education, defense, and welfare. They brought to politics two disaggregating qualities. First, they had their own power bases outside conventional party and government establishments, often their own prosperous consulting firms. Second, they brought expertise in techniques that could serve any candidate, party, interest, or cause just as well as another. Since their professional livelihoods depended less on serving any single client than in generating a rolodex of hundreds, even thousands, of separate, proliferating clients, disaggregation of political recruitment served the long-term career ambitions of this emerging elite more than would have interest aggregation. This is not to claim premeditation or conspiracy, but merely to note that professionalized politics has enhanced the destructuring of the polity.

Too Much and Too Little for Voters in Time and Space

The proliferation through time, space, and media of the electoral process contributes to dehistoricizing campaigns via paradox. Namely, more information is available to voters through an increasing number of sources, yet the information explosion destroys an historical baseline, a common knowledge base, for evaluating that information. Proliferation's contribution to the destructuring of campaigns produces another paradox: Interest articulation (Almond & Coleman, 1960) has become increasingly egalitarian and democratic as heretofore undefined and unrepresented claims and demands emerge; yet that very equality of opportunity in articulation undercuts a key function of politics when destructuring shatters the consensus-building processes of interest aggregation.

Dehistoricizing and destructuring combine with a third consequence of the shifting relationships between politics, media, and democracy in the United States. Sociologist Orrin Klapp designates this trend as "social inflation," specifically "symbolic inflation" (1991, p. 3). Innovations in communication media—be they oral, print, electronic, or in the larger sense of campaigns themselves—as political phenomena do not merely provide new means of transmitting messages. In Pearce's (1993) terms they act as an infrastructure enabling different sets of events and relationships to occur than were possible before their arrival.

So conceived, the media constitute a *place* where things happen. To say that a person or event is "in the media" captures that sense of media as place. That place possesses its own unique dimensions of time and space, but has no location. Media time, as noted above, is "fractured into many splinters" (Pearce, 1993, p. 66). Media space is not a forum for a reasoned debate, but a place for hawking wares, a "county fair, with the din of competing shills seeking to entice momentary curiosity and separate the unwary from their money," a space "not conducive to dialogue" (Pearce, 1993, p. 67).

As with other areas of life's endeavors, in the time-fractured and space-for-hawking place that constitutes campaigns as media, the "flood of information" (Klapp, 1982, p. 57) inundates, yet does not bring with it the nutrients required to replenish the over-tilled, bored cultural soil of the polity (Klapp, 1986). Hence, there is again a paradox, that is, a *flood* of information leaves a residue of *missing* information (McKibben, 1992). U.S. campaigns produce an inexhaustible supply of claims and counterclaims, appeals and counter-appeals, statistics and counterstatistics, and factoids and counterfactoids. In the end, however, no matter how large their number or how often their repetition in the place that is indeed a county fair, they are not all that different. They are not all that informative.

Proliferation in U.S. campaign politics has produced a proliferation of symbols as a by-product, symbols inflated by hype, hyperbole, redundancy, euphemism, jargon, and the abuse of negative campaigning. To cut through the clutter, as Popkin asserts, voters employ informational shortcuts that permit them to "go without data" (1991, pp. 44–71); for example, a focus on current party claims rather than past performance, or a concern for personal morality of candidates rather than institutional morality—perceived competence rather than performance. Voters also "go beyond data" (pp. 72–74) by using representative heuristics, simple cues, and rules-of-thumb to judge if candidates will do the right thing.

The result, at least in Popkin's analysis, is that voters make choices through a "drunkard's search," a search "among obvious differences" (p. 92). Like the inebriate searching under a street lamp for a lost house key, voters look in unlikely places for clues as to how to choose between obvious differences. Asked why he didn't look for the house key where he had dropped it, rather than under the street lamp where he had not even been, a voter might reply as did the drunkard, "Because the light is better there."

A CONCLUDING QUESTION: THE DISCARNATE VOTER?

None of the previous material demeans voters' capacities for information processing. Indeed, behavioral scientists also follow the principle of the drunkard's search in their investigations, hopping from one hypothesis to another as the light turns on and off (Kaplan, 1964). Rather, if Popkin's likening of voters' choices to a drunkard's search has merit, it contributes to a concluding note regarding the consequences of contemporary campaigning for U.S. democracy. The paradoxical confluence in contemporary campaigns of an information overload and missing information brought about by symbolic inflation yields campaigns of play, of fanciful engineering, akin to Machiavelli's *fantasia*. Voters sedated by the spirits of campaigning are involved in the play of information. Like Marshall McLuhan's "discarnate" beings (Marchand, 1989, p. 238), they are as small children fascinated by a kaleidoscope, seduced by the shifting, transitory play and passage of images in a phantom electronic world.

McLuhan's discarnates as voters are accustomed to having political hawkers in their living rooms, and discarnate voters are present, minus their bodies, in many different places simultaneously through electronic passage. The consequences of this discarnate state were, for McLuhan, not pleasant. The discarnate "loses touch with a geographic location and a social function" and is "uncontrollable" (McLuhan & Powers, 1989, p. 124). Discarnates are "identityless inhabitants of the acoustic world," reacting "to their state by acts of violence, physical and psychological" (Marchand, 1989, p. 238).

We need not go so far as McLuhan and prophesy that, should the dehistoricizing, destructuring, and discarnating trends speculated upon continue, blood will ultimately flow—even though the growing amount of domestic violence in the United States tempts one to do so. Democratic processes may as easily be strengthened by people voting their emotions as threatened by the practice (Marcus & Mackuen, 1993). Yet we know overindulgence with drink takes a toll on the identity. Even W. C. Fields, a.k.a. Cuthbert J. Twillie, after a particularly bad night, found himself in bed with a goat rather than "My Little Chickadee." Who is to say that the heady spirits of contemporary campaign communication, messages, and media that taste great but are indeed less filling, might not have their own deleterious side effects for the body politic of the United States that is now our Greasewood City?

REFERENCES

Almond, G. A., & Coleman, J. S. (1960). *The politics of the developing areas*. Princeton: Princeton University Press.

Anderson, W. (1970). *Campaigns: Cases in political conflict*. Pacific Palisades, Calif.: Goodyear.

Bartels, L., & Brady, H. E. (1993). The state of quantitative political methodology. In A. W. Finifter (Ed.), *Political science: The state of the discipline II* (pp. 121–159). Washington, D.C.: American Political Science Association.

Bennett, W. L. (1992). *The governing crisis: Media, money, and marketing in American elections*. New York: St. Martin's Press.

Bentley, A. (1908). *The process of government*. Chicago: University of Chicago Press.

Bentley, A. (1935). *Behavior knowledge fact*. Bloomington, Ind.: Principia.

Binford, M. B. (1983, November). *Electoral campaigns: Contextual adaptation and candidate image development*. Paper presented at the meeting of the Southern Political Science Association, Birmingham, Ala.

Blumenthal, S. (1982). *The permanent campaign*. New York: Touchstone Books.

Campbell, A., Converse, P. E., Miller, W. E., & Stokes, D. E. (1960). *The American voter*. New York: John Wiley & Sons.

Campbell, R. (1993). Don Hewitt's durable hour. *Columbia Journalism Review, 32*(3), 25–28.

Crick, B. (1962). *In defense of politics*. Chicago: University of Chicago Press.

Downs, A. (1957). *An economic theory of democracy*. New York: Harper & Row.

Ellul, J. (1964). *The technological society*. New York: Vintage.

Eulau, H. (1981). The proliferation of American politics. *The Key Reporter, 46*(3), 2–4.

Evry, H. (1971). *The selling of a candidate: The winning formula*. Los Angeles: Western Opinion Research Center.

Ferejohn, J. A., & Noll, R. G. (1978). Uncertainty and the formal theory of political campaigns. *American Political Science Review, 72*, 492–505.

Freeman, J. L. (1958). Local party systems: Theoretical considerations and a case analysis. *American Journal of Sociology, 64*, 282–289.

Gilliatt, S. (1987). Being political: A quarrelsome view. *International Political Science Review, 8*, 367–384.

Gronbeck, B. (1978). The functions of political campaigning. *Communication Monographs, 45*, 268–280.

Guzzetta, S. J. (1981). *The campaign manual: A definitive study of the modern political campaign process*. Alexandria, Va.: Campaign Publishing Co.

Innis, H. A. (1951). *The bias of communication*. Toronto: University of Toronto Press.

Jamieson, K. H. (1992). *Dirty politics: Deception, distraction, and democracy*. New York: Oxford University Press.

Jensen, R. (1980). Armies, admen, and crusaders: Strategies win elections. *Public Opinion, 3*(5), 44–49, 52–53.

Kaplan, A. (1964). *The conduct of inquiry*. San Francisco: Chandler.

Kelley, S., Jr. (1956). *Professional public relations and political power*. Baltimore: Johns Hopkins University Press.

Kessel, J. H. (1988). *Presidential campaign politics* (3rd ed.). Chicago: Dorsey.

Key, V. O., Jr. (1949). *Southern politics*. New York: Knopf.

Klapp, O. E. (1982). Meaning lag in the information society. *Journal of Communication, 32*(2), 56–66.

Klapp, O. E. (1986). *Overload and boredom: Essays on the quality of life in the information society*. Westport, Conn.: Greenwood.

Klapp, O. E. (1991). *Inflation of symbols*. New Brunswick, N.J.: Transaction Books.

Klapper, J. (1960). *The effects of mass communication*. Glencoe, Ill.: Free Press.

Lamb, K. A., & Smith, P. A. (1968). *Decision-making: The presidential election of 1984*. Belmont, Calif.: Wadsworth.

Lang, K., & Lang, G. E. (1968). *Voting and nonvoting*. Waltham, Mass.: Blaisdell.

Lee, E. C. (1960). *The politics of nonpartisanship*. Berkeley: University of California Press.

Maddox, W. S., & Lilie, S. A. (1984). *Beyond liberal and conservative*. Washington, D.C.: Cato Institute.

Madison, J., Hamilton, A., & Jay, J. (1937). *The federalist* (E. M. Earle, Ed.). New York: Modern Library.

Marchand, P. (1989). *Marshall McLuhan: The medium and the messenger*. New York: Ticknor & Fields.

Marcus, G. E., & MacKuen, M. B. (1993). Anxiety, enthusiasm, and the vote: The emotional underpinnings of learning and involvement during presidential campaigns. *American Political Science Review, 87*, 672–685.

Mauser, G. A. (1983). *Political marketing*. New York: Praeger.

McKibben, B. (1992). *The age of missing information*. New York: Random House.

McLuhan, M., & Powers, B. R. (1989). *The global village: Transformations in world life and media in the 20th century*. New York: Oxford University Press.

Minogue, K. R. (1972). Theatricality and politics: Machiavelli's concept of fantasia. In B. Pareth & R. N. Benk (Eds.), *The morality of politics* (pp. 148–162). London: George Allen & Unwin.

Newman, B. I. (1994). *The marketing of the president*. Thousand Oaks, Calif.: Sage.

Nie, N. H., Verba, S., & Petrocik, J. R. (1979). *The changing American voter* (2nd ed.). Cambridge, Mass.: Harvard University Press.

Nimmo, D. (1992, November). *Socio-political myths as the enactment of voters' fantasies*. Paper presented at the meeting of the Speech Communication Association, Chicago.

Nimmo, D. (1993). Politics and the mass media: From political rule to postpolitical mediarchy. *Current World Leaders, 36*(2), 303–320.

Nimmo, D., & Combs, J. (1990). *Mediated political realities* (2nd ed.). New York: Longman.

Olson, D. M. (1967). The structure of electoral politics. *Journal of Politics, 29*, 352–367.

Patterson, T. E. (1993). *Out of order*. New York: Alfred A. Knopf.

Pearce, W. B. (1993). Achieving dialogue with "the Other" in the postmodern world. In P. Gaunt (Ed.), *Beyond agendas: New directions in communication research* (pp. 59–74). Westport, Conn.: Greenwood.

Popkin, S. L. (1991). *The reasoning voter*. Chicago: University of Chicago Press.

Pratkanis, A., & Aronson, E. (1991). *Age of propaganda*. New York: W. H. Freeman.

Riker, W. H. (1986). *The art of political manipulation*. New Haven: Yale University Press.

Sartori, G. (1976). *Parties and party systems* (Vol. I). London: Cambridge University Press.

Schattschneider, E. E. (1960). *The semisovereign people*. New York: Holt, Rinehart & Winston.

Smith, J. A. (1991). *The idea brokers*. New York: Free Press.

Sorauf, F. (1988). *Money in American elections*. Boston: Little, Brown.

Sorauf, F. (1992). *Inside campaign finance: Myths and realities*. New Haven: Yale University Press.

Sproule, J. M. (1988). The new managerial rhetoric and the old criticism. *Quarterly Journal of Speech, 74*, 468–486.

Trent, J. S., & Friedenberg, R. V. (1991). *Political campaign communication* (2nd ed.). New York: Praeger.

Wattenberg, M. J. (1992). *The rise of candidate-centered politics*. Cambridge, Mass.: Harvard University Press.

Wayne, S. J. (1992). *The road to the White House 1992*. New York: St. Martin's Press.

Chapter Three

Modern Communications versus Traditional Politics in Britain: Unstable Marriage of Convenience

Jay G. Blumler, Dennis Kavanagh, and T. J. Nossiter

The editors of this volume have advanced twinned hypotheses for our comparative consideration. One is that a global process of far-reaching change is inexorably if unevenly transforming competitive political communication campaigning in many modern democracies. According to its companion, the "Americanization" hypothesis, this process has been spurred by the export of many key features of campaign communications in the United States to "sister democracies" elsewhere, serving as a role model of publicity excellence. The relationship of the British case to this framework is highly complex, however, both confirming and challenging it. Of course, in dynamic conditions, not all the returns are yet in on these matters.

It is undoubtedly true that, since the 1950s, British campaigning practices have "changed fundamentally, . . . albeit slowly and cumulatively" (Butler, 1986, p. 3), conforming at each successive election ever more closely to a "professionalized" paradigm. It is all a far cry from the television interviewer who, in 1950, asked the Prime Minister, Mr. Clement Attlee, if he had anything to say on the eve of the election campaign. Attlee replied, "No," and that was the end of the interview. There remain significant and possibly enduring differences from the American archetype, however, and the causes of the trends concerned have been more indigenous than extraneous. Not all *similarities* to American patterns should be confused with *sources*.

Moreover, in the United Kingdom, the professionalized campaign model was introduced into a strongly formed political system and culture, which, however absorptive of new assumptions and emphases, has also been more resistant to the ways and values of *realpublizistik* than its U.S. counterpart. Characteristic features of Britain's traditional system are consequently in some tension with characteristic imperatives of the modern publicity process, yielding an unstable coexistence. Modernized political communication processes, with solid and institutionalized footholds in the British system, are curbed and tamed by contextual factors, which are themselves in flux and under some strain.

Much is at stake in the future course of this mixed marriage, including the contribution of communication to British democracy and citizenship. We consider those prospects in the conclusion to this chapter.

THE MODERN POLITICAL COMMUNICATION
PROCESS IN BRITAIN

Observers in different societies may provide varying accounts of the main trends of campaign change, reflecting differences of empirical reality and/or what they personally find significant. From a U.K. perspective, we would define the modern political communication process through the following nine features, all of which seem to apply "in trumps" to the United States and have taken some hold in Britain, albeit less completely in most respects.

An Upgrading of Publicity Priorities per se, Involving the Devotion by Political Actors of More Thought, Energy, and Resources to Media Strategies and Tactics

Many British examples of this tendency can be mentioned. Between 1979 and 1989, there was a tenfold increase, in real terms, in government spending on advertising, making government one of the country's top advertising clients. What Americans term "the permanent campaign" is now extending the British electoral calendar. Thus, as build up to the April 9th Polling Day for the 1992 General Election, the strategists of both major parties devised, from January onward, what was called a "near-term campaign," in which they bombarded the electorate with a host of preplanned events designed to channel and fix opinion before the three-and-a-half-week campaign officially opened in mid-March. The internal functions of the three main parties' annual conferences (one week each in early autumn) are being displaced by their external purposes. As Kavanagh has explained,

Traditionally, a party conference was a relationship between the platform and the floor. But intense media coverage has transformed that relationship into one between the conference as a whole and the viewer at home. . . . Conferences are [therefore] increasingly media events, stage-managed for television. More than ever they form part of the perpetual election campaign and the projection of a positive party image and strong leadership. (1990, p. 22)

It is increasingly alleged that even government and party policy decisions are influenced by how they might play in the arena of media-filtered impressions, favoring attention to the short-term dimensions of problems over their structural and long-term bases.

The Adoption by Political Competitors of Profoundly
Media-Centered Publicity Strategies

As a Conservative "war book" for the 1992 campaign tersely emphasized, "the most important target group is the media." Intriguing for scholars, a key thrust of this feature has academic roots in the tradition of media-effects research initiated by McCombs and Shaw (1972) in their classic article on "The Agenda-Setting Function of the Mass Media." Campaign managers have thoroughly absorbed their core assumption—namely, that the issues given most attention and prominence in the news media will tend to become the ones that voters think are most important, and in light of which they will judge the adequacy of politicians' performance and claims to power—as a pragmatic guide. They now see it as a prime task to try as best they can to shape the mass media news agenda for politics. As Crewe and Harrop declared after the 1987 election, "Election campaigns are agenda-setting games" (1989, p. xiii), a proposition which Labour publicists Hewitt and Mandelson echoed, maintaining in the same volume that, "Competition between rival agenda-setting is at the heart of modern campaigns" (1989, p. 53).

BBC journalists observed at work during the 1987 and 1992 elections testified that the parties' attempts to set the television news agenda had become "a more central, considered and concerted element in [their] strategies than ever before" (Blumler, Gurevitch, & Nossiter, 1989, p. 159). Battle commences early in the day, with the party researchers looking at first editions of the daily press and analyzing overnight television coverage. The aim is to pick up the latest stories and give them a spin or relate them to the party's chosen issue of the day. The party's position on that issue is presented by spokespersons at an early morning press conference and woven into subsequent events and interviews of the day. So far as possible, initial questions from journalists are confined to it, and the major television reporters are always called very early, in the expectation that their channels will carry the answer.

The Adaptation of Much Political Rhetoric to the
Presumed Imperatives of Television News

Since the 1970s, for example, the parties' campaign events have been synchronized to BBC-1 and ITV bulletin schedules, aiming to catch the midday news with material from the morning press conferences, staging leader "walkabouts" in visually appealing settings in the afternoons for early evening news coverage, and inserting passages into leader speeches at party rallies in the evening for inclusion in the main nightly news (Blumler, Gurevitch, & Nossiter, 1986, p. 104).[1] Recourse to "soundbites," involving the inclusion of "nuggets," "nutshells," and "golden phrases" in speeches on the stump or in Parliament for relay onward to news viewers (Blumler, Gurevitch, & Ives, 1978, p. 29), is now standard practice. Of course, not all British politicians have been good at this. Speechwriters were frustrated with Michael Foot and James Callaghan,[2] for example, but acknowledged that both had been reared in an earlier age.[3] An increasing personalization of party combat has also resulted, since television seeks to cast familiar and important characters as leading players in the unfolding political drama. As Hewitt and Mandelson confirmed for the 1987 election, "the media circus following each leader ensured that the leaders' tours were the principal device for telling the story of the campaign" (1989, p. 53).[4]

Politics as a Sort of "Virtual Reality," in Which Mass Perceptions of Politics Are All that Matter

Such a "nightmarish" formulation may seem less applicable to the mentality of elite circles in London than in Washington, D.C., from David Gergen's remarkable account of which it derives:

It has come to be held that what sort of person a politician actually is and what he actually does are not really important. What is important is the perceived image of what he is and what he does. Politics is not about objective reality, but virtual reality. (Quoted in Kelly, 1993, p. 64)

Nevertheless, the British literature includes many references to pressures on leaders to adjust their images to presumed media requirements, even when this went against their temperamental grain. Resulting feelings of role distance have reportedly afflicted such diverse personalities as Sir Alec Douglas-Home (urged to be less patrician), Edward Heath (to be less formal and cold), Margaret Thatcher (to be less harsh), and Neil Kinnock (to be more succinct). In just three years of Prime Ministerial office, Mr. Major has donned and discarded numerous personae, ranging from the caring to the tough. There is also an emphasis on keeping less voter-friendly politicians away from the screen, as with John Prescott and Gerald Kaufman for Labour and Norman Lamont for the Conservatives in 1992.

Why do some British politicians have difficulty in coping with television? Likely explanations include their frequent involvement in parliamentary debate, in which the main aim is to rally your own side (i.e., be partisan); the early party grooming of leaders as platform orators, as with Michael Foot and Neil Kinnock, who were more natural and energized when faced with live audiences; and the strong policy orientation of some politicians, such as Edward Heath, who loves facts and details and cannot talk down to people.

The Translation of Electioneering into Political Marketing

According to Harrop, the 1980s "were pivotal years in the development of political marketing in Britain," such that, by the end of the decade, "it would have been . . . big news if a major party had chosen not to use professional marketing expertise in an election" (1990, p. 277). This approach treats the voter more as a consumer to be pleased than as a citizen to be enlightened or engaged in debate. It equates the party message with a product suited to meet consumer needs and allay people's worries and fears (Butler & Collins, 1993). In particular, it encourages the party to define its message clearly, choose the medium through which it will be expressed, and specify the target for it, which is what is routinely done in commerce. British politicians have thought in these terms for a long time, but in an unsystematic way. The contribution of the marketing adviser has been to concentrate their thinking along these lines. Of course, extensive opinion research is a "foundation upon which the marketing concept has been built in British politics" (Scammell, 1991, p. 53). This introduces the next, further-defining feature of the process under consideration.

Data-Driven Campaigning

A sixth feature of the modern political process is data-driven campaigning, or an increasing use of public opinion polling, survey research, and focus-group exercises to discover voters' perceptions, moods, needs, and desires and their ratings of rival parties and leaders. Such data are then used, on the one hand, by the news media to report which parties and leaders are ahead or behind in the polls, and, on the other hand, by the political parties to shape, fine-tune, and monitor their campaign efforts. According to Butler and Kavanagh, public opinion polls "made more front-page news stories than almost any other topic in the [1992] campaign" (1992, p. 131). Though at an estimated "ten percent of all election coverage," journalistic "horse racism" was still far less dominant in British than in U.S. campaign reporting (Robinson & Sheehan, 1983; Patterson, 1980, 1993). Kavanagh treats the parallel "rise of private opinion polls by political parties [as a] symptom of how [they] more self-consciously attempt to orchestrate and manage their campaigns":

The parties incorporate private opinion polling in an overall communications strategy, along with advertising, election broadcasting, rallies and press conferences. Polling is used . . . by parties to test and enhance their images, target voters, present policy, track issues and themes, and generally improve their political communications with voters. (1992, p. 518)

The Professionalization of Publicity Management and Campaigning

The parties increasingly call on independent technical experts for skills of media presentation, as well as opinion-poll design and interpretation and the production of political advertising. Such professionalization has two dimensions. One is the injection of a new role, that of the specialized political consultant, into modern democratic politics, the occupants of which may enjoy high technical authority and access to top-level power holders. Butler and Kavanagh consider that campaign management by "experts in opinion polling, advertising and public relations . . . reached a new peak [in Britain] for the Conservatives in 1979 and for Labour in 1987" (1992, p. 77).

Their position is still far less dominant than in the United States, however, as documented by a recent American inquiry and survey (Hagstrom, 1992). This study showed that every serious candidate standing in a recent Presidential, Senatorial, or Gubernatorial race had hired a pollster and a media consultant, and that the trend was spreading fast to campaigns for lower offices. When a candidate decides to run for office, his or her first act after initial fund-raising is usually to hire a media consultant. Most surveyed candi-

dates also said that choosing a media consultant was the most crucial decision they made during a campaign. This is a far cry from the British situation, where such specialists are expected only to be on tap, not on top.
Moreover, campaign consultancy cannot be so flourishing a profession in
Britain as in the United States. Even in an election year, political polling does
not amount to as much as 5 percent of total business for such opinion research firms as Gallup, National Opinion Polling (NOP), and Market and
Opinion Research International (MORI). There are also fewer opportunities
for campaign consultants to practice their skills in Britain, since local elections are effectively off limits to them, and General Elections are run only
every four or five years.

Nevertheless, a second dimension, an ethos of professionalization, is now
firmly entrenched in the British parties. Butler and Kavanagh (1992, p. 77), for
example, repeatedly point out how, "By 1992 all parties were in the business
of orchestration," in which the buzz words were "thinking strategically," "coordination" of all communication activities, and "discipline" in sticking to
preconceived plans for unleashing campaign events and messages (although
such intentions were not infrequently upset and sidelined in the heat of campaign battle).

Resulting Dilemmas for Political Journalists in Defining
Autonomous and Constructive Roles for Themselves
to Perform in Campaigns Dominated by Media-Savvy
Politicians and Consultants

Although setting the media agenda is supposed to be the journalists' job,
they find the politicians almost doing it for and through them. The root problem is that political journalism steered by news values converts all too readily
into news management for politicians. Gurevitch and Blumler (1993) have
traced the interactions of British politicians and journalists over election news
through several stages. The 1970s witnessed an increasing adaptation of the
parties to news media demands; in the 1980s, they tried more proactively to
manipulate the journalists; and from the 1987 election onward the journalists
increasingly responded by "unmasking" the politicians' propaganda efforts.

Certain dimensions of British campaign coverage may now be regarded
therefore as attempts by journalists to reassert their control over their own
product. The commissioning and reporting of ever more opinion polls is one
expression of such a tendency. Another is inordinately heavy coverage of
any blunders that the professionalized parties may happen to commit. A case
in point was a Labour Party broadcast in the 1992 campaign about "Jennifer's
ear." This compared the different experiences of two small girls suffering
with blocked ear canals, such that one got immediate treatment using private medicine, while the other had a National Health Service operation repeatedly delayed. However, as faulty Labour research on the family
background to the case and then a poorly substantiated Conservative counterattack came to light, the entire British press broke loose in a three-day
"feeding frenzy" (Sabato, 1991) that submerged the message of the original
broadcast. Proliferation of behind-the-scenes stories about the parties' cam-

paign teams, strategies, and image-making efforts also belongs in this category. Most telling, however, are practices of "disdaining" election news, or
ways of writing stories that imply the reporters are distancing themselves from
the propagandistic purposes of a campaign event by suggesting that it has
been contrived, describing how it has been crafted, and presenting it as a public-relations effort to be taken with a grain of salt (Levy, 1981). Observers at
BBC Television News first noticed a disposition among reporters to attach
such "health warnings" to stories of party events in the 1987 campaign (Blumler,
Gurevitch, & Nossiter, 1989). By 1992, the "unmasking" of electioneering ploys
had become a more explicit part of their campaign coverage policy—though
it was still hedged about with reservations not apparent among American
campaign reporters (Blumler, Gurevitch, & Nossiter, 1995).

Accenting the Negative

Accenting the negative includes both a belief among political publicists that
attack campaigning is more effective than positive appeals, and more negative constructions of the campaign process by journalists. The first newspaper
ads, run by the Conservatives before 1959, were overwhelmingly positive—
presenting them as the party for all the people, one that would deliver prosperity, that believed in home ownership, and the like. The Labour message in
1964 was also largely positive—stressing its plans to "get Britain moving again"
through increased economic growth. But Kavanagh cites recent interviews
with many British advertising consultants who claim that only negative campaigns work nowadays. According to one,

Knocking adverts work. People are so disillusioned with politicians that you cannot
convince them of your good points. But they are prepared to believe that the other lot
are worse. . . . People are so fed up with politics that you are now pushing at an open
door. If they have doubts about the other side you have to make them hold them even
more strongly. (1995, p. 160)

Certainly, such an approach was wholeheartedly embraced in the 1992 campaign by the Conservatives, who mounted emotive and high-profile attacks
on the Labour Party's supposedly high taxation policies. The onslaught appeared sufficiently effective for Butler and Kavanagh to conclude after the
election that Conservative negative campaigning had "worked and Labour's
[more] 'positive' methods failed" (1992, p. 264).

ORIGINS AND SPURS

What forces lie behind the emergence of these trends in Britain? Are they well
explained by the editors' Americanization hypothesis? In our view, British
experience shows that, although there is "something to it," that hypothesis
must be heavily qualified.

It is true that officials of all Britain's main parties have visited the United
States to talk to campaigners there and to pick up electioneering tips and ideas;
have adopted American campaign practices that seemed promising; and have
hired or brought over American experts to help with British campaigns. Knowl-

edge of American campaigning is spread partly by the vast literature on the subject, partly by international media coverage of Presidential campaigns, and partly by personal contacts between campaigners in both countries. In planning for the British General Election of 1970, Conservative media advisers set up televised question-and-answer sessions for Edward Heath, with invited audiences along lines pioneered by Richard Nixon in 1968. When the Social Democrats were formed in 1981 as a brand new party by a group of breakaway leaders from the Labour Party, advice from sympathizers in advertising agencies ensured that many of its techniques of organization, funding, data collection, news media cultivation, and publicity appeals were based on what they perceived as advanced American models (Semetko, 1987). In 1987, a much remarked Labour Party film, *Kinnock*, was inspired by a television profile of Hubert Humphrey for the Democrats in 1968. In advance of the 1992 General Election, Labour strategists drew on the advice of such American campaign consultants as Joseph Napolitan, Bob Shrum, and Robert Doak, and the Conservatives on U.S. Republican Richard Wirthlin's ways of researching voters' values. After working on the Clinton campaign, British consultant Philip Gould wrote a lengthy memo on the lessons for the late Labour leader, John Smith. These included the need for the following:

- A rapid response to opposition attacks. To be done effectively, this requires a good research base—lacking in 1992.
- A clear consistent message, as Clinton had with his themes of change, economic recovery, and health care reform. Labour lacked such a message in 1992.
- Flexibility. Clinton's campaign dispensed with press conferences, and his schedule was decided only a day in advance.
- A campaign structure which is open, friendly, and mutually supportive. Again, the contrast with tensions in the Labour team in 1992 was stark.

Clearly, then, British campaigners are prepared to tap U.S. experience, perceived as on the cutting edge of electioneering innovation. Nevertheless, four major reservations apply to the Americanization hypothesis. First, the root sources of campaign-publicity change are indigenous to British politics. One has been the weakening allegiance of voters to the main parties since the 1960s, accelerating electoral volatility and increasing the importance of campaign planning, through which more votes can be won (or lost). Another has been the growth of television as the main source of Britons' information and entertainment, enabling less politically committed viewers to be reached by crisp messages, and obliging politicians to acquire new tricks of the rhetorical trade. A recent proliferation of channels in both television and radio (national and local) has reinforced the need for professional assistance and advice by multiplying the outlets and demands for political material and appearances. Increased competition across all media has in turn increased pressure on politicians to provide more arresting material to ensure headline coverage. Yet another factor may have been the onset of relatively intractable political issues, that is, problems of economic management; the accelerating demands and costs of social provision (health, education, care of the elderly); increasing rates of crime, drug-taking, and other indicators of social breakdown; as well as the eruption of a host of foreign trouble spots. An ever-ready ability to cope with journalism and the rapidly changing flow of front-page news has consequently become indispensable for politicians of all stripes.

Second, the Americanization hypothesis fails to take account of the fact that the direction of cross-national influence is not simply a one-way U.S.-Britain street. Sir Tom Bell, Gallup, and Saatchi personnel, active in the Conservative campaign in 1992, have been employed by parties fighting elections in Russia and South Africa in 1993 and 1994. Conservative Party officials helped the Bush campaign in autumn 1992, while Labour's Philip Gould worked on the Clinton campaign and has advised many West European Socialist parties. Britons have also gleaned bright ideas from campaign practices in such other countries as Sweden, Germany, and Australia. Since broadly shared political affinities structure many of these contacts, we witness, in a sense, not simply an Americanization of campaigning but its globalization along partisan lines.

Third, in Britain at least (and possibly elsewhere), Americanization is not a straightforward positive model. It also serves as an "antimodel" with pejorative connotations, provoking ambivalence and hostility. Such reactions may even be prompted by features of British media coverage of the American electoral process, which is not always framed in positive terms but is sometimes presented as grubby, gimmicky, exotic, odd, sensational, and so on.

Fourth, although the United States has been a pacesetter in the incorporation of proactive public relations, sophisticated news management, and professionalized marketing techniques into politics, the Americanization hypothesis ignores those features of American society that have made it exceptionally hospitable to such practices—and more so than elsewhere. One is the role of primaries in the U.S. election system, in which candidates must achieve name recognition and an impression of momentum within a low turnout. This plays into the hands of campaign consultants, makes media attention vital, and ensures that, "The road to nomination now runs through the newsroom" (Patterson, 1993, p. 33). By contrast, British parliamentary candidates are chosen from within closed party circles by activists and signed-up members, while national political leaders attain consideration for the highest offices of state largely by developing reputations for effectiveness in parliamentary debate. Pervasive cultural support for commercialism in the United States has ensured not only that advertising and the use of marketing techniques are more widespread in American society, but also that candidates have had full commercial freedom to buy access to electoral audiences through political advertising on television. In Britain, however, advertising is a lower-status occupation relative to the higher status that politicians have traditionally enjoyed, and a legal ban on all political advertising in television and radio remains in force despite the recent exposure of British broadcasting to market forces in many other respects. Again, the separation of powers in U.S. government has imposed a continual pressure on the President to court mass opinion through the mass media in order to keep the heat of popular support for his measures on the backs of ever-awkward Congressmen. In Britain's parliamentary system, however, the Prime Minister and his or her Cabinet can count on party discipline to ensure passage of almost all proposed legislation in the House of Commons. Moreover, the reduction of elections to races between many individual candidates—each developing his or her own campaign, spending from her or his own war chest, and hiring their own consultants and pollsters—is also special to the United States. In Britain's more centralized political system, even voting for local MPs largely depends on the balance of national opinion, and constituency parties are both financially and legally incapable of spending more than a pittance on their local campaigns. Finally, a relatively strong party system within a traditionally organized parliamentary framework has tended to "close" the British system to outside public opinion more than is the case in the United States.

CONTEXTUALIZATION OF BRITISH CAMPAIGNING

As the foregoing passages show, political communication serves and is shaped by a society's political structure and culture. Probably five system-level factors are most significant as contextual influences on the organization, uses, content, and limits of communication in British politics.

The Relative Strength of the Party System

Although the age of the mass party has weakened in the United Kingdom as elsewhere, British political parties are still much stronger than their American counterparts. It is true, for Conservatives and Labour alike, that voter identifications are less sure and strong, membership rolls have been falling, fund-raising has been more difficult, and newspaper partisanship, once remarkably staunch and strident, is now more contingent. The appeal of third parties (especially various centrist ones—Liberals, Social Democrats, and Liberal Democrats successively in the 1980s—as well as Scottish and Welsh Nationalists), though up and down, has been greater since the early 1970s. Pressure groups without party commitments have also sprung up on numerous single-issue fronts (the environment, housing, poverty, gender and race relations, etc.), attracting activist energies that in previous generations would have been expended in party channels.

Nevertheless, British political parties are still relatively cohesive, programmatic, and disciplined, and the center has great control over nominations and the local campaign. Leading figures in British parties derive their standing primarily from their ability in the House of Commons—in debate, mastering a brief, defending a policy, and the like. Even the new generation of politicians who are skillful in using television, like Kenneth Clarke, Tony Blair, Gordon Brown, and Robin Cook, all have a high standing in the House of Commons. Impressing one's parliamentary colleagues is thus still the route to promotion. The conduct of business in the House of Commons lies in the hands of the party leaders and whips, and the overwhelming majority of MPs vote in every division for their own parties. In the constituencies, candidates stand on national party programs. These are handed down by the leadership and impose limits on the kind of distinctive electoral appeals that the candidates can make. If they are denied recognition by the party headquarters, their candidacy is sunk, for most Britons vote for a national party label.

Similarly, national election campaigns are almost entirely organized through political party auspices. Their central events—press conferences, leader tours, rallies—are party-sponsored affairs. To seek interviews and appearances in campaign programs, broadcasters must approach party headquarters.

A Political System of Parliamentary Democracy

Parliament has enjoyed a relatively elevated status in the British political culture, particularly its elite culture (Blumler, 1991). It has attracted grandiloquent labels, like "the Grand Inquest of the Nation" (Lock, 1988) and "the mother of Parliaments" (Grigg, 1988). Even Margaret Thatcher's notoriously hard-headed Press Secretary was wont to assert "the primacy of Parliament as the channel for the communication of information by the Government to the nation" (Ingham, 1991, p. 203), underlining the tradition that government policy statements should initially be presented to the House of Commons—not through a televised press conference or anything like *Larry King Live*.

Consequently, the structure of British political reporting is Parliament centered. The national political press corps is physically based at Westminster, with offices away from their organizations' editorial headquarters. Many correspondents (some 150 strong) are "privileged" to belong to the so-called "Lobby," the members of which are issued passes giving access to parts of the Palace of Westminster that are otherwise restricted to MPs, peers, and their staffs; receive official publications even before their release to MPs; and enjoy many opportunities for purposive and informal exchanges with the country's elected leaders on what are called "Lobby terms" (Hennessy & Walker, 1987).

All this helps to explain three features of British political journalism. One is that Parliament, when in session, is rarely out of the news—although verbatim reporting of key debates, formerly a staple of quality press coverage, has become less frequent and full in the last decade (Straw, 1993). Another arises from the way in which national political systems define authorized spokesmanship roles with implications for politicians' access to media outlets. In a parliamentary system like Britain's, where the media are accustomed to reporting the pronouncements of Government Ministers and their Opposition shadows, there may be less pressure on leaders to fight their way into news reports with specially crafted media events (Blumler & Semetko, 1987). Discourse style, even in the mass media, may also be influenced. The standards and practices of relatively vigorous, sharp, sustained, and serious debate, which have developed in the House of Commons, tend to rub off onto exchanges in discussion programs and relatively long single political interviews (sometimes lasting up to fifty minutes) on radio and television.

Organization of the British Mass Media

Compared with other national press systems that are only barely accountable to political agencies (as in the United States), in Britain there have been more elements of subordination of the media system to the political system. In the 1992 General Election, for example, the Fleet Street press was fiercely partisan (although some Tory papers have since become sharply critical of the Major government). The fact that British public-service broadcasting was ultimately a creature of Parliament also inculcated among some of its practitioners a sense of responsibility for supporting the political system, seeing to the health of civic discourse generated in it, and showing sensitivity to some of its leaders' communication interests and concerns. It is true that political reporting in the mass tabloid press has been highly sketchy and sensational. Broadcasting, however, has taken its political vocation seriously and treated news and current affairs programming departments as a protected species with sizable claims on funds, talent, and airtime.

A General Election, specifically, has also tended to be viewed not just as an exceptionally long news story or as a parade of dramatic episodes, but as a time of critical choice for the nation. The coming of a campaign has been regarded by the broadcasting organizations as a transforming event, for which extraordinary measures are justified. In addition to deciding broadly how much coverage should be provided, schedules have been re-jigged, special programs introduced, specialist political staff redeployed, and news programs extended, with steps taken to strengthen their analytical component. For the 1992 campaign, for example, the BBC's *9 O'Clock News*, normally twenty-five minutes long, was extended to forty-five to fifty minutes and given a three-part structure: part I to report the day's campaign news; part II to report the day's nonelection news; and part III to present a range of more reflective approaches to the campaign, including preprepared films, often a report on the latest opinion-poll results, and a two-way exchange on the overall politics of the current situation between the news reader and the BBC's political editor. Wherever possible, efforts were also made to ensure that the coverage was substantive and informative; for example, by adding background comment and analysis from relevant specialist correspondents to news packages on party events and politicians' statements (Blumler, Gurevitch, & Nossiter, 1995).

Complex developments in Britain's broadcasting system since the passage of a Broadcasting Act in 1990, however, call into question its continuing ability to uphold the integrity of civic communication. Various changes to advertising-financed Independent Television—its commercialization, awareness of involvement in a more free-wheeling competition for viewers' patronage, relative deregulation, and the increased subordination of ITN (its news-program provider) to the network companies' scheduling and ratings needs—all entail the break up of Britain's public-service duopoly. Observers claimed to detect some signs of ITN differentiation of its political provision from BBC approaches during the 1992 campaign, screening shorter campaign packages and worrying more about audience holding (Nossiter, Scammell, & Semetko, 1995). Such a tendency may be braked, however, by persistence among its staff of an ITN self-image as a serious and intelligent news service, and an assumption that the British audience has been acculturated to expect and welcome such a service. Meanwhile, complex crosspressures are even reshaping the BBC: to take a public-service programming lead, achieve good ratings, pursue efficiency savings, and expand its commercial activities at home and abroad. Although it has identified "Informing the National Debate" as a prime future purpose (BBC, 1992, pp. 28–31), marked signs of competitive strain over its audience appeal have been surfacing, even in some sectors of its Current Affairs Division.

Regulation of Campaigning: Spending Limits

Two features of regulating campaign spending are very important. First, although there is no cap on campaign expenditure by British parties nationally, legal limits on expenditure in the constituencies are tight. In 1992, for example, the average maximum expenditure allowed per candidate was in the order of £6,000, and the average expenditure per main-party candidate was around £5,000 (Butler & Kavanagh, 1992, p. 245). Such figures mean that a candidate cannot commission a local opinion poll and stay within the limits.

Second, political advertising is not permitted on television and radio. Instead, the political parties are given free quotas of broadcasting time during campaigns (party election broadcasts) and also for the rest of the year (party political broadcasts). The allocations, which are distributed in rough proportion to the parties' electoral support at the previous election, are made for ten-minute broadcasts, though, if they prefer, individual parties can devote only five minutes to them but not *less than that*; thus, thirty-second spots are barred. On a typical campaign evening, then, a television channel is unlikely to carry more than one five- or ten-minute party broadcast. This is exceptionally important, partly because the television campaign is not distorted by differences of financial muscle between the parties, partly because a brake is set against wildly escalating campaign costs, but especially because the heart of competitive campaign communication is not lodged within party broadcasts, but in the broadcasters' main news and discussion vehicles. Even if party election broadcasts resemble political commercials in style more than they did in the past, these cannot be anywhere near so central or impoverishing to election communication as the heavy flow of thirty-second spots that can dominate even campaign news in the United States (Jamieson, 1992).

Characteristic Features of Britain's Elite Political Culture

One characteristic feature of Britain's elite political culture is a tendency to value political activity, not only as an arena of high-stakes combat and power gain, but also as a sphere of social purpose and commitment, to which convictions and considered principles are applicable. Margaret Thatcher's determination to lead her party and country as a "conviction politician" is just an extreme example of a more modest tendency among other leading figures to regard politics partly as a sociointellectual challenge. This was shown in Edward Heath's determination to engage Britain closely in the European Community project, Neil Kinnock and Tony Blair's efforts to modernize and redirect the Labour Party's policy commitments, and Roy Jenkins' ambition to transform the British party system. It can therefore be regarded as a weakness when top leaders are thought to be lacking in such aims and qualities.

Of course, things have changed from the days of Attlee and Churchill, politicians who were both born at the height of the Victorian age. But leaders today are still expected to be dignified, as befits a serious activity. There was nothing populist about Heath, Foot, or Callaghan. Even though Mrs. Thatcher fondled a calf in a field for fifteen minutes for photographers in 1979, nobody doubted that she was a serious politician. There were such doubts about Neil Kinnock, however, and because of them he tried to curb his extrovert and spontaneous nature.

Consequently, British politicians are uneasy about it being known that they receive help with presentation. They fear that it may provide ammunition for charges that they lack principles and convictions. Speech writers, pollsters, and advertising people are expected to keep a low profile. Indeed, the memoirs of party leaders (see Wilson, 1971, and Thatcher, 1993) make only perfunctory references to such assistance.

In addition, the culture generates expectations that positions taken by leaders on issues of political direction and problem solving will be based on intellectually defensible foundations that are testable in debate against similarly formed alternatives. Such expectations, to some extent, undergird evaluations of both parliamentary discourse and studio discussion. Party manifestos and policy documents are subject to more sustained discussion and scrutiny than in the United States. Issues are debated more seriously, and parties are expected to have well-prepared policies. Faced with such criteria, Labour's campaign came apart over defense in 1987 and over taxation in 1992.

British conditions have also allowed a relatively "enclosed" culture to develop among elites, including the lack of a First Amendment notion of freedom, strict rules of parliamentary privilege, and strong libel laws. And although British journalism has lately become more aggressive, this development is of more recent vintage than in the United States.

IMPACT ON THE POLITICAL SYSTEM

As befits a complex case, the impact of modern publicity imperatives on British political life is uneven, mixed, and not easy to specify. The difficulties are compounded by a paucity of empirical research charting trends over time in the amount, focus, and tone of media coverage of Britain's institutions and their responses to such coverage. This section can therefore only present our provisional "best estimate" of latter-day communication effects on the structure and culture of British politics.

Although changes in the assumptions and rules of the publicity game must have implications for most organized political relationships in any democratic society, in Britain, certain institutions appear to have been only marginally affected by recent developments, while others have been more deeply influenced.

The role of the Prime Minister in British government, for example, has probably changed little, although his or her perceived effectiveness as publicist and media handler may have become somewhat more important. With a strong reputation for this, the Prime Minister can be almost impossible to dislodge; without it, he or she becomes vulnerable (Blumler, 1990, p. 106). On this point, Mr. Major's reputation has fluctuated—high after his surprise victory in the 1992 election, but shaky in 1995. In early 1994, a belief that poor publicity was responsible for a historically low Tory opinion-poll standing obliged the Prime Minister to replace a low-key Press Secretary with someone known for more proactive media adroitness.

The civil service has also been relatively impervious to media penetration, though all departments are more concerned nowadays to get their policy messages out to the public through advertising, press releases, and ministerial statements (Franklin, 1994). None of the reforms that revamped the Whitehall machine substantially in the 1980s and 1990s were driven by publicity considerations. Potentially more significant for the future is the fact that the culture of confidentiality and secrecy, in which higher civil servants have hitherto operated comfortably, has seemed increasingly anomalous in an age of ubiquitous communications and come under closer scrutiny and attack. Administrations have sought to hold the line by promising more open and accountable government and by amending the Official Secrets Act without espousing so alien a concept as freedom of information.

The British Parliament has engaged more deeply, albeit tardily, hesitantly, and defensively, with the media sphere. For many years, it agonized over the admission of broadcasting to its precincts, torn between relegation to a civic side show if television was kept out and being demeaned and sacrificing its best traditions if it was let in. In late 1989, the House of Commons finally agreed to the televising of its proceedings.

No dramatic effects of television on parliamentary activity have yet been reported, however. The institution continues to perform many of its traditional political functions in traditional ways. Some observers attribute only relatively cosmetic changes to Commons television (e.g., higher standards of dress). Probably because the BBC decided to televise the twice-weekly session of Prime Minister's Questions live, the number of questions tabled has increased, and the heated atmosphere that has always surrounded these exchanges has intensified. The coming of television may also have helped to consolidate the place in the parliamentary system of a new structure of fourteen departmentally related Select Committees (introduced in 1979) to examine the expenditure, administration, and policy of the principal government departments (Barnett & Gaber, 1992). Straw (1993) also claims that more MPs are cultivating their own public-relations techniques and media contacts, instead of relying on Commons contributions to further their positions.

So far, however, none of this can remotely compare with the far more advanced publicity orientations prevalent in the U.S. Congress (Cook, 1987; Robinson, 1981). British MPs lack, and are not known to be seeking, anything like the lavish apparatus of press secretaries, computerized mail, television and radio studios, and satellite links to home-town stations that their American counterparts take for granted.

Thus, the modern publicity process has had a significant impact in Britain largely on those institutions that have a central raison d'être which has been to campaign for public support, namely political parties and pressure groups. As to the former,[5] four themes stand out from a rich quarry of available evidence on the complex interactions, since the late 1950s, between communication developments and party structures.

First, over that period, despite many fits and starts, the forces of publicity professionalization have moved into the major parties in impressive strength.

They have been given a somewhat easier, less complicated, less contested, and less uneven passage in the Conservative Party than in Labour ranks, however, where beliefs in communication as education for socialism do not sit easily with the shorter cuts of publicity tactics. Acceptance of new methods has been easier for Conservatives, due to more money to spend on publicity; greater sympathy for a commercial ethos among leaders and activists; a simpler, more hierarchical structure, which produces speedier decisions; and a more single-minded priority on winning elections. Nevertheless, for both parties similar developments can be traced between the 1960s and the 1990s.

One trend has been an increasing readiness to exploit numerous uses of public-opinion polls. These have been deployed to guide decisions on the most advantageous time to call an election (as with Mrs. Thatcher in both 1983 and 1987); to chart a party's strengths and weaknesses of public image and prompt thought on how to overcome the latter (crucial for Labour, particularly in the 1960s and again during Mr. Kinnock's leadership in the 1980s); to inform the party about its agenda's standing with the public and to suggest which issues it should try to project and which contain (for Labour, since 1979, this meant pressing social issues and unemployment and taking guard over taxation and economic management); to target electoral sectors amenable to wooing from opposition support (as with members of the skilled working class and their wives by the Conservatives in 1979); and to track within-campaign opinion shifts for day-to-day publicity initiatives. Thus, the findings of opinion polls about significant issues have driven party agendas—negatively for Labour on defense in 1987 and for the Conservatives on the local government poll tax in the early 1990s. Even so, British pollsters have nothing like the influence or access of their American counterparts. Their advice about election timing, for example, was ignored by Edward Heath in February 1974 and by John Major in 1991. Their message about Labour's weakness on taxation was ignored by the party leadership throughout 1991.

The growth of professionalism has had profound implications for party workings beyond the influence of any particular contributions. It has undermined the importance of feedback about opinion on the ground from constituency agents and activists. It has countered partisan blinkers by revealing at times a different state of public opinion from what some politicians and activists had fondly assumed. As new and unexpected findings with publicity positioning implications emerged, dependence on polls (and those who could design them) to learn yet more increased. At crucial moments, communication specialists had access to the party's top leaders.

A related trend has been the broadening scope and increasing authority of publicity experts in both parties. A turning point was reached in this respect by the Conservatives in 1979, when the advertising agency, Saatchi and Saatchi, was for the first time given responsibility for planning and coordinating all facets of the Party's publicity effort, including polling, press advertising, posters, and campaign broadcasts. The Labour Party's disastrous defeat of 1983, when its poll only barely topped that of the third-party SDP-Liberal Alliance, marked a similar moment for Her Majesty's Opposition. Wide-ranging authority was invested in an ex-broadcaster, Peter Mandelson, who was appointed Director of Communications, to determinedly transform and modernize the Party's approach to campaigning, in harness with Mr. Kinnock's Press Secretary (Patricia Hewitt) and with the support of a Shadow Communication Agency of volunteer specialists of differing publicity backgrounds and skills.

Second, this incursion sometimes triggered or overlapped with internal party differences, some policy-based, some turf-based, and some pertinent to publicity professionalization per se, including tensions and disputes between proselytizers for such modernization and doubters and skeptics about its real value. In the British parties, then, communication specialists did not simply slide smoothly into positions of publicity command. When, for example, it appeared that Peter Mandelson was becoming the most important official in the Labour Party, or Gordon Reece in the Conservative Party, this was resented and resisted by others. This is partly a natural outcome of the institutional strength of British parties, with a number of established officials in place. In both parties, senior officials sometimes express resentment of the working methods of the professional communicators, particularly objecting to their concentration on responding to survey findings about the voters' mood and the willingness to cut corners (often bypassing party committees) in the interest of speed. But even though new elites have moved into the party organization while others have been sidelined, politicians still jealously guard their autonomy. The loyalty credentials of the Labour modernizing professionals were also questioned at times, since some had other fish to fry than just their political contracts (Kavanagh, 1995).

There were thus many structural bases for in-party conflict. More ideologically minded politicians did not always respect or welcome the professionals' evidence and ideas. The professionals mistrusted politicians' subjectivity, egoism, and lack of tactical single-mindedness. The most frequent criticism that the politicians tended to make of advertising professionals latched onto their naivety. "Advertisers are not always sensitive in recognizing what messages can blow you out of the water," said Shaun Woodward (the Conservative client for Saatchi and Saatchi in 1992) in a conversation with one of us. Some Saatchi advertisements were rejected by party officials in September 1991 as too hard hitting. Policy suggestions by individual members of Labour's Shadow Communication Agency were also regarded by politicians as lacking in political judgment.

Third, despite its entrenchment, from which there can be no going back, the modern publicity process has not "taken over" the heart and soul of British party life. Leading politicians still think of themselves as public-opinion experts, prepared to back their own intuitions, lessons of experience, what they feel comfortable with, and the like. Publicists must tread warily when touching on policy making, even when they feel obliged to challenge policy positions for publicity unsuitability. No publicity expert achieves the kind of influence in Britain that his or her counterpart enjoys in the United States. Politicians occupy key positions in the main decision-making committees, and specialists' suggestions cannot be implemented without top politician approval. Even with increased publicity planning and orchestration, the notion of the fully programmed candidate on U.S. lines is alien in Britain. Various reservations are still entertained about publicity excesses and vulgarities—they may be seen as alien, unethical, usurping politicians' proper roles, demeaning and gimmicky, and short-changing the citizen. Not all is yet fair, therefore, in British campaign communication wars. And despite the dominance of soundbites and visual symbols in politicians' offerings to newscasters, it is still supposed that much campaign communication material should center on substantive issues and policies.

Last, professionalized communication approaches may have played some part in reducing the ideological basis of British political conflict. Kircheimer (1966) predicted some time ago that West European parties would increasingly resemble the "catch-all," programmatically weak parties that have long prevailed in the United States. Certainly, the Labour Party's adoption of opinion polling and related techniques has helped to propel it in such a direction. Both Hugh Gaitskell, the first Labour leader to use polling, and Neil Kinnock hoped that the evidence would educate all levels of the party to the electoral implications of social changes and the need for the party to modernize itself. Under Neil Kinnock, the following modernization measures, covering policy, campaign style, and party structure, were assisted by the new professionalism:

- Distancing the party from the trade unions—a connection which, surveys reported, was unpopular with voters
- Appealing to voters beyond the party's core constituency of organized labor and the working class
- Shifting the emphasis from grassroots campaigning via party activists and policy documents to reliance on the mass media and public relations
- Reducing the authority of the mass membership at the annual party conference and giving more discretion and flexibility to the parliamentary leadership
- Abandoning left-wing policies on defense, public ownership, and trade union rights, all of which, according to polls, alienated Labour's target voters

It is not surprising, therefore, that many of the new campaign methods have so often been opposed by Labour's left wing and, indeed, are viewed by some commentators as contributing to an erosion of substantive differences between the main political parties.

Finally, the political culture of a society may be more vulnerable than its political structure to corrosive communication effects. Not all that long ago, Britain's political sphere enjoyed considerable respect and her politicians tolerably assured status—unlike the United States where politicians, as a breed, have always been almost automatically viewed with suspicion as potentially corruptible (Semetko, Blumler, Gurevitch, & Weaver, 1991, p. 5). Deference to Conservative politicians was ascribed to a section of the working-class electorate (McKenzie & Silver, 1968); and among some political journalists, "sacerdotal" attitudes to Parliament were noticeable (deserving coverage as "something a bit different and special," Blumler, 1984).

Today, those seemingly enduring cultural bearings appear to have been swept away. Opinion-poll readings indicate widespread political mistrust, dissatisfaction with available leaders, lack of faith in government's ability to solve pressing problems, and a very low place for politicians on the pecking order of social status. Never have elite and mass political culture seemed so far apart.

Although the various causes of such disenchantment are difficult to identify and weigh against each other, two points may be made with some confidence. First, it is not implausible to implicate modern publicity conditions in the fraying and decaying of Britain's formerly more supportive political culture. The emphasis on perceptions rather than reality, the fractured integrity of political language, the visibility of manipulative publicity efforts, and the increased flow of negative messages all provide an ample supply of oxygen for public cynicism. Some part may also be played in this by the increasing tendency for the British press to project itself as an independent critical force in British politics. Its job (it implicitly claims more often now) is to be representative of its as-if-defenseless readers, examining and questioning authority. It should disclose matters of public interest which people in power might wish to conceal or downplay for one reason or another. Contemplating the resulting flood of scandals, exposure, criticism, and resignations from office, a leader writer for the traditionally Conservative *Daily Telegraph* concluded that, "There is a great invisible struggle going on as to who really has the most power—the Government or the newspapers" (Deedes, 1994, p. 12).

Second, in this situation, the British media are continually projecting the systemically influential *perception* that the respect of many ordinary Britons for their leaders and institutions is plummeting like a stone. On this point they could almost be said to be *constructing* for audience members how they are, and therefore should be, regarding their politicians and institutions. And whatever its validity, to the extent that such a perception prevails, it may undercut media policies of sustained and serious coverage of politics, weaken confidence in the audience appeal of extended discussion, and appear to justify the stereotyping in factual and fictional materials of politicians as cynical manipulators.

IMPLICATIONS FOR DEMOCRACY

According to the editors, the modernization of election campaigning transforms the role of the citizen from personal involvement to spectatorship. What light does recent British experience shed on that proposition? Is the offspring of a marriage of convenience between modernized communications and traditional politics likely to be a vigorous or an anemic democracy?

On such prospects, immediate alarmism is probably inappropriate. Overall standards of debate in the British Parliament remain impressive, and there are still many outlets for high-quality exposure and discussion of political problems on television, radio, and in the broadsheet press, served by thoughtful and civic-minded editors and journalists. By international standards, the British media score relatively well for substantiveness of content and commitment to dialogue and accountability (Semetko, Blumler, Gurevitch, & Weaver, 1991). In General Elections, large numbers of British voters still turn out on Polling Day.

Complacency, however, is also inappropriate in the developing situation. When given their head, many of the trends reviewed in this chapter have been productive of a widely recognized crisis of communication for citizenship in the United States (Swanson, 1992). Concerned journalists, some politicians, a raft of academics, and even a few political consultants now acknowledge that, in communication terms, the 1988 Presidential election was "the pits" and that, despite signs of improvement in 1992 (centering largely on the political roles of new communication forms—talk shows, CNN, MTV, C-SPAN, etc.), reform is needed, though its prospects are unclear. In Britain, awareness of similar problems has not reached crisis proportions, possibly because, in a more mixed system, the trends have not been so uniformly downhill as in the United States, and Britain's elite political culture has always been less supportive of populist values.

Nevertheless, there have been troubling signs lately of some impoverishment of civic communication in Britain. These include the following:

1. The increasing difficulty that even conscientious public-service broadcasters have experienced in providing constructive campaign coverage in the face of orchestrated party publicity management, determined not only to beat them at their own agenda-setting game, but also to back this up (should they be tempted to step out of line) with a barrage of complaints to show they are being watched (Blumler, Gurevitch, & Nossiter, 1995).

2. The near irrelevance of the modern campaign to post-election tasks of government. The unprecedentedly narrow range of issues on which the main parties thought it advantageous to concentrate in 1992 (chiefly, economic prospects, taxation, health, and education) ensured scarcely any coverage for such subsequently important problems as the country's relations with Europe, local government finance, defense, law and order, and management of the public deficit (Kavanagh & Gosschalk, 1995).

3. Emergence of a "public sphere commandeered by insiders" (Rosen, 1992; see also Mancini, 1993) through the increased preoccupation of politicians and journalists with their own complex patterns of collusive conflict. As a BBC producer acknowledged during a team post mortem on the 1992 coverage, "We were in no position with our dispositions to understand what was moving voters. We were almost entirely focused on the press conferences, the Leaders on the trail, reporting how the campaign was going as if it were primarily a media-party based affair" (Blumler, Gurevitch, & Nossiter, 1995, p. 77).

4. A tendency for the principal campaign communicators—politicians and journalists—to bring the worst rather than the best out of each other: soundbites, news management, and spin doctoring from the former and an increasingly disdainful attitude toward such features of party-organized electioneering from the latter.

5. Suppression, by an overly orchestrated campaign, of some of the essential ingredients of attractive and meaningful communication: spontaneity, a bit of unpredictability, a sense of adventure that could lead to discovery, and a sense of wrestling with reality instead of always trading smoothly in appearances and perceptions.

What lies ahead? The forces playing on civic communication in Britain are too numerous and diverse to support any firm prediction about its future. It is unfortunate, however, that most of the dynamic trends seem so retrogressive. Nor does the new found American "escape hatch"—emergence of a spirited, public-involving New Journalism—seem a likely starter. Furthermore, some of Britain's characteristic dams against the worst features of American campaign experience are not necessarily unbreachable. The floodgates could be opened, for example, if the ban on broadcast party advertising was lifted, or if the position of the BBC as a principled public-service broadcaster was to be drastically weakened through internal irresolution or external attack.

NOTES

1. In 1992, in response to the advent of breakfast television programs on BBC-1 and ITV, the parties retimed their morning press conferences to start at 7:30 A.M. each campaign day.

2. The British politicians named in the text are as follows:

Paddy Ashdown	Leader of Liberal-Democratic Party, 1988–
Clement Attlee	Labour Prime Minister, 1945–1951
Tony Blair	Leader of the Labour Party, 1994–
Gordon Brown	Labour spokesman on the economy, 1992–
James Callaghan	Labour Prime Minister, 1976–1979
Winston Churchill	Conservative Prime Minister, 1940–1945, 1951–1955
Kenneth Clarke	Conservative Chancellor of Exchequer, 1992–
Robin Cook	Labour spokesman, trade and industry, 1992–1994, and foreign affairs 1994–
Michael Foot	Leader of the Labour Party, 1980–1983
Hugh Gaitskell	Leader of the Labour Party, 1955–1962
Edward Heath	Conservative Prime Minister, 1970–1974
Alec Douglas-Home	Conservative Prime Minister, 1963–1964
Roy Jenkins	Founding Leader, Social Democratic Party, 1981–1983 (leading ex-Labour politician)
Gerald Kaufman	Labour spokesman, foreign affairs, 1987–1992
Neil Kinnock	Leader of the Labour Party, 1983–1992
Norman Lamont	Conservative Chancellor of Exchequer, 1991–1993
John Major	Conservative Prime Minister, 1990–
John Prescott	Labour spokesman for transport at 1992 election; Deputy Leader 1994–
John Smith	Leader of the Labour Party, 1992–1994
Margaret Thatcher	Conservative Prime Minister, 1979–1990
Harold Wilson	Labour Prime Minister, 1964–1970, 1974–1976

3. Television journalists were also frustrated with Michael Foot's speeches, complaining in 1983, in response to one such effort, that "it's difficult to get the scissors into it" (Blumler, Gurevitch, & Nossiter, 1986).

4. After counting politicians quoted on television and radio news during the 1992 campaign, Harrison (1992, p. 169) found that 45 percent of Conservative soundbites were drawn from statements by John Major, 52 percent of Labour's from Neil Kinnock, and 62 percent of Liberal Democrats' from Paddy Ashdown.

5. Space limitations prevent us from dealing with the growth of media awareness among pressure groups, where scholars have noted "parallels between the United States and the United Kingdom in the evolution of public relations, especially in recent years" (Corner & Schlesinger, 1993, p. 340). Suffice it to say that, like the political parties, British pressure groups mount campaigns, believe in soundbites, commission surveys, buy advertising space, and try to use the latest communication techniques. No detailed research has been yet published, however, on the implications of such developments for the internal purposes and organization of the groups concerned.

REFERENCES

Barnett, S., & Gaber, I. (1992). Committees on camera: MPs and Lobby views on the effects of televising Commons Select Committees. *Parliamentary Affairs, 45*(3), 409–427.

BBC. (1992). *Extending choice: The BBC's role in the new broadcasting age.* London: Author.

Blumler, J. G. (1984). The sound of Parliament. *Parliamentary Affairs, 37*(3), 250–266.

Blumler, J. G. (1990). Elections, the media and the modern publicity process. In M. Ferguson (Ed.), *Public communication: The new imperatives* (pp. 101–113). London: Sage.

Blumler, J. G. (1991). *Parliamentary communication in Britain.* Paper presented to a conference on "Parliamentary Information in the 1990s," Rome, Italy.

Blumler, J. G., Gurevitch, M., & Ives, J. (1978). *The challenge of election broadcasting.* Leeds: Leeds University Press.

Blumler, J. G., Gurevitch, M., & Nossiter, T. J. (1986). Setting the television news agenda: Campaign observation at the BBC. In I. Crewe & M. Harrop (Eds.), *Political communications: The general election campaign of 1983* (pp. 104–124). Cambridge: Cambridge University Press.

Blumler, J. G., Gurevitch, M., & Nossiter, T. J. (1989). The earnest vs. the determined: Election newsmaking at the BBC, 1987. In I. Crewe & M. Harrop (Eds.), *Political communications: The general election campaign of 1987* (pp. 157–174). Cambridge: Cambridge University Press.

Blumler, J. G., Gurevitch, M., & Nossiter, T. J. (1995). Struggles for meaningful election communication: Television journalism at the BBC, 1992. In I. Crewe & B. Gosschalk (Eds.), *Political communications: The general election campaign of 1992* (pp. 65–84). Cambridge: Cambridge University Press.

Blumler, J. G., & Semetko, H. A. (1987). Mass media and election campaigns in a unitary democracy: The case of Britain. *Legislative Studies Quarterly, 12*(3), 415–443.

Butler, D. (1986). The changing nature of British elections. In I. Crewe & M. Harrop (Eds.), *Political communications: The general election campaign of 1983* (pp. 3–16). Cambridge: Cambridge University Press.

Butler, D., & Kavanagh, D. (1992). *The British general election of 1992.* London: Macmillan.

Butler, P., & Collins, N. (1993). Campaigns, candidates and marketing in Ireland. *Politics, 13*(1), 3–8.

Cook, T. E. (1987). Show horses in House elections: The advantages and disadvantages of national media visibility. In J. P. Vermeer (Ed.), *Campaigns in the news: Mass media and Congressional elections* (pp. 161–182). Westport, Conn.: Greenwood Press.

Corner, J., & Schlesinger, P. (1993). Editorial to issue on "Public relations and media strategies." *Media, Culture and Society, 15*(3), 339–344.

Crewe, I., & Harrop, M. (1989). Introduction. In I. Crewe & M. Harrop (Eds.), *Political communications: The general election campaign of 1987.* Cambridge: Cambridge University Press.

Deedes, B. (1994, January 17). Interviewed for "It's War," *The Guardian*, tabloid section, p. 12.

Franklin, B. (1994). *Packaging politics: Political communications in Britain's media democracy.* London: Edward Arnold.

Grigg, J. (1988). Making government responsible to Parliament. In R. Holme & M. Elliott (Eds.), *1688–1988: Time for a new Constitution.* London: Macmillan.

Gurevitch, M., & Blumler, J. G. (1993). Longitudinal analysis of an election communication system: Newsroom observation at the BBC 1966–1992. *Osterreichische Zeitschrift fur Politikwissenschaft* [Austrian Journal of Political Science], *22*(4), 427–444.

Hagstrom, J. (1992). *Political consulting: A guide for reporters and citizens.* New York: Freedom Forum Media Studies Center, Columbia University.

Harrison, M. (1992). Politics on the air. In D. Butler & D. Kavanagh (Eds.), *The British general election of 1992* (pp. 155–179). New York: St. Martin's Press.

Harrop, M. (1990). Political marketing. *Parliamentary Affairs, 43*(2), 277–291.

Hennessy, P., & Walker, D. (1987). The Lobby. In J. Seaton & B. Pimlott (Eds.), *The media in British politics* (pp. 110–130). Aldershot, England: Avebury.

Hewitt, P., & Mandelson, P. (1989). The Labour campaign. In I. Crewe & M. Harrop (Eds.), *Political communications: The general election campaign of 1987* (pp. 49–54). Cambridge: Cambridge University Press.

Ingham, B. (1991). *Kill the messenger*. London: HarperCollins.

Jamieson, K. H. (1992). *Dirty politics: Deception, distraction and democracy*. New York: Oxford University Press.

Kavanagh, D. (1990, October 9). Keeping the lions away from the circus. *The Guardian*, p. 22.

Kavanagh, D. (1992). Private polls and campaign strategies. *Parliamentary Affairs, 45*(2), 528–544.

Kavanagh, D. (1995). *Election campaigning: The new marketing of politics*. Oxford: Blackwell.

Kavanagh, D., & Gosschalk, B. (1995). Failing to set the agenda: Election press conferences. In I. Crewe & B. Gosschalk (Eds.), *Political communications: The general election campaign of 1992* (pp. 160–174). Cambridge: Cambridge University Press.

Kelly, M. (1993, October 31). The game. *The New York Times Magazine*, pp. 64–103.

Kircheimer, W. (1966). The transformation of the West European party system. In J. Palombara & M. Weiner (Eds.), *Political parties and political development*. Princeton: Princeton University Press.

Levy, M. (1981). Disdaining the news. *Journal of Communication, 31*(3), 24–31.

Lock, G. (1988). Information for Parliament. In M. Ryle & P. G. Richards (Eds.), *The Commons under scrutiny*. London: Routledge.

Mancini, P. (1993). Between trust and suspicion: How political journalists solve the dilemma. *European Journal of Communication, 8*(1), 33–51.

McCombs, M. E., & Shaw, D. L. (1972). The agenda-setting function of the mass media. *Public Opinion Quarterly, 36*(2), 176–187.

McKenzie, R. T., & Silver, A. (1968). *Angels in marble*. London: Heinemann.

Nossiter, T. J., Scammell, M., & Semetko, H. A. (1995). Old values versus news values. In I. Crewe & B. Gosschalk (Eds.), *Political communications: The general election campaign of 1992* (pp. 85–103). Cambridge: Cambridge University Press.

Patterson, T. E. (1980). *The mass media election: How Americans choose their President*. New York: Praeger.

Patterson, T. E. (1993). *Out of order*. New York: Knopf.

Robinson, M. J. (1981). Three faces of Congressional media. In T. E. Mann & N. J. Ornstein (Eds.), *The new Congress* (pp. 55–96). Washington, D.C.: American Enterprise Institute.

Robinson, M. J., & Sheehan, M. A. (1983). *Over the wire and on TV: CBS and UPI in campaign '80*. New York: Russell Sage Foundation.

Rosen, J. (1992). Politics, vision and the press: Toward a public agenda for journalism. In J. Rosen & P. Taylor, *The new news v. the old news: The press and politics in the 1990s* (pp. 3–36). New York: Twentieth Century Fund.

Sabato, L. J. (1991). *Feeding frenzy: How attack journalism has transformed American politics*. New York: Free Press.

Scammell, M. (1991). *The impact of marketing and public relations on modern British politics: The Conservative Party and Government under Mrs. Thatcher*. Unpublished Ph.D. dissertation, University of London.

Semetko, H. A. (1987). *Political communication and party development in Britain: The Social Democratic Party*. Unpublished Ph.D. dissertation, University of London.

Semetko, H. A., Blumler, J. G., Gurevitch, M., & Weaver, D. H. (1991). *The formation of campaign agendas: A comparative analysis of party and media roles in recent American and British elections*. Hillsdale, N.J.: Lawrence Erlbaum Associates.

Straw, J. (1993). *The decline in press reporting of Parliament*. Privately circulated paper, London.

Swanson, D. L. (1992). The political-media complex. *Communication Monographs, 59*, 397–400.

Thatcher, M. (1993). *The Downing Street years*. London: Collins.

Wilson, H. (1971). *The Labour Government, 1964–70*. London: Weidenfeld & Nicholson.

Chapter Four

The Modernization of Swedish Campaigns: Individualization, Professionalization, and Medialization

Kent Asp and Peter Esaiasson

The significance of election campaigns in a democratic society has to do with at least two things. First, election campaigns are important as instruments for selecting individuals who will govern the country. Second, election campaigns are important in their role as an institutionalized and regularly recurring communication process between political representatives and voters. In other words, during a particular time period or in a certain political system, the significance of the election campaign can be empirically established on the basis of how decisive it is for the election results and how involved the electorate becomes in it.

Two ideal types of election campaigns can be distinguished according to their political significance. The first is characterized by an election campaign's complete lack of significance for the election results and the small involvement of the citizens in the campaign. The vast majority of citizens knows long in advance how they will vote, and standpoints are not based on active information gathering during the campaign, but on group affiliation or other social determinants. The election campaign is a ritual whose primary function is to give the individual citizen an occasion to practice an established and habitual rite without the necessity of participating or in any way becoming engaged in it.

According to the second ideal type, the election campaign is decisive for the outcome of the election and many citizens become involved in it. The citizens take an active part in the politics presented, and no voter has a prior conviction that determines how he will vote. Voters adopt their positions according to the information they register during the election campaign. The campaign is then an occasion for independent and rational decision making, and its primary function is to convey individual preferences on who will govern the country during the election period to come.

It is a matter of discussion as to whether modern Swedish election campaigns can be considered meaningless rituals, the results of which have been determined in advance by forces that work in the long term, or meaningful political events whose results cannot be predicted and are determined entirely by short-term factors. In their pure form, of course, neither of the two election campaign models agrees with reality. However, considering the empirical findings that can be used to shed light on the significance of Swedish election campaigns, it is no exaggeration to say that campaigns have shown a successive development, between the mid-1950s and the mid-1990s, from something similar to the first model toward something that likens more the second model, and that this shift occurred at the end of the 1960s and beginning of the 1970s.

Election campaigns have thus become more important in Sweden during the past decades. They are playing an increasingly significant role for the election outcome and as a channel of communication between voters and the elected representatives. It is against this background that we will consider developments in Swedish election campaigns in the past thirty or so years. The aim is to shed light on the most important political changes that have taken place in Sweden, changes that have been decisive in the modernization of its election campaigns.

There have been three central modernization processes: (1) an individualization of politics, (2) a professionalization of politics, and (3) a medialization of politics. To speak of the individualization of politics is a means of recognizing and describing the most important events as regards the main actor in the election campaign—the Swedish electorate. The analysis of the professionalization of politics is an attempt to summarize what has happened to the election campaign's two other actors—the political parties and the mass media. Finally, the discussion of the medialization of politics is meant to describe the most significant change that has taken place in the distribution of power between the three actors, in the social setting in general and during election campaigns.

THE SETTING

In all important senses, Sweden has been a parliamentary democracy for many years. However, even though the constitutional basis for the representative democracy is stable, the legal and political settings have changed in certain notable respects since the 1950s, reflecting a growing political complexity that falls into the general pattern of modernization. The tempo of political life is faster, there are more demands on citizens who strive toward treating politics in a rational manner, and the political parties have become more dependent on federal actions.

Until the 1970s, the Swedish Riksdag was composed of two equal chambers, a directly elected lower chamber and an indirectly elected upper chamber. The chambers were elected on separate occasions, and thus the results of the direct elections to the lower chamber had no immediate significance for how the government was formed (Stjernquist, 1992). The upper chamber was abolished before the 1970 parliamentary elections, and the Riksdag now comprises one directly elected chamber with 349 members. The key consequence of this constitutional reform was that the relationship between the results of the elections and the formation of the government was strengthened. Thus, each individual parliamentary election has become more important.

The election period is now three years, having been four years before 1970. Since the 1930s, elections have been held on the third Sunday in September, and extra elections are held only in certain exceptional cases (two times during this century). Thus, there is little possibility for government parties to set elections at a time that would allow them some strategic advantage. At the same time, of course, the parties do have ample opportunity to prepare their election campaigns.

The most important legislative restriction on campaigning is that there is a ban on paid political commercials on radio and television. As cable television has grown and permits have been granted to commercial television and radio channels in addition to the public-service channels, the question of political commercials has again been raised. At present, it is uncertain what will happen concerning paid political commercials in future election campaigns.

The Swedish party system has traditionally been one of the most stable in the West (Petersson, 1994). Since the "freezing" of the party system in the 1930s, the same five parties have been represented in the Riksdag. The parties, reflecting the conflicts between labor and capital and between urban and rural areas, could be arranged in a clear left–right pattern: Left Party (the former Communist Party), Social Democrats, the Center Party (the former Farmer's League), Liberals, and Conservatives. The party system began to change at the end of the 1980s, however, and new cleavages were introduced. It started with the entrance of The Greens into the Riksdag in the 1988 elections. In the following election, in 1991, this party lost its seats, but a typical right-wing populist party, New Democracy, and a new centrist party, the Christian Democrats, won Riksdag seats. At the beginning of the 1990s, the Swedish party system showed similarities with other Western multiparty systems, with a number of crosscutting cleavages.

THE INDIVIDUALIZATION OF POLITICS

There have been great changes in the behavior of the Swedish electorate in recent decades. Behavior was essentially predictable in the 1950s, and has since become more volatile, unstable, and refractory. While the trends in change are the same in Sweden as in other Western countries, the pace of change has been faster there than in most other places.

The findings of nearly four decades of election studies give several indications of the electorate's greater volatility. Among a number of indicators, the most telling change is the increase in the share of party switchers. At the end of the 1950s, less than 10 percent of voters switched parties between two consecutive elections. At the beginning of the 1990s, the figure was 30 percent (Gilljam & Holmberg, 1993; Granberg & Holmberg, 1991).

The following reasoning is based on the notion that the increasing volatility of the electorate is an expression of an ongoing *individualization* of politics (e.g., Toffler, 1980). In turn, the individualization of the electorate has to do with the voters' relation to two different but overlapping structures. During the 1950s, voters were strongly rooted in both party-related and class-related structures. They were loyal to their "natural" party, and voted largely according to class affiliation. Today, in the 1990s, voters give less consideration to old party loyalties, and class-based voting is less widespread.

The weakened influence of the party structure is expressed in the voters' greater criticism of and independence from the political parties. In the beginning of the 1960s, two-thirds of voters still reported that they identified with a certain party; in international comparisons, Swedish political parties ranked at the top as regards loyal supporters. Now, less than half the voters are prepared to call themselves supporters of a particular party, which corresponds to a middle position in European comparisons. What is more, party loyalty is strongly generation related, making the parties' cadres of adamant supporters successively melt together (Holmberg, 1993; Schmitt & Holmberg, in press).

The exceptionally strong influence of class structure on Swedish voters up to the end of the 1960s—in international comparisons, Sweden topped all other countries in terms of the strength of class voting—was conveyed by strong organizations. Blue-collar workers were organized in the Swedish Trade Union Confederation, which cooperated closely with the Social Democrats; the farmers' interest organizations were allied with the Center Party; and employers' interests were defended by the Conservatives. The decline of class-based voting goes hand in hand with the facts that there are fewer traditional socioeconomic lines of differentiation among voters and that the organizations no longer have the same control over how their members vote. The tendencies toward change are again particularly obvious among the younger generations (Oskarson, 1992, 1994).

Class affiliation as a direct determinant of voters' choice of party has chiefly been replaced by increased ideological voting and issue voting. Until the end of the 1960s, class was more significant for party choice than opinion in left–right issues. At the beginning of the 1970s, the pattern changed. Now, conservative blue-collar workers and radical white-collar workers tend to follow their ideology more than their class (Gilljam & Holmberg, 1993).

What, then, has the individualization of politics meant for the running of election campaigns? A conceivable consequence might be for the campaigns to come closer to the American situation, with candidate-centered politics. However, no such tendencies toward Americanization can be noted in the Swedish election campaigns. At the same time that the parties' position has become weaker among the electorate, their position has actually become stronger among the political elite; for example, members of parliament now more easily accept a strong party discipline than was the case during the 1960s (Esaiasson & Holmberg, 1994).

Instead, the most important consequence of individualization is, as was indicated in the introduction, the increased importance of campaigns. As traditional structures have become weaker, events during the short weeks of campaigning have become increasingly important for the results of the election.

THE PROFESSIONALIZATION OF POLITICS

The second major trend in the development of Swedish election campaigns is the professionalization of politics. This trend relates to the two other main actors apart from the voters: the political parties and the media.

The Professionalization of the Political Parties

Amidst the turbulence of the past decades, the political parties have been the least changeable factor in election campaigns. Parties have worked in very much the same way for a long time: There is a central party leadership that establishes political guidelines and is responsible for the national campaign, and regional and local organizations that, in cooperation with the central party leadership, have the job of running campaign activities in the districts.

In terms of the parties, the trend toward professionalization is related to the financing of election campaigns. Since the introduction of a system of public financing in the mid-1960s, the parties have become successively less dependent on the financial support of party members; tax revenues are now their primary source of income (Gidlund, 1991). What this public support means for the parties is that they have been able to maintain operations on a high level, despite a decreasing number of active members—most important, in this context, is that at least the largest parties have had the means to employ individuals with relevant knowledge of campaigning.

However, while the parties are purchasing external expertise more and more (chiefly to design the commercial portion of their campaigns), the central party leaderships have still been able to retain the final say on the overall campaign design. The professionalization of activities has thus not resulted in parties' losing control over their campaigns to different independent political consultants (Esaiasson, 1992).

Another significant factor underlying the continuing strong grasp of the party leadership over campaigns is the democratic doctrine that dominates in all the established parties. Parties to the left and the right adhere to the Responsible Party Model: The parties go to elections on different programs, the voters take a position on the programs, and the party or group of parties that receive the greatest support form the government and carry out their program.

Belief in this essentially rational model of representative democracy has had a conservative effect on campaigns. Large groups in the parties are skeptical of the American type of consultant-operated campaigns with their emphasis on collecting a great deal of information about voters' sentiments and fine-tuning political messages. According to the skeptics, rather than adapting the messages to temporary sentiments among marginal voters, it should be up to the party organizations and party members to formulate programs that they believe in and that the voters are then given the occasion to either accept or reject.

During the campaign, the parties have access to two principal types of channels for voter contact: *direct* and *indirect* channels. As used here, direct channels refer to face-to-face contact between parties and voters, whereas indirect channels refer to contacts through the mass media. The indirect channels can in turn be classified into *controlled media* (pamphlets, advertisements, and other paid media under the total command of the parties) and *free media* (primarily news coverage in radio, television, and daily newspapers).

The main trend in Swedish campaigns is that the parties have become increasingly dependent on free media for spreading their messages. In fact, one of the greatest peculiarities of Swedish election campaigns is the relationship between the parties and the broadcasting system. In contrast to most other Western countries, Sweden does not allot its parties any free broadcasting time in public-service television and radio. These two media instead supplement traditional news coverage with different special programs before elections. The two most important types of programs are a series of hour-long interviews, in which two journalists take on each of the party leaders separately, and a number of debates between leading party representatives (Esaiasson, 1992; Esaiasson & Moring, 1994).

Of particular significance is a final debate, lasting several hours, between the leaders of all the important parties, which takes place a few days before the election. This debate is usually followed by a clear majority of the voters and marks the high point of the campaign. The tradition of a final free-format debate between the parties was begun in the era of the radio during the 1930s, and thus was well established long before the "Great Debates" between Kennedy and Nixon prior to the 1960 presidential election in the United States. Altogether, the Swedish political parties have a large number of opportunities to address the voters in radio and television, although their ability to control the contents of the programs is limited.

The growth of commercial media parallel to the traditional public-service channels has had an effect on campaign conditions. The new channels, that started broadcasting toward the end of the 1980s, have tried some different types of special programs, allowing the parties greater freedom.

In addition to news coverage, the parties run traditional campaign work via candidates and activists with rallies, canvassing, and workplace activities (Esaiasson, 1991). These activities have remained on the whole unchanged since the 1950s, even though shifts have occurred in types of activities between different campaigns.

The greatest change was the drop in the number of public meetings at the breakthrough of television at the beginning of the 1960s. Public meetings have become more popular again, however, as the parties tried a new tactic in arranging short meetings in places where many people tend to gather. These are called "town square meetings," at which a speaker, usually a member of parliament or a candidate in local elections, talks in the midst of a crowd of people out for a stroll or shopping, and are one of the clearest signs that an election campaign is going on.

Altogether, the direct campaign influences about one-fifth of the voters (Gilljam & Holmberg, 1993). The parties' direct activities are thus sufficient to be of some significance in the campaigns, but cannot be said to be decisive.

Similarly, paid media channels such as brochures, newspaper advertising, and posters have been a part of the parties' campaigns for a long time (Esaiasson, 1991), and the parties have traditionally invested much of their budgets there.

The largest sums go toward advertising in the daily press and magazines.

Despite other efforts, it is still the news coverage in the free media that is most significant for the results of the elections. The major responsibility for contact with the increasingly independent national news media has been given to a small number of top politicians, primarily party leaders. Since the end of the 1960s, party leaders have more than doubled their campaign activities—for the most part, by arranging press conferences and photo opportunities—and are now almost constantly in action in efforts to satisfy the news media's demands for appearances (Esaiasson, 1991).

While party leaders have held a leading position in campaigns during most of this century, their appearances have undergone a fundamental change in the past twenty-five years. Attempts to personalize campaigns have been the main strategy for tackling the complicated requirements of today's campaigns.

Since the 1960s, the parties have had to deal with harder competition in their campaigns. During the 1950s, the parties had almost a monopoly on shaping opinion; election discussions and debates were internal issues for politicians. Now, however, other actors want to be in on influencing the campaign process. The news media, which will be discussed in the following section, are the most important example of new actors wielding their power in election campaigns. In addition, different interest organizations have begun to systematically launch lists of demands during the weeks before elections. This increasing competition has changed campaign conditions considerably.

Opinion polls, an important means by which competition has grown, illustrate the new situation. Their existence heightens the tempo of the political debate; each shift in opinion can be registered and commented upon. Parties have thus far been slow in adapting to the new situation. A concrete example is the hesitance to systematically exploit qualitative and quantitative opinion-poll methods in campaign planning. The professionalization of the political parties has not yet led to a professionalization of their campaigns.

Still, at this point in the mid-1990s, there are signs that campaigning is starting to change. The Social Democrats and Conservatives in particular have begun to borrow impulses from outside the country. Obtaining inspiration from other countries is nothing new in itself—protests against Americanized campaigns were heard as early as during the 1800s, and most parties have long had established international contacts—but recently these imports have become more obvious. The Social Democrats were in contact with Jacques Séguéla, the well-known French consultant, before the 1991 elections, and they have since hired American consultants, something that would have been unthinkable only a few years ago.

Party campaigns in Sweden are coming to a breaking point. Hard evidence that old badges are no longer sufficient is that a "flash party" such as the populist New Democracy succeeded in entering the Riksdag in spite of the fact that it was created only six months before the election and lacked any actual member organization. Other new moves will probably be tried during the years to come. The influence is, of course, from the United States, but Sweden is also picking up impulses from France, Great Britain, Germany, and even smaller European countries. The most important trend in future campaigns may well be "internationalization."

The Professionalization of Journalism

Two important changes in the Swedish media system took place at the beginning of the 1990s. An extensive deregulation and demonopolization of the broadcasting media was begun, making way for the commercialization of radio and television. Sweden now has some of the most liberal legislation in respect to the broadcasting media. In addition, the de–party-politicization of the daily newspapers—a process that had started during the 1970s—reached its high point at the same time (Asp, 1982; Hadenius & Weibull, 1991). The professionalization of journalism can be seen as both a cause and a result of this development.

The professionalization of journalism is a multidimensional concept (Larson, 1977), but one important feature is the independence of journalists—the fact that they stand free in terms of different social and political interests. The increasing independence of journalism in Sweden has expressed itself on many different levels. It is seen on the structural level: Deregulation has limited politicians' power over the broadcast media, and the de–party-politicization of the newspapers has further weakened the ties between this medium and the parties. It is also seen in the attitudes of journalists, in which an ideology of professionalism is becoming more obvious (Melin, 1991). And it is seen in the journalism that is actually practiced.

The professionalism of journalism has led to greater conformity in the different news media and pluralism within individual news media. The Swedish Media Election Studies have been able to empirically register this professionalization in journalism in that, in current election campaigns, the Swedish party press has favored their own party in news items to a distinctly lesser degree than during the 1950s and 1960s. This is particularly true for the Social Democratic provincial newspapers. Nevertheless, the editorial pages still show evidence of strong ties with the party. Sweden can therefore still be said to have a party press to a certain extent, but it is much less identifiable in the news pages than in the editorial pages (Asp, 1988). Moreover, in the Swedish daily press there is now a very weak relationship between the political color of the newspaper in which the journalist works and the journalist's own political feeling (Asp, 1991).

The professionalism of journalism is an important factor in the role that journalists play in current election campaigns in Sweden and the design of the media's campaign coverage. The next section offers a closer analysis of how this important component of the professionalization of politics is expressed.

THE MEDIALIZATION OF POLITICS

The increasing importance and power of the media in politics is the third distinguishing feature of the modernization of Swedish election campaigns. The comprehensive concept used here to identify this development is the medialization of politics (Asp, 1986, 1990). The medialization of politics can be seen as a three-stage process in which there is a development toward increasing media influence. The different stages of medialization can be viewed as mutually necessary, if not sufficient, conditions, and thus indicate the degree of the media's power and influence in politics and society as a whole.

The first stage of medialization is seen in a society or political system in which the mass media constitute the dominant communication channel between those who govern and those who are governed. A large and growing part of the world with which people come into contact is brought forth via the media; a media world based more on representations and pictures than on real experience, and in which peoples' relationship with politics is better described as a spectatorship than a citizenship.

The second stage of medialization has been reached when the mass media become independent actors who exercise great influence on the governing body and the people. This society or political system is characterized by the media as a communication structure being the dominant source of influence in politics, and also by the actors in the media setting their own stamp on the picture of politics that they mediate via their power of selection and interpretation. The media not only have power over their public, but also have independent power over the picture that influences the audience.

This is the visible face of the media power or the manifest power of the media. But the media also exert another kind of power, in which the active mechanism is not direct influence, but adaptation. This represents the invisible face of media power. It is this invisible exercising of power that constitutes the third stage of medialization. This society or political system is not only strongly affected by the media. Developments have gone a step further, and the society or system adapts itself, to a large extent, to the working routines of mass media and the conditions that the media set up; for example, the demands that the media place on simplifying an issue, on confrontation and personification, and so on. The adaptation on the part of society to the logic of the media can be said to be the final stage in the medialization of politics.

To what extent is the development of Swedish election campaigns distinguished by the medialization of politics and its three different stages? Seen in an international perspective, the Swedish media system demonstrates three special features. First, there is a privately owned daily press with a very strong position among its readers and in the advertising market, as well as a public-service broadcasting system that also holds a strong position in society and among its public. Second, the coverage of politics and social issues occupies a central position in both the broadcast media and newspapers. And third, there is a deep equality in citizens' consumer habits regarding the mass media.

At the end of the 1980s, however, this stable system began to change. This applies to all three features. At the beginning of the 1990s, the public-service company's two channels (Channel 1 and TV2) started having to compete with a third commercial, terrestrial television channel (TV4), and a further terrestrial channel is planned to start broadcasting in 1996. Since the middle of the 1980s, there has also been a large selection of cable channels, among them two Swedish channels (TV3 and TV5/Nordic) that reach about 40 percent of the Swedish population. In addition, during the 1990s, a large number of private, commercial radio stations has been established all over the country that compete with the channels of the public-service company.

Although the position of the Swedish daily press in the reader market is still strong in an international perspective, the number of copies sold during the last ten to fifteen years has stagnated and even fallen slightly (Weibull & Anshelm, 1992). However, Sweden is still among the most newspaper-reading nations in the world, with about 510 newspapers per 1,000 inhabitants as compared with 275 in the United States, 350 in Germany, and 150 in Italy (*World Press Trends*, 1991).

The traditionally strong position that the coverage of national politics and public affairs has held in the press, radio, and television has also weakened. The increasing competition for viewers and listeners has resulted in a greater commercialization of television programs and in a certain effect on journalism in the daily press. The number of serious programs of current affairs on television has fallen strongly since the end of the 1980s, in numbers and proportionally, after a high point at the beginning of the 1970s.

Sweden shows great equality in media consumption (in comparison with the United States, for example), which may be explained, at least in part, by the relatively high journalistic quality of the local daily press and its strong position among readers, and by a public broadcasting company with good coverage of politics and social issues (Miller & Asp, 1985). In the first years of the 1990s, there has been much evidence that equality in the consumption of media, where high-quality coverage of public affairs can generally be said to be available to all Swedish citizens, began to break down and that the gap between information-rich and information-poor citizens is increasing.

Although the Swedish media system underwent considerable change and fragmentation—became Americanized, if you will—during the first half of the 1990s, this does not mean that its position among its public and in society became weaker. On the contrary, the media have become more significant. There are more newspapers and magazines and more radio and television channels today than there were ten years ago. The time that the public devotes to media consumption has also increased (Weibull & Anshelm, 1992).

If we concentrate on the exposure of the voters to the election campaign, for example, 70 percent of the voters reported that they had watched the final television debate between the party leaders in the 1991 elections, while only a total of 18 percent of the electorate reported that they had had direct contact with the parties at their workplaces or in their homes, or had attended any campaign rally. The news media are the citizens' most important source of information on politics, and it is primarily via the media that voters come into contact with their politicians.

Thus, establishing that the Swedish mass media constitute the dominant and most significant channel of communication between those who govern and those who are governed may appear to be a somewhat trivial conclusion. But is the medialization of politics, in this simple but fundamental sense, more conspicuous in the 1990s than it was in the 1970s, or the 1950s? Are the media, as a channel of communication, more significant and more dominant in the election campaigns of today than thirty or forty years ago?

The answer is, of course, dependent upon which time we choose as a starting point. However, in general, it can be seen that no decisive quantitative changes have occurred in terms of the Swedish voters' exposure to the election campaign since the beginning of the 1960s, when television had its great public breakthrough. In the 1950s, the final debate between the party leaders gathered as large a public before the radio—about 70 percent of the population—as the same debate on television during the 1990s (Gilljam & Holmberg, 1993). In fact, television programs that have focused on elections in this decade have actually had a lower number of viewers than they did in the 1960s (Findahl, 1993). Neither do we see any decisive changes in exposure to the election campaign via the newspapers.

The scope of citizens' direct contact with the election campaign is no smaller today than it was during the 1950s. Actually, today's voters are more active in political discussions during election campaigns and try more to recruit votes than was the case thirty or forty years ago. Neither is there evidence that interpersonal communication during election campaigns is less extensive now than during the 1950s. Exposure to election campaigns in discussions in the family and with friends, acquaintances, and fellow workers seems to be a very stable social behavior that shows little variation over time or between countries.

The medialization of politics, and thus also of election campaigns, in Sweden can consequently be established to have occurred in its first stage during the first years of the 1960s. The 1960 election campaign usually is counted as the first television election campaign in Sweden (Sjödén, 1962). The introduction and growth of television has not only meant a general increase in the significance of the media as a channel of communication between voters and elected representatives, but also implies that new groups of uninterested citizens or citizens with low education have been exposed to election campaigns to a greater extent than earlier.

One of the two most important changes since the 1960s in respect to the media as a channel of communication between voters and elected representatives is that there now is "more" of politics in the media, in both quantitative and qualitative terms. The mass media in Sweden now devote a great deal more attention to election campaigns than before. The space allotted to coverage in newspapers tripled between the mid-1950s and the end of the 1970s. A similar development can be noted for television programming. Election coverage on the two public-service channels, Channel 1 and TV2, in the 1990s is about three times that of the beginning of the 1960s.

Thus, Swedish voters have received more of politics in quantitative terms, and the politics they are given in the media is of a more insistent nature. The media proffer politicians everywhere in news and entertainment programs, and citizens are confronted constantly with politics—during all hours of the day and night, every single day of the year—although the flow of information does culminate during election campaigns.

The second important change that has occurred in the past decades is that the media representation of politics is much more negative than it has been before. These politics are filled with conflict and drama, conducted at an increasingly rapid pace, and dominated by personages more than issues—politics in which the boundaries between private and public are successively disappearing.

Because of the enormous dominance of the media as a channel of communication between politicians and citizens, because the media constitute the most important source of information on the world of politics, because of the huge coverage and constant presence of political issues and politicians in the media, and because politics has simply become so obtrusive in the media, it is not remarkable that, for most citizens, the real world of politics is synonymous with the world of politics they are shown in the media, and that the true election campaign is the same for them as the campaign presented in the media. This is the sense in which there is reason to speak of the medialization of politics.

The political parties still play the leading role in media election coverage. The parties' statements and actions receive the greatest attention, and party representatives are the major participants in debates and question-and-answer programs on radio and television. However, the representatives for the political alternatives that citizens have to choose from at election time are among the actors that actually lose ground in the media. In the last decade, politicians have lost attention because the media's own commentators, experts, and researchers—and so-called ordinary people—more and more frequently come forth as important actors in campaign coverage by the news media.

Party leaders are political actors who have not been losers in the media. The concentration on party leaders as central actors in election campaigns has increased strongly during the past thirty to forty years. Notable changes did take place in the exposure of party leaders in the newspapers on two occasions. During the 1964 elections, the portion of coverage given to party leaders relative to the total coverage of the parties in the city newspapers increased to 25 percent from barely 15 percent in the mid-1950s. The next change occurred in the 1976 elections, when the focus on party leaders increased to about 35 percent (Esaiasson, 1990). A further increase has occurred since then, but not a particularly large one.

A qualitative change occurred at the end of the 1980s and beginning of the 1990s, however, as regards personification in election campaigns, in the sense that there has been a focus on party leaders as private persons. Previously, party leaders appeared mainly as spokesmen for their parties. With this personification of political parties, intimacy has been introduced into media coverage of the political leadership.

Issues are still central in media campaign coverage in Sweden. It is difficult to directly compare the results of American studies, which have investigated the relationship between game and substance (Patterson, 1980, 1993), but the Swedish news media, especially the television news programs, do appear to be oriented more toward issues than the American media. In rough terms, six of ten television features on election campaigns primarily treat issues. The portion is somewhat higher in the morning city newspapers, but considerably less, about 40 percent, in the evening papers. The trend that can be made out, however, is toward more of a game and horse-race journalism.

An important feature or quality of the media's campaign coverage is its nonpartisan attitude. The primary result, which is based on studies of the five most recent election campaigns, is that the picture the media gives of an election can very strongly support or disfavor a political party. And this happens in each election. But there is no systematic bias in the partisanship of the public-service broadcasting company. It is not possible, using the findings of the election campaign studies, to say that any party or political orientation is systematically favored or disfavored in the news broadcast on radio and television.

The Swedish news media thus function as both "co-players" and "counter-players" for political parties during election campaigns (Holmberg & Asp, 1984). Sometimes the media work with a party, and sometimes they work against it. Their role as team player or opponent shifts beween different parties and elections, and the parties can never be certain of which role the media will play. Chance and nearly random phenomena many times determine whether the media will be with or against a party. Marginal events during an election campaign can, through the agency of the media, be quickly introduced into the general election debate and transformed into central political issues of decisive importance for the election results.

The possibilities that the mass media have to treat different actors favorably or unfavorably via their selection and presentation of news material give them tremendous power (Asp, 1983a). Studies of the partisanship of the media thus also become studies of a key aspect of the power of the media and their influence in society. And thus we come to the second stage of medialization.

The power of the media is related to two different questions. The first has to do with the media's power to influence; the power the media have over the audience. The second has to do with to what extent it is the journalist or the media that determine or control what is aired or printed; the power the media exercise over the contents of what they present (Asp, 1986). The media are powerful, in that what they present affects peoples' thoughts, feelings, and actions, at the same time that they can be powerless, in the sense that it is not the journalists themselves who determine the appearance of the picture that affects the people. A complete answer to the question of the power of the media—or the lack of power—thus requires both questions to be answered.

In regard to the power of the media over the public, the results of the Swedish Election Media Studies show that the picture that the media gives of the parties and election campaigns plays a very important role in the parties' election results. There is a clear relationship between the successes and failures of the parties in elections and how they are treated in radio and television. A "better" treatment from one election to another results in success; a "poorer" treatment from one election to another is followed by dismal results (Asp, 1988). The direction of the casual arrow is not obvious, however. Successes in public opinion can also lead to more favorable treatment in the media, and setbacks to less favorable treatment. There is an interaction between the treatment of the party in the media and its support in public opinion, in which each affects the other. Still, the conclusion must be that media treatment is the most important factor.

However, the decisive role of the media in the results of an election is also demonstrated by the fact that new parties can, with the media's help, be successful in gaining seats in the Riksdag. In the 1988 elections, the environmental party—the Greens—succeeded in this. Their success can, to a very great extent, be traced to the media's emphasis on environmental issues during the entire election year and during the campaign itself. The strong dominance of environmental issues during the election campaign not only ushered in the Greens, but influenced the electorate as well, and thereby became an important factor in all the parties' successes and setbacks in 1988.

The 1991 elections saw the introduction into the Riksdag of still another new party, New Democracy. This party, best described as populist with strong feelings against immigrants, can be said to have been directly created by the media. The party was given very unfavorable press during the election campaign, when news staffs discovered its great popularity as the election drew closer. Despite this, the media laid the foundations for the party's success: first, by functioning as an obliging platform, allowing the party's strongly media-adapted leadership to bring its message to the public, and second, by long having been a part of creating a very favorable opinion climate for the party, with strong skepticism toward politicians and political measures.

The picture that the Swedish media give of the parties and election campaigns has a strong effect on the results of an election. The media do have power over their public. Still, it is not necessarily the journalists or the media that form the picture that affects the public. The parties, and even individual candidates, also have a hand in it.

It is impossible to give a simple and clear answer as to whether journalists or politicians determine the picture that news media present of election campaigns. The empirical findings in the Swedish Media Election Studies can be interpreted in different ways. That media's role as team player or opponent varies between different parties and between different elections and situations, and the fact that nearly random phenomena can be decisive in whether the media will play one or the other role can, of course, be interpreted to mean that journalists are active, independent, and influential during election campaigns. But it can also be interpreted as a sign of the media's dependency on, and great susceptibility to, leaks and outbursts from the parties; that is, that the media are easily manipulated. This changing of roles, in other words, would be chiefly achieved by forces outside the media.

The great similarity between the different news media's ways of covering election campaigns can be seen as a sign of their independence and power, in the sense that the media can only be measured against themselves; where their professional news evaluation principles determine what events will be given attention, what issues will be taken up in the election debate, what conclusions citizens will draw, and so on. A different interpretation can be found here as well, however. While the media do not passively convey the cues that the parties themselves wish to bring out, they do keep themselves within the framework of issues that the parties set up. The media's news evaluation principle of focusing on the parties according to their position in public opinion can also be viewed such that the media maintain their sphere within a framework of choice that is much determined by external conditions and not by the media themselves.

The struggle over who determines the media's agenda—one of the most decisive features of an election campaign—is a further example that explains the power relationship between politicians and journalists (Asp, 1983b). Here, the empirical results show that the media's agenda in all five elections (1979–1991) strongly agrees with the agenda of the parties as a group. In other words, it seems as though the parties determine the framework of choice for the media; they determine the limits within which the media may work. However, the results also indicate that the agenda of the media shows very little agreement with the agenda of individual parties. The parties are often forced to express themselves on questions they would prefer not to deal with, and are not allowed to make statements on questions they would like to discuss. In this perhaps still more central respect, the parties seem, as individual actors, to have very limited power and the journalists very great power.

The power of the media has been seen as a function of the extent to which the media have power over their audience and the extent to which the media themselves have power over what they present. Consequently, there are four possible answers to the question of the media's power: (1) In what they present, the media have little or no power over the audience and, as an actor, the media have little or no power over what they present; (2) the media have great power over the audience, but little or no power as an actor over what they present; (3) the media have little or no power over the audience, but as an actor great power over what they present; or (4) the media have great power over the audience, and as an actor great power over what they present. Among these possibilities, it is most reasonable to place the current Swedish media and their election coverage in the fourth category: The Swedish mass media are not only powerful in the sense that their picture of the election campaign has a considerable effect on the election results, they are also powerful in the sense that they very much participate in characterizing the picture that is such an important instrument of power in the election campaigns.

It is difficult to precisely determine when the second stage of medialization took place, but at the beginning and middle of the 1970s, after a development that had started at the end of the 1960s, a clear change occurred toward a more independent journalism and an increase in the influence of the media in politics. This development has continued, though, granted, not without resistance. Still, this mainly addressed one aspect of the media's power and influence, the visible face of media power. The media also have another kind of power. They exercise power by their mere existence. The simple fact that powerful people must give consideration to the way in which the media react affects their actions. There is an invisible side to the media's power as well.

The invisible face of media power not only restricts action, but also leads politicians and other powerful people to adapt themselves to the media and the conditions they raise, such as the media's demands for simplification, incisiveness, confrontation, and personification. This adaptation of the logic of politics to the logic of the media and the thought patterns and norms that journalists apply in their work is the most sophisticated form of power exercised by the media.

The third stage of medialization is expressed in many areas of Swedish society and politics, even if it is especially obvious during an election campaign. As in earlier questions, it is difficult to indicate exactly when this medialization of politics became obvious in Sweden. It can be observed that, at the end of the 1970s and beginning of the 1980s, the political game—the contention for power and tactics—was placed more and more in the center; the public debate was limited to a few simple, clear-cut controversial issues; politics became increasingly personified and party leaders were given a more intimate face; and the initiatives, the hunt for popularity, and short-term opinion politics to a greater and greater extent replaced long-term politics aimed at results, discussion of special issues, and statesmanship.

The adaptation of politicians to the logic of the media has also led to a kind of spiraling effect. In the struggle for the voters' attention, the politicians first adapt themselves to the conditions placed by the media and the techniques used by the media for reaching their voters. In this way, politicians learn how the media think and how they can be exploited but the media, in turn, also learn how to defend themselves against the politicians' manipulation, which leads to the politicians having to use even more refined methods to gain media attention, and so on. What arises is something that could be called a spiral of medialization that results in an even greater dominance of the logic of the media on the political scene.

SUMMARY AND CONCLUSION

Three important modernization processes have been distinguished here in order to summarize and describe the most significant changes that have taken place in terms of Swedish election campaigns during the past decades: the individualization of the Swedish voters, the professionalization of the parties and the mass media, and the medialization of politics. The three trends hold together and are mutually dependent, and it is thus actually meaningless to distinguish one of the three modernization processes by designating it as absolutely the most important change in Swedish politics in general and in Swedish election campaigns in particular. But should one be forced to such a choice, it would probably be the increasing influence of the mass media in politics via the medialization of politics in its three different guises.

How can the medialization of politics be explained? There is not sufficient space here to give an exhaustive theory for the increasing power of the media in society or during election campaigns. It is nevertheless clear that the stronger and stronger power position of the media must be seen against the background of the increasing struggle for attention in society. Politicians and other powerful people in business, central authorities, and organizations are simply more dependent on publicity and attention today than they were twenty or twenty-five years ago. It is modern society's surplus of information and deficit of attention that determines the basic choices, or prerequisites, for the media's growing power. If these prerequisites did not exist, or if they ceased to exist, then the basis for the power of the media would vanish.

The greater importance of publicity and attention in society, and in election campaigns, is in turn explained by the increasing political volatility or, if you wish, the individualization of politics. Thus, it has become increasingly important to gain competence and to control the power that creates opinion, of which the professionalization of politics can be seen as one expression. A shift of power toward the media can also be explained in this way. The explanation largely lies in the simple fact that journalists and the media control something politicians and other holders of power have become increasingly dependent on, publicity and attention. And to get this publicity they are forced to adapt to media logic and the conditions the media impose.

However, explanations of the medialization of politics cannot be sought only in objective social changes, such as the individualization and professionalization of politics. More subjective factors must be considered as well. One important factor is the notion, especially among people with power, of the media's increasing power in society. That which is ascribed power, or is rumored to have power, does indeed get power.

Regardless of what can be thought to explain the medialization of politics in its three different guises, it is clear that this development creates a political system built, to a large degree, on the media as the dominant channel of communication, where both those who govern and those who are governed are not only influenced by the media but also, to a great extent, adapt themselves to the conditions established by the media. Thus, perhaps the term that best expresses the most remarkable feature of Swedish democracy in the 1990s is "Mediarchy" (Asp, 1990).

REFERENCES

Asp, K. (1982). Väljarna och massmediernas partiskhet [The voters and media bias]. In K. Asp, S. Hadenius, S. Holmberg, R. Lindahl, B. Molin, O. Petersson, & L. Weibull, *Väljare partier massmedia: Empiriska studier i svensk demokrati* [Voters, parties, mass media: Empirical studies in Swedish democracy] (pp. 139–195). Stockholm: Liber.

Asp, K. (1983a). On the influence of journalists in election campaigns. *The Nordicom Review of Nordic Mass Communication Research*, No. 2, 27–31.

Asp, K. (1983b). The struggle for the agenda: Party agenda, media agenda and voter agenda in the 1979 Swedish election campaign. *Communication Research, 3,* 333–355.

Asp, K. (1986). *Mäktiga massmedier: Studier i politisk opinionsbildning* [The powerful mass media: Studies in political opinion formation]. Stockholm: Akademilitteratur.

Asp, K. (1988). Politisk journalistik: Studier i mediernas partiskhet och makt [Political journalism: Studies in media bias and media power]. In U. Carlsson (Ed.), *Forskning om journalistik* [Research on journalism] (pp. 7–51). Stockholm: Nordicom-nytt/Sverige 4.

Asp, K. (1990). Medialization, media logic and mediarchy. *The Nordicom Review of Nordic Mass Communication Research*, No. 2, 47–50.

Asp, K. (1991). *Journalisternas åsikter: En jämförelse med politiker och allmänhet* [The opinions of journalists: Compared with politicians and the public]. In L. Weibull (Ed.), *Svenska journalister: ett grupporträtt* [Swedish journalists: A group portrait] (pp. 58–87). Stockholm: Tiden.

Esaiasson, P. (1990). *Svenska valkampanjer 1866–1988* [Swedish election campaigns, 1866–1988]. Stockholm: Allmänna Förlaget.

Esaiasson, P. (1991). 120 years of Swedish election campaigns: A story of the rise and decline of the political parties and the emergence of the mass media as power brokers. *Scandinavian Political Studies, 14,* 261–278.

Esaiasson, P. (1992). Scandinavia. In D. Butler & A. Ranney (Eds.), *Electioneering* (pp. 202–221). Oxford: Clarendon Press.

Esaiasson, P., & Holmberg, S. (1994). *Parliamentarians: Members of Parliament and representative democracy in Sweden.* Unpublished manuscript.

Esaiasson, P., & Moring, T. (1994). Codes of professionalism: Journalists versus politicians in Finland and Sweden. *European Journal of Communication, 14,* 171–189.

Findahl, O. (1993). Nationell television [National television]. In U. Carlsson (Ed.), *Mediesverige 1993: Statistik och analys* [Media Sweden 1993: Statistics and analysis] (pp. 267–276). Stockholm: Sveriges Radio.

Gidlund, G. (1991). Public investments in Swedish democracy: Gambling with gains and losses. In M. Wiberg (Ed.), *The public purse and political parties: Public funding of political parties in Nordic countries* (pp. 13–54). Helsinki: Finnish Political Science Association.

Gilljam, M., & Holmberg, S. (1993). *Väljarna inför 90–talet* [Voters in the 1990s]. Stockholm: Norstedts Juridik.

Granberg, D., & Holmberg, S. (1991). Election campaign volatility in Sweden and the United States. *Electoral Studies, 10*, 208–230.

Hadenius, S., & Weibull, L. (1991). *Partipressens död?* [The death of the party press?]. Helsingborg: SIM.

Holmberg, S. (1993). The undermining of a stable party system. In P. Gundelach & K. Siune (Eds.), *From voters to participants* (pp. 22–36). Arhus, Denmark: Politica.

Holmberg, S., & Asp, K. (1984). *Kampen om kärnkraften: En bok om väljare, massmedier och folkomröstningen 1980* [The struggle for nuclear power: A book about voters, mass media and the 1980 referendum]. Stockholm: Liber.

Larson, M. S. (1977). *The rise of professionalism: A sociological analysis.* Berkeley: University of California Press.

Melin, M. (1991). Journalisternas syn på sin yrkesroll [The journalists and their perceptions of the professional role]. In L. Weibull (Ed.), *Svenska journalister—ett Grupporträtt* [Swedish journalists: A group portrait] (pp. 101–126). Stockholm: Tiden.

Miller, A. H., & Asp. K. (1985). Learning about politics from the media: A comparative study of Sweden and the United States. In S. Kraus & R. M. Perloff (Eds.), *Mass media and political thought: An information-processing approach* (pp. 221–266). Beverly Hills, Calif.: Sage.

Oskarson, M. (1992). Sweden. In M. Franklin, T. Mackie, & H. Valen (Eds.), *Electoral change: Responses to evolving social and attitudinal structures in Western countries* (pp. 339–361). Cambridge: Cambridge University Press.

Oskarson, M. (1994). *Klassröstning i Sverige—Rationalitet, lojalitet eller bara slentrian* [Class voting in Sweden—Rationality, loyalty or just habits]. Stockholm: Nerenius & Santérus.

Patterson, T. E. (1980). *The mass media election: How Americans choose their president.* New York: Praeger.

Patterson, T. E. (1993). *Out of order.* New York: Alfred E. Knopf.

Petersson, O. (1994). *The government and politics of the Nordic countries.* Stockholm: Fritzes.

Schmitt, H., & Holmberg, S. (in press). Political parties in decline?. In H-D. Klingemann & D. Fuchs (Eds.), *Citizens and the state.* Oxford: Oxford University Press.

Sjödén, R. (1962). *Sveriges första TV-val* [The first Swedish TV-election]. Stockholm: Sveriges Radios förlag.

Stjernquist, N. (1992). The Swedish bicameral system and beyond. In H. W. Blom, W. P. Blockmans, & H. de Schwepper (Eds.), *Bicameralisme. Tweekamerstelsel vroeger en nu* [Bicameral parliamentary systems of yesterday and today] (pp. 423–438). The Hague: Sdu Publishers.

Toffler, A. (1980). *The third wave.* New York: Morrow.

Weibull, L., & Anshelm, M. (1992). Indications of change: Developments in Swedish media, 1980–1990. *Gazette, 49*, 41–73.

World press trends. (1991). Paris: FIEJ.

Chapter Five

The "Americanization" of German Election Campaigns: Any Impact on the Voters?

Klaus Schoenbach

A VOLATILE ELECTORATE

One of the most significant observations to emerge from studies of electoral behavior in advanced industrial democracies over the past thirty years is the declining importance of the voters' social characteristics as an influence on the vote. Traditional social cleavages or group identification, and social class in particular, once established as the determinants of the voting decision (e.g., Lipset & Rokkan, 1967), have become less relevant (e.g., Budge, Crewe, & Farlie, 1976; Crewe, 1983; Crewe & Harrop, 1986; Dalton, 1988; Heath, Jowell, & Curtice, 1985, 1990).

Among West Germans, religiosity and social class had represented the traditional social cleavages for the voting decision (Baker, 1974). Those who were religious were more likely to support the Christian Democrats (CDU), the major (moderately) conservative party, than the nonreligious (Pappi, 1973). Catholics, in particular, were leaning toward the CDU—especially those who attended church services frequently. On the other hand, skilled workers and union members more often supported the major liberal party, the Social Democrats (SPD).

Although there has been no significant change over time in the proportion of West Germans identifying themselves as Catholic or Protestant, the frequency of church attendance has declined dramatically since the 1950s (Berger, Gibowski, Roth, & Schulte, 1983, 1986). The proportion of the electorate described as working class has also shrunk considerably during this period (Berger, Gibowski, Jung, Roth, & Schulte, 1990). As a consequence, in West

Germany, as in other Western countries, unquestioned party identification has decreased (e.g., see Dalton & Rohrschneider, 1990). Instead, images of the political parties—impressions of how they handle relevant issues, for instance—and characteristics of their candidates have become more important for the vote. Baker, Dalton, and Hildebrandt therefore argued that, in West Germany, "issue images" and "values" were replacing "the old sociostructural cues" as guides to the voting decision (1981, p. 252).

COMMUNICATING TO VOTERS IN ELECTION CAMPAIGNS: THE ROLE OF TELEVISION

In a highly concentrated and even ritualized fashion, election campaigns provide opportunities for parties and candidates to present those images to the electorate that have seemingly become more important for the voting decision. Political parties in Germany still use a large variety of channels for communicating to voters during election campaigns: town meetings, canvassing, information stalls at markets and in pedestrian zones, posters or billboards in cities and towns, as well as advertising in newspapers and magazines. But classical election-campaign strategies have lost some of their significance—rallies and the distribution of leaflets, for example. Paralleling the decline of social determinants of the voting decision, the willingness of party members and followers to campaign for their party has also decreased. In Western societies, this gap in support has been filled by an increasing *professionalization* of election campaigning. Savage describes this process: The "voluntary foot soldiers of the party organization" have been relieved by the "mercenaries of the marketing companies" (1981, p. 5).

In the course of this process, the news media have become more important. They can serve both as carriers of paid advertising and of information on candidates and parties via their regular political coverage. The latter is said to be particularly effective, because of the seeming impartiality of news reports as opposed to advertisements. As a consequence, newspapers, radio, and television have become the target of many political public-relations efforts. Among the news media, television often is deemed particularly significant. The following are often claimed as reasons for its superiority over other media (e.g., Noelle-Neumann, 1970): the suggestive power of pictures; the credibility of television as a consequence of its seeming authenticity; and the plausible idea that a medium such as television, with a great reach into the audience (compared to newspapers, for instance), must also have widespread political effects. Plus, television is said to be particularly powerful in election campaigns. First, it is assumed to not only reach many voters, but particularly those not very interested in politics. These are the voters who are said to be most susceptible to media effects (Blumler, 1970, 1983). Second, television seems to be best suited to convey personal images—for instance, those of the candidates, that are so important for the voting decision nowadays (Noelle-Neumann, 1970; Blumler, 1983).

Interestingly, the empirical evidence of a general superiority of television in election campaigns is not particularly convincing, as studies comparing political effects of television and print media have revealed (e.g., the synopses by Weaver & Buddenbaum, 1980, and Schoenbach, 1983; see also the studies by Patterson & McClure, 1976, and Semetko & Schoenbach, 1994). Even the important prerequisite for such an effect—the reach of political information on television into a wide audience—has been challenged (e.g., Feist & Liepelt, 1986, Schoenbach, 1983, Semetko & Schoenbach, 1994). However, this does not keep many politicians and campaign managers from believing that their public-relations and advertising efforts are best invested in television.

TELEVISION AS A CHANNEL FOR ELECTION COMMUNICATION

How, then, do politicians and parties in Germany get on television? Of course, commercials are one way. In the two nationwide public service channels (ARD and ZDF), party commercials have even been free. But severe restrictions applied to both their length (no more than two-and-a-half minutes) and their number (up to eight at most, depending on the size of the party's fraction in the parliament). Commercials on the private television channels are of course less restricted, but have to be paid for (see Schoenbach, 1992). And, since the technical possibilities to receive these channels had been limited until recently, advertising in them was not a very attractive alternative. So, public-relations efforts to get the parties' messages into the regular news coverage of the media have not only been sensible, because of the seemingly nonpartisan nature of this type of information channel, but also a necessity in order to appear on television sufficiently often.

These public-relations efforts are enhanced in Germany by the electronic media's legal obligation to provide politically balanced news coverage—usually meaning a roughly equal amount of time devoted to each of the major parties and its candidates in the totality of a station's programming over the course of a campaign, rather than in each program and newscast offered during a campaign. The parties have monitored their coverage and have sometimes even counted the seconds to ensure that their share of time is not less than that of their opponents (see Schoenbach, 1992). In the 1970s and 1980s, complaints by the parties even extended into the domain of entertainment programming, resulting in the cancellation of some programs which might have been too controversial during the final weeks of an election campaign.

Another avenue for a German party to encourage frequent and positive coverage on television is direct contact with the journalists who are sympathetic with the party. In the two nationwide public television channels, ARD and ZDF, the political sympathies of most journalists are widely known, and many journalists are party members.

In Germany's public-service broadcasting system, the parties have even had a great deal of influence over the hiring of television and radio managers and journalists. Many of the top positions in German public broadcasting corporations are filled according to party affiliation. In theory, this means that if one important post is occupied by a CDU member or sympathizer, then a second post will eventually be filled with an SPD member or sympathizer. In practice, however, only one of two national public television channels, ZDF, is reputed to hold fairly closely to this balance model. In the member stations of the other channel, ARD, positions are often given, more or less completely, only to those whose party is presently in the respective state government.

The new competitive electronic-media environment in Germany—with the introduction of private television channels in the mid-1980s—may have had the consequence of somewhat diminishing television journalists' fear of political retribution. Two nationwide commercial television services with a notable portion of political programming, SAT.1 and RTLplus, were added to the two public-service channels in 1984. The journalists of the new commercial channels cannot be pressured the same way that journalists in the public-service institutions could. As a consequence of the new competition, public-service broadcasting organizations are now likely to fear losing viewers more than they fear political pressure. Already, one result of this is a reduction in the amount of political programs on public-service channels, with the time devoted instead to entertainment, which has the potential for higher ratings.

As a result, the German parties have to secure more regular television coverage in a more subtle way. Instead of directly pressuring television journalists and managers, politics has to be "staged" more often in a way that will attract the strongest possible attention from television news. For this purpose, German campaign managers have increasingly looked at campaign strategies in the United States, whose media system has begun to resemble the one in Germany more closely than before, now that commercial broadcasting is an important presence in the German system.

One of the campaign strategies German campaign managers discovered in the United States concerns the visual nature of television. As a visual medium, television demands pictures, including pictures of politics, if political events are to receive news coverage. Of course, this is sometimes difficult, because politics often consists of processes or events with little visual appeal as defined by the conventions of television. In order to cope with this problem, "pseudo-events" are contrived to make politics more visible and visually appealing on television (see Boorstin, 1963). Such events include, for example, rallies, press conferences, or travels to foreign countries during election campaigns. Pseudo-events are surprisingly successful in German television coverage (Mathes & Freisens, 1990; Semetko & Schoenbach, 1994).

A second important strategy for visualizing politics is *personalization*, which has long been an important, even defining, feature of American election campaigns (e.g., Graber, 1980; Patterson, 1993; Patterson & McClure, 1976; Wattenberg, 1990, 1991). Since the 1970s, concentration on candidates' personalities has become increasingly popular among German campaign managers (e.g., Radunski, 1980; Riegger, 1983; Schroeder, 1983; Wolf, 1980).

To be sure, personalization of politics—creating and using the prominence of leaders—has always had an important function in politics; it adds "visibility" to the policial process (e.g., Sarcinelli, 1987, pp. 177 ff.). With television as the central medium of election campaigns, however, personalization has gained even more importance for Germany than before: "The modern mass media, particularly television, provide *faces* to political power" (Radunski, 1980, p. 16). One could argue now that a stronger personalization of politics—because of television—may have two important consequences for the German political system. First, more than ever before, parties have to consider whether a candidate promises enough "telegeneity," that is, a good performance on television (Boorstin, 1963; Sarcinelli, 1987, p. 180). Second, the voting system of proportional representation for most elections in Germany could be de-legitimized.

Why de-legitimized? The holders of top executive positions in the Federal Republic—the chancellor, the state prime ministers, and most of the mayors—are not selected by the people directly but by majorities of the members of the national, state, or community parliaments. In order to see specific persons elected, Germans have to vote for the parties to which the desired candidates belong. For German voters, in national (Bundestag) elections, most statewide (Landtag) elections, and the European elections, a voting system of "personalized proportionality" applies. Voters must choose both a local candidate and a state-party list. The number of votes for the party list determines the size of that party's fraction in the parliament and how many persons from the list obtain seats. Only the composition of the fractions is, to some (usually small) extent, determined by which local candidates the voters prefer.

In the U.S. political system, the personalization of election campaigns is virtually a self-evident consequence of the way in which elections are decided, among other structural factors. Candidates are selected individually and directly by voters in a pluralist voting system. Thus, news coverage and political advertisements on U.S. television naturally concentrate on the presentation, even the "packaging," of persons, the individual candidates. The same kind of campaigning on TV in Germany, however, could make it increasingly difficult for the electorate to understand why they are not allowed to vote for the chancellor or his challenger directly, but instead must vote for a more or less anonymous party list. In this way, the growing presence of personalization in German politics may run counter to the proportional voting system. At its base, the idea of a personalized proportional voting system is self-contradictory.

THE CASE OF 1990

The 1990 National Election in Germany provides the opportunity to examine more closely both the amount and the impact of political personalization on the voters in German campaigning (see also Semetko & Schoenbach, 1994). The first all-German National Election saw a competition between Helmut Kohl from the CDU, incumbent Chancellor since 1982, and his challenger from the SPD, Saarland Prime Minister Oskar Lafontaine.

In the two months before election day (December 2, 1990), all news media in the western part of Germany mentioned the two politicians fairly often. At least a fourth of all political reports contained at least one of them—mostly the incumbent, however, as Helmut Kohl was covered up to four times more often than his challenger. These are results from an extensive content analysis of eleven newspapers and four prime-time television newscasts originating in West Germany. The time of that analysis was the "hot phase" of the campaign—from October 1, 1990, to Election Day, December 2, 1990.

The eleven newspapers analyzed consisted of the "prestige" press (the *Frankfurter Allgemeine Zeitung* [FAZ] and the *Sueddeutsche Zeitung*), eight local newspapers, and the *BILD*, Germany's national tabloid, which were the newspapers with the highest circulation in West Germany. All stories in those papers that at least mentioned one German politician or party were coded as "political"—news articles, commentaries, and cartoons—except for those stories that appeared only in the local news sections of the newspapers. Also, all the ads that the parties published in these newspapers were added to our analysis. (For a list of the analyzed papers and their 1990 circulation, see Table 5.1.)

For television, all political reports were analyzed on the main evening news programs of the public-service channels ARD ("Tagesschau" at 8 P.M.) and ZDF ("Heute" at 7 P.M.), and the two widely available (in more than 60 percent of all households) private channels RTLplus ("Aktuell" at 6:45 P.M.) and SAT.1 ("Blick" at 7:30 P.M.).

Our codebook included variables such as the subjects of news stories, the main political actors in the news, and the visual components (i.e., who was pictured in the news and in what way?). We also assessed whether the 1990 national election was the topic of a story or was at least mentioned in it.

In all media groups, but also in every single medium, Helmut Kohl enjoyed a *Kanzlerbonus*—in other words, a bonus for the incumbent chancellor

Table 5.1
West German Newspapers Included in the Content Analysis of Political Coverage, October 1 to December 2, 1990

Newspaper	1990 Circulation (IV/1990)
"Prestige Papers"	
Frankfurter Allgemeine Zeitung	385,900
Sueddeutsche Zeitung, Munich	383,400
Local Newspapers	
Augsburger Allgemeine	361,500
B.Z., Berlin	286,800
Express, Cologne	310,300
Hannoversche Allgemeine Zeitung	409,300
Nuernberger Nachrichten	349,000
Rheinische Post, Duesseldorf	397,000
Suedwestpresse, Ulm	369,200
Westdeutsche Allgemeine Zeitung, Essen	655,000
National Tabloid	
BILD-Zeitung, Hamburg	4,339,400

candidate. He was mentioned sometimes much more often than his challenger, Oskar Lafontaine. Quite plausibly, the national tabloid *BILD* was the strongest personalizer of politics (see Table 5.2).

In stories which explicitly mentioned the 1990 election, there were many more references to one or the other of the two top candidates. But even there, the *Kanzlerbonus* prevailed: The chancellor continued to be more visible than his challenger. Lafontaine gained some ground in those reports; the gap separating him from the incumbent became smaller (see Table 5.3).

The two major parties also concentrated their advertising heavily on the top candidates. There were virtually no CDU press ads without a reference to the chancellor. Even about a third of the SPD ads at least mentioned Helmut Kohl (not very favorably, of course). The Social Democratic candidate, on the other hand, appeared in only 60 percent of all the ads of his own party, the SPD. The CDU ignored him completely in its advertising. On television, virtually all the party commercials concentrated on the two top candidates in 1990 (Holtz-Bacha & Kaid, 1993).

Voters' Interest in the Top Candidates

Blumler and McQuail's (1968) classic study of the 1964 British general election campaign identified different types of general orientations voters take toward campaign information, based on audience members' specific "needs" for attending to the media. Refining this typology, Gurevitch and Blumler (1977) distinguished, among others, "spectators" and "monitors" among media users

Table 5.2
Helmut Kohl and Oskar Lafontaine in Political News Stories: The Proportion of Stories where the Candidate Was at Least One of the First Ten Actors in the Text or in Photos/Film of a Story (Percentage)

	TV News	Local Newspapers	National Tabloid	"Prestige" Newspapers
Actor in the Text				
Kohl	22	24	32	21
Lafontaine	6	9	17	9
At Least One of the Two	25	28	41	24
Actor on Photos/Film				
Kohl	14	5	7	2
Lafontaine	4	1	6	1
At Least One of the Two	17	5	11	2
Total Number of Political Stories	1,135	4,918	346	2,357

Note: There was virtually no story containing more than ten political actors.

Table 5.3
Helmut Kohl and Oskar Lafontaine in Stories Mentioning the Election: The
Proportion of Stories where the Candidate Was at Least One of the First Ten
Actors in the Text or in Photos/Film of a Story (Percentage)

	TV News	Local Newspapers	National Tabloid	"Prestige" Newspapers	Press Ads CDU	Press Ads SPD
Actor in the Text						
Kohl	39	41	47	35	93	30
Lafontaine	20	26	49	25	--	62
At Least One of the Two	46	50	62	45	93	62
Actor on Photos/Film						
Kohl	29	8	10	3	44	--
Lafontaine	15	4	18	1	--	38
At Least One of the Two	38	10	24	3	44	38
Total Number of Stories Mentioning the Election	123	979	79	487	55	47

during election campaigns. Spectators are stimulated by the excitement of the
electoral race. They regard the campaign primarily as a thrilling game, and
use the media largely for information about campaign events. Media monitors, on the other hand, are interested in more substantive information on the
political parties and their candidates. We can distinguish between two types
of media monitors in West Germany in 1990: those who were interested in
what the parties planned to do if they came to power (i.e., whose interest was
largely "issue-oriented"), and those who were more concerned with the characteristics of the top candidates (whom we call "candidate-oriented").

As a whole, West German electors were generally more issue oriented than
candidate oriented in 1990. Most people claimed to be strongly interested in
what the parties would to do if they came to power. The top candidates were
of secondary interest. On average, both types of interest remained at the same
level over the course of the campaign. These results stem from a two-wave
panel survey during the hot phase of the campaign, in October and November 1990. In collaboration with the *Forschungsgruppe Wahlen* in Mannheim,
the first wave of the panel study was conducted by telephone between October 22 and 26, 1990, among a sample of 1,196 respondents, eighteen years
and older. The sample was representative of the voting-age population in
West Germany. The second wave was fielded four weeks later, between November 19 and 23. Of the 1,196 persons originally contacted, 892 remained in
the panel for the second contact, a response rate of over 81 percent. Both
interviews lasted about twenty minutes (for more details, see Semetko &
Schoenbach, 1994).

The two different forms of a monitoring interest in the campaign can be represented by indexes based on the level of interest expressed in party plans and candidates, respectively. The questions read as follows: "Are you interested (in what the parties plan to do if they come to power after the election) (in the top candidates for the Bundestag election on December 2): Strongly, somewhat, or not at all?" This was followed by, "Would you like to know more about (what the parties planned if they come to power) (about the top candidates), or would you not like to know more?" Scores of the two answers for each interest were multiplied to form our index. Those who were both interested "strongly" (score of 3) in one of the topics and wanted to know more about it (score of 2), scored highest (6, or 2 × 3). The lowest score was attributed to those who claimed not to be interested in that topic at all (score of 1) and, consequently, did not want to know more about it (score of 1) (see Table 5.4).

The Impact of Personalization on Voters' Orientations

Personalization in the 1990 national election campaign was not very successful with the voters. Exposure to media and other campaign channels did not particularly stimulate greater interest in the top candidates, at the expense of a more "institutional" interest in the parties' plans if given power. We used the two panel waves in order to establish the relationship of information exposure to changes in individuals' interest over time (for more details, see Semetko & Schoenbach, 1994). A number of measures of routine exposure to information sources were the independent variables:

- Routine exposure to the *BILD*, the national daily tabloid newspaper
- Routine exposure to the "prestige" newspaper, *Frankfurter Allgemeine Zeitung*
- Routine exposure to any other "prestige" paper (*Sueddeutsche Zeitung, Die Welt, Frankfurter Rundschau, Tageszeitung [taz]*)

Table 5.4
Interest in Top Candidates and Party Plans: Mean Scores

	Interest in Top Candidates ("Candidate-oriented")	Interest in Party Plans ("Issue-oriented")	Average Difference Between Interest in Top Candidates and Interest in Party Plans
October	3.7 (1.7)	4.6 (1.7)	-0.9 (1.8)
November	3.6 (1.7)	4.5 (1.7)	-1.0 (1.8)
Stability (Correlation between October and November Scores)	.55	.46	.30
N	892	892	892

Note: Range 1–6; standard deviations in parentheses.

- Routine exposure to any local daily newspaper
- Routine exposure to any one of the main evening television news programs (ARD's "Tagesschau," ZDF's "Heute," RTLplus's "Aktuell," SAT.1's "Blick")

These routine types of exposure had been measured at the first wave of our panel survey, in October, with questions worded in an analogous way to the question for local newspapers: "How frequently do you read a newspaper covering what is going on here where you live: Every day, almost every day, several times a week, once a week, less often, or never?"

During October and November 1990, voters could also find information specifically on the election. Campaign exposure had been gauged by asking respondents how frequently ("often," "occasionally," or "never") they had recently noticed something about the election in each of the previously mentioned sources of information. In addition, we had posed questions on how often they had noticed the following:

- Posters and leaflets from the political parties
- Party TV spots
- Party press advertisements
- Something about the election on TV programs other than the newscasts

We had also asked how often respondents discussed the election with their friends or family. These campaign exposure questions were each asked in both waves of our study, in October and November, with response options of "often," "occasionally," or "never."

The two types of exposure measures—exposure to political coverage in general and to election information in particular, the latter at two points in time—comprised the independent variables in our model of the effects of exposure to information on the voters' interest in the top candidates. The dependent variable was the wave-two (November) individual difference between the interest in the top candidates and in the parties' plans. The design of the analysis was not used to predict simply the amount of this difference in November, however. Instead, we wanted to know whether this difference widened during the campaign in favor of a stronger candidate orientation once people were exposed to campaign information. Thus, we controlled for the difference in each respondent's level of interest in the two areas (party plans and top candidates) at the time of the first panel wave in October. Therefore, the wave-one difference is included as an independent variable in the equation (see Achen, 1982). As a result, the impact of the interest difference in October on the one in November is partialled out, leaving only the *change rate* in the dependent variable to be explained by the exposure measures. Simultaneous multiple regressions were used to assess the influence of exposure to various media and campaign news, as well as of the prior difference in orientation on the difference in respondents' levels of interest in the parties' plans and the top candidates at the end of the campaign.

Only three exposure behaviors turned out to be significant predictors of whether people became more or less interested in the top candidates during the campaign relative to their interest in the parties' plans. Two of those behaviors actually decreased candidate orientation and increased issue orientation. Both concern news-media exposure: watching television news coverage of the election and listening to radio news reports on the election. Seeing party ads in newspapers, on the other hand, is the only exposure behavior that made people more interested in candidates at the expense of an orientation toward party plans. This is not very surprising: We know that newspaper ads were much more personalized than the reporting of the media (see previous discussion). What is surprising, however, is that none of the types of television information led to more personalization in the minds of the electorate, but print ads did. On the contrary, news on television even diminished personalization (Table 5.5).

CONCLUSION

The 1990 German national election campaign was definitely a personalized one, although we do not know whether it was more personalized than earlier campaigns. Its impact on what the electorate deemed important, however, was not very impressive. The gap between the amount of voters' interest in the top candidates and in the parties' plans did not widen considerably under the influence of exposure to the campaign. Obviously, one cannot argue that the 1990 German election campaign reduced interest in issues at the expense of interest in candidates—counter to the rationale of the German election system. There may have been four reasons for this result:

- Voters had already become strongly interested in the candidates before the hot phase of the campaign began, so that the efforts during the campaign to increase voters' interest faced a "ceiling effect."
- The 1990 campaign may simply not have been personalized enough to stimulate increases in voters' interest in the top candidates. Offering some support for this explanation is the fact that it took the heavy concentration of newspaper ads on the top candidates to raise more voter interest in the incumbent chancellor and his challenger.
- Changes in voter orientation, either toward the candidates or toward the parties' plans, may take more time than the brief (four weeks) hot phase of the campaign investigated here to "sell" persons successfully.

Table 5.5
Impact of Information Exposure on the Difference between Interest in the Top Candidates and Interest in Party Plans

Frequency of	Beta*
Seeing parties' press ads (October)	.10
Listening to radio news coverage of the campaign (October)	-.10
Viewing television news coverage of the campaign (November)	-.08

Note: Significant betas from a multiple regression, N = 842.
*$p < .05$.

- German voters are resistant to the impact of personalization. They are still aware of their voting system. They know that top candidates are important, but that, in the end, it is the parties one has to vote for.

Is there no real danger of a de-legitimization of the German voting system? Has the Americanization of campaigning in Germany not led to an Americanization of the German election process? Our case study suggests that Americanized, highly personalized election campaigns, such as the 1990 campaign, do not lead German voters' to fixate on candidates instead of on issues.

But what about the cumulative nature of the electorate's experience with personalized campaigns in Germany? It is likely that voters in 1990 had been interested in candidates from the start. A single election campaign, then, could not change such an orientation very much, especially in a period of two months. Nevertheless, even if interest in candidates may have been stronger than ever, it still did not surpass interest in issues in 1990.

REFERENCES

Achen, C. A. (1982). *Interpreting and using regression*. Beverly Hills, Calif.: Sage.

Baker, K. L. (1974). The acquisition of partisanship in Germany. *American Journal of Political Science, 18*, 569–582.

Baker, K. L., Dalton, R., & Hildebrandt, K. (1981). *Germany transformed: Political culture and the new politics*. Cambridge, Mass.: Harvard University Press.

Berger, M., Gibowski, W. G., Jung, M., Roth, D., & Schulte, W. (1990). Sieg ohne glanz: Eine analyse der bundestagswahl 1987 [Victory without glamour: An analysis of the 1987 national election]. In M. Kaase & H.-D. Klingemann (Eds.), *Wahlen und politisches system: Analysen aus anlass der bundestagswahl 1987* [Elections and the political system: Analyses of the 1987 national election] (pp. 689–734). Opladen: Westdeutscher Verlag.

Berger, M., Gibowski, W. G., Roth, D., & Schulte, W. (1983). Stabilitat und wechsel: Eine analyse der bundestagswahl 1980 [Stability and change: An analysis of the 1980 national election]. In M. Kaase & H.-D. Klingemann (Eds.), *Wahlen und politisches system: Analysen aus anlass der bundestagswahl 1980* [Elections and the political system: Analyses of the 1980 national election] (pp. 12–57). Opladen: Westdeutscher Verlag.

Berger, M., Gibowski, W. G., Roth, D., & Schulte, W. (1986). Legitimierung des regierungswechsels: Eine analyse der bundestagswahl 1983 [Legitimizing the change of government: An analysis of the 1983 national election]. In M. Kaase & H.-D. Klingemann (Eds.), *Wahlen und politisches system: Analysen aus anlass der bundestagswahl 1983* [Elections and the political system: Analyses of the 1983 national election] (pp. 251–288). Opladen: Westdeutscher Verlag.

Blumler, J. G. (1970). The political effects of television. In J. D. Halloran (Ed.), *The effects of television* (pp. 70–104). London: Penguin.

Blumler, J. G. (1983). Election communication: A comparative perspective. In J. G. Blumler (Ed.), *Communicating to voters: Television in the first European elections* (pp. 359–378). London: Sage.

Blumler, J. G., & McQuail, D. (1968). *Television in politics: Its uses and influence*. London: Faber & Faber.

Boorstin, D. J. (1963). *The image*. Harmondsworth, Middlesex: Penguin.

Budge, I., Crewe, I., & Farlie, D. (Eds.). (1976). *Party identification and beyond*. New York: John Wiley.

Crewe, I. (1983). The electorate: Partisan dealignment ten years on. *West European Politics*, 6(4), 75–102.

Crewe, I., & Harrop, M. (1986). *Political communication in the 1983 British general election campaign*. Cambridge: Cambridge University Press.

Dalton, R. (1988). *Citizen politics in Western democracies*. New York: Chatham.

Dalton, R. J., & Rohrschneider, R. (1990). Waehlerwanderung und die abschwaechung der parteineigungen von 1972 bis 1987 [Changes in the electorate and the decline of party attachment 1972–1987]. In M. Kaase & H.-D. Klingemann (Eds.), *Wahlen und Waehler* [Elections and voters] (pp. 297–324). Opladen: Westdeutscher Verlag.

Feist, U., & Liepelt, K. (1986). Vom primat des primaeren: massenkommunikation und wahlkampf [On the primate of the primary: Mass communication and election campaign]. In H.-D. Klingemann & M. Kaase (Eds.), *Wahlen und politischer prozess* [Elections and the political process] (pp. 153–179). Opladen: Westdeutscher Verlag.

Graber, D. A. (1980). *Mass media and American politics*. Washington, D.C.: CQ Press.

Gurevitch, M., & Blumler, J. G. (1977). Linkages between the mass media and politics: A model for the analysis of political communication systems. In J. Curran, M. Gurevitch, & J. Woollacott (Eds.), *Mass communication and society* (pp. 270–290). London: Edward Arnold.

Heath, A., Jowell, R., & Curtice, J. (1985). *How Britain votes*. Oxford: Pergamon.

Heath, A., Jowell, R., & Curtice, J. (1990). *Understanding political change*. Oxford: Pergamon.

Holtz-Bacha, C., & Kaid, L. L. (1993). Wahlspots im fernsehen: Eine analyse der parteienwerbung zur bundestagswahl 1990 [Party commercials on television: An analysis of party advertising in the 1990 election campaign]. In C. Holtz-Bacha & L. L. Kaid (Eds.), *Die massenmedien im wahlkampf: Untersuchungen aus dem wahljahr 1990* [Mass media in the election campaign: Studies from the election year 1990] (pp. 46–71). Opladen: Westdeutscher Verlag.

Lipset, S. M., & Rokkan, S. (1967). Cleavage structures, party systems and voter alignments. In S. M. Lipset & S. Rokkan (Eds.), *Party systems and voters alignments* (pp. 1–64). New York: Free Press.

Mathes, R., & Freisens, U. (1990). Kommunikationsstrategien der parteien und ihr erfolg: Eine analyse der aktuellen berichterstattung in den nachrichtenmagazinen der oeffentlich-rechtlichen und privaten rundfunkanstalten im bundestagswahlkampf 1987 [Communication strategies of the parties and their success: An analysis of the news coverage in the news magazines of the public and commercial broadcasting channels in the 1987 national election campaign]. In M. Kaase & H.-D. Klingemann (Eds.), *Wahlen und politisches system: Analysen aus anlass der bundestagswahl 1987* [Elections and the political system: Analyses of the 1987 national election] (pp. 531–569). Opladen: Westdeutscher Verlag.

Noelle-Neumann, E. (1970). Der getarnte elefant: Ueber die wirkung des fernsehens [The hidden elephant: On the impact of television]. In D. Stolte (Ed.), *Fernsehkritik: Die gesellschaftliche funktion des fernsehens* [Television criticism: The societal function of television] (pp. 79–90). Mainz: v. Hase & Koehler.

Pappi, F. U. (1973). Parteiensystem und Sozialstruktur in der Bundesrepublik [Party system and social structure in the Federal Republic of Germany]. *Politische Vierteljahresschrift*, 14, 191–214.

Patterson, T. E. (1993). *Out of order*. New York: Knopf.

Patterson, T. E., & McClure, R. D. (1976). *The unseeing eye: The myth of television power in national elections*. New York: Putnam's Sons.

Radunski, P. (1980). *Wahlkaempfe: Moderne wahlkampffuehrung als politische kommunikation* [Election campaigns: Modern election campaigning as political communication]. Munich: Olzog.

Riegger, V. (1983). Medien im wahlkampf der SPD [Media in campaigns of the SPD]. In W. Schulz & K. Schoenbach (Eds.), *Massenmedien und wahlen* [Mass media and elections: International research perspectives] (pp. 146–154). Munich: Oelschlaeger.

Sarcinelli, U. (1987). *Symbolische politik: Zur bedeutung symbolischen handelns in der wahlkampfkommunikation der Bundesrepublik Deutschland* [Symbolic politics: On the significance of symbolic action in the election campaign communication of the Federal Republic of Germany]. Opladen: Westdeutscher Verlag.

Savage, R. L. (1981). From selective distortion through minimal effects to media election: Four decades of media/voting research. *Political Communication Review, 6*, 1–12.

Schoenbach, K. (1983). *Das unterschaetzte medium: Politische wirkungen von presse und fernsehen im vergleich* [The underestimated medium: Comparing the political impact of press and television]. Munich: Saur.

Schoenbach, K. (1992). Mass media and election campaigns in Germany. In F. J. Fletcher (Ed.), *Media, elections and democracy* (pp. 63–86). Toronto: Dundurn Press.

Schroeder, P. (1983). Medien in den wahlkampfstrategien der F.D.P. [Media in the campaign strategies of the F.D.P.]. In W. Schulz & K. Schoenbach (Eds.), *Massenmedien und Wahlen* [Mass media and elections: International research perspectives] (pp. 155–161). Munich: Oelschlaeger.

Semetko, H. A., & Schoenbach, K. (1994). *Germany's "unity election": Voters and the media*. Cresskill, N.J.: Hampton Press.

Wattenberg, M. (1990). *The decline of American political parties*. Cambridge: Cambridge University Press.

Wattenberg, M. (1991). *The rise of candidate-centered politics*. Cambridge: Cambridge University Press.

Weaver, D. H., & Buddenbaum, J. M. (1980). Newspapers and television: A review of research on uses and effects. In G. C. Wilhoit & H. de Bock (Eds.), *Mass communication review yearbook 1* (pp. 371–380). Beverly Hills, Calif.: Sage.

Wolf, W. (1980). *Der wahlkampf: Theorie und praxis* [The election campaign: Theory and practice]. Cologne: Verlag Wissenschaft und Politik.

PART II

Campaign Innovations in
New and Restored Democracies

Chapter Six

Television, Campaigning, and Elections in the Soviet Union and Post-Soviet Russia

Ellen Mickiewicz and Andrei Richter

THE MEDIA CONTEXT

With extraordinarily rapid tempo, the Soviet Union dissolved, fifteen independent republics took its place, and the vast Russian Federation quickly became the most powerful player in the post-Soviet constellation of nations. To a significant degree, the key decisions affecting the initiation of this process were related to the operation and content of the mass media. As competitive, multiparty elections became legitimized, the traditionally central role of the media was maintained but, increasingly, with an overlay of practices modeled on those of the West. As in the West, television, which had become the "large caliber" medium (as Soviet officialdom referred to it), was at the center of the parties' and candidates' strategies. In post-Soviet Russia, the primacy of television was heightened by the near collapse of the newspaper market. It is for these reasons that we focus this chapter on the medium that overshadowed all others: television.

Soon after the Bolshevik victory in the Russian Revolution, Lenin, recognizing that a revolution required resocialization and remobilization and understanding the twin problems of illiteracy and dispersion of population across a vast territory, decreed the rapid development of the new technology of radio. Radio—like electrification, center of a key campaign—would be a prime instrument in Lenin's program of revolutionary transformation, reaching the entire population, even the illiterate majority. Together with the reinforcing process of personal agitation, the new electronic medium would carry the message of Moscow's new leadership to a largely rural and ethnically heterogeneous country.

Stalin transformed the media system into a highly centralized and uniform set of interrelated structures. Like Lenin, Stalin retained the view that the principal role of the media is resocialization and social change, and he did not fail to appreciate the importance of media penetration. The Stalinist pattern functioned until the process of liberalization, initiated by Mikhail Gorbachev, loosened its strictures. The most important features of the Stalinist model were centralization of media organs and personnel, Communist Party control (utilizing government levers) of information, and saturation. All media were subject to dual authority. They operated under a government ministry or state committee (such as the State Committee for Television and Radio Broadcasting, *Gosteleradio*), but were also subordinated to the Ideological Department of the Central Committee of the Communist Party and, ultimately, to the "second secretary," the second most powerful individual in the ruling Politburo. For the most part, control was exercised through "telephone law," direct voice communication from Party headquarters, exploiting timeliness and eliminating documentation and accountability. Ministerial control provided allocations to the media as "budgetary organizations," without any viable system of cost accounting or incentives to contain costs or meet audience demand. The Committee on State Security (KGB) had a particularly strong interest in media organizations with significant foreign connections (Mickiewicz, 1984).

Newspapers in the Soviet period were printed and distributed in huge numbers, particularly the national newspapers published in Russian (such as *Pravda, Izvestia, Komsomolskaya pravda, Trud,* and *Krasnaya zvezda*). Beneath the national level, there were republic-level newspapers for the Russian-speaking and the titular ethnic groups, regional- or province-level papers, city and district papers and, within organizations or factories, wall newspapers. By the mid-1970s, 8,000 newspapers of all kinds were published, with a total circulation of almost 170 million copies annually. With a fundamentally successful crash program to eliminate illiteracy, newspapers could now saturate the population.

Television, on the other hand, developed rather late, and it was not until the first communications satellites were launched in the late 1960s that it became possible to saturate the huge country. Turning significant resources to building broadcasting facilities and producing television sets for individual ownership, the government had achieved near total penetration by the time Gorbachev came to power. In 1960, only 5 percent of the Soviet population could watch television; but by 1986, the second year of Gorbachev's administration, fully 93 percent were viewers, and the prime-time audience for the nightly news was estimated at about 150 million people. Like newspapers, television was organized at the central (all-Union), republic, regional, and city levels. Two national channels (Channels, or Programs, One and Two) broadcast programs in Russian to all of the republics, but Channel One had significantly greater penetration. Republic television stations broadcast both in Russian and in the language of the titular nationality, and in the centralized administrative structure, each station was responsible to the higher-level organization. Sub-republic broadcasting was minimal, consisting of "windows" of programming on the second channel or on the republic channel. From the standpoint of the leadership, no program was more crucial than the evening news, and no station at any level was permitted to broadcast competing materials during that time slot. In a country where the newspaper was revered for its close association with revolutionary antecedents and for the desirable skills it required (elite political cultural values placed reading very high in the hierarchy), it is remarkable how quickly television displaced the venerable newspaper (Mickiewicz, 1981).

In 1985, Mikhail Gorbachev and his Politburo initiated a drive for radical reform, the eventual outcome of which the authors neither foresaw nor desired (Mickiewicz, 1988). They were determined to effect a change more profound than the numerous abortive policies of past leaders, although the profound dissensus among elites on issues of media autonomy was not apparent at the outset. The differences between those who favored rehabilitating the status quo and those with more radical agendas typically set off unforeseen results (DiPalma, 1990). Divisions arose among elites over the instrumental use of glasnost to reform and retain the fundamental system and the more far-reaching aim of (still limited) democratization. The increasing importance attached to television by a growing number of political contenders made the inelastic resource of air time a prime political asset. Perhaps the most significant development in the battle over television was the rise of an alternative source of political power in the election of Boris Yeltsin, first to the Congress of People's Deputies, then to the chairmanship of the Russian Federation Supreme Soviet, and, finally, to the presidency of the Russian Federation. It is important to note the effects of a contending political power base. In an effort to deprive the new challenger of a politically valuable instrument of communication, the Gorbachev government restricted Yeltsin's access to Channel One and delayed until May 1991 the pledged allocation to the Russian Republic of state television's Channel Two. Even then, only six noncontiguous hours daily were provided to the rival Yeltsin government. Television programs broadcast under the aegis of the Russian parliament were both an expression of and a catalyst for an independent and competitive power base.

In the Stalinist system, political parties other than the single Communist Party carried the opprobrium of the "factionalism" so decried by Lenin. In 1989, in the first genuinely multicandidate elections in the Soviet Union, candidates ran as individuals, not party nominees (and one-third of the seats were reserved for mass organizations such as the Communist Party and the Communist Youth League, and professional bodies such as the Academy of Sciences).

In contemporary Russia, political parties are often equivalent to discussion clubs that lack, for the most part, infrastructure and strong grassroots organizations. Most of their leaders (as well as candidates on the party lists in the 1993 elections) and the largest share of their activity are concentrated in Moscow and St. Petersburg. Russia's Choice, Yabloko, Women of Russia, and some other parties were formed by Russian politicians in October 1994 in order to draw votes in the Parliamentary elections on party lists. This electoral process, in which competitive parties had not yet been developed, gave a powerful impetus to the personalization of the political process.

ELECTIONS AND CAMPAIGNS: FUNCTIONS, LAWS, AND PRACTICES

The Communist understanding of elections lay in the Marxist formula of the ruling Communist Party as vanguard of the workers, destined, because of its insight into the predetermined course of history, to lead the masses into the future. Thus, the ideological concept, not the practical contest at the ballots, was the foundation of the power structure of the regime. Elections were viewed as a confirmation of the exercise of popular will in conformity with the process of history. Existence of a single political party (small traditional parties in several socialist states were, in fact, obedient wings of the ruling Communist Party) was routinely explained by the absence of ideological or political conflicts in the societies of victorious socialism and exemplified, in the Soviet Union, by the electoral bloc of "communists and non-party people" (Furtak, 1990, pp. 4–5). As noted, the Gorbachev-era reform was originally aimed at, among other things, bringing new winds into the political process by giving some real power over the day-to-day affairs to the soviets (councils) and involving more people—directly and through public organizations—in decision making with the ensuing responsibility for its results. Controlled democratization culminated in elections to the Congress of People's Deputies, the new super-parliament, in 1989. This policy, however, spun out of control during the 1990 elections to republican legislatures of the USSR, when spontaneously formed anti-Communist political groups won majorities in the Baltic republics and Georgia, and numerous seats in other regions. Eventually, entire union republics led or threatened by these groups seized upon Gorbachev's liberalizing policies to pursue their respective ethnic, nationalist, and, in several cases, secessionist agendas. Still, the basic functions of the elections during perestroika, as viewed by the Kremlin, remained the same as before.

Nonetheless, Communist-sponsored elections were neither a purposeless ritual nor an empty expression of the rhetoric of democratic procedure. First, they served to legitimize Soviet communist power by showing to the nation and the world that the majority of the population (99%, prior to Gorbachev's reforms) supported the ruling elite. Due to the representation of a large number of workers and peasants, Soviet leaders could claim success in achieving the class cooperation their doctrine asserted.[1] In fact, after the 1989 and 1990 elections, Gorbachev and other leaders of the country publicly complained that too few workers, peasants, and women had been elected, and suggested establishing quotas—this time, overt ones—for these categories of the population.

Second, elections were an important propaganda campaign, exercised through the canvassers and the mass media. In this case, the latter clearly fit the pattern of the "collective propagandist, collective agitator, and collective organizer" functions designed by Vladimir Lenin. The campaigns were used to educate the people on the latest Party directives, advance new goals, and by leading electors to vote in the right way, to ratify readiness to participate in the implementation of communist ideas.[2] Some lesser functions of the elections and the campaigns of the last decades present special interest as they appear to be preserved in post-Soviet Russia.[3] Thus, the preelection period was used by the electorate to present its minor nonpolitical problems as bargaining chips to the authorities. These complaints would usually regard water supply, absence of telephones, inadequate heating (if elections were held in winter), leaking roofs (in the fall), and the like. As they did earlier, the voters exercised this chance to petition the government before the 1993 elections to the Russian Federal Assembly, by claiming that they would not go to the polls unless glass was put in doorway entrances or delayed wages were paid. And the authorities did promise to meet the demands (Sargin, 1993). The durability of these practices, as will be noted, created opportunities for the inheritors of the old party structure to utilize nonmedia-related electoral campaign advantages in the December 1993 Russian Federation parliamentary elections. The elections also served to execute police control (with the help of the canvassers and housing administration) regarding voters' possession of residence permits and violations of the "passport regime" and, in rare cases, to register overt opponents of the official candidates to the soviets and those brave enough to declare their refusal to participate in the elections. In the December 1993 elections, fear of this kind of police control of the process was voiced when the Ministry of the Interior was assigned the responsibility for validating the parties' lists of signatures (without the requisite number, the party could not register). In addition, reports of the strange disappearance of such lists and turning off the telephones of anti-Yeltsin leaders raised fears that the police would take note of supporters of the opposition (as was reported in *The Financial Times* [as quoted by Slater, 1993], *Megapolis-Express* [Pestrukhina, 1993], and *Interfax* [1993]).

In the Soviet period, most of the election campaigning was performed with the help of canvassers as well as the press and broadcasting. Some 8 million canvassers (*agitatory*) were selected by managers and party committees of every enterprise, farm, and institution in the USSR to perform duties assigned by *agitpunkty*, or voters' clubs, which themselves were under the strict control of local communist bodies. The canvassers checked the lists and informed voters about the elections, met with every family in the country, registered complaints and reasons for nonvoting, staffed the *agitpunkty*, posted announcements with official biographies of the candidates in every doorway, assisted in staging meetings of candidates with the electorate and other propaganda events to provide political and social involvement of the population, and monitored the attendance on voting day of "their voters." They were also charged with making last-minute attempts to guarantee 100 percent participation in the elections (Friedgut, 1979, p. 101).

The election campaign in the mass media was strictly formalized in accordance with certain unspoken rules. After the official announcement of the elections, the campaign for nominating candidates was announced by the Central Election Commission. In the case of elections to the Supreme Soviet, the nominating campaign began with numerous nominations of the top politicians in different constituencies: General Secretary of the Central Committee of the CPSU, chairmen of the Supreme Soviet and the government, and members of the Politburo. Each nomination was accompanied by a report in the press and on TV and radio which carried a summary of the nominating speech praising the candidate's political virtues. Then came smaller media reports on nominations of local candidates who had been selected for their unanimous support of party policies. As soon as the nomination stage was over, the time came for the official meetings; usually one meeting with the voters for each of hundreds of candidates, usually held in a local public auditorium. Coverage of the meetings tended to present a refrain of the same propaganda speeches, but this time with pledges and slogans from the nominees who promised to follow the wishes of the masses. In the last days of the campaign, just two meetings a day took place; those of the party leaders, which received full-page coverage by the press and extensive broadcasting by radio and TV. The climax occurred when the General Secretary took the floor at the Kremlin Palace of Congresses to speak to the workers who had nominated his candidacy. His speech was broadcast live by all channels, replayed in full later in the evening news, printed on the front pages of all newspapers and, in a matter of days, produced in the form of a brochure. Thus, the campaign began at the top, brought a wide but shallow wave of heterogeneous candidates, and ended with the major political speech of the year.

The first Law on Elections, adopted in the wake of the constitutional initiatives of Brezhnev in 1978, added nothing substantial to the earlier regulations, but it did formally recognize the right of citizens "to free and all-round discussion of the political and personal qualities and competence of candidates, and the right to campaign for [but not against] them at meetings, in the press, and on television and radio." All candidates had "an equal right . . . to make use" of the mass media (Legislative Acts of the USSR, 1981, Article 9, p. 214). The nomination process, however, was a monopoly of the ruling party.

A calibrated departure from Marxism, initiated by Mikhail Gorbachev in the late 1980s, affected electoral procedures. The first experiment—with just 4 percent of the delegates to the local Soviets—occurred in 1987, when a choice of candidates was permitted in selected districts in politically safe rural constituencies in Russia, Ukraine and Central Asia. This was followed by a new electoral law and constitutional changes in 1988, which paved the way for the creation of the "super parliament," the Congress of Peoples' Deputies of the USSR. A genuine contest was permitted, both at the nomination stage and during the actual balloting. Another new feature was the addition of a third of the deputies elected by the social organizations, which was widely criticized at the time as a contravention of the principle of equal suffrage. The 1988 Law on Elections of People's Deputies of the USSR brought slight but important changes in the regulation of election campaigns. In the spirit of glasnost, it guaranteed journalists the right of access to all meetings and sessions connected with the elections, including all sessions of electoral commissions. The right to campaign—not just for, but also against candidates in the press, on TV, and on radio—was another new feature. Supporters of a candidate received the "guaranteed opportunity" of free access to the mass media, while candidates themselves not only could but were obliged to publish their programs, the content of which was restricted only by the Constitution and the Soviet laws (Zakon SSSR o vyborakh narodnykh deputatov SSSR, 1993). This obligation was very important, since it excluded the possibility of programs directed against the Communist Party or the Socialist regime in the USSR (both provisions were then parts of the basic law). It also meant that candidates could not run without an openly stated program. At the same time, it gave a real opportunity to moderate liberals to publish their programs without interference of the censors.

The referendum of April 25, 1993, was an attempt by the Yeltsin administration to break the deadlock of the two-headed power structure pitting the President against an increasingly recalcitrant parliament, the Congress of People's Deputies, and its subset, the Supreme Soviet. The Russian people were asked four questions: about confidence in President Yeltsin; about support of his economic reforms; about the desirability of holding an early presidential election; and about support for early parliamentary elections. On March 29, 1993, the Congress adopted a ruling governing the referendum; ordering, among other requirements, that there be "access to state mass media guaranteeing their equal use for agitation [campaigning] for and against the questions appearing in the referendum" (O vserossiiskom referendume 25 aprelya 1993 goda, 1993). The decree of the Federation Supreme Soviet, proceeding from the will of the Congress, ordered that

state mass media . . . be given equal opportunities to campaign for and against the questions submitted to the all-Russian referendum. The Russian Federation Ministry of the Press and Information is to ensure that the aforesaid provision is carried out by all state mass media. (*Rossiiskaya gazeta*, 1993)

Within months, the referendum vote was followed by a national parliamentary election, the rules for which were published by presidential decree, since the legislature had been dissolved. The statute obliged all state-run or state-subsidized media to provide equal opportunities for the candidates, including the right of appearing on the state television and radio, and banned publication of the results of public-opinion polls related to the elections within ten days of the ballot day (Article 8 of the statute). For the first time in Russian history, the election statute was supplemented by special regulations concerning the role of the mass media in election campaigning. The "Regulations on Information Guarantees in the Election Campaign" of October 29, 1993 established standards governing both the conduct of the campaign by the politicians and parties, and the impartiality of state broadcasting companies and their personnel in the campaign. The regulations also established a procedure for providing access to free and paid airtime on television and radio. Article 28 stipulated that an hour of free television time in the morning and an hour in the evening on weekdays be made available to all registered political parties.

To oversee these and other rules during the election campaign, the regulations established an Information Arbitration Tribunal, with mainly advisory powers. A growing concern, both in the West and inside Russia, over equal opportunities for media access for all parties and candidates resulted from the suspension of several opposition newspapers, the firing of "inharmonious" anchors from Ostankino, and open support of the Russia's Choice party by leaders of the state-run media. Freedom of the media, especially television and the major daily newspapers, emerged then as a key issue in the run up to December elections, and Yeltsin was under pressure to demonstrate that his critics and rivals would have fair access to the media. Described by its chair as an "ethical-legal structure" which would use public opinion as its primary weapon, the Tribunal issued expert opinions, provided advice about ethical practices, and made recommendations for improving coverage of the campaign. With one or two exceptions, all nine members of the Tribunal were chosen from among the associates and students of President Yeltsin's counselor and press-law expert, Yuri Barturin. Despite its makeup, the Tribunal proved to be an impartial body by criticizing, as will be discussed, both Yeltsin proponents and opponents for what it considered as violations of appropriate campaign practices. The Tribunal's dozen or so verdicts were not much criticized, in part because, although sessions of the Tribunal were open and widely publicized, its decisions and warnings had no major restraining effect on the violators of acceptable campaign procedures. By the time the Tribunal reached a conclusion on a case, new accusations of misconduct surfaced and, in effect, negative campaigning and smear tactics were treated after the fact.

TELEVISION AND ELECTORAL CAMPAIGNS

When an authoritarian regime loses power or mandates change with unexpected rapidity, as happened in the Soviet Union, new rules for television use in electoral contests have to be devised swiftly and often in the midst of crisis. In particular, rules have to be conceived concerning coverage by regular news programs, allotment of free time, and participation in candidate debates. Since, in the Soviet transition, the Communist Party had monopolized partisan politics, the structure of competition was only very weakly developed, relying on highly personalized movements or parties. With interest aggregation still largely nominal, a proliferation of views and stances—hence candidates—was the likely result. The 1989 elections to the Congress of People's Deputies marks the debut of televised campaign coverage. Paid commercials were not then allowed, and campaign coverage seemed little concerned with achieving a balance of views. Decisions were decentralized and often spontaneous. Televised electoral debates seemed to be significant factors in the elections, though the evidence is largely impressionistic.

As has been noted, in the Soviet Union in 1989, candidates were to be guaranteed access to promote their programs in the mass media. But the broad electoral law provided no rules for specific events. Ad hoc practices were improvised to fill the gap. In order to prevent Boris Yeltsin, a candidate in Moscow, from gaining airtime on national television, it was decreed that, since so many candidates were running in each electoral district, debates and other campaign activities would be most appropriately covered on local television systems. When Yeltsin did finally meet his opponent, a Moscow factory director, the debate was shown on the Moscow city channel, where it had a significant impact. Even though the debate resembled two separate interviews rather than a confrontation, the viewers could compare the men and their views. During that threshold year of 1989, the Moscow news program, "Good Evening, Moscow," also featured debates in other electoral districts in the city.

It is important to note that the debates were aired live. The importance of live broadcasts in buttressing the credibility of television and reducing the fear of censorship is extremely important. Lacking specific laws and practices at the time, urban television stations developed their own rules for candidate debates. Some commonalities emerged: All debates were broadcast live, a key element in gaining the trust and credibility of an audience which had long been accustomed to censored materials. All candidates were invited to appear on the air, and some eighteen or twenty would gather in the studio at one time. There were no formal time constraints; a moderator was umpire. In these spontaneously developed debates, the audience played a critical role, posing questions from the studio or by telephone. There is no doubt that, during these exuberant days of the first elections, the guiding principles of television coverage were inclusiveness, spontaneity, and audience participation. At the same time, the process needed honing or adjusting. The net amount of information the public received was reduced by the static of so many contenders sharing the stage.

In some ways, the newness and the ad hoc measures by which local television debates were structured in 1989, at the beginning of the transition in the Soviet Union, resulted in a degree of audience participation that has not been characteristic of older democracies. Furthermore, the elastic time limits and the inclusiveness of the debates gave viewers a very wide spectrum of political positions. With genuine political parties not yet permitted, the electoral contests necessarily were highly personalized. Conversely, the personalization of politics that television tends to produce may itself militate against the development of the political party as a mediating institution (Lang & Lang, 1984). This tendency was enhanced by the close relationship of television to an executive that spurned political parties as unworthy of a nationally elected leader, in a country which, by national doctrine, viewed parties as divisive factionalism. But in part, the uneasy relationship between television and political parties was a result of lack of procedural norms for determining the operational limits of political tolerance and for granting exposure fairly under conditions of great political and economic crisis that strained the very notion of tolerance. Indeed, the idea of tolerance was a concept launched by the more reformist faction of the Gorbachev government as part of what would be an unintended revolution.

Television coverage of the 1989 and 1990 elections and parliamentary proceedings was riveting for a country that had not before heard officially sanctioned political disagreements of great substance. Television greatly aided the campaigns of those who lacked the structure and resources of the single party and its auxiliary organizations. Though the contenders were drawn from the ranks of party members, for the most part, they most often represented the liberalizing wing and utilized the electronic medium to even their chances. Very soon, the contenders for political power would self-consciously begin to shape their campaigns with television in mind.

The political significance of the April 25, 1993 Russian Federation referendum was soon overshadowed, as the country faced, within eight months, the first fully competitive parliamentary election. However, the prominence of television in the referendum campaign, and the particular relationship of the state-run medium to political power, profoundly affected the choices that were made in the later parliamentary election campaign of December 1993.

The greatly exaggerated prominence given to television by leaders and observers alike bespeaks the continuing weakness of other channels of mobilization and the increasing concentration on the medium. The referendum campaign on television, as in earlier campaigns described previously, was carried out in the absence of a developed party system and organized party structures. It was, moreover, highly personalized, addressing the issue of confidence in the person of the President, who was deeply involved in the campaign.

A systematic content analysis of television messages related to the referendum shows the heavy hand of state direction of the campaign. The clear preponderance of pro-Presidential positions on news and public-affairs programs on the state-run television channels is impressive, as determined by content analyses of all referendum-related stories on these programs on the national Channels One and Two and the Moscow channel between April 5 and 15. Directed in Moscow by Vsevolod Vilchek, with the collaboration of Ellen Mickiewicz, the analysis included all such messages broadcast from 3:00 P.M. to midnight on Sundays and from 6:00 P.M. to midnight on all other days. On the Russian Federation–wide national channels One and Two, state television clearly supported the President in about 20 to 25 percent of the news and public-affairs coverage. Support of the parliament's positions, by contrast, was recorded in just under 10 percent of referendum-related messages. In a news story about voting procedures, it was not unusual to see a sample ballot with the pro-Yeltsin responses clearly marked, or an official presenting the pro-Presidential view with no opposing side presented. In programs that carried messages supporting the President, Boris Yeltsin most often spoke for himself. When parliament speaker Ruslan Khasbulatov was shown, an off-camera voice usually summarized his statement. Thus, on Channel One, 26 percent of the messages were in support of the President, with Yeltsin or another newsmaker speaking for himself; only 5 percent of the messages relating to the referendum were in support of the Supreme Soviet and showed a newsmaker speaking for himself. On Russian television (Channel Two), the figures were 17 percent pro-Yeltsin and 9 percent opposed; and on the Moscow channel, 21 percent and 8 percent, respectively. When newsmakers did not speak for themselves, journalists usually quoted or summarized their speeches or statements.

The arguments advanced by each side in the referendum campaign as covered by television were, to a considerable degree, mirror images. The majority of the arguments made on behalf of the President's side were positive: They outlined the successes of his and his allies' policies, but they were also cautionary, warning of dire consequences if he were defeated. The positive arguments positioned Yeltsin as guarantor of democracy and freedom, while the negative arguments saw a Yeltsin defeat setting loose the forces of reaction. On the other hand, the majority of the messages supporting the Supreme Soviet were negative, critical of the opposing side. Arguments supporting the Supreme Soviet referred to the ruin of the economy toward which Yeltsin was leading the country, the corrupt influences derailing production and trade, and the dangerous fracturing of society Yeltsin's policies had produced.

Of all the newsmakers on programs relating to the referendum, by far the most frequently covered was Boris Yeltsin, who appeared in nearly a fifth (18%) of the stories on Channel One, 12 percent on Channel Two, and 11 percent on the Moscow channel. In addition, members of Yeltsin's government accounted for another 9 percent on Channel One, 6 percent on Channel Two, and 13 percent on the Moscow channel. In contrast, then-Vice President Alexander Rutskoi, the most popular of Yeltsin's opponents, was the newmaker on 2 percent of stories on Channel One, 5 percent on Channel Two, and none on the Moscow channel. Then-Speaker of the Parliament Ruslan Khasbulatov appeared in 6 percent of the stories on Channel One, 5 percent on Channel Two, and 3 percent on the Moscow channel. Journalists were the other large group of newsmakers. By providing their own views, journalists became newsmakers in 10 percent of the stories about the referendum in support of the President on Channel One, 5 percent on Channel Two, and 3 percent on the Moscow channel. They were also newsmakers in 2 percent of the stories in support of the Supreme Soviet on Channel One, 2 percent on Channel Two, and none at all on the Moscow channel. These percentages are based on the total number of referendum-related pieces on each channel. They do not include stories in which newsmakers were not shown (about a quarter of the total); stories were coded for multiple newsmakers if each was in the news for at least five seconds. The phenomenon of journalists becoming newsmakers by announcing their own views was not repeated during the later parliamentary elections, when journalists were reined in so thoroughly that they found it difficult to perform professionally.

Almost all of the referendum messages on state television were placed in news and public-affairs programs, but some appeared in unexpected, even bizarre, places. During the April 6 show, "Music Soundtrack," the host called on young people to vote for the President. During the half-time in a soccer game, a telegram was read announcing that the coach and the team supported President Yeltsin. By all accounts, perhaps the most popular public-affairs program, one that broke new ground by personalizing the President and his family, was the April 20 broadcast of "A Day in the Life of the President." Directed by the well-known film director Eldar Ryazanov, it presented to the Russian viewers an unaccustomed look at the family and home life of their leader. It was a clear break with the customary remoteness that had been maintained by previous leaders. Political advertising during the referendum campaign was aimed at getting out the vote in public-service announcements, but also at supporting the Yeltsin platform. A U.S. advertising firm planned and executed Yeltsin's advertising campaign. No advertising supporting the parliamentary side was shown.

One other point is worth noting about the televised campaign of the April referendum: As before (and as would be the case in the future), the great heartland of the country was ignored by television. In the coverage of this referendum campaign, state television followed the traditions of Soviet television: excessive concentration on the capital city, with only cursory attention to the rest of the vast and highly differentiated country. About three-quarters of all coverage of the referendum was centered on Moscow.

Less than one-fifth related to other places in the Russian Federation. And just under 10 percent of the stories were generated by former Soviet and more distantly foreign locales. Since the two national networks, Channels One and Two, utilized a correspondent corps outside Moscow and had the capacity to offer more varied and geographically balanced coverage, the continued overrepresentation of Moscow was a result of a (perhaps unexamined) policy, rather than happenstance. To be sure, the seat of government generates more politically newsworthy stories than the provinces, and the sharp opposition between president and parliament was voiced in the capital city. Nonetheless, the referendum was to be a national vote. The Soviet period saw an exceedingly Moscow-centric pattern of news coverage, one that was criticized by those concerned with the disaffection of the rest of the country. Little changed during the call to the referendum in the spring of 1993. By its neglect of provincial cities and the countryside in general, state television and, to some extent, therefore, the political elite of which it was a part, was deprived of needed information about and communication with a very large constituency.

Another instrument of modern political campaigns also developed around the referendum. Public-opinion polling had been proscribed for decades and slowly "rehabilitated" (Benn, 1989; Shlapentokh, 1970). During the referendum campaign, polls rose to prominence. Television, radio, and newspapers all reported surveys; the results favored the President, as did the final tally. Exit polls were discussed on the Sunday news program, "Itogi" (Results), before the polls closed. The relatively great predictive power of these surveys before the referendum helped to legitimize and accelerate their use in future political contests. However, because of the extraordinary volatility of the electorate and the harshly adversarial parameters introduced by the armed rebellion of October 1993 and the outlawing of certain political parties, analysis of preelection public-opinion surveys became much more problematic during the December parliamentary election campaign.

THE TELEVISION CAMPAIGN IN THE RUSSIAN PARLIAMENTARY ELECTIONS: 1993

In the Russian parliamentary elections of December 1993, the many strands of an evolving pattern of campaign coverage came together. In contradistinction to past elections, this was to be the first multiparty parliamentary election. Though the earlier 1989 and 1990 parliamentary elections had offered opposing candidates, there had not been formalized parties, except for the Communist Party. By the end of 1993, there were a large number of parties, reduced for the electoral campaign by two processes: Some failed to gather the requisite number of signatures to be put on the ballot; others were judged by the Yeltsin government to constitute extremist threats to the constitutional system and were proscribed. Still, some thirteen parties did make it to the ballot. They were mainly loose and sometimes new entities united by (shifting) loyalty to their popular leaders, rather than by defined political or economic positions and policies. A number of existing parties reorganized, formed coalitions, and renamed themselves, thus leaving Russian voters disoriented and poorly informed about their political options (Corning, 1993).

The country's largest political party, the Russian Communist Party, claiming just half a million members, was briefly "suspended" by Yeltsin two months before the elections in the wake of the bloody "October events." Although the population did have a free choice among several alternatives, the pattern for Russia differed dramatically from that of Western Europe and North America: Having had no competitive party system for over seventy years, there was little opportunity to create new parties in the brief periods leading up to critically important elections. Nor was there any real possibility of resurrecting pre-Soviet parties, with their symbols and platforms. Such attempts, though perhaps promising at the beginning of perestroika, had been abandoned for the most part by the time of the 1993 elections. To complicate the task of the parties in the December 1993 elections, the person of the President was not engaged. Rather, in a de Gaulle-like posture, he viewed his office as standing above party politics and representing the nation at large.

Whereas in the Western model, political parties may be increasingly detached from the popular roots from which they grew, the Russian parties were detached from the people by never having established grass roots. Two parties were able to maintain connections with various groups on the basis of previously crafted relationships in which they had enjoyed positions of power. The Agrarian Party and the Communist Party (close allies, with the former being an outgrowth of the latter) did exploit the old structures and the old economic levers of the Soviet system. They did so by continuing, wherever possible, to monopolize or adapt instruments of local power. The Communist Party deliberately declined to utilize the tools of the modern, Americanized campaign. It bought no time for political advertising, but instead relied on the cadres of mobilizers and local networks that were the legacy of its monopolist past. Whether that strategy represented a genuine alternative for the future or a vestigial holdover from past campaigns remains to be seen.

The obtrusive partisanship of state television in the referendum campaign had justly called forth criticism from all sides. It is likely that, were it not for state television's blatant partisanship in April, the pendulum of campaign-coverage practices would not have swung so far in the other direction in December. The rules for the December 1993 campaign were to be substantially different. In fact, neutrality was to be so strict that television journalists were reduced to being mere traffic police. They were not allowed to provide commentary, analysis, or even to pose searching questions. In short, their training and role as journalists were to be nullified. The candidates and their parties were to enjoy unimpeded direct contact with the public: They could choose the form of that contact—the interview setting, a speech to the camera, a celebratory popular show format—but their message would be undisturbed by anyone in the television studio posing questions about the reliability, feasibility, consistency, or desirability of any of the goals put forth by the candidates (Regulations on Information Guarantees in the Elections Campaign, 1993, Article 15, p. 9). This policy left the viewing public to listen to a succession of platforms without any assistance from journalists in comparing them or even in clarifying their exact meaning. Vladimir Zhirinovsky squarely faced the viewing public on the program, "Voter's Hour," on November 25, and said (with deliberate mystification), "I use Aesopian language. . . . I could say other things," and after December 12, "I will say more about what I think about the former republics. . . . Sometimes I speak more softly than I think and than I want. . . . After the election, we will completely show our cards." Statements so provocative and deliberately obfuscatory would, for most communities of journalists, have called forth the most vigorous criticism and pressure for the candidate to reveal hidden plans. In this campaign, the journalists were ordered to refrain from journalism.

In terms of the amount of time devoted to news coverage of the different parties, the lion's share still went to the party favored by the President's administration; the dramatic change was in removal of editorial partisanship, not in news time. Though the imbalance in time is extreme, it should be recalled that this is one of the advantages of incumbency. Table 6.1 shows the amount of coverage that the two national channels, Channels One and Two, devoted to the leading political parties from November 1 though December 10. (The data are drawn from a collaboration between Vsevolod Vilchek, who directed the project, and Ellen Mickiewicz.)

According to one television critic, ten- to fifteen-minute current-affairs programs began to appear on Channel One (Ostankino Broadcasting) after the evening news. "They were called 'Topical Interview' and 'Topical Report' but there wasn't anything especially topical about them except that their participants belonged to the Russia's Choice Party" (Petrovskaya, 1993, p. 1). Equal time in news coverage of the contending parties clearly was not observed by state television. The Gaidar party, the choice of the Yeltsin administration, was strongly advantaged, especially on the larger network of Channel One, as was acknowledged even by the Deputy Chairman of Ostankino Television

Table 6.1
Time Allotted to Selected Parties in News Coverage of 1993 Parliamentary Campaign on Channels One and Two, November 1 to December 10, 1993

Party	Channel One	Channel Two
Russia's Choice*	90 mins., 45 secs.	43 mins., 00 secs.
Unity and Accord*	25 mins., 55 secs.	10 mins., 05 secs.
Movement for Democratic Reforms*	12 mins., 20 secs.	05 mins., 05 secs.
Yabloko#	12 mins., 45 secs.	05 mins., 00 secs.
Communist Party**	04 mins., 00 secs.	06 mins., 25 secs.
Agrarian Party**	03 mins., 50 secs.	01 mins., 20 secs.
Liberal Democratic Party**	01 mins., 50 secs.	03 mins., 55 secs.
Democratic Party#	06 mins., 40 secs.	04 mins., 40 secs.

* Party generally supporting presidential reform platform.
\# Centrist party.
** Party opposing presidential reform platform.

(Tolz, 1993). Despite the continuing imbalance in allotting time to the party favored by Yeltsin, however, two very significant changes in news coverage took place. First, a significant amount of time was allotted to other points of view, even if substantially less time than was accorded to the favored party. Second, there was a near-total change in the incidence of opinionated or biased reporting. This time, scrupulous neutrality was maintained by most of the news correspondents and anchors.

The glaring—and illegal—exception to this pattern of prohibition of partisan editorializing was, undoubtedly, a desperate reaction to the perception of a rapidly accelerating swing of undecided voters to the Zhirinovsky side in the last days of the campaign. State television violated clearly stated rules prohibiting campaigning just before election day. One of those violations was the broadcast on Channel One of a prime-time documentary film called "Hawk." State television officials undoubtedly hoped that presenting Zhirinovsky through his own words would repel the voters, particularly since this documentary was strategically placed immediately following a hysterical and brutal fictional film, "Stalin's Legacy," which depicted the madness and horror that a hypothetical, but very dramatic, return to Stalinism would entail. Whatever the intentions of the television officials, "Hawk" gave Zhirinovsky an extended platform for his harangues. Whether the message was received by the audience as the bureaucrats intended is doubtful. In any case, the practice of the television officials' substituting their own views for reliable indicators of public opinion was familiar from earlier times.

Astonishingly, during the entire period of our study there was not a single rural-based story about a political party. There was only one story that concerned the countryside at all, and it provided some general election information. This inattention undoubtedly worked to the benefit of the largest and best organized "voice" of the rural population, the Agrarian Party, inheritor of the old collectivized structure. As before, Moscow generated far more stories about political parties than did any other location in Russia. St. Petersburg also became a player, but the rest of the country was very spottily covered and clearly underrepresented, in spite of the fact that parliamentary, unlike presidential, elections could be conceived of as fundamentally local, especially when the country's President remained aloof from the process.

The degree to which the televised campaign personalized the contest is an important element of our discussion of the effects of "modern" campaigning in a "quasi-party" system. In the election postmortem, it was evident that even though the party of Yegor Gaidar, Russia's Choice, had the overwhelming advantage in news coverage and purchase of nonnews time, the party's strategy was to present itself through appearances by the many candidates it fielded. Russia's Choice could be seen in the faces of literally dozens of its candidates, while its leader, Yegor Gaidar, appeared in only a fraction of stories and programs about the party. Since many of Gaidar's colleagues in the party were also ministers and other government officials, they were bound to make news, and Gaidar apparently was neither able nor willing to define, in his person, the promise of the party and its platform. In fact, in cinéma vérité- style campaign ads, Gaidar appeared distinctly uncomfortable. As a result, Russia's Choice became a kaleidoscope of the faces of famous politicians. This was both the advantage and disadvantage of incumbency. Gaidar's appearance on television screens was counterproductive for two reasons. First, he was viewed by the public as responsible for the worsening economic situation of the population. Second, as the grandson of a well-known Communist writer, he was perceived as "having been born with a silver hammer and sickle in his mouth" (Rahr, 1994, p. 35). He tended to speak about complex economic policies of his party, instead of about the simple needs of voters. In this way he followed a Soviet political tendency "to start with what . . . the candidate wants to say, rather than what . . . the electorate wants to hear" (Sloane, 1993, p. 6). On the other hand, Vladimir Zhirinovsky's Liberal Democratic party had no such problem: Out of power, staffed mainly by people little known to the public, and without substantial political influence, the news concentrated on the energetic showman and his extreme ideas, and he chose to fill his paid and allocated free time by spending most of it talking directly to the public.

Perhaps the most important innovation in the Russian coverage of elections was the rule governing the allocation of free time and procedures for buying time for political advertising. Although advertising time was initially limited to a half-hour of paid time, that ceiling was later revoked by the government and replaced by no ceiling at all. Interestingly, some new parties adopted a strategy of relying almost entirely on television to get their message across and gain name recognition with the electorate. New Names/Future of Russia, a group of largely conservative politicians opposing the reformers, used substantial amounts of free and paid time. They did not even qualify to have seats in the parliament by passing the threshold of gaining 5 percent of votes. Similarly, the Movement for Democratic Reforms, with some highly visible political figures and substantial paid time, also did not qualify for representation in the State Duma, and neither did the fast-fading Civic Union.

Much has rightly been made of the innovation of political advertising. As we have noted, however, political advertising was introduced during the referendum campaign of 1993. At that time, its use was restricted to supporting only one position. President Yeltsin's October 1993 ruling governing state television in the parliamentary campaign provided for access by lot to unpaid time and money for any additional time the parties wished to purchase at reduced rates (see Table 6.2). During this campaign, foreign political consultants kept a very low profile, since the issue of foreign intrusiveness had become salient after the referendum campaign and after criticism of a U.S. AID-funded proprivatization spot that aired for a short time in the form of a rewritten spot supporting the Russia's Choice party. However, Moscow-based film directors were prominent participants in shaping advertising messages: Russia's Choice used Eldar Ryazanov, who had directed the popular documentary visit with the Yeltsin family at home. Noted documentary director Stanislav Govorukhin was both a strategist and a candidate for the Democratic Party of Russia. When he charged that Gaidar had paid people to turn out to support the President during the October 1993 rebellion, the Information Tribunal accused Govorukhin of "unethical behavior" and of making "insulting unsubstantiated statements about Yegor Gaidar" and the draft Constitution. The Tribunal ruled that if he violated the rules again and were

Table 6.2
Advertising Time in 1993 Parliamentary Campaign: Media Buys of Selected
Parties

Party	Channel One	Channel Two
Civic Union	88 mins., 30 secs.	34 mins., 00 secs.
Unity and Accord	88 mins., 00 secs.	12 mins., 15 secs.
Russia's Choice	87 mins., 30 secs.	156 mins., 50 secs.
LDPR	84 mins., 00 secs.	90 mins., 00 secs.

Source: Treteisky informatsionny sud i pervye vybory, 1994.

elected to the Federal Assembly, it would "request the Credentials Commission of the future Parliament to assess the methods used" in his campaign (Radio Moscow World Service, 1993).

As has been noted, not all parties bought time for advertising, even though rates were extremely favorable. Yavlinsky and the Communist Party did not buy time and still achieved the threshold for participation in parliament. "Our ads are designed to reflect on people's emotions and consciences. They are not supposed to have any logical effect," said the campaign publicity head for Russia's Choice (Sloane, 1993). The most frequent of Russia's Choice ads showing a rosy-cheeked boy romping happily with a furry—and expensive—St. Bernard in a lavishly outfitted playroom. When a slick poster appeared showing Party leader and Economics Minister Yegor Gaidar with the slogan, "Everyone talks. He listens," some, due to the subtleties of the spoken Russian language, interpreted the slogan as "Everyone says he's to blame" (Fireman, 1993).

Political advertising itself became a campaign issue to the extent that it represented the imposition of a foreign model. For example, a consultant advised the reformist party Unity and Accord to portray its leader as a man who cares about his family and, by association, voters' families by showing him with his wife and children. This consultant, who runs a public-relations company, conceded that he had learned all he knew from watching news clips of U.S. Presidential campaigns (Fireman, 1993). Further, the form of the political advertising was central to this issue: Imitating Western-style product advertising necessarily invoked the rather complex associations surrounding those newly imported messages. Viewers were ambivalent about their style and about the products, often unavailable locally or well beyond the reach of the household's income.

Zhirinovsky's ads were long homilies. He sat before the camera, on a modest set, speaking without notes and without pause about a selected subject announced in advance. He spoke, in turn, to believers, to the military, and to youth. His points were often disjointed and absurdly egocentric, but he displayed energy and eschewed the abstract language and vague promises of his competitors. When he appeared in the company of other candidates, his voice was often the only direct and forceful one. He carefully rejected the *appearance* of the Americanized model of political campaigning, while adapting its advantages for his campaign and his targeted electorate.

CONCLUSION

The extension of the franchise was achieved early in the life of the Soviet regime. But the transformation of the franchise from nominal to real was a revolutionary change some seventy years after the Bolsheviks came to power. Genuinely competitive elections for parliamentary representatives and president dramatically altered the political map of Russia. This profound change was accomplished over the span of less than five years, and even if no other change of note had accompanied it, the electoral revolution might well have been dislocating quite by itself.

In fact, however, the transformation of the franchise was accompanied by changes of enormous magnitude: The very definition of the polity was altered suddenly, and citizens of the Soviet Union became citizens of other countries or, in some cases, foreign nationals where they lived. Together with this profound reassessment of individual identity and culture, the disintegration of the economy created hardships for dependent populations and those on fixed incomes. The move to a market economy added the further burden of rapid and uncontrolled change in prices and real wages, while the security provided by the old state sector disintegrated. With many deracinated; others, declassed; and few able to predict the course of internal or foreign politics, the citizens participated in elections.

The legacy of the Soviet regime was also manifest in the absence of secondary associations, which had been proscribed. Thus, there were no developed microstructures or political party channels in place by which to aggregate interests. At the same time, the network of relationships the Communist Party had built up, particularly outside the principal cities of Russia, proved to be durable, at least in the near term. Other elements of the Soviet legacy were also important as the new age of televised electoral campaigns was ushered in: The personalization associated with televised political campaigns amplified and enhanced the traditional Soviet focus on the individual leader. Even though that leader was always pledged, in doctrinal terms, to perform the will of the Communist Party as a collective, in fact, the leader personalized his rule. One other element of the Soviet legacy was to be important in the televised electoral contest: The primacy of television and its unambiguous centralization under the authority of the political leadership was not easily altered in the post-Soviet phase. Though newspapers were the first to be decentralized and pluralized, television remained close to state authorities and subject to their oversight. The quest for autonomy is a difficult and protracted process.

Television has been a key factor in the changing politics of the Western world. In Russia, this has been equally true and, perhaps, more singularly so because of the deterioration of the newspaper market, a practical result of the collapse of the "central" papers and substantial drops in press circulation over the past few years (Richter, 1995). Television has been left as the primary structure for disseminating information, including the critical flow of information about candidates, parties, and elections. New to the television/elections equation has been the introduction of modern campaigning, including political advertising, and this raises the issue of the modernization or Americanization of the society. The massive social, political, and economic change referred to has been associated with the end of socialism and the introduction of the market. Democracy and market economics have been paired together in the pronouncements of the reformers, though that consonance may be problematic. Thus, the very reversal of the system itself is seen by many as modernization in the American mode. This means not just the introduction of the market, but a startling change in the hierarchy of values and symbols; one that separates generations. The Americanization of the electoral campaign, then, is a subset of a more destabilizing process, the manifestations of which are clearly "American." To the extent that political advertising is linked to this larger revolution à l'américaine, a whole host of cultural and political cues is triggered.

As might be expected, the changes are not universal, and the revolution has not been completed. A difficult transition lies ahead. Television plays a major role in that transition, particularly during phases of plebiscites and elections. The strategies of individual candidates and their consultants are self-consciously linked to basic positions concerning the direction of the society at large and its newly forming or reforming political identity. Positioning oneself closer to the Americanized end of the spectrum or moving in the direction of the older, more durable elements of the Soviet legacy—these options produce very different campaign strategies. Determining how to represent a specifically, distinctively Russian, pre- or non-Soviet set of values and images, given the mode and tempo of the post-Gorbachev change, is even more challenging.

In the Western world, television has had the effect of nationalizing elections; the old whistlestops, when candidates could craft their messages only to limited groups in the population, are a thing of the past. Television standardizes and magnifies. Television coverage of electoral campaigns in Russia has done the same, but without popular consensus on the definition of the nation. With its traditional disinterest in the countryside and small towns, television in Russia has tended to exacerbate the rural/urban cleavage and create a layering of (metropolis-based) national identities and names over an as yet underdeveloped base, without the firm underpinning of locally based organizations in the provinces. In the West, the tendency of politics in the television era to weaken parties, with their attendant networks of patronage and local support organizations, has been noted. In Russia, television electoral politics, with its emphasis on personalization drawing from both Soviet traditions and Western imports, plays to a nation uncertain of its future and lacking the secondary associations that can act as brakes or firewalls. Though it is only one variable in this complex model, television, the most powerful medium and desired political asset, could well retard the development of the very political parties that render the electoral system efficacious.

NOTES

1. For representation of party/nonparty people, men/women, ethnic groups, and the like in the Soviets as required by the central authorities, and changes of the ratios as a sign of changes of national policies, see Friedgut, 1979, pp. 83–91.

2. For a broader description of the main functions, see Furtak, 1990, pp. 10–11; Friedgut, 1979, pp. 137–147; Zaslavsky and Brym, 1978, pp. 362–363.

3. For a broader list of minor functions, see Zaslavsky and Brym, 1978, pp. 367–371.

REFERENCES

Benn, D. W. (1989). *Persuasion and Soviet politics*. Oxford: Basil Blackwell.

Corning, A. (1993, December 3). Public opinion and the Russian parliamentary election. *RFE/RL Research Report*, pp. 16–23.

DiPalma, G. (1990). *To craft democracies: An essay on democratic transitions*. Berkeley: University of California Press.

Fireman, K. (1993, December 4). Campaign advertising bombards Russia voters. *The Ottawa Citizen*, p. B1.

Friedgut, T. H. (1979). *Political participation in the USSR*. Princeton: Princeton University Press.

Furtak, R. K. (Ed.). (1990). *Elections in socialist states*. New York: St. Martin's Press.

Interfax. (1993, October 19). Dispatch.

Lang, G. E., & Lang, K. (1984). *Politics and television re-viewed*. Beverly Hills, Calif.: Sage.

Legislative Acts of the USSR. 1977–1979. (1981). Book one of *The law of the Union of Soviet Socialist Republics on elections to the Supreme Soviet of the USSR (of July 6, 1978)* (pp. 212–238). Moscow: Progress.

Mickiewicz, E. (1981). *Media and the Russian public*. New York: Praeger.

Mickiewicz, E. (1984). The functions of communications officials in the USSR: A biographical study. *Slavic Review, 43*(4), 641–656.

Mickiewicz, E. (1988). *Split signals: Television and politics in the Soviet Union*. New York: Oxford University Press.

O vserossiiskom referendume 25 aprelya 1993 goda, poriadke podvedeni a ego itogov i mekhanizme realizatsii rezultatov referenduma [On the All-Union referendum of April 25, 1993, on the order of qualifying its results, and the mechanism on implementation of referendum results.] (1993). Reported in *Rossiiskaya gazeta*, April 1, 1993, p. 6.

Pestrukhina, Y. (1993, November 17). Baburin i ko. proidut v gosdumu po odinochke [Baburin and company will make their way into the State Duma one by one]. *Megapolis-Express*, p. 17.

Petrovskaya, I. (1993, November 19). Vyacheslav Bragin i drugie funktsionery 'Ostankino' agitiriut za svoi vybor [Vycheslav Bragin and other functionaries campaign for their choice]. *Nezavisimaya gazeta*, p. 1.

Pravda. (1988). December 4, p. 2.

Radio Moscow World Service. (1993, December 2). *BBC Summary of World Broadcasts*, p. 15.

Rahr, A. (1994). The implications of Russia's parliamentary elections. *RFE/RL Research Report, 3*(1), 33–35.

Regulations on information guarantees in the election campaign. (1993). *Post-Soviet Media Law and Policy, 2*, 8–11 (Russian text published in *Rossiiskaya gazeta*, November 2, 1993, p. 4).

Richter, A. (1995). The Russian press after Perestroika. *Canadian Journal of Communication, 20*(1), 7–23.

Rossiiskaya gazeta. (1993, April 20). FB15-SOV-93-074, p. 1.

Sargin, A. (1993). Chudesa v izbirkome [Miracles at the Election Commission]. *Argumenty i fakty, 48*(December), 2.

Shlapentokh, V. E. (1970). *Sotsiologia dlya vsekh* [Sociology for everyone]. Moscow: Sovetskaya Rossia.

Slater, W. (1993). Allegations of corruption in election campaign. *RFE/RL News Briefs,* *2*(45), 5.

Sloane, W. (1993, December 2). Roll the cameras—Russia's politicians are on the air. *The Christian Science Monitor*, p. 6.

The text of the draft constitution. (1993). *The Current Digest of the Post-Soviet Press,* *45*(45), pp. 4–16.

Tolz, V. (1993). Yeltsin meets media chiefs. *RFE/RL News Briefs, 2*(46), 1.

Treteisky informatsionny sud i pervye svobodnye vybory [Information tribunal and the first free elections]. (1994). Moscow: Iuridicheskaya literatura.

Zakon SSSR o vyborakh narodnykh deputatov SSSR [The USSR Law on election of peoples' deputies of the USSR]. (1993).

Zaslavsky, V., & Brym, R. J. (1978). The functions of elections in the USSR. *Soviet Studies, 30*(3), 362–371.

Chapter Seven

Television and Elections in Post-1989 Poland: How Powerful Is the Medium?

Karol Jakubowicz

THE MEDIA AND ELECTIONS: SOME APPROACHES

Election campaigns are obviously a very special case of political communication, defined by Wolton as "the space in which contradictory discourse is exchanged between three actors with the legitimate right to express themselves in public on politics, namely politicians, journalists and public opinion" (1990, p. 12). As Mickiewicz and Firestone (1992) point out, during an election campaign in a democratic society, each of these actors has different interests: The candidate is interested in reaching the electorate; the media take an interest in elections as journalists and as media; and the public is interested in receiving the information necessary to participate knowledgeably in an election.

Assuming that they are not associated with any political parties and are not dedicated to furthering any political cause, the media's interests can be further defined in terms of three goals: first, to serve the candidates and the audience by making available facilities for direct access by candidates to airtime or news and/or opinion and editorial pages of newspapers and periodicals, as provided for by electoral law and dictated by the newsworthiness and importance of an election in general; second, to serve the audience by covering the election campaign and providing additional information, background, analysis, and commentary which help the audience make an informed choice on polling day; and third, to avoid being caught in political controversies or becoming a battleground for competing parties, and to avoid compromising their credibility by biased or unbalanced coverage of the campaign.

This approach views media performance in elections in terms of the purposive action of their managerial and editorial staff, that is, of the media organization itself. This is just one way of looking at the issue, however, because the mass media play several distinctly different roles in elections. As *communication media*, their generic properties and structural characteristics have by themselves helped remake the shape of election campaigns and have, in general, played an important role in shaping the political process. The media also are *channels for communicating* ideas and images existing or created independently of themselves, that is, channels of communication between the politicians and the public (hopefully this will be two-way communication)[1] and among the politicians themselves. Politicians seek to reach out to the public with their images, election platforms, and views on election issues; in turn, the public in various ways voices, to and through the media, its views on the candidates and parties contesting the election. Similarly, the candidates respond to messages spread by other politicians and directly or indirectly engage in a debate with them. And, of course, the media also function as *communicators*, originating messages and images and introducing them into social discourse, that is, as initiators of political communication and as communicators of their own messages (e.g., coverage and analysis of the campaign, staging of debates, interviews with candidates conducted at the media's own initiative).

Using McQuail's (1987, p. 25) typology of media functions, we can see that different dimensions come into play in each of these roles of mass media (Table 7.1). On the first question, there is no doubt that the structural characteristics of the modern news media, and especially television, as sets of technical arrangements for delivering content to the audience with unprecedented speed, reach, and immediacy, have played an important role in shaping the political process. Abramson, Arterton, and Orren (1988, pp. 66–121) ascribe to them an important role in the general transition of the American political system from the original communitarian through the pluralist to the present individualist, plebiscitarian vision of democracy. At a more practical level, the media have promoted a decline of attention to face-to-face political campaigning and consequently a de-localization of politics, more attention to the personality of the leader, a form of competition between parties which stresses

Table 7.1
Functions of Mass Media in Electoral Campaigns

Media roles in elections	Dimensions of media definitions (aspects of media playing the main role in each case)
Media as media of communication	Organizational and technological features; conditions of distribution, reception and use
Media as channels	Political: Relations to state and society
Media as communicators	Political: Relations to state and society; Normative: Social and cultural values; Social relationship of sender and receiver

performance rather than ideology, and some de-politicization of local government, among other things. All of these developments have been part of what has been described more generally as a transition from statesmen to politicians to personalities. This is known as the "medialization" of politics, that is, the tendency of the political system to change and adapt to the circumstances of a society in which the media are the main source of public information (see McQuail, 1983), where the political system takes advantage of the norms and working logic of the media system for its own purposes. At the risk of oversimplification, this could be described as one case in which the medium, is indeed, the message. Abramson, Arterton, and Orren (1988) predict that the new media, because of their own generic properties (great volume of information, speed of its transmission, receiver control, decentralization, targeting and interactivity) will similarly affect the political process, potentially reversing some of the earlier processes.[2] Paradoxically, we may say that the media's major, long-term impact on the very shape and functioning of the political system has been due to their properties as media of communication, leaving aside their content or the messages they deliver.

Media effects can be both deliberate and nondeliberate (McQuail, 1987). It would thus seem that the influence of the media as media on the political scene and election campaigns belongs to the category of nondeliberate effects, which does not detract from the fact that they have played a major role in promoting fundamental changes in these fields.

The role of the media in election campaigns as channels of communication between the politicians and the public and among the politicians themselves is also largely passive, especially as far as direct access by candidates is concerned. Rules of such access are usually decided outside the media themselves (Jakubowicz, 1991). Of course, an element of editorial policy is involved in selecting which views expressed by members of the public to convey to the audience, but these are still views and ideas existing or created independently of the media themselves.

The influence of a medium as a communicator is another thing altogether. This influence results from the medium's editorial policy and its choice of messages to introduce into social discourse:

In addition to performing a service to both sides of election-time communication (i.e., the candidates and the voters), the media also appear as *a separate communicator, a third force*, as it were, which exerts a significant influence on the course and effects of this process. Of course, they perform this role only if they are relatively independent of the two other participants, and particularly the candidates and the parties or political movements which support them. And they perform it to the extent to which *they actually bring influence to bear on societal attitudes and behaviour*. (Bralczyk & Mrozowski, 1993, p. 145, emphasis added)

Recognition of the media's role in elections as communicators raises a new set of issues concerning their ability to act independently in that capacity. There seems to be widespread acceptance in the literature of the view that the impetus which decides what role the media will play comes largely from outside the media system. If so, their role in the political process may turn out to be secondary and derivative in many cases.

This, of course, is an element of a broader problem—that of the relationship between the media and the power structure. The fundamental question here is whether the relationship is symmetrical (i.e., both are social actors in their own right, with an independent—and roughly equal—power base in society) or asymmetrical (i.e., the power base and importance of one far outweighs that of the other).

Following Gurevitch and Blumler (1983), we may identify at least three sources of the media's power: *structural*, stemming from their ability to deliver an audience that is not available by any other means, and, more generally, from their characteristics as a means of communication; *psychological*, based on the relationship of credibility and trust that the media have developed with their audience and which enables them to intervene in political processes in their own right, as it were; and *normative*, deriving from the respect in a democratic system for the principle of free speech and media independence, which legitimates the media's own role in the political process.

The media can direct or divert attention to particular problems, solutions, or people; they can confer status and legitimacy; and they can be a channel for persuasion and mobilization. By virtue of their contents, the media can affect the relationships between the individual and the political system (by affecting the individual's knowledge and view of that system), between the individual and the institutions of the political system (by supporting particular institutions or gaining support for particular politicians), between the constituent institutions of the political system (by affecting their relative strength), and between the political system and its constituent institutions (by giving prominence to some institutions and not to others).

The question, however, is to what extent the media perform these functions and so exercise the power inherent in them, independently and of their own volition, and whether the power gained in that manner accrues to the media alone. In general terms, while the nature of the media–power structure relationship changes from case to case, depending on the social and political situation, it is usually asymmetrical, with the power structure able to bring much more influence to bear on the media than vice versa. If one looks at the media–society relationship in general, what one usually finds when the media are influencing society is either that an active segment of society has influenced the media to influence society, or that a change in society has triggered media action to influence society or created conditions in which media could influence society (Jakubowicz, in press). Of course, this is not to say that every instance of the power elite seeking to use the media to influence society will bring the desired effect. Those effects may be functional, but they can turn out to be dysfunctional as well.[3]

A useful framework for examining the crucial aspects of the interactions between the power structure and the media in elections is provided by the two major perspectives in European political-communication research: one concerned with institutional politics, the other with cultural politics. These are summarized in Table 7.2.

The institutional-politics perspective concentrates on the procedures and mechanisms of power structure–media relations and the methods applied by

Table 7.2
Two Approaches to Political Communication

Institutional politics perspective	Cultural politics perspective
Concern with processes and relations in government, laws, parties, candidates and communications, opinions and votes	Concern with social origin and functions of all widely disseminated symbolic forms that convey images about our organized relations with one another
Concern with struggles over the power to govern	Concern with struggles over meaning
Concern with messages that refer overtly to choices framed and faced by power holders and those wishing to influence them	Concern with texts
Receivers of media messages: side takers	Receivers of media messages: reading and meaning makers
Rooted in political sciences	Rooted in anthropology, literary criticism, semiotics, economics, etc.

Source: Adapted from Blumler, Dayan, & Wolton, 1990.

the power structure and other social actors to gain as much influence over the media as is needed to have the power to govern. Let us note in this context that Gurevitch and Blumler (1983) distinguish legal, normative, and structural constraints applied by the state to fix the position of the media on the continuum between subordination to, or autonomy from, the authorities.

However, institutional control of the media themselves offers no guarantee of the power to govern unless it is accompanied by cultural control (i.e., control over meaning and definitions of reality) as disseminated by the media and (even more important) as subsequently interpreted and assimilated by receivers. It is only this dimension of control which gives real power. As a consequence, the institutional politics involved in gaining control of the media should be seen not as an end in itself (though, in fact, many politicians mistakenly assume that institutional control in and of itself guarantees cultural control over meaning), but as a means to an end, that of gaining the ability to successfully engage in cultural politics. Institutional and cultural politics must go hand in hand.

In order to reformulate the interests of the three participants in election-time political communication in the light of the institutional–cultural politics framework, it will be useful to recall a typology of media roles, functions, and goals which offers some clues as to the purposes of institutional and cultural politics with regard to the media. This typology is presented in Table 7.3.

As can be seen, this typology correlates the main types of journalists' social and occupational roles with modes of communication relationships, goals, and functions pursued by the media and with audience roles (based on Gurevitch & Blumler, 1983). On this basis, the interests of the three parties can be reformulated, as in Table 7.4.

Table 7.3
Media in Society: Roles, Relationships, Goals

Role vis-à-vis the audience	Mode of communication relationship	Functions, goals of media system	Audience roles
Hegemony	Command	Mobilization, political education, manipulation (coercive)	Passive object of mobilization
Leadership	Associational	Fight for common goals (normative)	Partisan follower
Guardianship/ Stewardship	Command/ Associational	Teacher, watchdog, combatting social ills, champion of causes (mixed)	Citizen, monitor, "pupil"
Service	Service	Neutral reporter of events, provider of content demanded by audience (utilitarian)	Monitor, spectator

Disregard of the different roles played by the media in elections and of the role of external factors in determining their impact on society can easily lead to a misrepresentation and misunderstanding of specific cases when the media are seen to have played a role in an election. One case in point is the recent Italian election won by Silvio Berlusconi's *Forza Italia* movement, largely, it would seem, on the strength of Berlusconi's ownership of, and campaign on, three national television networks. However, this is a classic case when the manner of operation of a television organization and its effects are determined by outside factors. First of all, Berlusconi's television networks performed primarily as channels for messages imposed on them by their owner in his role as a social and political actor. Second, this was precisely a case when a change in society created conditions in which media could influence society. Exactly this point is made by Wolton, who rebuts all the talk of "telecracy" or "videocracy" in Italy:

It is not the media we should look to for an explanation of this phenomenon, but the general context. In other words, instead of condemning the tyranny of the media, should we not rather analyze the historical, sociological and economic roots of the upheaval in Italy? Are the media really the cause for this earthquake? In comparison with what is written about Berlusconi's control of the media, how little analysis is really conducted of the structural reasons for his success: the collapse of the political class, the delegitimation of the State, the corruption of the elites. Silvio Berlusconi appeared after all of that had happened; he did not create those phenomena, he merely took advantage of them. To ascribe to the media and to this one man a crucial role in producing such election results is to disregard the reasons for the Italian malaise. (Wolton, 1994)

In other words, television could appear so powerful because the voters, thoroughly disgusted with the now discredited political system and its entire leadership, were looking for a change. In other circumstances, Berlusconi would probably not have stood a chance of successfully challenging the established order, all his mastery of television notwithstanding. As it was, television certainly helped project himself and his movement, but its role was secondary compared to that of the general structural factors which created circumstances in which it could play the role it did in the Italian election.

This would suggest that external factors determine, to a large extent, whether the media can affect the course or results of an election campaign. Factors which ordinarily enhance the media's persuasive effectiveness include their overall high credibility; the fact that the audience has no direct, personal knowledge of an issue and cannot verify media messages from first-hand experience; and the fact that the audience does not hold firm views on the given subject. While the first two factors are, of course, important, the third one would seem to be of primary significance in our case. We could hypothesize that the higher the degree of political partisanship among the electorate (resulting, for example, from existing social divisions and conflicts), the less of a chance the media have in affecting (i.e., changing) the popular mood and thus influencing election results.

By the very fact of transmitting, as a channel, messages attuned to the existing mood the media may, of course, intensify already existing sentiments, mobilize the electorate around an issue on which it already feels very strongly, give exposure to an individual or a symbol, help provide a previously unavailable focus for those sentiments, or even help counteract an existing spiral of silence by making individuals and groups who felt isolated by virtue of their views aware of how many others share those views, and thus create or fuel a bandwagon effect (see Note 1).

However, the media's ability to affect the voters in other ways is limited. We could thus say that the media's influence on election results is in inverse proportion to the gravity of issues facing the voters, the stakes involved for them personally in the election result, and the extent of their political commitment. Therefore, the more that depends on the outcome of the election for the voters personally, the more interested they will be in the issues, the more intense their political commitment will be, and the less they will need to rely on the media to make sense of the dilemmas involved or to make up their mind who to support. As a general rule, this means that the content delivered by the media, and especially television, in their role as channels and communicators, can be a relatively powerful force at election time in societies marked by a general social consensus on the shape of the country's political and economic system (this is usually a feature of stable, prosperous, and democratic societies). In such circumstances, the general level of political awareness and commitment in society will be low, and there will not be a fundamental difference between the election platforms of leading contenders or much at stake in the outcome of the election for most voters personally. Therefore, receptivity to media-delivered and media-originated information and persuasive messages may be high. And conversely, where these conditions do not obtain, this receptivity may be low. We will treat this as a hypothesis to be tested by examining elections held in Poland in and after 1989.

Table 7.4
Journalists' Roles, Modes of Communication Relations, Media Goals and Functions, and Audience Roles

	Institutional Politics
Candidates' media-related interests in an election	**Media as media:** Seek to understand and turn to advantage* the generic properties of the media
	Media as channels: Seek to obtain best possible terms for direct access† in a way that benefits the candidate and disadvantages opponents, as well as to control or influence the extent and manner (as well, hopefully, as orientation) of the public's views conveyed by the media.
	Media as communicators: Seek to control the media so they will favor the given party, its platform and candidates
The media's interests in an election	**Media as channels:** Maintain strictly regulated and clear, legally defined relations with candidates and their party organizations; obtain from outside regulators or develop together with parties generally accepted rules for direct access; fight off attempts for political control of media's role as a forum for public debate.
	Media as communicators: Retain autonomy and independence in coverage of the election, impartially mediate between the candidates and the public.
The public's media-related interests in an election	Practically identical to those of the media themselves.

* One obvious and much quoted example is the Nixon-Kennedy debate, when Nixon's refusal to have theatrical makeup applied to his face is reported to have affected the "result" of the debate in terms of the viewers' judgment of who "won."

† During the 1990 presidential election in Poland, discussions on the format of the television debate among candidates proved to be unsuccessful because Tadeusz Mazowiecki's representatives wanted a highly structured format, giving their candidate advance warning and time needed to ponder and express his views on any issue, while Lech Walesa's representatives wanted an open, unstructured format, giving their candidate the opportunity to shine in the heat of a fast-flowing, give-and-take debate, his preferred style. The interests were so incompatible that the result was no debate at all.

Cultural Politics	Media Role vis-à-vis Public Mode of Communication Relationship	Audience Role
Seek to control the representation and interpretation of reality so as to set campaign issues, influence perceptions of problems facing society, persuade that the party's platform offers best solution for those problems and the candidate is best suited to lead.	Overt: Leadership-Associational (normative) Covert: Hegemony-Command (coercive)	Overt: Citizen, partisan, follower Covert: Object of mobilization, manipulation
Provide opportunities for all representations and interpretations of reality, symbols, and meanings to reach audiences, and provide keys to decoding these representations of reality, symbols, and meanings to make them, and the intent behind them, intelligible to the audience.	Service (in electoral broadcasts) Service + Associational (mixed) Guardianship-Stewardship-Leadership (in news and current affairs	Citizen Monitor Spectator "Pupil"
Obtain texts from the totality of election-related media content that provide full information on the parties' and candidates' views of the country's situation, sources of and reasons for its problems, ways of resolving them, results that their election platforms will bring.	Service (in electoral broadcasts) Service-Associational (mixed) Service-Guardianship-Leadership (in news and current affairs)	Citizen Monitor Spectator "Pupil"

POLAND: ELECTIONS REVOLVING
AROUND FUNDAMENTAL ISSUES

Three general elections (1989, 1991, and 1993), two local government elections (1990 and 1994), and two presidential elections (1989 and 1990)[4] in one country in the space of five years; if that is not a record, it must come close. At the time of this writing in August 1994, Poland is coming up to another presidential election in 1995 and, on past form, another early general election cannot be entirely ruled out.

The June 4, 1989, general election, conducted according to the rules worked out during the Round Table Conference in the spring of 1989 between the Communist leadership and representatives of Solidarity (it was described as an exercise in "contractual democracy" by Wiatr, 1991), was the first in Poland's postwar history which involved a real contest between opposing political forces and an active role of the media. In particular, state radio and television helped mediate the conflict and provide a forum for both sides. Since then, elections have been fought in the media, and primarily on television, to a growing extent. So, Poland is an interesting case study of the role of the media in a newly reborn democracy, offering, at the same time, rich material to test the hypothesis that has been formulated. For reasons of space, it will not be possible to deal at length with the learning curve of Polish politicians in finding out how to use the media to best advantage. Suffice it to say that, to begin with, their skills in using the medium of television especially were very limited, resulting in very static, uninteresting electoral broadcasts, using wooden political jargon and making practically no use of the possibilities offered by the medium. Let us only note in passing that consideration of the power of the television medium must also include the ability (or lack of it) to use the features and properties of the medium. With time and the greater availability of money in some cases, parties began to hire consultants, public-relations and advertising companies, as well as professional directors and producers. However, even greater media and public-relations savvy did not, as we will see later, prevent some of them from making what are considered to be grave mistakes and miscalculations in designing their election campaigns.

What makes the matter even more interesting is the self-restraint and, in fact, timidity of Polish Television in acting as a communicator in election-time political communication. Paradoxically, the abolition of the Communist system in 1989 did not relieve but, if anything, intensified political pressures on the state broadcasting system. The government, having "lost" the now-privatized printed media, sought to retain broadcasting as a means of communicating with society. The new breed of politicians proved as willing as the old to exert pressure on Polish Radio and Television to get their views across.

Seeking to pacify its critics, the management of Polish Radio and Television chose the easy option of playing safe, staying out of trouble, and provoking critics as little as possible. It was doubly cautious during election campaigns, so it usually refrained from interviewing candidates and from discussing election platforms, the course of the campaign, and possible results. News programs provided very little coverage of various campaigns, reporting few rallies, press conferences, and other events. Another reason for this policy was low professionalism and high political commitment among the staff, who could not always be trusted to stay impartial and were prepared to declare their political preferences and voice support for their favorite candidates on the air. The difficulty of monitoring what each journalist was doing in election-related programs was another reason for the general policy concerning coverage of elections.

Polish Television's policy becomes more understandable when we realize the extent of the fragmentation of the political scene in Poland (at the time of this writing, some 250 parties or party-like organizations have been registered in the country). Seeking to analyze their political identities, Jerzy J. Wiatr (1993) points out that these parties exist in a "three-dimensional space," in which differences among them can be measured by their placement on three continua: strongly monetarist to anti-monetarist, pro-state interventionism; secularism to religious, moral fundamentalism; and for de-communization[5] to against. Zukowski (1993a) offers a somewhat more extended catalogue of the range of choices facing Polish voters after 1989, which can usefully be combined with Wiatr's continua, as in Table 7.5.

The pro-lustration movement may seem to be strangely placed, but it combines its virulent opposition to the continued presence of former Communists in public life, the "Round Table Conference sellout" and the Solidarity forces which negotiated it, with a pro-Church orientation and an economic stance which sees a role for state interventionism and distrusts the monetarist policies of the Solidarity governments.

While the dilemmas are presented here in a much simplified form, and not all of them became equally important in every post-1989 election, it is clear that each involves a fundamentally different range of choices, so much so that anyone committed to one alternative is not likely to be easily persuaded by electoral propaganda to abandon it and embrace the other.

Table 7.5
Polish Election Dilemmas

Accept Communist past (Lustration: No)	Support European integration (Secularism)
Anti-monetarism	Monetarism
Reject free market (Lustration: Yes)	Pro-free market
Defend traditional & religious values (Fundamentalism)	Support Solidarity (Governments)

The 1989 General Election: A "Solidarity" Landslide

The Round Table Conference decided that a general election would be held in which the opposition could contest 35 percent of the seats in the Diet (the lower chamber of parliament) and all the seats in the Senate (on the understanding that only the next election would be free, with no predetermined allotment of seats).[6]

The 1989 election was the first general election in decades in which voters had a real choice. Only one of the dilemmas shown in Table 7.5 faced the electorate: whether to support Solidarity or to support the old system. According to the mood of the time, it was a choice between "us" and "them," and the result was a forgone conclusion: Solidarity and other opposition forces won all the seats they could contest in the Diet, and all but one of the one-hundred seats in the Senate.[7]

Electoral support for Solidarity candidates was a symbolic, reflexive and spontaneous gesture which had little to do with election platforms or issues. On June 4, 1989, a visit to a polling station constituted a celebration of the ethos of the right cause and an act of opposition to the existing socio-political order. That celebration brought to the fore the traits of the Poles' collective subconsciousness: a reserved attitude to the institutions of the official order (which could easily become a denial of that order) and a compensatory respect for the institutions, or, better yet, the values of a moral order and principles of justice. (Lipinski, 1990, p. 60)

Nevertheless, the 1989 electoral campaign was very interesting and deserves some attention. It was marked by a curious role reversal. The Communist party and its allies sought to put major emphasis on the personalities and individual features of particular candidates, to avoid clear identification with any political force or ideology, and to demonstrate democratic intent by putting up a few candidates for each seat. By contrast, Solidarity was almost totalitarian in putting up only one candidate for each seat, playing down individual candidates, stressing their membership in "Walesa's team" and their role as representatives of Solidarity, and focusing on the big political and ideological issues rather than on what the candidates wanted to do for their constituencies or their voters. Under the agreement worked out at the Round Table, Solidarity was given access to airtime on radio and television in proportion to the number of seats it could contest, and was able to produce its own electoral broadcasts. Solidarity activists, many of them former Polish Radio and Television journalists who had been fired in one of many political purges, were now given access to studios and equipment to produce the broadcasts as they saw fit. They were assisted by intellectuals, artists, and social scientists associated with Solidarity, who also helped mastermind its general election strategy. So, electoral broadcasts consisted of two clearly separate parts: segments devoted to official candidates and, after separate opening credits, the Solidarity part.

Content analyses of these electoral broadcasts (Jedrzejewski, 1990; Kowalski, 1990; Mrozowski, 1990) stress several distinguishing features of the persuasive strategies applied by both sides. First, the official campaign was individualistic in orientation; the Solidarity campaign was collectivistic: Its candidates all spoke as duly authorized[8] representatives of one organization, united by the same views and pursuing the same goals. In that way, the Solidarity message was homogeneous and very forceful. Second, segments devoted to official candidates focused for two-thirds of the time on the candidates themselves;[9] their message was vague and defensive. Segments on Solidarity candidates devoted two-thirds of the time to general issues, which reinforced the stress on Solidarity's substantive message concerning the need for fundamental political reform. Finally, the Solidarity campaign was very rich in symbolic content, with patriotic, religious, and historical symbols and references creating a potent message which stirred the imagination, integrated individuals, and created a sense of collective identity.

The role of state radio and television in the Solidarity campaign was clearly that of a channel. Of course, they were also communicators in their own news and current-affairs programming, seeking to do what they could to undermine Solidarity's credibility. That role was imposed on them by their political masters in the Communist party. However, the very fact that Solidarity candidates could appear on the air and speak freely was such a major change and signified such a breakthrough that nothing else mattered. In any case, "the quality of election propaganda was of secondary importance, at best, and so its impact on election results does not seem especially significant. The election turned out to be a plebiscite for or against change, and in this situation propaganda proved helpless" (Kowalski, 1990, p. 134).

The Presidential Election of 1990: Electing a Favorite Son

The arrangement worked out at the Round Table provided (though not in so many words) for General Wojciech Jaruzelski, the architect of martial law and the leader of the reformist wing of the Communist party which realized the need to share power with the opposition, to be elected as President of the country for a six-year term. His role was, in part, to be a guarantor in Soviet eyes that change in Poland would not jeopardize Soviet interests.

General Jaruzelski was elected President by the General Assembly in July 1989. Soon afterward, the entire context which was seen as necessitating his holding of the post (and as justifying Solidarity support for his election)[10] began to fall apart. One country after another in Central and Eastern Europe staged a "velvet" or "singing" revolution and ended Communist rule. Internally, the two parties which had always been junior partners in a "coalition" with the Communist party under the Communist system now changed sides and allied with Solidarity. The Communist party itself disbanded in January, 1990, and transformed itself into two separate social–democratic parties.

Meanwhile, there were also rising tensions within the Solidarity movement. The Solidarity-led government of Prime Minister Tadeusz Mazowiecki and the intellectual wing of Solidarity grouped around it sought to preserve the movement as one, mass "catch-all" party, providing necessary backing for the program of economic shock therapy pursued by the government. They felt that the extraordinary difficulties and hardships created by the shock introduction of market reforms justified delaying the normal emergence of many different political parties and orientations out of the Solidarity movement, once united primarily by its opposition to the now defunct Communist system. As part of the same strategy, they sought to marginalize the Solidarity trade union proper and to isolate its leader, Lech Walesa, who had no formal position in the State.

That strategy was challenged by a new party, Centre Alliance, which wanted an early presidential election and sought to divide the political scene between itself, as a right-of-center party, and the left-of-center movement emerging out of the political grouping revolving around the government (it was to have been a bipolar system of movements originating out of Solidarity, which would stabilize the political scene and marginalize all other political forces). At the same time, Lech Walesa himself declared "war at the top" as a way of challenging what he perceived to be artificial unity promoted by the progovernment grouping as a way of maintaining its hold on power, and declared in April 1990 that he would run for President.

The original plan had been to adopt a new constitution first, then hold an early general election and complete the process with a new presidential election. However, pressure for "acceleration" became irresistible. Parliament decided that an early presidential election would be held first, in December 1990, and an early general election second, in the spring of 1991.

That set the stage for a highly acrimonious and increasingly personal campaign which could leave few politically involved people indifferent. Many of the dilemmas listed in Table 7.5 were alive in that campaign, including bitter debates concerning market reforms, the choice between "us" (Solidarity supporters) and "them" (former Communists), the meaning of the legacy of the Communist years, and the role of the Church.

The campaign was fought largely on television for two reasons. First, political parties or movements backing the six candidates[11] who collected the 100,000 signatures of support required by electoral law were either very new or in disarray, so they were incapable of mounting full-fledged campaigns throughout the territory of the whole country. Second, the press scene was, just at that time, undergoing profound transformation, with many titles changing hands or political affiliations, which prevented many newspapers from being able to cover the campaign well and to take a clear stand on the candidates.

So, television "dominated the course of the campaign to an unprecedented extent, though at the same time it was in a highly awkward situation in that among the six candidates was the incumbent Prime Minister [Tadeusz Mazowiecki] to whom [state] radio and television were subordinated" (Bralczyk & Mrozowski, 1993, pp. 145–146). For that reason, as well as for the general reasons already explained, Polish Radio and Television sought to stay as neutral as possible, reducing its communicator role to a minimum. Hence, coverage of the campaign was confined to brief news reports. Polish Television reported the results of public-opinion polls, but generally refrained from commenting on them or from speculating on the possible results of the election. That was also a feature of the one regular current-affairs program devoted to the election ("Around the Election"), in which well-known journalists and commentators discussed the campaign. However, they, too, steered clear of politics and of commenting on the platforms of particular candidates, preferring to concentrate on campaign tactics and media coverage of the campaign, stressing the passive behavior of journalists generally. An analysis of all Polish Television programs which contained references to the election campaign before the first round of balloting results is presented in Table 7.6.

Although electoral law provided for equal access to airtime for all candidates as far as electoral broadcasts are concerned, when the entire airtime devoted to candidates is added up, some of them had more time than others. If one discounts Mazowiecki's appearances in his capacity as Prime Minister, Lech Walesa is at the top of the table, which reflected not only his success in the polls (in which he was favored to win), but probably also television journalists's own preferences. The order of the other candidates roughly reflects their standing in the polls.

However, the orientation of statements about the candidates run or quoted by Polish Television was predominantly neutral, and statements in favor usually outnumber statements of opposition. Differences among candidates are not really significant and conform to no clear pattern. The one exception is Stanislaw Tyminski, who was the object of more negative than positive statements, due in part to his attacks on the Prime Minister. In general, however,

Table 7.6
Polish Television's Coverage of the 1990 Presidential Campaign

	Mazowiecki	Wałęsa	Tymiński	Cimoszewicz	Bartoszcze	Moczulski
Shows with candidates' statements	138	122	77	75	70	66
Time (in seconds) devoted to candidates	10,632	8,220	4,010	2,353	2,336	2,125
Statements concerning candidates	376	377	174	104	100	94
Quotes of candidates' statements	22	43	4	10	6	6
Statements of support	66	73	24	16	10	10
Statements against the candidate	49	59	43	6	6	6
Neutral statements about the candidate	254	242	104	78	80	77

Source: Bralczyk & Mrozowski, 1993.

Polish Television was able to maintain a neutral stance before the first round of balloting. Clearly, none of the candidates had won the institutional-politics battle for control of Polish Television or, to be more precise, for a change in its general political affiliation. Its management and journalists were generally pro-Solidarity.

The results of that first round were astounding. Everyone had expected a two-way race between Walesa and Mazowiecki. In fact, Mazowiecki came in third, suffering a humiliating defeat at the hands of Stanislaw Tyminski, who thus passed into the second round to face Walesa, who had received the most votes but not enough to win the presidency on the first ballot.

"If it had not been for television, there would have been no Tyminski" (Jasiewicz, 1993, p. 115). There is general agreement that Tyminski's candidacy and popularity were almost entirely creatures of television. That, of course, is true, but mainly in the sense that his views and appearances on television struck a chord with disaffected voters—a passive and apolitical group—outsiders who for social, political, psychological, and cultural reasons found themselves beyond the Solidarity camp and the reach of its reforms.

The Walesa–Mazowiecki conflict, which introduced dissent into the movement on which the nation had pinned its hopes, shocked many Poles, weakening the power of Solidarity symbols to rally the population. That, added to the sense of disenchantment and anticlimax caused by both the shock of market reforms and the inevitable mistakes of the new government, convinced many that "the government and its Prime Minister are ineffective, the Chairman [i.e., Walesa] and his supporters are irresponsible, and all of them are incompetent" (Zukowski, 1993b, p. 76). The appearance of Tyminski, who created an image of himself as an independent candidate uncompromised by any ties to Solidarity, a successful businessman, and a man of the world—honest, truthful and disciplined—gave them hope and triggered their emergence as a third force in Polish politics. This force was composed largely of younger, less educated people from among the unemployed; and generally from less integrated communities, least affected by the impact of Solidarity and the Church, who were opposed to economic liberalism and the power of the Church, and had been hit particularly strongly by the Solidarity austerity program involved in the introduction of market reforms.

Thus, Tyminski's cultural politics had been particularly effective in offering those people both a diagnosis of their own situation and a promise that something could be done to remedy it, as well as an image of himself as the person capable of offering them, and the whole country, new hope. He was thus a Berlusconi-like figure, capitalizing on the self-destructive blunders of the political establishment and answering a deeply felt need for a different alternative. And very much like Berlusconi, he would have gotten nowhere if developments in the country had not delivered to him a "silent, apolitical minority" (Zukowski, 1993b).

After the first ballot, Polish Television shook off its passive role and became a communicator. Two reasons accounted for the change. First, it had been generally criticized for its passivity and inability (for the reasons explained) to bring the candidates to a debate. Second, and more important, Solidarity elites in Polish Television and elsewhere were horrified to discover that Tyminski stood a real chance of doing well in the second round, perhaps even of winning. Therefore, they staged a counterattack. Polish Television sought to confront Tyminski, whose Polish, after many years spent abroad, was halting, with the fast-talking Walesa. That produced not so much a debate, but a joint press conference, packed with opponents of Tyminski who mercilessly probed his every weakness and exploited any inconsistency in his platform. Tyminski refused to attend the second, already scheduled debate, whereupon Polish Television showed a background report on him, purporting to provide evidence of his ill treatment of his wife and children, his refusal to provide them with money for living expenses, and the like. That, together with a second such film, was a dirty-tricks campaign designed quite openly to discredit him. At the same time, Polish Television showed background reports on Walesa, portraying him as a great statesman and a historic and charismatic figure who almost single-handedly overthrew Communism.

That campaign, aided by a similar one launched by the Church, helped secure victory for Walesa on the second ballot. Walesa would have won anyway: There was no way he could be defeated by the "man from nowhere." Mazowiecki had asked his supporters to vote for Walesa, and most of them did. However, the anti-Tyminski campaign did persuade some former Solidarity supporters who had voted for him to return to the fold, and discouraged more traditionally minded voters from supporting him. The nation's favorite son, Lech Walesa, became President.

The 1991 General Election: Confusion Reigns Supreme

As has been mentioned, the Polish parliament decided, in 1990, that as the product of the rigged, only partly democratic election of 1989, it no longer had legitimacy in the fundamentally changed national and international context to perform its role. It dissolved itself in the summer of 1991, and an early election was called to make sure that the new parliament would truly represent the people.

The war at the top waged by Lech Walesa had by now destroyed the somewhat artificial unity of the Solidarity movement and set the stage for the appearance of scores of new splinter parties. The electorate found itself with an unaccustomed *embarras de richesse* in the form of 111 parties, associations, and ad hoc citizens' groups contesting the election, of which only twelve were known by name to most voters (Raciborski, 1993). By now, all the orientations shown in Table 7.5 were represented by different parties, sometimes in several shades of intensity and variation. Five axes were most important: attitudes to the Communist legacy, now being redefined as attitudes for or against de-communization; attitudes to market reforms, privatization, and inegalitarian social and welfare policy; the issue of the role of the Church in society (with the Church itself and Catholic-oriented parties growing in importance); the issue of a strong versus a weak presidency, revolving around the role of Lech Walesa in the country's public life; and the issue of integration with Europe versus the defense of traditional values.

Polish Television continued its policy of giving very limited coverage to the campaign and campaign issues. Parliament was dissolved in early summer, and the general election was set for late October. It was clear that the intervening months would be crucial in terms of clarifying the issues and helping voters obtain the information and knowledge needed to make a conscious, informed choice about which party to support. Yet Polish Television followed its standard practice of removing most current-affairs programs from its summer schedule, reducing its ability to offer the kind of service needed by the voters, should it decide to do so. Clearly, that was not the intention.

In July 1991, 34 percent of respondents to a public-opinion poll said they knew which party to support. In October of that year, three weeks before election day, that figure was 41 percent. That did not, however, mean a growth of just 7 percent because, meanwhile, 20 percent of the electorate had developed a preference as a result of the campaign, but 13 percent changed their mind and decided to back a different party than before (Raciborski, 1993). On election day, voter turnout was very low; only 42 percent.

The conclusion to be drawn from this is that voters found the issues and the platforms of particular parties so confusing that the campaign's impact in helping voters make up their minds and decide to go to the ballot turned out to be only slightly stronger than its impact in confusing and demobilizing them:

In their mass the voters did not identify the program *positions* of the individual parties, they did not understand "what was at issue in these elections." The divisions turned out to be too complicated to be understood by the man-in-the-street, especially when the previous ways of thinking about the world of politics had been shattered during the earlier presidential elections . . . [there was no longer] the [simple] polarity between Solidarity and the forces associated with the old regime. (Raciborski, 1993, p. 40)

Perhaps, that is why level of education turned out to be the factor which correlated most strongly with a clear voting preference: It was simply too much for many uneducated people to make sense of what the different parties were saying.

The result of the election was equally confusing. With a straight proportional system laid down in electoral law, a total of twenty-eight parties succeeded in getting into the two chambers of parliament. The party with the largest number of seats in the lower chamber had won only 12 percent of them. Representatives of all orientations got in, making for a fragmented, highly volatile parliament and political scene, where it was difficult to put together a stable coalition of like-minded parties. Two years later, after several changes of government, this parliament was dissolved by the President.

The Parliament of 1993: A Relapse of Communism?

In order to prevent the 1991 situation from repeating itself, the electoral law was changed to prevent the fragmentation of parliament.[12] In consequence, many parties failed to clear any of the thresholds required to win even a single seat, even though they received a total of 34.5 percent of the vote.

As the date of the election drew near, it became clear that it could produce a major political upheaval. According to one social scientist, the mood and sentiment which ultimately accounted for the results of the election resulted from the fact that

We are a disillusioned and for that reason a deeply frustrated society . . . [most people] feel estranged and helpless in the present situation. They sense that the ground is slipping out from under their feet, that they are losing their bearings and confidence in the future. Even many of those who are not directly affected by social ills like unemployment express lack of hope and confidence in the future. They are not predisposed to trust the rulers because reality is different from their promises. They feel abandoned because they believe that the ruling elite is less concerned with the public interest than with its own interests. (Wiatr, 1993, pp. 10–11)

While this somewhat overstates the case, in that not all strata of the population are affected by the country's situation in the same way, awareness of how widespread such feelings nevertheless are raised the stakes for parties contesting the election and made a successful campaign doubly important for them. More than ever, that put a premium on their ability to tailor their message to what the public expected.

All the dilemmas presented in Table 7.5 faced the voters, though, of course, their relative importance had changed. Public-opinion polls showed that resentment against the Communist past and those who claimed a link with it had clearly waned. Support for, or tolerance of, market reforms had also weakened and, as we have seen, produced a strong feeling of frustration among many people. That strengthened those who opposed privatization, introduction of market mechanisms, and reduction of the welfare state, and could conceivably have created favorable conditions for another wild-card candidacy, a Tyminski figure from outside the political establishment to gain the support of the same, but potentially larger, group of outsiders who constitute a third force in Polish politics. Relative withdrawal of support for the modernizing, pro-European tendency could have produced a wave of support for nationalist and religious tendencies.

Practically all parties sought to respond to those trends, with the opposition parties obviously trying to capitalize on them. However, several parties miscalculated and adopted unsuccessful campaign strategies. Several examples can be mentioned. One case in point is Stanislaw Tyminski's Party X and others like it, which went for very dramatic imagery in portraying the situation of the country (e.g., the "Self-Defense" organization of indebted farmers whose main campaign slogan was "Poland is perishing" and which used in its electoral television broadcasts the image of the historic Polish bell, which tolls only on occasions of momentous importance for the country). As it turned out, the voters rejected this radical rhetoric:

In Poland, despite the emotions which sometimes overtake people, voters clearly prefer to support those who speak calmly and without emotions, who appear sound and unlikely to make radical demands. . . . It is becoming a tradition that radical rhetoric and radical slogans or images fail to win support, however faithfully they may reflect everyday discourse and emotions. Radical rhetoric has been regularly defeated and even popular politicians see their support ebb when they cross that intangible line which separates moderation, realism and responsibility from everything else. (Krzeminski, 1994, p. 23)

The efforts of both the Roman Catholic Church and Catholic parties to reaffirm the role of religion and religious values in social life also failed to secure a good showing during the election. They had aroused resentment and fears of possible "re-ideologization" of life, with another set of strict rules replacing those in force during the Communist years.

The Liberal–Democratic Congress, which had spearheaded the monetarist, market-oriented, pro-European orientation, suffered a defeat all the more spectacular for the care and effort which went into planning their election campaign. It was a media- and public relations–minded campaign, planned with the assistance of Saatchi and Saatchi, full of media events, geared to newspaper and television deadlines, and seeking to provide appealing and dynamic images (Kozlowski, 1993). However, it was misguided: The campaign was based on a misreading of the public's opinion of the liberals and therefore concentrated on providing images and arguments which alienated the voters instead of winning them over (Krzeminski, 1994).

The fractious center-right parties, embroiled in never-ending internal disputes, together received roughly the same number of votes as the Democratic Left Alliance, which won the largest number of seats, but separately, each of them failed to introduce a single deputy into parliament. One could thus say that the situation of the 1989 election reversed itself: This time the post-Solidarity forces contributed to their own defeat, while the united and well-organized left emerged triumphant. A public-opinion poll conducted a few days before polling day found that 63 percent of the nation believed that the program of reforms conducted over the previous few years had failed and should be changed. Nearly 60 percent agreed that the previous four years had been wasted, that there were few prospects for improvement, and that people cannot be expected to agree to further sacrifices. Those feelings predominated over all attempts to persuade voters otherwise, even though, when translated into votes, they meant support for parties like the Socialist Left Alliance, whose backbone is the Social–Democratic Party (a successor to the former Communist party), and the Polish Farmers' Party (a successor to the United Peasant Party; largely a puppet organization, which under the Communist system was allied with the Communist party in a ruling "coalition," together with another puppet organization, the Democratic Party).

As for the role of television in that campaign, "It would be difficult to point to a clear interrelationship between the campaign in the media, and especially television, and the voters' decisions. Most constituencies backing particular parties coalesced and grew or diminished independently of the media campaign" (Krzeminski, 1994, p. 21).

A few days before the election, 60 percent of the electorate knew who they would support. Before the campaign had started, that proportion stood at 50 percent, confirming its limited effectiveness. The parties which ultimately won the election were generally said to have waged rather boring campaigns on television (Bralczyk, 1993).

Polish Television continued its play-safe policy. At the beginning of summer in 1993, when parliament had been dissolved and an early election was scheduled, it followed its normal practice of taking most of its current-affairs programs off the air during the vacations. So, it virtually deprived itself of the opportunity to interview candidates on current-affairs programs and discuss election platforms, the course of the campaign, and possible results on its own programs and in its own way. News programs provided very little coverage of the campaign, reporting few rallies, press conferences, and other events.

Polish Television did run a number of election-related series. Two dealt with electoral law and the election process itself and were strictly factual in nature. One was a series of discussions among sociologists on issues facing Poland and on the elections in this context. Yet another was a vox-pop program with brief soundbites on people's expectations concerning what MPs and senators should be like and how they should serve the public.

Only two series were really oriented to the election issues and to offering viewers a chance to better understand the parties' election platforms. One, called "Two on Two," featured two Polish Television journalists, who, for ten minutes, would grill two representatives of one of the fifteen election committees which registered national lists of candidates. The journalists looked for holes in their election promises, reminding them of their past behavior and trying to trick them into telling the truth about themselves. This was good in design, but bad in execution. Ten minutes is not enough time to analyze a party's election platform and to get to the bottom of its views and ideas of how Poland should be governed. So, the result was confusing rather than enlightening.

The other series of five programs involved debates among three parties in each program. In the course of an hour, first party experts, then party activists, and finally party leaders would join the debate—the idea being, of course, to sell the party's own ideas to the public and discredit the ideas and record of the other two parties taking part in the debate. Polish Television journalists involved in those programs were "traffic cops" more than anything else, making sure that the programs went smoothly but contributing practically nothing of substance.

It was only two days before the polling day, after all the electoral broadcasts had been transmitted, that some of those journalists put on a special programme, "Without Emotions," in which they took a hard look at some of the election promises and statements of some of the candidates and parties and exposed their propagandistic, demagogic nature. The problem with that program was that the journalists editorialized on these matters, clearly expressing their own personal views and displaying their own political preferences—which is the last thing they should have done.

The National Broadcasting Council, the newly appointed broadcasting regulatory body, censured Polish Television for failing to perform its duties properly. The Council found that Polish Television failed to adequately perform as required by its role in democratic society and by the law. Among other things, Polish Television was charged with broadcasting too few current-affairs programs in which uncommitted experts could present and discuss the current situation in the country and, in this context, to assess the election platforms of particular parties. In general, low professionalism (erroneous interpretation of electoral law, poor quality of journalistic work and lack of preparation among reporters covering the campaign, excessive stress on personal conflicts rather than substantive debates in the campaign) contributed to a failure to make sense of the election for the benefit of the viewers.

CONCLUSION

The process of fundamental, systemic transformation in Central and Eastern Europe is analyzed and interpreted in many ways. Jadwiga Staniszkis (1994) believes that it has taken three forms: a "top-down" revolution, decreed and managed from above; an implosion, involving a collapse of all or most institutions and general disintegration of the state; and an evolutionary change, involving formal and symbolic continuity with the past while gradual change of the sociopolitical context gives old institutions new meaning and new patterns of functioning. She considers the Polish case to be one of a top-down revolution, with all the tensions this implies, especially since it is proving less effective and thorough-going than expected. The state is caught between the need to achieve a breakthrough and the continuation of old laws and institutions resulting from the nature of the top-down revolution. It has shown itself to be comprehensively unable to control and manage the process of change, especially in the spheres of social consciousness, people's attitudes, and convictions. Hence, the modernizing elite is out of touch and largely unable to communicate with the majority. Meanwhile, other processes (the birth of "political capitalism," promoted by the takeover of economic power by former Communists and the impact of world economic and political processes) dictate developments in ways uncontrolled by anyone.

Wojciech Lamentowicz (1994) seeks to develop ways of explaining the cultural and institutional dimensions of democratic transformation and, to this end, formulates the following hypotheses:

- Short-term adaptive shock, which is natural in the conditions of such far-reaching change
- The heritage of the past, with the legacy of the Communist past weighing heavily on the present
- The revolution of rising expectations
- Arrogant elites
- Uncompleted institutional transformation
- The crisis of legitimization

Central and Eastern European countries, says Lamentowicz, face different prospects for the future. Some will consolidate their democratic institutions. Others will get bogged down in a stalemate between democracy and creeping authoritarianism. In still others, the state will be abolished by a massive bureaucratic explosion and/or implosion.

All this will reflect on voting behavior in a variety of ways, including a refusal to vote for reasons of political apathy or alienation or loss of faith in the democratic process. The floating vote and the unpredictability of election results may grow as the electorate searches for answers to problems besetting the country. In its role as a channel, television will play the important role of enabling voters to come into contact with politicians offering the promise of providing such answers. It will also continue to play its role as a medium, reshaping the political system in ways known from other countries. Its role as a communicator will probably grow as the old play-safe policies and incompetence in dealing with complex political issues become things of the past.

However, it is argued here that, for a long time yet, voters will be primarily influenced by their conditions of life, the socioeconomic and political situation resulting from the progress (or otherwise) of the process of transformation. When television begins to play a crucial role in elections and the more telegenic candidates stand a better chance of getting elected, we will know that the process of transformation has been successfully completed.

NOTES

1. Wolton (1990) assumes that the public should express itself solely by means of public-opinion polls, but that seems to unnecessarily restrict the range of choices open to the public to articulate its views and interests and join the public discourse.

2. For example, they contend that, in the United States, the decentralized nature of the news media and their greater ability to target particular audiences may result in the following trends: reducing the role of New York and Washington in prescribing the agenda and content of election coverage; greater attention by the public to local politics; greater emphasis on ideological and issue-oriented politics; and a greater tendency to interpret public opinion in group terms (see also Swerdlow, 1988).

3. The media's intervention into the political process may, indeed, be counterproductive. One case in point is the Russian general election of 1993, when Russian Television (or whoever was its political master) decided to discredit Zhirinovsky by running long documentary films meant to expose him as an irresponsible, nationalistic, and dangerous rabble-rouser. As it happened, Zhirinovsky's views struck a chord with the voters, and the films won him a lot of support, turning him from a still insignificant figure into a major force in Russian politics.

4. The 1989 election was conducted by the National Assembly (i.e., the two chambers of parliament), and only the 1990 election (as discussed later) was decided by a national ballot.

5. De-communization is a term for some form of vetting (also known as "lustration"; see Truth and Justice, 1993) which would remove former Communist cadres from political and public life. Strong supporters of de-communization formed a group of parties and groupings which opposed the contract arrived at during the Round Table Conference and accused post-1989 Solidarity governments and the parties which formed them of "selling out" to former Communists and ensuring their continued, and increasingly important, role in the country's political and economic life.

6. Spring 1989 was a time when the collapse of the Communist system had not yet begun. It was assumed by all concerned in Poland that it would continue in the Soviet Union and elsewhere for a long time yet. Hence, the pragmatic wing of the Solidarity movement which worked out the Round Table compromise was prepared to accept such a limited step toward full democracy.

7. The one seat that Solidarity failed to win did not go to a representative of the old order, but to a businessman who had enormous powers of patronage in his constituency.

8. One famous stratagem was to put up election posters all over the country showing each candidate in the company of Lech Walesa (who did not run for election himself), putting on the candidates Solidarity's seal of approval, as it were.

9. A fair number of them were television and other public personalities, drafted by the party to provide added attraction to the official ticket.

10. Fearing that opposition to him would be so strong as to prevent his election and wreck the whole arrangement, several Solidarity leaders turned in invalid ballots to ensure his victory. He was elected by a majority of one vote.

11. They were as follows: Lech Walesa, leader of the Solidarity union; Tadeusz Mazowiecki, a Catholic journalist and intellectual, previously a Solidarity adviser and now Prime Minister; Wlodzimierz Cimoszewicz, chairman of the social-democratic parliamentary caucus, composed of former Communists; Roman Bartoszcze, representing the farmers' movement; Lech Moczulski, leader of the Confederation of Independent Poland; and Stanislaw Tyminski, the "man from nowhere," a Polish businessman with interests in Peru and Canada, leader of the small Libertarian Party in Canada.

12. This included a provision that single parties must win at least 5 percent of the vote (or at least 3 percent if no party has won 5 percent) and coalitions at least 8 percent of the vote (or at least 5 percent if no coalition has won 8 percent) to win seats in parliament. In terms of the division of seats among national lists put up by parties and coalitions, the latter must have won at least 7 percent of the vote for their national lists to be included in the distribution of seats (all these thresholds are waived in the case of national minorities). The d'Hondt system of calculating election results was applied, additionally favoring the parties which received the most votes.

REFERENCES

Abramson, J. B., Arterton, E.C., & Orren, C. R. (1988). *The electronic commonwealth.* New York: Basic Books.

Blumler, J. G., Dayan, D., & Wolton, D. (1990). West European perspectives on political communication structures and dynamics. *European Journal of Communication, 5*(2-3), 261–284.

Bralczyk, J. (1993). Ksztaltowanie obrazu "sceny politycznej" w programach wyborczych Telewizji Polskiej [Shaping images: The "Political Scene" on Polish Television]. In *Telewizja–pieniadze–wladza* [Television–Money–Power]. *Proceedings of a conference organized by the Institute of Culture and NTP Plus* (pp. 39–42). Warsaw: Institute of Culture, NTP Plus.

Bralczyk, J., & Mrozowski, M. (1993). Prezydencka kampania wyborcza w telewizji. Konstruowanie (auto)portretów kandydatów [The presidential election campaign on television: Construing the (self-)portrayals of the candidates]. In S. Gebethner & K. Jasiewicz (Eds.), *Dlaczego tak glosowano. Wybory prezydenckie '90* [Why did the vote go this way? Presidential election '90] (pp. 144–178). Warsaw: Instytut Studiów Politycznych PAN, Instytut Nauk Politycznych UW.

Gurevitch, M., & Blumler, J. G. (1983). Linkages between the mass media and politics: A model for the analysis of political communication systems. In J. Curran, M. Gurevitch, & J. Woollacott (Eds.), *Mass communication and society* (pp. 270–290). London: Edward Arnold.

Jakubowicz, K. (1991). Electoral campaigns on radio and television: General principles. In A. Pragnell & I. Gergely (Eds.), *The political content of broadcasting* (pp. 48–55). Manchester, England: The European Institute for the Media.

Jakubowicz, K. (in press). Media as agents of change. In D. Paletz, K. Jakubowicz, & P. Novosel (Eds.), *Glasnost and after: Media and change in East and Central Europe* (pp. 19–47). Cresskill, N.J.: Hampton Press.

Jasiewicz, K. (1993). Polski wyborca—w dziesiec lat po sierpniu [The Polish voter—Ten years after August]. In S. Gebethner & K. Jasiewicz (Eds.), *Dlaczego tak glosowano. Wybory prezydenckie '90* [Why did the vote go this way? Presidential election '90] (pp. 91–117). Warsaw: Instytut Studiów Politycznych PAN, Instytut Nauk Politycznych UW.

Jedrzejewski, S. (1990). "Studio Wyborcze," Polskiego Radia: Studium przypadku ["Election Studio," Radio Poland: A study in coincidence]. *Przekazy I Opinie* [Transmissions and Opinions], *3–4,* 135–145.

Kowalski, T. (1990). Wybory '89 w Telewizji: "Studio Wyborcze, Kto w Twoim imieniu" Studium przypadku [Election '89: "Election Studio, Who acts in your name?" A study in coincidence]. *Przekazy I Opinie* [Transmissions and Opinions], *3–4,* 121–134.

Kozlowski, J. (1993). Telewizyjne kampanie partii politycznych w Polsce [The television campaigns of political parties in Poland]. In *Telewizja-pieniadze-wladza* [Television-money-power]. *Proceedings of a conference organized by the Institute of Culture and NTP Plus* (pp. 34–38). Warsaw: Institute of Culture, NTP Plus.

Krzeminski, I. (1994). Najlepiej nieudana kampania [The perfectly unsuccessful campaign]. *Krytyka, 43,* 21–32.

Lamentowicz, W. (1994). Perspektywy spoleczenstwa obywatelskiego w Europie srodkowej: U zródel pesymizmu politycznego [Social perspectives on civil society in Central Europe: The sources of pessimism in politics]. In W. Jakóbik (Ed.), *Kontynuacja czy przelom? Dylematy transformacji ustrojowej* [Continuity or rupture? Dilemmas in the transformation of the political system] (pp. 100–112). Warsaw: Instytut Studiów Politycznych PAN, Friedrich Ebert Stiftung.

Lipinski, A. W. (1990). *Plebiscyt I odmowa: Studium terenowe reakcji wyborczej 1989 roku* [Plebiscite and refusal: A field study of reaction in the election of 1989]. Warsaw: Centralny Program Badan Podstawowych.

McQuail, D. (1983). The influence and effects of mass media. In J. Curran, M. Gurevitch, & J. Woollacott (Eds.), *Mass communication and society* (pp. 70–94). London: Edward Arnold.

McQuail, D. (1987). *Mass communication theory: An introduction.* London: Sage.

Mickiewicz, E., & Firestone, C. (1992). *Television and elections.* Queenstown, Md.: The Aspen Institute.

Mrozowski, M. (1990). Analiza zawartosci programów "Studia Wyborczego" nadanych przez Osrodek Telewizyjny w Lodzi (10 maja–4 czerwca) (Studium przypadku) [Content analysis of the program, "Electoral Studies," broadcast by the Television Center in Kodz (10 May–4 June) (A case study)]. *Przekazy I Opinie* [Transmissions and Opinions], *3–4,* 97–120.

Raciborski, J. (1993). Whether and how to vote? Confused voters. In J. J. Wiatr (Ed.), *The politics of democratic transformation: Poland after 1989* (pp. 32–43). Warsaw: Scholar Agency.

Staniszkis, J. (1994). Czy rewolucja odgórna jest mozliwa? [Is revolution from the top possible?]. In W. Jakóbik (Ed.), *Kontynuacja czy przelom? Dylematy transformacji ustrojowej* [Continuity or rupture? Dilemmas in the transformation of the political system] (pp. 89–99). Warsaw: Instytut Studiów Politycznych PAN, Friedrich Ebert Stiftung.

Swerdlow, J. L. (Ed.). (1988). *Media technology and the vote: A source book.* Washington, D.C.: The Annenberg Washington Program.

Truth and justice: The delicate balance. The documentation of prior regimes and individual rights. (1993). Working Paper No. 1, Central European University, Budapest.

Wiatr, J. J. (1991). *Zmierzch systemu* [Twilight of the system]. Warsaw: Wydawnictwo Fundacji im. Kazimierza Kellesa-Krauza.

Wiatr, J. J. (1993). Fragmented parties in a new democracy: Poland. In J. J. Wiatr (Ed.), *The politics of democratic transformation: Poland after 1989* (pp. 108–121). Warsaw: Scholar Agency.

Wolton, D. (1990). Political communication: The construction of a model. *European Journal of Communication, 5*(1), 9–28.

Wolton, D. (1994, May). *L'écran alibi: Le Monde des débats* [The screen alibi: The world of the debates]. *Le Monde*.

Zukowski, T. (1993a). Przed podniesieniem kurtyny [Before the raising of the curtain]. *Polityka* [Politics], *28*, July 10.

Zukowski, T. (1993b). Wyniki glosowania: Mapa polityczna Polski jesienia 1990 r [Voting results: A political map of Poland in Fall 1990]. In S. Gebethner & K. Jasiewicz (Eds.), *Dlaczego tak glosowano. Wybory prezydenckie '90* [Why did the vote go this way? Presidential election '90] (pp. 61–90). Warsaw: Instytut Studiów Politycznych PAN, Instytut Nauk Politycznych UW.

Chapter Eight

Political Communication and Electoral Campaigns in the Young Spanish Democracy

Juan I. Rospir

The Spanish democracy is a late fruit in Europe. Supported by a national consensus, the transition to a parliamentary monarchy was made very quickly, through reforms that began in 1976 and the founding elections that took place in 1977. Political parties were established in short order, without the long traditions of ideological debate; historical ties to class and group interests, grassroots organizations, or network of client relations; and personal links to voters that characterize political parties in other Western European democracies. Television was already well established as the primary medium of communication and information before 1977, and it immediately became the focus of political and electoral communication in the fledgling democracy. When democracy came, it came in a flood. Since 1976, Spaniards have been called to the ballot boxes for six general elections, four municipal elections, three national referenda, two elections for the European Parliament, and numerous regional referenda and elections for the regional legislatures. During the same period, the media system has been transformed by a steady increase in the number of newspapers, radio stations, and television stations. Rapid expansion of the media system was supported by a boom in the Spanish advertising market, with foreign communications groups spending the equivalent of 245 million U.S. dollars in 1992 alone to advertise in Spain. Private, commercial television arrived only recently, but, beginning with the June 1993 election, seems to be increasing the focus on television in electoral campaigning even more.

Given these circumstances, it is perhaps not surprising that, as we shall see, the democratic political institutions and electoral practices that have emerged in Spain bear the typical marks of modernism: a multiparty system that is dominated by centrist "catch-all" political parties whose support rests on voters' opinions and is therefore heavily dependent on effective use of communication; great emphasis on television as the medium for building, maintaining, and enhancing political support; personalization of politics through the principal party leaders; and so on. The interesting aspect of these practices in Spain is that they developed very quickly, without the conflict between traditional forms and new media that often have been seen in older democracies. From its comparatively recent beginnings, democratic politics in Spain has been tied to contemporary communications media, strategies, and priorities.

At the same time, Spain is similar to older democracies in Western Europe and elsewhere in many respects. Spain's is a parliamentary democracy with multiple political parties. Seats in the parliament are apportioned based on the distribution of votes in each electoral district, where voters choose between lists of candidates presented by the parties. There is public financing for political parties and election-campaign expenses. The official election-campaign period is quite short, lasting only three weeks. Political advertising is prohibited on television but allowed in print media and radio, and the public television system allocates free time to the political parties during election campaigns.

These similarities and differences to other democracies make it worthwhile to explore the Spanish experience as, alternately, an example of a comparatively modernist system of political communication that was born in the media-centered age, and as a case study in what happens when a modernized political communication system is constructed in a society and system of government for which it may not be entirely suited.

THE ELECTORAL SYSTEM AND ITS CONSEQUENCES FOR POLITICAL PARTIES

In order to understand how electoral communication is practiced in Spain, the place to begin is with an appreciation of how some structural features of the system of electoral representation shape the political parties and their relationship to the voters.

The Electoral System

Spain has a proportional electoral system that follows d'Hondt's formula for distributing the 350 seats in the national parliament among fifty-two electoral districts. In each of the districts, the political parties present lists of candidates equal to the number of seats allocated to the district, plus any supplements. These lists are closed and blocked, that is, voters are not allowed to make any modifications or alterations to the lists. The electoral districts vary greatly in size: from very large districts, such as Madrid with more than 4 million inhabitants and thirty-four representatives to be elected, to very small districts. In the June 1993 election, for example, one representative was elected in Madrid for every 115,466 voters, compared to one representative for every 26,093 voters in the small Soria district.

Such striking differences in the size of electoral districts imply corresponding differences in the possibilities for effective campaigning. In large districts, the sheer size of the electorate makes it virtually impossible for the candidates to develop any direct or personal relationship with the voters. Instead, the parties and the politicians must rely on the mass media to communicate with the public. Face-to-face communication between candidates and voters is more feasible in the smaller districts, yet the opportunity in small districts to establish a more personal relationship between candidates and voters is largely ignored. Instead, campaigns are heavily centralized under the control of the leadership of the political parties, and are standardized based on the model that is appropriate to the largest districts. As a result, campaigns everywhere are heavily focused on mass media, and electoral propaganda is not adapted to the concerns of individual districts but, instead, addresses general, national topics. The practice of standardizing campaigns in this way accomplishes some useful goals for the large political parties, such as maintaining firm party control of the content of campaigns and making expensive media-centered campaigns more cost effective by employing the same materials nationwide rather than only in the largest districts. However, these goals are obtained at the price of forgoing the more compelling approaches to campaigning that would be possible in smaller districts, such as direct contact between candidates and voters, with appeals based on the issues that are most important in each district. By applying everywhere a media-centered campaign model created for large urban areas, the parties may needlessly distance their candidates and propaganda from the voters' local concerns. Such a practice may well compound the lack of connection between voters and candidates that often occurs when candidates are selected, not by the voters, but rather by the parties for the parties' own purposes.

An exception to the general rule of centralized, standardized national campaigns is the efforts of smaller, minor parties. Unlike the large centrist catch-all parties that compete for control of the government, smaller parties often represent more narrowly defined interests, such as regional, more extreme, more sharply partisan or ideological interests, and particular socioeconomic, religious, or ethnolinguistic cleavages (Lane & Ersson, 1987). These parties are sometimes able to win small numbers of seats in the parliament by breaking with the standardized approach of the large parties' campaigns and instead offering to represent the specific interests of voters in particular districts. The potential for success of this "targeting" strategy is limited, however, by the tendency of some voters to engage in what is called "strategic" voting. Rather than "waste" their vote for a party that has no chance of winning a large number of seats, some voters in districts that elect only three to five representatives would rather have their district represented by candidates of the victorious party and thereby secure a more influential voice for the district within the governing party. Voters who cast their ballots on this basis are said to engage in strategic or "sophisticated" voting (in Spanish, "useful" voting). Some studies estimate that the incidence of strategic voting is as high as 10 percent (Gunther, 1989). The practice of voters casting their ballots for the party they prefer among those parties that have a realistic chance of winning a substantial number of seats attenuates the normal relationship between voters' preferences and their voting choices, and also reduces the possibilities of success for all but the largest parties.

The Relationship of the Political Parties to the Voters

The nature and types of political parties reflect structural features of the electoral system. On the one hand, there is a profusion of political parties. The number of parties winning seats in the parliament ranged from a high of fifteen parties in 1979, to a low of eleven parties in 1993. On the other hand, the method by which seats are apportioned in the parliament disproportionately rewards parties that are able to win large majorities of votes nationally. In all six national elections through 1993, the two leading parties in each election together won a minimum of 64.7 percent of the vote and a maximum of 73.5 percent. With only one exception, however, the method of apportioning seats based on these elections awarded the two leading parties together a substantially larger proportion of the seats in parliament than their share of the vote (in five of the six elections, the two leading parties won from 80.5% to 87.4% of the seats). Only in the 1986 election did the two leading parties receive seats in the parliament equal to their share of the national vote, at 70.2 percent. Thus, the electoral system is structured in a way that disproportionately favors broad, centrist parties that can capture large, homogeneous majorities of voters.

Reflecting the way in which the electoral system discourages true multiparty competition in favor of bipartisan competition, the Spanish political scene is dominated by two major parties which have a broad, centrist political orientation and appeal to the nation as a whole. In order to win the large majorities that are favored by the electoral system, these parties are constituted as catch-all or "opinion" parties, which endeavor to win by capturing the support of the widest possible range of voters. Accordingly, their programs are wide and inclusive and address a national agenda, rather than being specifically ideological and addressed to narrower agendas. Internally, these parties are characterized by clear structure, centralized organization and leadership, and strong unity. More extreme, narrow, or ideological interests and programs are the province of minor parties that play only a peripheral role in the context of the situation in Spanish elections.

Because the return of democracy occurred so recently, the voters have no historical affiliations to the political parties. And because the dominant parties are centrist rather than sharply ideological, there is no history or encouragement of ideologically based voting. As a result, elections in Spain tend to be referenda on the performance of the governing political party, a situation which makes for a volatile and changeable electorate in Spain, as in the United States. Moreover, Spanish voters have a comparatively low level of interest in politics, reflecting in part the great frequency with which elections have been held in the short history of Spanish democracy. This low level of interest perhaps makes the electorate even more volatile.

Low levels of political interest combined with the lack of any history of party affiliation or ideologically based voting give particular prominence to the mass media because of the role they can play in shaping political opinions. The advent of democracy and of political parties coincided with growth of the media in Spain. From the beginning, political parties regarded television as the great instrument of mobilization and electoral influence. As is explained in more detail later in this chapter, a particular result has been a high degree of "political personalization," or emphasis on the images of the party leaders, and "political spectacle" (Edelman, 1988) in Spanish campaigns, both of which may be seen as responses to demands imposed by the media in return for ample and favorable coverage of campaigns.

The political parties' reliance on mass media, especially television, to form and maintain their relationship with the voters is also explained by the public financing that the political parties receive. The parties are financed with public money in three ways: party subsidies given annually, subsidies of electoral expenditures in each election, and subsidies of parliamentary groups in the two houses of parliament. Thanks to public financing, the parties can mount media-centered campaigns unhindered by the need to raise funds to pay for them, particularly since the prohibition of political television advertising reduces the cost of such campaigns.

However, there is evidence that the large parties' reliance on television to build their relationship with voters by projecting a national message has not been completely effective. In a national survey conducted in 1988, more than 50 percent of those who voted for the two major parties described their party as having had "little" or "no" success in explaining to the country what problems are most important and how the party would solve them (Sociological Research Center, 1988). The failure of campaigns to engender strong attachments to the parties is suggested by other national studies which showed that, in the 1989 and 1993 elections, only 15 to 34 percent of the voters for each of the major parties reached their voting decision because of party loyalty (Sociological Research Center, 1989, 1993).

Despite limited success in building party loyalty among voters, the large parties continue to be committed to a centralized and media-focused campaign strategy. Staffs of communications experts, consultants, and journalists work the parties and their groups of representatives in the parliament. The activities of these communications professionals are directed by the small group of most important party leaders, which rarely numbers more than five people. It is the party leaders, not individual members of parliament, who direct communications efforts and play the most important roles in electoral campaigns.

THE ORGANIZATION AND AUDIENCE OF THE MASS MEDIA

In order to understand fully the preoccupation with television in Spanish electoral campaigns, it is useful to also recognize the broad outline of the organization and audience of the mass media in Spain. At present, there are 115 daily newspapers, 1,650 radio stations, and thirteen television channels—ten public channels and, since 1990, three private channels. The public channels are divided between the two national, state-owned channels—TVE-1 and TVE-2—and regional public channels. The daily audience of each medium, in 1993, is shown in Table 8.1.

Television

It is clear from Table 8.1 that television is the hegemonic medium of communication in Spain. Ninety percent of Spanish homes have at least one television set, which is close to the average of other countries in the European Community. Unlike other countries in Western Europe, however, television viewing is limited mostly to broadcast television; only 12 percent of Spanish homes receive satellite services, and only 500,000 homes subscribe to cable television services. Television is also the only mass medium that reaches nearly all of the general public without regard to age, social class, sex, or place of residence. Spaniards watch television an average of more than three hours per day. This high level of viewing is distributed about equally between men and women, and among persons living in urban areas, smaller towns, and rural areas, as Table 8.1 indicates.

Table 8.1
Composition of Daily Audience for Mass Media

Audience Attribute	Percentage of Population Aged 14 and Older Consuming Daily			
	Newspapers	Magazines	Radio	Television
Sex				
• Men	44.6	53.7	57.2	89.3
• Women	23.3	61.9	47.9	89.7
Social Class				
• High-middle class	56.7	70.7	62.7	87.3
• Middle class	38.6	65.1	56.8	90.9
• Middle-lower class	18.9	44.9	43.4	80.0
Place of Residence				
• More than 200,000 inhabitants	41.9	64.8	58.4	88.1
• Less than 200,000 inhabitants	29.9	54.9	49.8	90.1
Age				
• 14-24 years	32.9	79.8	61.9	89.4
• 25-44 years	42.9	67.0	56.8	88.0
• 45-64 years	28.9	42.3	45.4	90.4
• 65 years and older	22.9	33.2	41.3	91.2
Total Daily Audience	33.6	57.9	52.4	89.5

Source: Fundesco, 1993, p. 21.

Among the thirteen broadcast television channels, the two national public channels (TVE-1 and TVE-2) attract an average of 40.8 percent of the television audience. Since 1993, the three private channels attract 42.2 percent of the audience, and the public regional channels 17 percent of the audience. However, the main public channel, TVE-1, is the primary source of news nationally. The three private channels are relatively new and were available for the first time in the 1993 general elections.

Radio

Spain is one of the three largest radio markets in Europe (the others are France and Germany) and takes the largest share of total radio advertising expenditures (*European Planning Guide*, 1993, pp. 38–41). The country has almost twice as many commercial stations (1,640) as France, its nearest rival, and has the largest number of national stations in Europe, with fourteen across the public and private sector (Breaking the Sound Barrier, 1993). The average time spent by Spaniards listening to the radio was 137 minutes per day in 1992. Considering these figures and the radio audience profile shown in Table 8.1, radio is a more useful medium for politics than newspapers, but is less important than television.

Spanish radio broadcasts two main types of informational programs, traditional news and news bulletins, and the "tertulias" or "chat shows." The latter are a meeting place where, for thirty to sixty minutes during the morning and late-night periods, journalists, commentators, and political experts analyze the daily political situation, reporting and commenting on news from newspapers, television, and magazines. Government and party leaders and important officials sometimes attend this radio get-together. Listeners tend to be citizens who are interested in politics, for whom the chat shows are becoming the main source of political information. Given their audience, it is easy to understand why these programs have become an important information source during recent electoral campaigns. However, they have received criticism from those who do not approve of the journalistic methods used or the political opinions given.

Radio has assumed additional importance during electoral campaigns because, unlike television, where political advertising is banned by law, paid political advertising can be broadcast on radio at any time of the day. As indicated in Table 8.1, radio offers a means by which political parties may reach a large and heterogeneous audience that includes more than 40 percent of the members of every age, socioeconomic, gender, and geographic group. Thus, the advertising budgets of the political parties in electoral campaigns are spent mainly on radio and the press.

Newspapers

As Table 8.1 reflects, newspaper readers are skewed toward males of high to upper-middle class in large urban areas. Newspaper readership is highest, at 57.7 percent of the population, in the areas served by the thirteen largest newspapers (more than 50,000 copies printed), and lowest, at 15.9 percent, in areas served by the seventy-eight smallest newspapers (fewer than 15,000 copies printed). Overall, newspaper readership is comparatively low and is growing only slowly. A national average circulation of 100 newspapers for each 1,000 inhabitants was reached for the first time in 1991, compared to an average circulation of 232 newspapers for every 1,000 inhabitants in the European Community. Today, there are still thirty-seven provinces (electoral constituencies) in Spain that have not reached an index of 100. Circulation throughout these thirty-seven provinces ranges from 32.6 to 93.8 for every 1,000 inhabitants.

Only three newspapers print more than 200,000 copies daily. Two of these are in Madrid, and the third is in Barcelona. The average number of copies printed daily for all newspapers was 29,000 in 1990. Compared with other European countries, this number is very small (*European Planning Guide*, 1993).

Unlike what has been observed elsewhere, and what one might suppose based on the skewed nature of the newspaper audience, in Spain there does not appear to be a strong relationship between newspaper reading and political participation or activity. Thus, heavy concentration on television as the medium of choice in electoral campaigns appears to be justified by the role of newspapers in Spanish society. This does not mean that newspapers are regarded as unimportant in Spanish political campaigns, however. To the contrary, they serve several important functions that are described later in this chapter.

POLITICAL COMMUNICATION IN SPANISH ELECTION CAMPAIGNS

Communication practices in Spanish election campaigns reflect the nation's political culture and recent history, and also the implications for campaigning of the electoral and media systems described above. As noted in the introduction to the chapter, these influences are in some respects similar to what is found in other countries and in some respects quite unique. It is not surprising, then, that they have shaped a set of communication practices that also are in some respects familiar and in other respects different from common practices elsewhere. The following description of political communication in Spanish election campaigns highlights the similarities and differences and endeavors to relate both to attributes of the Spanish context.

The Parties' Approach to Campaigns

For reasons already described, the political parties have practiced the modern media-centered model of campaigning from the beginning of Spanish democracy. In some countries, such as the United States and Italy, the rise of mass media as the preeminent channels for campaign communication has been accompanied by a decline in the power and authority of the political parties. In other countries, such as Germany and the United Kingdom, parties have retained their position, while focusing their communication efforts on mass media. One important factor that seems to influence how media-centered campaigning affects political parties is whether the parties retain the power to select the candidates who are presented to the voters. Increasingly, the power to select candidates has been ceded by the parties to the voters in the United States and Italy, through expansion of primary elections in the former and adoption of a majoritarian voting system in the latter. On the other hand, Germany and the United Kingdom are examples of political systems in which the power to select candidates remains firmly under party control. In this respect, the situation of the political parties in Spain is similar to that found in Germany and the United Kingdom. Party leaders choose the candidates who appear on the party lists that are presented to the voters, and this feature of the electoral system may help explain how Spanish parties are able to control campaign strategies and communication practices while being firmly committed to media-centered campaigning.

In fact, the design and leadership of campaigns are thoroughly centralized. Usually, campaigns are directed and executed by "campaign committees" at the parties' headquarters, aided by staffs of communications experts and other campaign professionals. Decisions about campaign expenses, media planning, slogans, posters, party program, and political strategy are made in the central party offices and applied in a uniform way throughout the entire country.

As is common where media-centered campaigning is practiced, polls have great influence in party decision making. Tracking and targeting polls have been conducted since 1989, and leaders and strategists in every party rely on poll results concerning voting intentions, popularity, and so on. Because of the circumstances of their creation and development, as mentioned previously, the political parties never had the grassroots organization that, in other countries, was the parties' traditional source of information about the voters' beliefs and attitudes. Thus, from their beginnings, the Spanish parties have been very dependent on poll data, and their political decisions are heavily involved with electoral polls and advice from the pollsters. Indeed, the parties' campaign strategies seem to be based more on poll figures than on the parties' political ideas and programs. The pollsters' influence is greatest in the opposition parties, where their advice is regarded as a useful guide for campaign strategy. The ruling party relies more on the advantages of incumbency and is perhaps less influenced by pollsters.

As in other countries where the modern model of campaigning is practiced, Spanish political campaigns are highly personalized. Although Spain has a parliamentary system, electoral campaigns focus mainly on the political leaders who lead their party lists as candidates for Prime Minister. Campaign agendas are shaped primarily by the records that each party has developed in the legislature. Naturally, the parties endeavor to integrate the personal appeal of their leaders with the most favorable representation of the parties' accomplishments in the legislature, in order to offer a seamless and compelling campaign message to the voters. This approach to designing campaigns is thought to be well suited to the Spanish situation, where voters lack historical, ideological, or group-based loyalties to the parties. In effect, political campaigns are referenda on party performance colored by the personal appeal of party leaders.

To communicate their message to voters, the political parties follow the practice that has become common in other countries which have relatively short official campaign periods; namely, the parties begin their campaigning long before the "official" campaign period starts. The "real" campaign begins when the government calls the elections and swings into high gear when the parties publish their definitive lists of candidates.

The parties' communication efforts are oriented chiefly to what are perceived as the requirements of using television most effectively. From the first free elections in 1977, the visibility of the campaign on television has increased constantly. Additional electioneering activities (Butler & Ranney, 1992), including direct mail, billboards, and posters, are engaged in, as well as some traditional methods of campaigning, such as circulating leaflets and holding public meetings (until recently, the bullrings have been popular venues for party-sponsored public events). There is no door-to-door canvassing, although the two leading parties do mobilize about 40,000 poll watchers—one for every voting table—on election day. Among these varied communication channels, however, there is no question that television is the preeminent campaign medium.

Television in Campaigns

As has been noted, political advertising is forbidden on television, both state-owned and private channels. Electoral law does provide some free television time to the parties, however, for programs that are broadcast in prime time, after the evening newscasts. The amount of time allotted to each of the parties is based on each party's success in the most recent elections. The parties produce their own video messages, which typically feature the most important statements of the party leaders about their main political issues, proposals, and programs, interwoven with video publicity spots. Party programs are highly personalized, with party leaders being the clear center of attention and the nation's problems typically relegated to the background.

As elsewhere, television news is a major target of campaign strategies and activities. In television news programs, a block of ten minutes is usually devoted to information about the campaign. Many campaign events are designed to attract favorable coverage, with spectacular activities and compelling visuals for television. Political speakers are adept in their speeches and television interviews at offering the short messages and sound bites that are thought to be well suited to television. The great importance given by campaign strategists to "sound bite rhetoric" and visually appealing events reflects, of course, an effort to manipulate television news in order to receive as much coverage of a favorable nature as possible. To a large extent, in Spain, as in other countries where television is the principal intermediary between politicians and the public, the campaign is shaped by the requirements and preferences of television news (see, for example, Semetko, Blumler, Gurevitch, & Weaver, 1991).

The 1993 election was the first in which privately owned, commercial television was available, and it led to the emergence of two new forms of informational programs. The first televised electoral debates took place in 1993—the most important being between Felipe González, the incumbent Prime Minister, and José Mª Aznar, the opposition leader—and were organized by private channels. The first such debate was broadcast by Antena 3 on May 24th, and the second by Tele 5 on May 31st. Both were broadcast in prime time and attracted very large audiences. Less-important electoral debates were broadcast on the second public channel, TVE-2. In 1993, in addition to debates, the Prime Minister and the opposition leader were also interviewed by a pool of journalists on the private television channels. Both the debates and the interviews attracted large audiences of viewers.

To this point, readers who are familiar with the roles of television in political campaigns elsewhere will have found the description of television in Spanish campaigns to be familiar. Now, we turn to a less familiar attribute of the Spanish experience. Remember, as we noted earlier, that the state-owned national television channels, especially TVE-1, offer what are, by far, the most important national television news programs. As is always the case with state-owned media, questions of objectivity and neutrality in coverage given to the government and the ruling party are critical. From the first democratic elections, discussion in the parliament and between the political parties of the appropriate role for television has centered on the ideal of public service. However, accusations of partisanship and bias in state-owned television news and of manipulation of the news by the government and the government's party have been constant. The accusations have been well founded. In each electoral campaign, public television has been blatantly partial in favor of the incumbent government and its political party. The party in power receives substantially more, and more favorable, news coverage and more opportunities to present its program in a favorable light. The government's agenda dominates public television news coverage of campaigns, the images that are shown overwhelmingly favor the government party, and the government party is depicted as representing the "natural majority" in the country. In short, public television attempts to mobilize support for the government. This practice reinforces the general tendency to interpret electoral results as a kind of plebiscite over the Prime Minister and a referendum over the record of the government. Because the most important communications medium for political news and information and for political campaigning is not impartial, opposition leaders and parties labor under a very substantial disadvantage in getting their message to the voters.

The Press

There are no nationally circulated newspapers in Spain. Three large-circulation local newspapers are published in Madrid and Barcelona, and these newspapers command 85 percent of the country's comparatively small newspaper readership. Despite the geographic concentration of newspaper readership and the low overall average circulation of newspapers throughout the country, newspapers play significant roles in Spanish political campaigns.

The relationship between the political establishments and print journalism is nearer to an exchange model than an adversary one (Blumler & Gurevitch, 1981). Spanish newspapers do not officially endorse political parties or candidates for office, and newspapers endeavor to insert their own journalistic agenda into campaign coverage. Journalistic priorities have led, in Spain, as in other countries, to news reporting that gives great emphasis to the horse race aspect of campaigns that is thought to inject interest and excitement into political contests. At the center of horse race coverage is, of course, the great attention given to public-opinion polls, which are always front-page news. Such polls are relatively recent phenomena in Spain, having increased in importance steadily throughout the seventeen-year history of the democracy, following roughly the pattern that Kavanagh (1981) described for a dozen other European countries. Despite the attention given to them, news coverage of poll results is flawed by oversimplification and lack of attention to methodological matters that ultimately determine the reliability of polls—shortcomings of journalists' handling of poll results that have been noted elsewhere (see Holley, 1992; Worcester, 1987). Exit polls have been common since 1986, and the most important poll is always taken on the Sunday before the election. The Electoral Law does regulate some aspects of the publication of polls, and it forbids publishing poll results during the five days that immediately precede the voting.

The journalistic rather than partisan orientation that newspapers take to covering campaigns produces more balanced and objective coverage than public television offers. Politicians regard the press—especially the largest and most prestigious newspapers—as playing a key role in shaping public opinion, despite comparatively low levels of newspaper readership, and the political parties and the government make great efforts to influence the newspaper agenda. One reason for the importance given to newspapers is that they are the primary site where the "long" campaign occurs, the jockeying for position that takes place during the prolonged period preceding the three-week official campaign.

Reflecting a blending of the parties' priorities and journalists' own agendas, the journalistic agenda of the Spanish press produces campaign coverage that is characterized by qualities which are similar to those noted in other countries: heavily personalized coverage focusing on political leaders; coverage preoccupied by the horse race; and, increasingly through the campaigns of 1986, 1989, and 1993, "bad news" about politicians and their campaigns (compare to Patterson, 1993).

In fairness, it should also be noted that press coverage of election campaigns has become progressively more sophisticated as the appurtenances of precision journalism have come into play through enterprising use of technological information sources and other means. Indeed, the prestige press' political coverage has become a routine reference source for radio and television news coverage of campaigns.

Spanish newspapers and magazines are also important as a vehicle for political advertising in campaigns. With such advertising banned from television, a very significant portion of the political parties' publicity budgets is devoted to the press.

CONSEQUENCES OF THE MODERN MODEL OF CAMPAIGNING: THE SPANISH EXPERIENCE

Spanish democracy has undergone important changes despite its very short history. Many of these changes have to do with electoral campaigning. Unlike older democracies, where change has been driven by and reflected in the transition from traditional to modern models of campaigning, change in Spain has been caused by the implementation and subsequent development of the modern model. Although much of what has happened in Spain reflects unique aspects of the Spanish situation, the experience of Spain also casts light on some of the more general consequences of the modern model of campaigning.

The first electoral campaign, conducted in 1977, had great symbolic significance for Spaniards, representing a return to the freedom and democracy that had been abandoned more than forty years before. Few citizens remembered the last time they had been able to vote in a democratic election, which had occurred in February 1936 in a very different political and historical context. The current constitutional monarchy was thus launched with intense popular enthusiasm and commitment to elections as the symbols and instruments of democracy. Elections continued to be regarded in this way until the third campaign, in 1982, by which time voters had experienced a comparatively large number of campaigns at the various levels of government, and elections had come to seem more routine. The 1982 campaign also structured the actual system of political parties. Parties have been supported with public financing since 1977 and, initially, there was close competition among many political parties. Spaniards' strong desire for their country to become integrated with the other European democracies facilitated the introduction into Spain of electoral practices that were common in Europe and the United States. Unlike the case in some other countries, the use of methods and techniques from foreign campaigns received hardly any criticism. Through emulation and the aid of foreign consultants and political parties, the Spanish campaign model was not "made in Spain" but, rather, reflected many different influences from abroad. Initially, the parties concentrated their campaign efforts on providing information to political reporters in order to facilitate coverage, and on the political programs they prepared for broadcast media. Later, when the party system was consolidated and symbolically legitimized by the media, the parties kept pace with the modern model as it was developing elsewhere by creating campaigns that were targeted to the media, especially television, and intended to produce maximum favorable coverage. Spanish voters are now thoroughly accustomed to professionally designed, personalized campaigns that stress events which are constructed for media and promote appealing leaders and images.

Increasingly sophisticated campaigns have not increased election turnout. Turnout has remained relatively stable, varying from 68 to 80 percent across all national elections. The great majority of voters (78% in 1993) claim that they are not influenced by campaigns and that they decide how to vote before the campaigns begin (Sociological Research Center, 1993). As has been observed in other countries, however, many voters do believe that sophisticated campaigns produce a "third-person" effect, influencing other people but not themselves (Sociological Research Center, 1986, 1989, 1993; Davidson, 1983).

When we take the voters' perspective, we can see two different campaigns; one campaign centered on the mass media and a second campaign based more on political, religious, and historical subcultures. The second campaign is, for all practical purposes, an invisible expression of the traditional elements of Spanish culture and society. Beneath the media-centered hoopla, conversations with relatives, neighbors, and acquaintances within groups of all kinds continue to exert strong influence on the vote decision (O'Keefe & Atwood, 1981; Sociological Research Center, 1993).

In Spain, the modern model of campaigning has not produced a government that has solved the problems that beset the life of the average citizen, such as unemployment and inflation. To the contrary, these enduring problems play only a secondary role in campaigns that focus on promoting appealing images for party leaders. Modern campaigning has led to the emergence of modern political leadership; leaders who know how to make news and receive favorable media coverage in order to win popularity and the trust of voters. Ordinary members of parliament and journeyman party politicians have lost importance and prestige in the increasingly media-centered and leader-centered world of Spanish politics. Journalistic oversimplification, contrived drama, and preoccupation with the strategic game all make it more, not less, difficult for the public to understand the workings of the parliamentary regime itself.

Parliament is no longer the focus of political life. Instead, the primary axis of political life has shifted from the relationship between the government and the parliament to the conflict between the media and the parties, as the government and opposition parties battle for favorable media treatment. The government strives constantly to be the most important protagonist in the media; the opposition strives to be represented in the media as the center of parliamentary life. The media-centered model of campaigning has thus been generalized to a model of government.

Although Spain is a parliamentary monarchy, it practices a style of political communication and electoral campaigning that seems better suited to a leader-centered presidential system or a majoritarian electoral system than to its own multiparty and proportional system. By deflecting attention from problems to images and from the workings of government to telegenic leaders, media-centered democracy is favoring a kind of institutional change whose final consequences we do not know. At present, it appears that the media have won the battle.

REFERENCES

Blumler, J. G., & Gurevitch, M. (1981). Politicians and the press: An essay on role relationships. In D. Nimmo & K. R. Sanders (Eds.), Handbook of political communication (pp. 467–491). London: Sage.

Breaking the sound barrier. (1993, Autumn). Media and Marketing Europe, pp. 23–41.

Butler, D., & Ranney A. (1992). Introduction. In D. Butler & A. Ranney (Eds.), Electioneering: A comparative study of continuity and change (pp. 1–10). Oxford: Clarendon Press.

Davidson, P. (1983). The third person effect in communication. Public Opinion Quarterly, 47, 1–15.

Edelman, M. (1988). Constructing the political spectacle. Chicago: University of Chicago Press.

European Planning Guide, 1993–1994. (1993). London: M & M, in association with Initiative Media.

Fundesco. (1993). Communicación social 1993: Tendencies [Social communication 1993: Trends]. Madrid: Fundación Social para el Desarrollo de las Communicaciones.

Gunther, R. (1989). Electoral laws, party system, and elites: The case of Spain. *American Political Science Review, 3*, 835–858.

Holley, J. K. (1992). The press and political polling. In D. I. Lavrakas & J. K. Holley (Eds.), *Polling and presidential election coverage* (pp. 215–237). London: Sage.

Kavanagh, D. (1981). Public opinion polls. In D. Butler, F. R. Penninman, & A. Ranney (Eds.), *Democracy at the polls* (pp. 196–215). Washington, D.C.: American Enterprise Institute.

Lane, J. L., & Ersson, S. O. (1987). *Politics and society in Western Europe* (pp. 39–94). London: Sage.

O'Keefe, G. I., & Atwood, L. E. (1981). Communication and election campaigns. In D. Nimmo & K. R. Sanders (Eds.), *Handbook of political communication* (pp. 334–338). London: Sage.

Patterson, T. (1993). *Out of order*. New York: Knopf.

Semetko, H. A., Blumler, J. G., Gurevitch, M., & Weaver, D. H., with Barkin, S., & Wilhoit, G. C. (1991). *The formation of campaign agendas: A comparative analysis of party and media roles in recent American and British elections*. Hillsdale, N.J.: Erlbaum.

Sociological Research Center (CIS). (1986). *Post-election study no. 1,543*. Madrid: Author.

Sociological Research Center (CIS). (1988). *Study no. 1,740*. Madrid: Author. (Reprinted in *Revista Española de Investigaciones Sociológicas* [Spanish Sociological Review], 42).

Sociological Research Center (CIS). (1989). *Post-election poll, study no. 1,842*. Madrid: Author.

Sociological Research Center (CIS). (1993). *Post-election poll, study no. 2,061*. Madrid: Author.

Worcester, R. M. (1987). *Journalists' guide to publication of opinion survey results*. London: MORI.

PART III

Campaign Innovations in Democracies Facing Potentially Destabilizing Pressures

Chapter Nine

American-Style Electioneering in Israel: Americanization versus Modernization

Dan Caspi

AMERICANIZATION AND MODERNIZATION

There is almost no country today in which election time does not summon up familiar phenomena: Portrait photos of a smiling candidate, dressed in a tailored suit, tie, and blue-collared shirt, are plastered on billboards and the newspapers in France, Italy, the United States, Israel, Japan, or Venezuela. Every election time, parties arm themselves with an arsenal of consultants and professionals in the fields of communications and political marketing, storming the electorate with almost identical wooing strategies and tactics via the mass media and, alternatively, face-to-face contacts which are amazingly orchestrated and directed. There is not a political party today which can forego advertising in newspapers or television and radio commercials, just as politicians cannot refuse direct encounters with voters, whether these are planned visits covered by the mass media at public places or private homes, or public debates, generally broadcast on television.

The standardization of electoral campaigns in various countries, as expressed in the patterns of appeal to the voter and the use of similar persuasion tactics, gives rise to the feeling that a characteristic style of American politics, known as "the New Style" (Agranoff, 1972), has come about. In the time since the first stirrings of this new style emerged in the United States roughly thirty years ago, it has undergone considerable development and also has spread to many other countries in Western and Eastern Europe as well as the Third World, to the point where it has gained recognition as a sweeping phenomenon of Americanization. The introduction to this volume raises an interesting working hypothesis regarding the direct correlation between the Americanization of electoral campaigns and modernization, as follows:

Innovations in election campaigns over the last few years that resemble practices developed first in the United States result fundamentally, we believe, from transformations in the social structure and form of democracy in countries where the innovations have taken place. These transformations are part of the modernization process; the more advanced is the process of modernization in a country, the more likely we are to find innovations in campaigning being adopted and adapted. (Mancini & Swanson, introduction to this volume)

Social scientists are experts in analyzing and defining phenomena. Sometimes, our definitions shape our perceptions of the reality we study. In this chapter, I wish to reflect upon two issues simultaneously: the basic analysis of the central phenomenon and its significance (i.e., the Americanization of electoral politics), and the hypothesized relationship between this phenomenon and modernization.

AMERICANIZATION OR STANDARDIZATION?

The characteristics of the New Style have not passed over electoral politics in Israel. In Israeli electoral campaigns in recent decades, we have seen the accelerated adoption of characteristic components of electoral politics in the United States. Among these components, we may note especially the growing involvement of media professionals at the campaign headquarters of the parties, the massive use of mass communication media, and the dramatic changes which have taken place in electoral strategies. However, while the immediate facts may seem to encourage us to regard the considerable similarity between electoral campaigns in various countries as Americanization, surface appearances can be misleading. The McLuhan heritage and technological determinism have also contributed to defining this phenomenon as the Americanization of politics in Israel. Soon enough, someone will propose to name a book "Electoral Propaganda in the Global Village."

The tendency to find similarities between cultures is natural and even fulfills an understandable human need to bridge alienation and create common denominators. It encourages development of general models and frameworks for comparison. In the past, McLuhan's concepts seemed to be extremely efficient models for dealing with the increasing complexity of communications. Similar models are likely to facilitate our understanding of the ever-increasing political complexity of the jumbled world order resulting mainly from the collapse of the Soviet Empire, the blurring of differences between the Second and Third World, or the emerging buds of crisis affecting the Western World. Even the hierarchial order among the Three Worlds, as among the countries within each of these Worlds, represents a separate intellectual and value issue.

As distances between cultures shrink and the political boundaries between them disappear, it is inescapable that cultures will increasingly influence each other. From the beginning of time, intercultural contacts have led to an exchange of values, know-how, thought, and performance patterns. In our time, advanced technology further accelerates interaction between cultures in all spheres, including the areas of politics and communications.

The concept of a "global village" has come to seem plausible, not only because of similarities in the format and content of different countries' television broadcasts, but also, and perhaps more important, because of the standardization which encompasses other, even more significant areas of life, thanks to shared technology: People of different religious persuasions and races drive identical cars on different roads throughout the world, and drink almost the same beverages, often from the same plastic cups. Products and services are offered throughout the world in almost uniform wrapping, whether it is mineral water, catsup, telephones, automatic banking machines, or airports. Does the uniform outer wrapping necessarily reveal the inner content?

Other formal steps, such as the unification of Western Europe and the creation of an extended political community, also contribute towards increased standardization in most areas and effectively reinforce the illusion of the global village. However, the growing similarity between cultures and the obvious desire to stress this similarity have not eliminated the marked, traditional differences between them, both manifest or latent.

Therefore, we propose to view the spreading of the "New American Style" (i.e., the Americanization of electoral campaigns in various countries) within a wider context as an expression of an ancient, universal trend toward mutual fertilization between cultures; a trend which undoubtedly has been accelerated in our time by the more intensive and continuous encounters between cultures. We shall maintain that Americanization is not necessarily correlated with modernization but, alternatively, is related to a more general trend toward standardization, as presented in Table 9.1.

Table 9.1 proposes an alternative diagnosis for these numberless innovations in electoral campaigning: Standardization is the name of the game, here and in other areas. In this view, Americanization could be considered a sufficient, but not a necessary or required, condition for political modernization. Standardization implies a symmetrical and free exchange of practices, values, and norms among cultures. Moreover, standardization is a value-free term which, in this context, denies that deep changes in a country's political system necessarily accompany adoption of Americanized practices. Thus, the concept of standardization may overturn some ideological traditions in the American community, especially for those who still believe in the superiority of American culture and its political tradition.

The difference between Americanization and standardization is not of a marginal nature. The former awards preference to the source of the innovation over the adopter of the innovation, often out of a sense of superiority. The latter view assumes that the adopting unit controls the diffusion process; that is, the adopter decides if, to what extent, and how the innovation should be absorbed.

According to the former diagnosis, the adoption of the American style in electoral campaigns represents an almost inevitable stage in the general modernization process, possibly even a necessary prerequisite for anyone who is endeavoring to emulate the source of the innovation. On the other hand, the latter diagnosis regards the adoption of the American style as optional and

Table 9.1
Patterns of Innovation in Electoral Campaigning

	Americanization	Modernization	Standardization
Geographical Area	First World Countries	Second and Third World Countries	Everywhere
Value Orientation	USA/West	West/USA	Mixed
Source-Adopter Relationship	Vertical	Vertical	Horizontal
Source Attitude toward Adopter	Persuasive	Compulsive	Elusive
Pattern of Adoption	Imitation	Adaptation	Transaction
Degree of Impact	Superficial	Substantial	Moderate
Influence on	Strategies/Tactics	Institutions, Cultures, etc.	Various
Mode of Innovation	Purposive	Structured	Occasional

far from necessary or inevitable. Standardization occurs as a result of diversified forces, some outside of the immediate relationship between the source and the adopting unit. The former diagnosis is more than a little afflicted with determinism, as it seems to present Americanization as a chronological stage of modernization. In contrast, we believe that Americanization is not inevitable, at least in the case of Israel, as is subsequently discussed.

"AMERICANIZATION," ISRAELI STYLE

The New Style of electoral campaigns was formed in the unique cultural and political climate of the United States, within the regional direct elections, in a vast industrialized, urban, and mass society where electoral campaigns are almost continuous—for the presidency, the House of Representatives and the Senate, the state governorships and legislatures, numerous county and municipal offices, and so on. Sociopolitical conditions aggravated the communication needs of the candidates, who were required to reach large constituencies and to win the majority of their support. Within these unique circumstances, the candidates sought the assistance of the highly developed communications industry. Consultants, public relations professionals, and experts on political marketing who apprenticed at advertising firms excelled in applying and adapting an accumulation of ideas and experience from the area of consumer advertising to the political marketing campaign.

Within a short time, they provided the candidates with the tools to shape voters' preferences and mobilize their electoral support. Subsequently, commercial advertising and political advertising were differentiated, with advertising firms establishing special departments and professional consultancy roles in the political sphere. Later still, they were organizationally separated. The accelerated development of mass media further amplified the need for these new roles and increased the recognition that they were truly essential.

Every political candidate has had to deal with a growing number of reporters, respond to more of their queries, follow whatever appears in the press, and respond rapidly and effectively, especially during a campaign and on the eve of an election.

Every industry contains its own internal logic dictating growth and expansion; initially within the boundaries of its own country, during the industry's infancy, and later beyond national borders, depending upon the forces of the free market. As the American electoral industry grew and flourished, it became a model for envy and emulation, especially in the eyes of vigorous initiators from other countries, including Israel, who became enamored with it. These initiators visited the United States and spent a period of time within the electoral industry acquiring credentials, political ties, know-how, and experience. These newly acquired skills encouraged them to import the principles of the New Style to their countries of origin, with the aim of tapping their innate economic potential.

In some cases, the importing of electoral techniques was boosted by the needs of the local market, while in other cases their import came prior to communication demands that created a need for them. Thus, in the latter cases, professionals who had been enticed by the tempting aroma of the American electoral industry and then returned to their native lands first had to cultivate communication needs, develop recognition and awareness of their existence within political circles, and only then offer their services to meet those needs: a classic technique in the world of marketing.

The Israeli political culture is fundamentally different from the American political culture. These differences are of long standing. In contrast to the United States, elections for the Knesset (Israel's parliament) are secret, general, national, and proportional (Elazar & Sandler, 1992). The competition is between lists of candidates, rather than between individual candidates. Each voter selects a list of candidates and has very little say regarding the composition of the list or the order in which the candidates are listed, both of which are determined by party members.

In recent years, at least three significant changes have been introduced in the centralized character of the electoral system. Each of these changes may herald a process of personalization in Israeli politics. First, since 1977, most of the parties have established primaries which determine the composition of their Knesset lists and the order in which the candidates appear. This new arrangement comes as a welcome substitute for the former "placement committees," which were made up of a handful of leaders who were responsible for the final composition of the lists. In some cases, all members of the party are allowed to attend the primaries, as was the case within the Labor Party in 1992, when two-thirds of the 160,000 party members participated. In other cases, the order of the candidates is decided by elections held within the party's central committee and/or its convention.

The introduction of primaries has promoted democratization within the parties and redefined the candidate's basis of support, even to the extent of redefining the relationship between the electorate and the elected representatives. The candidates have been obliged to show evidence of personal achievement in order to win political support. Although the primaries are limited to party members and are not open to the general public, the candidates have learned the secret of personally wooing votes and the need to build and maintain personal appeal as a basis for winning political support. This being the situation, there are cases where individual candidates or groups of candidates prepare for the primaries by setting up campaign headquarters equipped with electoral and public-relations professionals and consultants.

Although confrontation in the primaries is of a personal nature, between individual candidates, this does not prevent factioning within the parties. Candidates are identified with particular factions, and the factions are active in opposing and supporting individual candidates in the primaries. The importance of factional support means that the basis of electing candidates for the Knesset party list is not purely personal. Moreover, even if, at some point, factioning is either weak or not evident, so that the internal elections are held completely or almost completely on a personal basis, voting in the primaries is still restricted to party members. Even in the absence of active factions, this restriction alone may introduce concerns beyond a candidate's purely personal appeal into voting decisions. In any case, the choices that ultimately are presented to the public in the Knesset elections are lists of candidates rather than individual candidates.

The primaries were not the only change which introduced personal elements into the Israeli electoral system. A second change was an amendment of the Election Law for Local Authorities of 1979, which separated mayoral elections from elections of council members for the same local authority. According to this amendment, every voter is required to vote twice, in two separate envelopes. In one envelope, the voter chooses a mayoral candidate of the local authority; in the other, the voter chooses from among the lists of candidates running for the municipal (or local) council. The double vote encourages the separation of support between the mayoral candidate and the lists which make up the city council. It is important to note that the lists of candidates for the local council are closed, just as the party lists for the Knesset elections are closed, so that the voter can only choose one list as opposed to another.

In many cases, mayoral candidates have won even though their faction has failed to achieve a majority in the local council and despite the fact that their party is only a minority component of the council. To be elected, a candidate for mayor must receive 40 percent of the votes cast. If no candidate receives 40 percent, a second round of balloting is held between the two candidates who received the most support in the first round. The very existence of the second round sharpens the personal aspect of the mayoral elections and underlines the basic difference between the former and the elections for the local council, which are based on lists.

A third change that certainly will lead to increased personalization is a recent amendment to the Knesset Election Law. This amendment provides for instituting personal—that is, direct—elections for prime minister beginning with the elections for the Fourteenth Knesset, which currently are scheduled for Autumn 1996. This amendment was introduced to fortify the status of the prime minister and to release the government leader from dependence upon the leader's party and coalitions of factions. To a great extent, this amendment will surely create the same sort of separation which typifies the municipal elections.

Elections for the prime minister will be held concurrently with the Knesset elections. According to clause 13 of the Knesset Election Law,

(a) The candidate who acquires more than half of the valid votes, on the condition that he is a member of Knesset, will be elected prime minister. (b) If no candidate acquires the number of votes mentioned in clause (a), a second round of elections will be held on the first Tuesday, two weeks after the announcement of the results of the first elections. . . . (f) If no candidate is elected as stipulated in this clause, special elections will be held.

According to clause 10(a), the special election must be held within sixty days.

Do these reforms leading to increased personalization in the Israeli electoral process mean that Americanization is under way in Israel? Admittedly, the ever-increasing importance of the personal dimension in Israeli campaigns may appear to reflect the Americanization process. However, it is important to recognize, at the same time, that the slow political reforms introduced into the electoral system were not necessarily inspired by Americanization but, rather, by dissatisfaction which had been felt for years. It is true that the introduction of some Americanized techniques into electoral campaigns preceded, by a few years, the reforms that are leading to greater personalization. But dissatisfaction with the electoral system also preceded the budding Americanization of the Israeli electoral process.

SOME CAUSES OF AMERICANIZATION

It would seem that, from the very beginning, Americanization was essentially a communication process which was imported to Israel, much like other social and cultural fads and fashions. However, a number of changes within Israeli society contributed to the lowering of cultural barriers and to softening the ground which then appeared to absorb thirstily the principles of the American New Style in electoral politics.

The adoption of American-style campaigning in Israel is closely associated with the professionalization of the electoral propaganda which, to a great extent, has been a product of several social developments and political shifts (Caspi & Eyal, 1983). First, the size of the Israeli electorate has grown significantly, from about half a million voters in the first elections of 1949, to over two and a half million in the tenth campaign in June 1981, three million in the twelfth campaign in 1988, and about three and a half million eligible voters in the 1992 elections. As the number of voters increased, candidates and parties have had to communicate with a larger public and, consequently, to utilize mass media and other novel techniques of persuasion in an efficient way.

Second, natural biological processes have brought about the emergence of a new generation of leaders. This young leadership possesses neither the historical reputability nor the charismatic personal qualities of its predecessors. Their political power rests and depends upon instrumental skills, such as the ability to carry out objectives and plans outlined by their predecessors. To secure political support, the rising new leadership has had to resort to manipulation and persuasion techniques which, almost always, have required the use of the mass media.

Third, the relationship between voters and the political parties has undergone significant changes over the years. Public support, usually a function of traditional loyalty to a party, has become an outcome of the voters' evaluations of the capabilities and qualities of the parties and their leaders. The images and evaluations of political figures and institutions presented to the public have often been the products of professional image makers.

Fourth, the development of the mass media, and especially the emergence of the private daily press, placed journalists in a pivotal position as mediators between the political elite and the rest of the population, as well as between the political elite and the other elites of Israeli society (Caspi & Limor, 1992). The increasing use of mass media for political mediation may be another force accelerating the adoption of American-style electioneering.

As if to provide for the new political needs, a significant development in the political use of broadcast media has taken place in the last two decades. Television as a public service, modeled on the BBC, was introduced in Israel shortly after the 1967 Six Day War. The monopolistic structure of the Israeli broadcast media for more than a quarter of a century guaranteed and amplified the centrality of election broadcasts in each successive election campaign. According to Paragraph 15 of the Election Law, "Each party and its candidates will be granted twenty-five minutes and each party represented in the outgoing Knesset will receive an additional four minutes per Knesset Member." Similarly, Amendment 3 to this law establishes the distribution of television time. According to Paragraph 15a of the amendment, "Each party and list of candidates will be awarded ten minutes, and each party represented in the outgoing Knesset will receive an additional four minutes per Knesset Member."

In the elections to the Twelfth Knesset in 1988, 1,151 minutes of radio broadcast time and 984 minutes of television time were allotted to the various parties, compared to 1,470 minutes of radio broadcast time and 662 minutes of television time in the most recent elections for the Thirteenth Knesset. The large amount of broadcast time obligated even the minor parties to prepare themselves to use their allotment well.

The time slot designated for election broadcasts followed the major evening news program. The electoral broadcasts of the various parties were aired for thirty to forty minutes every evening. Thus, the politicians were presented with free prime-time television exposure and enjoyed a high viewing rate (Levinsohn, 1988). The selection of this attractive time slot for election broadcasts was by no means accidental or pure happenstance, but instead reflected priorities of the political culture.

In the 1969 election campaign, politicians had already begun to utilize television, simply appearing full face on camera and "lecturing" their arguments before the curious viewers of the new medium (Gurevitch, 1972). The second election campaign that utilized television took place in the shadow of the 1973 Yom Kippur War and its aftermath, and the political parties curtailed their advertising expenditures drastically (Peri, 1975). Only during the 1977 electoral campaign did the nature of electioneering change significantly, mostly as a result of the substantial financial resources invested in the campaign. Almost every political list learned to use the mass media extensively (Elizur & Katz, 1979). They provided for ads in the newspapers and broadcast media. This trend continued during the following elections and became, as can be seen in the 1994 election campaign, a major trait of the electoral process in Israel (Caspi, 1984).

Fifth, a few advertising firms, undoubtedly in response to increasing demand, have introduced their professional services in the running of political campaigns. Reliance upon such professional services opened the parties' doors, for the first time, to professional communicators, consultants, advisors, copywriters, public-relations professionals, advertising experts, and their staffs. The presence of these professionals, and particularly their day-to-day involvement in party election affairs, had a significant impact upon the parties' styles of campaigning and on their techniques for mobilizing electoral support.

Each of these five changes ensured that the new fashion would not be flatly rejected, and so the New Style was found to be relevant to Israeli politics, a relevance which, over the years, proved to be the result of the political reforms.

THE CHARACTERISTICS OF AMERICANIZATION

Special circumstances created meeting points between political processes and communications processes. The encounter between the structural changes and the changes on the Israeli communications map facilitated the adoption of certain elements of the New Style menu, especially in electioneering but also on an everyday basis. The Americanization of the electoral campaign encompasses structural and content characteristics, electoral strategies and tactics, and the entire carnival atmosphere preceding election day as well. Several outstanding traits of the new style of campaigning in Israel can be observed in the last two decades (Caspi & Eyal, 1983).

Sophistication of Media Use Persuasion techniques previously used and tested in the American political culture have been adopted and adapted to the Israeli scene. Among these, the television debate is probably the best known format, and it appears to be the main event and the peak of an electoral campaign (Caspi, 1986). Style changes in the political broadcasts have also taken place. Over the years, the political broadcasts have lost their amateurish flavor. Instead of on-camera personal appearances and long speeches by political leaders, as in the first two electronic media-centered campaigns, most parties are now assisted by media professionals. Short and catchy jingles containing slogans and abridged messages are produced by trained writers and directors and acted out by attractive deliverers.

The overall level of visualization of political ads in newspapers has increased with perceptible regularity from one campaign to the next, at the expense of content-laden verbal messages (Gertz, 1986). This trend is characterized by the increased use of large and even double-spread presentations containing eye-catching visual elements, graphics, and slogans.

Personalization of the Political Dispute This aspect, to which the television debate probably contributes a great deal, has become a predominant factor (Caspi, 1986). Over the course of time, the personal attributes of the candidates progressively eclipse the content of the electoral propaganda. The actual ideological divergences between parties, no matter how strong, are gradually replaced by the greater importance accorded to personal traits and rhetorical skills (Nir, 1987).

"Pollsification" Reliance on polls has grown. There are at least two purposes for use of these polls: political manipulation, that is, trying to influence the development of public opinion and support by the use and misuse of poll findings; and formulating and refining campaign strategies, that is, shaping the tactics of persuasion, choosing the issues, learning the public's preferences, and checking the efficiency of the electoral strategy and tactics. During election campaigns, the print media are flooded with data from various polls, some of them conducted at the behest of the journalists themselves (Weimann, 1984). This practice has aroused no small degree of public controversy, especially as the predictions made on the basis of these data have often proved to be surprisingly inaccurate (Shamir, 1986). It seems that the publication of poll results has become an electoral tactic in the hands of the professional propagandists, even though the desired effects are not always achieved (Keren, 1986).

"Carnivalization" The reshaping of the electoral campaign into an interrupted political carnival is probably one of the most obvious results of the adoption of the American style of election campaigns. The general atmosphere appears to be aimed at stirring public interest in and excitement about the campaign. This is achieved by several tactics, such as initiation of media events; intensive public relations campaigns; sophisticated manipulation of information through mass media; creating perceptions of general support for the party or for a candidate; creating the illusion of plenty, hope, and undoubted victory; and organized interpersonal communication between candidates and voters, mainly designed for media coverage.

Even though these American-style campaign practices are widespread in Israel, it is important to recognize that they may divert public attention away from the real issues and their proper solutions. The professional gimmick of projecting a good-time scenario and an illusion of plenty amid numerous facile promises for a better future may narcotize large segments of the electorate.

THE EFFECTS OF AMERICANIZATION

The adoption of components of the New Style raises questions regarding their significance and impact upon Israeli society. Are the changes in style accompanied by structural changes? Is Israeli politics becoming more "American"?

Mutual influences are inevitable, especially in contacts between a strong culture with prolific resources and a young culture with poor resources. The ongoing contact between the cultures, the perpetual encounter between the elites and the politicians, nurtures the simulation and imitation of political patterns and customs.

Communications professionals are not the sole importers of American propaganda methods. Many Israeli politicians visit and spend extended stays in the United States. Perhaps it is not coincidental that both Prime Minister Yitzhak Rabin and Likud leader Binyamin Netanyahu served as Israeli Ambassador to the United States and, while in that post, undoubtedly absorbed elements of the American political culture.

Nevertheless, it is permissible to contemplate the extent of New Style influence in general, not just with regards to Israel: Is Americanization limited to the formal, stylistic practices of politics or does it reflect more extensive, structural change? In other words, is Americanization a fundamental change of structure and substance, or does it have to do merely with external wrappings? Does Americanization cause changes in the map of political parties, the political structure, the relationship between the electorate and its representatives, the electoral system, or the quality of government? At first glance, the accumulated evidence supports the conclusion that Americanization is more than just a formal, stylistic change. We shall elaborate on some of these lines of evidence.

The Decline of the Status of Political Parties   The growing involvement of professional consultants at campaign headquarters apparently diminishes the politicians' dependence on the party. Mass media offer alternative mediation channels and compete with the party as the traditional intermediary for contact with the public and the mobilization of its political support. This would seem to suggest a decline of party status and power.

Israeli experience does indeed indicate an increased number of "loners," politicians who, with very little prior warning and a limited or modest party apparatus, achieved impressive results; no less than lists rooted in well organized, veteran parties. In the elections for the Thirteenth Knesset, Raphael Eitan's Tsomet list surprised everyone and increased its representation fourfold in comparison to the previous Knesset, an achievement which was credited to a successful election campaign and wise election strategy. Indeed, the political campaign without at least one (or sometimes two) loners is rare. The following are just a few outstanding cases of successful loners. Uri Avneri entered the Sixth Knesset in 1965, with a list named for the weekly which he edited, "Haolam Hazeh." Shmuel Tamir, who left Gahal (the second-largest party), entered the Seventh Knesset with his colleague in the Free Center Party. Shulamit Aloni burst into the Eighth Knesset as the head of the three-member "Citizen's Rights" list. Millionaire Platto-Sharon succeeded in entering the Ninth Knesset after a short and costly election campaign. Amnon Rubenstein penetrated the Tenth Knesset with a new list called "Shinui." On the eve of the elections for the Twelfth Knesset, Rehavam Ze'evi set up a list called "Moledet" which unexpectedly won two mandates. Although the ability of these lists to endure over time and become long-term political players is still an open question, the very existence of the phenomenon lends credence to the conclusion that Americanization is associated with important structural effects in the political system.

Personification of the Ideological Conflict   Personification is the continuation and twin of personalization; they go hand in hand. Ideological and substantial conflicts between movements and parties are reduced to individual, personal conflicts between the party heads and leaders. This reductionist presentation of conflicts simplifies reality and helps propagandists to clarify differences between the various political alternatives for the general public.

Certain elements of the New Style are responsible for the personification of the political conflict. As the political controversy increasingly is enacted on the mass media, it is shaped more and more by constraints relating to broadcasting times and locations. By nature, mass media shorten and fit discussions into pigeonholes of time and place, thereby demanding the use of slogans and idioms which encapsulate the message and, in the process, simplify the ideas and arguments. In the media, ideas and arguments are identified with the writers and spokesmen who raise them. In this manner, the controversy is translated to a personal level, and ideological debates are ascribed excessive personal dimensions. Public support for or opposition to a certain list is becoming increasingly dependent on its spokesmen and their personal attributes, rather than on the ideas and arguments that the list represents.

Television debates further reduce profound ideological differences to the personal, and often shallow, level. And so, in the course of election campaigns, Likud propagandists aimed their arrows directly at Shimon Peres, perhaps even more than at the Labor Party. Similarly, Labor propagandists directed the blame towards Likud candidates, and particularly the prime ministers, Menahem Begin and Yitzhak Shamir. It would seem that, for similar reasons, Labor propagandists, during the elections for the Thirteenth Knesset, were careful to include Rabin's name in the list's official title, "Labor Led by Rabin." This reflected the strategists' assessment that many voters would prefer to vote for Rabin's party because of his personality and reputation as a "moderate security man." The propagandists took this reasoning a step farther and proposed the slogan, "The nation is waiting for Rabin," which reminded the older voters of the popular song from the Six Day War, "Nasser is Waiting for Rabin!"

Various preliminary polls seem to reinforce a "hit-parade" orientation, by focusing attention on the popularity of the top names on the lists. The tendency toward simplification becomes more justified as the cases of loners multiply. In the case of the latter, support is indeed more dependent on the personal attributes of the party leaders. But do the acts of pollsters and communications consultants have the power to bring about a structural political change such as reform in the electoral system?

Pseudoparticipation   Such possible media effects as narcotization and the creation of illusory participation have been dealt with extensively and over a long period in professional literature. Media coverage of political processes and heavy exposure to mass media are largely responsible for creating an illusion of involvement which may paralyze actual activity and represent what, to the voter, seems to be a satisfactory substitute. By following the campaign through the mass media, voters may cultivate a false sense of political involvement, while, in fact, they remain inactive and only receptive on their own couches. This effect of media-centered campaigns undoubtedly may have the power to leave a significant imprint on the quality of democratic debate, although the results are inconclusive.

When active participation is replaced by pseudoparticipation through mass media, the field may be opened for determined minorities and interested parties to silence the majority. As active participation withers, the traditional structures that hold decision makers accountable for their actions may loosen their grip. One result can be to expand maneuvering space for decision making, releasing decision makers of their immediate responsibility toward the constituents and their wrath in the event of a dramatic or unpopular decision. This may partly explain the Israeli government's ability to adopt a new policy toward the PLO during the summer of 1993 which is diametrically opposed to the traditional policy held over many years. The sounds of vigorous demonstrations, such as expressions of support for the peace talks with the PLO, echoed from various sectors of the political map against a background of silence or, perhaps, the wide support which prevailed in its center.

Obstructions between the Electorate and Its Representatives The increased involvement of professionals and various sorts of communications experts may create a barrier, rather than a bridge, between the political elite and the general population. The narcotizing effect is not limited to the general public. Political representatives and politicians may be misled by the illusion of being connected with the public while they are, in fact, detached from it. Sometimes the very use of the media and the concentrated presence of professionals create a "safety belt" around the campaigners and a false sense of having "a finger on the pulse."

The belief in the power of the mass media and communications experts can inspire an exaggerated sense of security regarding the possibilities of dictating issues to the public agenda. Suffice it to note the frequent cases in which the public agenda significantly differs from the agenda of the candidates (Elizur & Katz, 1979). The standard wrapping of electoral propaganda messages, notwithstanding their professionalism and polish, may only alienate voters who feel apathy toward an electoral campaign that fails to address issues they are concerned about. Moreover, proliferation of communications media may divert attention from campaigns. In the 1992 electoral campaign, for example, it became clear that audiences for electoral broadcasts were smaller than in previous campaigns, a decrease attributed to the new cable channels which provided an alternative to the public television service that had thrived as a broadcasting monopoly for almost twenty-five years (Lehman-Wilzig, 1994).

The Example of Jerusalem

Although the components of Americanization have been absorbed into Israeli politics in a highly visible way, we nevertheless witness many cases of incompatibility between them: The adopting units still have trouble adjusting to the innovations, and they sometimes seem to ashamedly reject the New Style. In this regard, the case of the local elections in Jerusalem may serve to balance the preceding discussion.

In November 1993, in the middle of intensive negotiations between Israel and the PLO, elections for the local authorities were held in Israel. Following the experience accumulated from the Knesset elections, political lists hired professional services, especially in the large cities and other locations where the races were expected to be close. And so, the election campaign on the local scale also adopted the New Style, but on a more limited scale than the elections for the Knesset. We saw, then, in local campaigns, a loud and vigorous advertising war, the intensive use of both national and local media, per-

sonal rebuttal and the exchange of verbal blows between the campaign headquarters of the various candidates, frequent publication of poll results, and
so on.

The Jerusalem campaign naturally aroused special interest, undoubtedly
because of the proximity of the campaign to the national government. The
Prime Minister himself took pains to create an affinity between the political
process and the local elections. A few days prior to the elections, Mr. Rabin
stated that he would regard the election results for the local authorities as a
test of the public's support for government policy, a declaration which later
proved to be a tactical error. The modest achievements of the Labor Party
and its candidates' losses in a number of local elections were interpreted as
public opposition to the government's political course.

But even without the national dimension, the Jerusalem local elections still
had the power to awaken national interest. After serving as mayor for over a
quarter of a century, the popular Teddy Kollek again appealed for the voters'
confidence. In contrast to the past, this time his challenger was an ambitious
and well-known candidate. After serving many years as a member of Likud
governments, M. K. Ehud Olmert decided to make his escape from the wil-
derness of the Opposition and challenge Kollek.

In every respect, the campaigns of both candidates were professional and
thoroughly American. Each candidate ran a campaign headquarters which
leaned upon advertising agencies, consultants, and professionals. Each side
ran an aggressive campaign loaded with personal attacks. Ehud Olmert's
propagandists focused on Kollek's advanced age of 83. They led his campaign with the battle cry, "Because everyone knows that the time has come,"
alluding to Kollek's age, which was well known to the Jerusalemites who
were his enthusiastic supporters. In keeping with the entire propaganda strategy of the Olmert campaign, this slogan combined admiration for the opponent with forgiveness toward him, as is appropriate for any elderly person.
Moreover, Olmert's propagandists tried to, and succeeded in, inserting a
wedge between Teddy Kollek and his campaign headquarters. The members
of his list were represented as forcing the exhausted and worn-our mayor to
run yet again, against his wishes. And so, they shaped a pathetic image of an
elderly mayor held captive by a group of power-hungry politicians who would
replace him immediately, if and when elected.

On the other hand, Teddy's propagandists did not allow themselves to be
outdone. They ultimately chose a more aggressive tone and conducted a negative campaign of vilification, focusing on Ehud Olmert's character and openly
questioning his personal integrity. This approach was well expressed in an
advertisement published during the final days of the campaign, in which a
smiling Teddy appeals to the voters with the striking question, "You must
choose between my age and his character." This ad was supposed to culminate the noisy campaign, during which the cover of a fifteen-year-old issue
of a political weekly brandishing Olmert's picture and a one-word headline,
"Liar," had been aired. Moreover, in contrast to previous municipal campaigns, the campaign headquarters of both candidates hung signs and advertisements bearing portraits and battle slogans throughout the city at
intersections and on advertising billboards, homes, and electric poles.

Despite the red-hot campaign and the major efforts of the propagandists, most Jerusalemites did not make their way to the ballot box and did not participate in the voting. It seems that even the professional propaganda machines of both the candidates could not infect the voters with their enthusiasm. Perhaps there was even a boomerang effect. Despite the red-hot campaign, a considerable part of the public remained indifferent and chose not to vote. Why the low turnout? In these two highly professional campaigns, the propagandists, perhaps consciously, ignored substantial issues which troubled the residents of Israel's capital.

For the most part, Jerusalem life revolves around three sources of suppressed conflicts, probably as a microcosm of the whole society: Jews versus Arabs; nonreligious versus religious residents; and Sephardim versus Ashkenazim (Oriental versus Western Jews). Surprisingly, the electoral propaganda touched only lightly on these issues. The autonomy talks between the PLO and Israel awakened considerable anxieties about the city's future and the relationship between the eastern Arab part of the city and the western Jewish part: Will the city be divided or remain as it is now? The campaign headquarters chose to sweep this issue under the carpet, but many voters tended to believe that a Likud candidate would make it difficult to redivide the city, if and when the issue were to be raised on the agenda.

When the results were announced, Ehud Olmert's overwhelming success was attributed to the low turnout among the nonreligious population as compared to the high turnout of the Haredi (ultra-orthodox) population. Although the Haredim represent a minority, they are a highly organized, disciplined minority with high awareness, which makes its presence felt in the city. On the eve of the elections, an agreement signed between the Haredi candidate for mayor, Meir Porush, and Ehud Olmert became public knowledge. The Haredi leader agreed to withdraw from the race and to transfer support to Ehud Olmert in exchange for promises regarding the composition of the new coalition and positions within the coalition. As opposed to the secular population, which was still debating "Kollek's age and Olmert's character," the Haredi residents streamed to the ballot boxes in droves, all in accordance with the rabbis' instructions. The complacency of the secular population proved to be the instrument of their own defeat: Upon the announcement of the results, it became clear that not only had Ehud Olmert won two-thirds of the vote and routed the popular mayor in humiliating fashion, but also that the Haredim had become the largest faction in the city council.

This case sharpens some of questions raised above: Despite the professional American-style propaganda of the two main contenders, or perhaps because of it, most of the public remained indifferent and detached. It is clear that the results of the election were predetermined in a political maneuver ironed out between two political entities far away from the spotlights of the mass media and without the professional strategists. The political agreement which enabled Ehud Olmert to win the election rested on decidedly old-fashioned bloc voting, power brokering, and organization. The ability of such a political agreement made on election eve to succeed so dramatically reflects the continuing importance within Israel of a political culture that is anything but Americanized.

In the end, the voters who cast the deciding vote between the candidates did so not because of the propaganda campaigns with all their strategies, tactics, arguments, and slogans, but, rather, because of the voters' identified interests and calculations. The recommendation to support Ehud Olmert was passed on to each Haredi voter not necessarily via mass media but, rather, through the traditional communication channels of the Haredi community.

DISCUSSION

The Americanization of electoral campaigns in Israel may provide a few important lessons to other young democracies which are inclined to idealize the experiences of the older ones. Most young democracies apparently need a model for imitation, and in some cases the import of tried and true democratic procedures may save time. It is not easy to resist the temptation to walk in the footsteps of an old and experienced democracy. On the other hand, imitating the ways of others can be a mistake if it fails to recognize the unique and valuable attributes of a country's political heritage. The case of election campaigns in Israel proves the fallibility of blind imitation of a "big brother." The price, as is proved by the changes in the nature of electoral campaigns in Israel, may be too high for a young democracy. Some dysfunctions of this rapid adoption of American-style election campaigns are illustrative.

First, following the continuing process of Americanization, the electoral campaign has become increasingly more expensive. The total of state budget allocations to parties for election campaigns has increased fourfold in the last decade, from $10 million in 1977, to $15 million for the Tenth Knesset, $30 million in 1984, and $42 million for the Twelfth Knesset elections held in 1988 (Kalcheim & Rosevitch, 1992, p. 219). In addition to the official budgets assured by law, parties and candidates need to raise the additional funds required to conduct expensive professional campaigns. Basically, the Law for the Financing of Parties—1973 guarantees the state financing for campaigning. Each party receives a proportional budget according to the size of its faction in the outgoing Knesset; allocations for both campaign financing and current expenditures are calculated on a standard "unit" per MK. In the case in which a faction's representation is decreased as a result of an election, excess payments are deducted from the current expenditure allocation to the faction. New lists are awarded budgets only after the election, on the basis of their achievements. Originally, this arrangement was aimed to minimize the need for contributions from outside sources. In fact, one of the results of the increased costs of Americanized campaigning is the dependency of the parties upon various economic and interest groups in addition to the official budget.

It is probably the fear of such dependency that convinced the politicians to amend Paragraph 10 to the Law of Election eight times, and to adapt it each time to the new circumstances. The last amendment, of March 1992, stipulates the following: The size of a print ad may not exceed forty inches; double-spread ads are not permitted; a list may publish only one ad per day in each newspaper; the ad may be printed in no more than two colors; and during the last three months before election day, the total space of a list's advertisements may not exceed 10,000 inches.

The professionals have left only a limited mark on the campaigning so far, influencing more the form and less the substance of political messages. It seems that a practical "division of work" between the politicians and the professionals has been made in each party's headquarters. It is plausible to conclude that the politicians, rather than the professionals, remain in charge at party headquarters, and it is they who shape election strategies. The specialists, on the other hand, may shape the tactics of mobilizing voters.

Second, even though the new American style appears to be an inevitable development in Israel, a number of questions arise regarding the accepted formats of broadcast political propaganda. Following seven televised election campaigns, a degree of routinization is evident in the public's reactions to these broadcasts, which have lost quite a bit of their initial magic and have undergone an erosion typical of other broadcasting formats.

Faced with this trend, the politicians and their propagandists may have to reconsider the format of electoral propaganda and, especially, how to refresh it. This pressing need may grow in future election campaigns in line with the current changes in the monopolistic structure of the broadcast media. The initiation of unconventional occurrences, such as media events, can serve to reengage the attention of radio listeners and television viewers to the election broadcasts.

The persistent contradiction between the interests of the propagandists and the voters can produce negative side effects, be they in the form of criticism of the electoral campaign or perhaps in the creation of alienation between voters and propagandists. Thus, two-thirds of the interviewees in a 1988 survey expressed their dissatisfaction with the agenda of the election campaign (Caspi & Levinsohn, 1992). In their view, the electoral advertisements in general, and those of both major parties, dealt insufficiently with the most important issues (the important issues that respondents thought were being neglected concerned security, peace and the future of the territories, and revitalization of the economy). Only slightly more than a quarter of the interviewees were satisfied with the place accorded in the electoral advertisements to what they deemed the most important issue.

Third, the last election campaigns for the Twelfth and Thirteenth Knessets restored general and research interest in interpersonal communication (Katz & Levinsohn, 1989). While the professionalization of electioneering attracts attention to the mass media, the electoral success of the Haredi parties reminds us of the status and importance of face-to-face communication in Israeli society, and particularly in its political life. This reminder is especially important, given that Israel retains many significant traits of a traditional society, and there continue to exist within the country many enclaves populated by traditional communities which are serviced by networks of interpersonal relations. The Haredi parties successfully addressed the different groups of the religious public through these alternative channels of interpersonal communication.

Study of a select number of electoral broadcasts revealed something of the electoral strategies and tactics adopted in interpersonal communications of Haredi parties. A typical electoral broadcast was that of the SHAS party, the "Absolution of Vows Broadcast," which was one of the more famous broadcasts of the election campaign for the Twelfth Knesset. In a "one-shot" broadcast lasting ninety seconds, a number of esteemed rabbis, including the former Sephardic Chief Rabbi Obadiah Yosef, appeared on the screen. The rabbis absolved their potential voters of the vows which they had taken to support political rivals. The purpose of this broadcast might have been to confirm rumors regarding similar political messages which seeped down rapidly through interpersonal communication networks such as synagogues and institutions of religious education and charity. It is quite likely that the main purpose of the broadcast was to reinforce the propaganda messages disseminated through the interpersonal channels.

The professionals of the major parties also attempted to make use of interpersonal communications, but apparently without major success. The public controversy which erupted surrounding these attempts limited their prospects for success in advance. Thus, for example, in 1988, the Alignment organized an ambitious campaign combining written and telephone approaches to the general public. For this purpose, they purchased computerized data banks, a step which provoked certain ethical dilemmas concerning confidentiality and the right to privacy.

At times, it is surprising just how little attention is accorded to fundamental issues concerning the effectiveness of democracy. To date, academic interest has focused almost exclusively on the geographical expansion of New Style components. But what is the significance of bumper stickers or television debates between contenders in young and poor democracies such as Poland, Hungary, or India? Does the Americanization of these electoral campaigns reflect structural political changes, or does it merely nurture an optical illusion resulting from only surface changes? Is Americanization accompanied by a significant structural reform of electoral politics?

Even though politicians today are more aware of the mass media and more sensitive to their manipulative uses, these factors do not have the power to negate unique and fundamental characteristics of the entire political system. The electoral system of the Knesset elections has yet to change. If it does change in the future, the structural changes undoubtedly will affect the political culture significantly. Even if the proportionate representation system is abandoned in favor of the regional-majority system, which is more compatible with the American-style election campaign, it remains unclear whether this change would represent any true degree of modernization.

The proportional electoral system is deeply rooted in Israel's political culture. Despite demographic changes, Israeli society conserves traditional patterns of organization with amazing strength. This applies to interpersonal communication channels as well, which cannot be negated by the admittedly greater hold of the mass media on Israeli society. The existence of traditional enclaves perpetuate both their exploitation and their effectiveness as political intermediary agents. Although even the religious and Haredi lists have made their electoral campaigns more sophisticated over the years—using radio and television broadcasts, graphic design of press and wall ads, catchy slogans, and the like—synagogues, wall papers, and study halls remain significant channels for the religious constituents. The Arab population also maintains an intricate system of interpersonal communications, which has proven its efficiency in times of elections and also during periods of crisis and distress. This does not prevent the lists wooing the Arab vote from adopting characteristics of the American electoral campaign.

These examples, which repeat themselves in every Israeli electoral campaign, sharpen the question of the relationship between Americanization and modernization. Which prevails, the political process over the communications process or vice versa? The adoption of American electoral principles does not necessarily herald modernization. While modernization represents an intensive, comprehensive, and structural process within society, Americanization can often reveal itself as a tactical, but not strategic, change of style in the social rite of distributing power. Just as elections represent a necessary but not sufficient condition for democracy, so Americanization does not signal modernization. The fact is that traditional regimes can selectively adopt American modes (and not only in the political sphere) without changing their lifestyles in the least, and use American modes to perpetuate traditional customs. Undemocratic regimes also may make use of American modes, such as colorful campaigns in a carnival atmosphere, in order to obscure malaise and internal weakness. Indeed, the "American" wrapping can be misleading and is capable of creating a temporarily distorted image of the regime.

Even if electoral politics has undergone a significant shift toward Americanization, it is still permissible to ask if this change is different in dimension and scope from similar processes which have taken place in other spheres in Israel—economics, culture, education, or even academia.

The phenomenon of reciprocal relations, the trend toward unification of lifestyles, and the creation of uniform organizational patterns is especially prominent in this era of "open boundaries" between peoples and cultures. Influence is the name of the game, whether it is Americanization, modernization, Westernization, or just standardization.

REFERENCES

Agranoff, R. (Ed.). (1972). *The new style in election campaigns*. Boston: Holbrook Press.

Caspi, D. (1984). Following the race: Propaganda and electoral decision. In D. Caspi et al. (Eds.), *The roots of Begin's success: The 1981 Israeli elections* (pp. 245–272). London: Croom Helm.

Caspi, D. (1986). Electoral rhetoric and political polarization: The Begin–Peres debates. *European Journal of Communication, 1,* 447–462.

Caspi, D., & Eyal, C. H. (1983). Professionalization trends in Israeli election propaganda, 1973–1981. In A. Arian (Ed.), *The elections in Israel—1981* (pp. 259–282). Tel Aviv: Ramot.

Caspi, D., & Levinsohn, H. (1992). To influence and to be influenced: The election campaign to the 12th Knesset. In D. Elazar & S. Sandler (Eds.), *Who's the boss in Israel? Israel at the polls: 1988–89* (pp. 153–171). Detroit: Wayne State University Press.

Caspi, D., & Limor, Y. (1992). *The mediators: The mass media in Israel, 1948–1990.* Tel Aviv: Am Oved Publishers.

Elazar, D., & Sandler, S. (Eds.). (1992). *Who's the boss in Israel? Israel at the polls: 1988–89.* Detroit: Wayne State University Press.

Elizur, J., & Katz, E. (1979). The media in the Israeli election of 1977. In H. R. Penniman (Ed.), *Israel at the polls: The Knesset elections of 1977* (pp. 227–254). Jerusalem: Jerusalem Academic Press.

Gertz, N. (1986). Propaganda style of election ads from 1977 to 1984. In A. Arian (Ed.), *The elections in Israel—1984* (pp. 209–234). Boulder, Colo.: Westview.

Gurevitch, M. (1972). Television in the election campaign: Its audience and function. In A. Arian (Ed.), *The elections in Israel—1969* (pp. 220–237). Jerusalem: Jerusalem Academic Press.

Katz, E., & Levinsohn, H. (1989). Too good to be true: Notes on the Israeli elections of 1989. *International Journal of Public Opinion Research, 1*, 111–122.

Kalchheim, C., & Rosevitch, S. (1992). The financing of elections and parties. In D. Elazar & S. Sandler (Eds.), *Who's the boss in Israel? Israel at the polls: 1988–89* (pp. 212–229). Detroit: Wayne State University Press.

Keren, M. (1986). Drafting the platform: The pollsters' race. In A. Arian (Ed.), *The elections in Israel—1984* (pp. 251–266). Boulder, Colo.: Westview.

Lehman-Wilzig, S. (1994). The 1992 media campaign: Toward the Americanization of Israeli elections? In D. Elazar & S. Sandler (Eds.), *Israel at the polls* (pp. 251–280). Lanham, Md.: University Press of America.

Levinsohn, H. (1988). *Exposure patterns to radio and TV programs—Summer 1988* (Report (S)HL/1039/H). Jerusalem: Israeli Institute for Applied Social Research.

Nir, R. (1987). *Electoral rhetoric in Israel—The televised debates* (Working paper no. 517/87). Tel Aviv: Open University of Israel.

Peri, Y. (1975). Television in the 1973 election campaign. In A. Arian (Ed.), *The elections in Israel—1973* (pp. 95–117). Jerusalem: Jerusalem Academic Press.

Shamir, Y. (1986). The prediction errors of the pre-election day polls. *State, Government and International Relations, 25*, 131–148.

Weimann, G. (1984). Every day is election day: Press coverage of pre-elections polls. In D. Caspi et al. (Eds.), *The roots of Begin's success* (pp. 273–293). London: Croom Helm.

Chapter Ten

Patterns and Effects of Recent Changes in Electoral Campaigning in Italy

Gianpietro Mazzoleni

The Italian General Election of March 27, 1994, has been identified as the end of the First Republic and the birth of the Second. The sweeping victory of a media tycoon, Silvio Berlusconi, marks this passage to a completely new phase in Italy's political history. The majority of voters gave credit to a political figure who, from the glamour of his commercial television channels, promised to rebuild the country's moral and economic well-being as well as its international image, blurred by years of domestic malaise.

The dramatic character of this event rests especially in the fact that the country's traditional, long-lasting, almost unmovable *nomenklatura* had been swept away by the prosecutors during the preceding two years on charges of corruption, bad administration, and even ties with the Mafia. The crumbling of the establishment, and of the party system that had governed Italy since the end of World War II, created a serious vacuum in the political arena that was promptly filled by a brand new party, *Forza Italia*, that had been created in only a few weeks by Berlusconi. The ability of this leader to draw from the magician's hat, as it were, a new political creature that was entrusted to govern the country still intrigues adversaries, political scientists, and commentators.

There is no doubt that the Italian electorate was sensitive to the message of change expressed by Berlusconi and other new political leaders who had no ties with the old governing parties. The electorate was also ready, as never before, to switch voting patterns by the millions; to abandon the rigid allegiances to the old party system. By the standards of Italy's traditional voting dynamics, which have been anything but volatile (see Parisi, 1980), this was almost a revolutionary turnaround. Until the General Election of 1992, the fluctuations of votes from one party to the other had largely followed the previous pattern, although with the significant exception of the Northern League. Two years later, the situation had been turned upside down by numerous dramatic events, the last being the unexpected entry of Berlusconi into the political arena. Everything seemed to work in his favor, including the mistakes in the campaign strategies of his adversaries, the Progressives, who ridiculed and demonized Berlusconi, thus contributing to a sympathetic vote for him.

Whether what occurred in 1994 represents a "modernization" of Italy's campaign communication patterns is a complicated question. Answering this question requires close observation of the empirical evidence and the weighing of a series of indicators of modern campaigning. The crisis of the mass parties, the rise of media power, the personalization and scientificization of politics, the cleavage between parties and citizens, and the trend from citizenship to spectatorship are, according to the editors, some of the indicators of modernization. It is our assumption that the 1994 campaign represents a clamorous acceleration of the modernization of Italian campaign communication practices that had been under way since the 1980s. These indicators and more can be seen in the 1994 campaign. Perhaps the key indicator of modernization that was evident in 1994 was, in the editors' words, "the empowerment of individual figures at the expense of the authority of the political parties." In this sense, the Berlusconi phenomenon epitomizes the Italian path to Americanization and modernization of the political arena. For this reason, we shall focus on the 1994 campaign, the first campaign of the new political season in the era of the Second Republic.

ELECTIONEERING IN THE FIRST REPUBLIC

It is certainly not the case that, for the forty-five years of the First Republic, Italy's political arena remained stagnant but that, with the elections of 1994, everything suddenly changed. Like many other European countries, Italy in the postwar decades experienced turbulent periods of social unrest, political strife, and even political terrorism, not to mention the attacks of organized crime. Yet one cannot deny that the political parties established at the end of World War II maintained a steady and unchallenged control over the country for forty-five years. Even though governments lasted only one year (on average) during this long period, and many different coalitions formed them, it was always a matter of shuffling the same cards: The Christian Democratic Party (DC) governed uninterruptedly until March 27, 1994, with Mr. Giulio Andreotti being the symbol of their unending presence in power. The Socialists (PSI) played the part of the unfaithful ally (but an ally nevertheless), with the Christian Democrats sharing with them the responsibility for the policies that have shaped contemporary Italy. Other minor parties played the role of supernumeraries in the several weddings and separations (but never divorces) of the two major government parties. On the opposing side, the Communists (PCI), given the international constraints, never gained access to power. The prominent political leader and statesman, Aldo Moro, who was murdered by the Red Brigades, once depicted this state of Italian politics as a "blocked democracy."

Of course, the stability of political balances described above reflects the stability of the electorate's voting preferences during this period. With some temporary exceptions that did not jeopardize the existing political order, three Italians out of ten remained loyal to the Christian Democrats, three to the Communists, one to the Socialists, and the other three split their support among a myriad of tiny parties. Election results during these decades typically showed only scanty variations within this quite stable underlying pattern of party preferences.

Italian political scientists A. Parisi and G. Pasquino (1977) explained these patterns in terms of subcultural factors underlying the attitudes and behavior of Italian voters. The strong influence of Roman Catholicism in the country's culture, history, and character nurtured vast and stable political support for the Christian Democratic Party. The Communists were especially rooted in the so-called "red regions," which historically were hostile to the Church. The Socialists gathered votes in the followers of democratic Socialism (the adversary to Soviet Communism). This enduring pattern of partisanship was securely based on a stable structure of subcultures and associated political ideologies. The end of the Berlin wall and the melting of the traditional subcultures are the most recent facts that have changed the domestic political picture and voting behaviors.

The stability of voting patterns in the First Republic was also reinforced by the "exchange vote" (Parisi & Pasquino, 1977), based on patron–client relations. This was typical of the Southern regions, where the two major governing parties (DC and PSI) extensively engaged in bargaining favors for votes. Corruption was just one step away from this practice, as the criminal investigations and sanctions of the prosecutors of the early 1990s will unveil.[1]

Finally, according to the same authors, the comparatively small "opinion vote," that is, voting decisions that rested on citizens' evaluations of the parties' platforms and performance, relying to a large extent on the news media for their information, explained the limited vote switching between parties that took place between elections during this long period of general stability.[2] Beginning in the early 1980s, however, opinion voting has increased and has played an increasingly important role in domestic electoral dynamics.

To the list of factors underlying the long-lived political stability of the First Republic should be added the influence of the mass media. The Italian public broadcasting service (RAI) has always been closely watched over and directly controlled by the political establishment. This guaranteed that television would not challenge the established political balances. However, the rise of commercial television in the mid-1970s undermined the strong hold of the parties over the electronic media. The new mogul of private television, Silvio Berlusconi, did not himself wage a war against the political parties, from which indeed he managed to secure large favors (especially from the Socialist Premier, Craxi; see Mazzoleni, 1991a, 1991b). Instead, the challenge to the established balance of political power was represented by the commercial nature of independent broadcasting. Commercial broadcasting eventually attracted 50 percent of the former audience of the public channels. These viewers were exposed to models, values, and lifestyles that worked to further depoliticize the electorate. In this way, commercialization of broadcasting meant the weakening of the political power of RAI as a vehicle controlled by the parties and used to mold and maintain public opinion in support of the status quo.

In addition to undermining political control of both broadcasting and print media, the eruption of commercial television and rapid growth of its necessary handmaiden, the advertising industry, also provided fertile ground for the commercialization of politics and, eventually, of political communication. Increasingly since the early 1980s, political marketing and "showbiz" techniques have been introduced into Italian electoral campaigning. The key indicators of this conversion of political communication and propaganda to the marketing philosophy have been the *spectacularization* of campaigns and the *personalization* of political discourse. In the former case, massive use of television spot ads by parties and candidates, and the imposition of media logics, such as a preference for sensationalism in news coverage of campaign events and personages, were a major rupture with the traditional formal, stiff, and rather boring style of political campaigning and reporting. In the latter case, the greater attention given to the personalities of candidates by the media has personalized the party's message and exalted the position of the candidates, overshadowing the traditional centrality of the party (Mazzoleni, 1987).

The impact of these dynamics on the political system as a whole was remarkable in the last period of the First Republic, as they were slowly but steadily changing the traditional features of the political game, the political discourse, and the criteria for political leadership. It was during this time that the term "Americanization" was first used to describe the innovations that were appearing in Italian campaigning. However, the connotation of the term was negative, as the Left objected to the changes, considering them dangerous for the democratic process and alien to the "good old traditions."

NEW RULES FOR THE ELECTION GAME

A major thrust toward innovation in Italian political campaigns came in late 1992, when Parliament passed a bill that radically reformed mayoral elections. That was the start of a series of truly revolutionary reforms that gave birth to the Second Republic. The new system for electing mayors introduced majoritarian rule after decades of proportional voting. If no candidate received a majority, there was provision for a second ballot between the two candidates who received the most votes in the initial balloting.

This reform actually sanctioned the personalization of the election contest by encouraging the formation of alliances around the pivotal figures of prestigious candidates who might have sufficient appeal to win a majority of the votes. It was indeed a process that opened the way to an Americanization of electioneering in Italy, in the sense hypothesized by the editors. The new regulation, of course, was not inspired by any groundswell of opinion in favor of modifying domestic campaigns to fit American models, nor did it imply the adoption of campaign methods and practices that had been developed in the United States and widely publicized by the mass media. Rather, the reform was born simply out of a widespread popular demand for more efficient city administrations. Majoritarian rule was chosen by the legislators as the key to more stable local governments.

However, majoritarian rule entails an approach to campaigning that privileges electoral methods and practices that are well established in and perhaps are most closely associated with the United States, as well as the United Kingdom and France. In this modern model, the party machine and organization become secondary to the personal skills, appearance, and appeal of the mayoral candidate. So, it was no surprise that several candidates in the new mayoral elections in 1993 (in Milan, Turin, Rome, Venice, Trieste, and Genoa) relied extensively on the expertise of political consultants, media professionals, public-relations practitioners, and market analysts to organize their campaigning during the pre- and post-ballot weeks. There is evidence from news stories, interviews, and appearances on television that a number of those campaign professionals fit the editors' description as persons that "have visited the United States to study firsthand and report on election campaigns." Others simply drew insights and suggestions from the several books and manuals on the subject published in the United States. The news media themselves were greatly involved in the general game and enthusiastically "played it American," spectacularizing the campaign events and, especially, the television matches or debates between the finalists in the second, run-off balloting.

The reform of the mayoral election system injected heavy doses of innovation into the wider political system. However, this represents only the beginning of an institutional revolution that was intended to "modernize" Italian democracy. The mayoral campaigns of 1993 served as laboratories, in which could be detected signs of the decline of the party as an agency for gathering electoral consent and the rise of strong individual candidacies and of the scientificization of the candidates' communication.

It was in the campaign for the parliamentary elections of early Spring 1994 that almost all of the ingredients of the modernization of Italy's campaigning emerged. Before looking closely at the peculiar features of that precedent-setting campaign, it is useful to sketch briefly the background to the 1994 campaign.

Following a long debate about the so-called "Institutional Reforms" and the complicated issues raised by the question of electoral engineering, Italy's Parliament approved, in late 1993, a radical revision of the electoral system that abandoned almost completely the old system based on proportional rule. Now the MPs are elected through majoritarian rule, similar to the U.S. and British systems. However, 25 percent of the seats in the Parliament are still reserved for candidates elected with the old proportional rules. The voting constituencies for both the Chamber of Deputies and the Senate had to be completely redrawn, and their formerly large scope (sometimes comprising even two or three different provinces) was drastically reduced to districts containing no more than 100,000 to 120,000 inhabitants. Unlike the reform for mayoral elections, though, this change does not provide for a second ballot between the leading contenders. Thus, if no candidate wins a majority of the votes cast, the candidate with the plurality of votes wins, even if the plurality is but a single vote.

Among the many facets of the national reform, the most significant one to notice here is the multiplication of small constituencies. This new setting of the electoral game forces candidates to establish direct, strong ties with the local features of the electoral marketplace, whereas, in the old electoral districts, the parties often disregarded the recruitment of new voters and relied merely on the fairly stable support of certain sectors of the large constituency. In previous elections, it was the party that decided who were to be the winning candidates and directed their campaigns. The 1993 revolution pushed the parties to the background and exalted the role of the individual candidates, who now run mostly on their own.

The political scandals that brought to court or to jail several representatives of the old party system stirred a general outcry among the public— supported by the majority of the news media—against leaders, parties, politics, and practices that had characterized the history of the First Republic. The enormous amounts of public money that, as judicial inquiries discovered, had been misappropriated by politicians or by party organizations deeply impressed most Italians, who demanded an end to political corruption at the expense of taxpayers and the unemployed, and demanded more severe control over the flow of public money as well.

This political malaise also led, in 1993, to approval of a set of regulations restricting the expenditure of both public and private money in election campaigns. Law 515 imposed a series of finance and communication austerity measures. In addition, on the eve of the 1994 general election, the Guarantor for Broadcasting, Italy's authority for the media sector, issued further constraints on campaigns' media activities. These regulations and constraints represent a stumbling block to the process of Americanization that had been observed in the election campaigns of the First Republic and in the new mayoral elections. Paradoxically, one expected that the introduction of the majoritarian ballot would greet spectacularization, campaign hoopla, marketing, advertising, media use, and more as the right campaign weaponry for the new electoral system. On the contrary, the lawmakers of the last legislation of the First Republic attempted to interpret the mood of the country by placing severe restrictions on frivolous campaigning. Nevertheless, ways to circumvent these restrictions would soon be devised.

The law applies only to the period of thirty days preceding Election Day, which is the official campaign period in Italian elections. Some of the restrictions contained in Law 515 and in the decree by the Guarantor for Publishing and Broadcasting are the following:

- Candidates and politicians are forbidden to appear in any television show except for news programs and campaign debates, where the completeness and impartiality of the broadcast can be safeguarded.
- All paid propaganda or advertising in the press and on television (i.e., spot ads) as well as television messages aiming at impressing voters with spectacular features, are forbidden.
- It is forbidden to disclose results of political opinion polls in the last two weeks of the campaign.

- The total amount of money that may be expended by a single candidate is limited to 80 million lire (about 50,000 U.S. dollars), plus an additional 100 lire per each inhabitant of the constituency (to a maximum of 120,000 inhabitants), for a total spending limit of 90 million lire.
- Any fund-raising shall be done and funds disbursed under strict accounting procedures.
- All media organizations intending to cover the campaign with special programs, debates, news, and the like should adopt a code of practice in which they commit themselves to guarantee equal access to all contenders. A copy of the code should be presented to the Guarantor's office.
- Severe sanctions are threatened (including the withdrawal of the broadcasting license) for violations by the media, and heavy fines in the case of violations by the candidates.

In addition to these major restrictions, other minor ones (regarding, for example, a ban of outdoor advertising that does not conform to strict size limitations) contribute to the general austerity of election campaigning.

AN UNPRECEDENTED ELECTION CAMPAIGN

After the conclusion of the electoral reform and approval of limitations on campaigning, everything appeared ready for the first test of the new rules of the game. Elections were called for March 27, 1994, and the campaign period was set at February 25 to March 25. A one-month period for the first campaign of a new era in Italian political history was thought to be too short a time for the feared excesses of the new politics to emerge. Most of the old governing parties were dead, and new formations had to be founded. New leaders waited impatiently to be consecrated as celebrities by the media. The news media pressed to play a leading role in the contest. Voters, free from traditional loyalties, longed to try new emotions. The many constraints enforced on the official campaign were a serious obstacle to the unleashing of all this energy. If effective, the constraints would indeed restrict the movement to modernize the political arena, a move bolstered by the institutional revolution but slowed by the claims for austerity.

A clever way to circumvent the constraints was quickly found by all the involved actors: The real campaign would be staged in the months *before* the start of the official one. So January and February became the hottest months of what was named the pre-campaign. Most of the key events that marked the transition from the old system to the new system took place during the pre-campaign. The absence of any constraint allowed the drive for innovation to be given full rein and to fill the public agenda. In this regard, four phenomena deserve close attention: (1) Berlusconi's stepping into the election contest; (2) the creation from scrap of a new party, *Forza Italia*; (3) the strong commercialization of pre-campaign communication; and (4) the protagonism of the media.

The campaign warfare had its real start when, in the second half of January, Berlusconi disclosed his intention to run for office and to lead a new force to win a significant number of seats in Parliament. Berlusconi was a well-known industrialist and media tycoon who, until then, had manifested only cautious attitudes toward the domain of politics. In recent times, he had come under fire by the Left for his attempts to enlarge his publishing and television empire (see Giglioli & Mazzoleni, 1991). He enjoyed large popularity for his identification with the much beloved (in terms of audience ratings) commercial television, which, for a decade, undoubtedly contributed to building a big reservoir of positive attitudes toward him with millions of potential voters. The announcement of his candidacy was staged with a crescendo of suspense and turned out to be a real earthquake for the political balance of forces at the time. His simple platform would be to keep the Communists and the Left out of power, make a "new economic miracle," and revive the prestige of the nation in the world.[3]

The candidacy of a prominent figure who had enjoyed great successes in his industrial and financial activities and whose interest in politics was not at all clear was an utterly unprecedented event in Italy's post-war history. The calibre of personality, the wealth, and the style of presentation made Berlusconi's apparition on the political stage the most "American" event of the 1994 campaign. He was immediately compared to Ross Perot, and many commentators saw his candidacy as a strong sign of the Americanization that seemed to be favored by the new voting rules.

A further indicator of Americanization is the rise of Berlusconi's own party, *Forza Italia*. Unlike the old mass parties of the previous political era, which relied on solid capillary networks throughout the electorate and on heavy bureaucratic structures, the new party has very loose links with the voters and very volatile structures. It has been labeled the "light party" and the "media-centered party," and it has been pointed to by commentators as a product of the modernization of patterns of political and electoral organization. *Forza Italia* has much more in common with the electoral machines of American presidential candidates than with the traditional European party models. It exists mainly as a function of the strength or charisma of its leader, Berlusconi; it serves to amplify the leader's image; it activates mostly in election campaigns; and it relies primarily on media outlets to reach the electoral market.

The rise and electoral fortunes of this party were made possible by the scientific sales and promotion strategies carried out by highly professionalized experts that Berlusconi already commanded in his commercial and industrial empire. This is the first example of the "making" of an Italian political leader by means of marketing tools and media resources.

Other parties in the 1994 campaign also depended on mass media to reach the voters, although in varying degrees. It seemed clear that no party could remain in the contest without heavy use of mass communication channels for paid propaganda, for defending one's positions in public debates, and for maintaining the visibility of candidates and spokesmen. The sheer volume of campaign material conveyed by all media—public and commercial, news and entertainment, daily and periodical press, and local and national broadcasting stations—in the pre-campaign was enormous.

The launching of *Forza Italia* was by far the most "scientific" marketing operation ever seen in Italian election campaigns. Berlusconi inundated the screens of his three nationwide networks with hundreds of spot ads to sell his ideas, his personal image, and his own party. The slogans of *Forza Italia* hammered television audiences for weeks, and succeeded in making the new product (party) familiar to Italian consumers (voters). A new opinion-polling company was established by people linked to the tycoon and his movement. It continuously monitored the "positioning" of the new party in the electorate by means of cross-sectional surveys, panels, and focus groups.

Such a costly operation could not be duplicated by the other contenders because of both financial reasons and deep differences in political outlooks. The Progressives, especially, remained anchored to the old dislike for any commercialization of electoral communication as potentially inconsistent with and undermining their political message.

The pre-campaign was also characterized by an extensive use of polls. The media carried almost daily (often contradictory) figures on the opinion climate, the would-be voters' options, the ups and downs of the popularity of the main actors, and forecasts of the vote outcome. Many political circles close to the contending parties clearly used the polls to influence public opinion. The unprecedented intensity of this phenomenon was so high, and most polling was so biased, that one may say that Italian electioneering has now joined the community of other nations in the use of polls as new offensive weapons in modern election campaigns.

On February 25, one month before the ballot, the official campaign period began, and the restrictions described above took effect. The major contenders were forced to lower the volume of their personal communication and to reduce their television appearances. However, they did not totally disappear, as the public and private television channels scheduled a series of special election broadcasts (the so-called "Tribunes"), where candidates and leaders had the opportunity to speak or to be interviewed on formal bases of equal opportunity and fairness.[4] But the spot ads did end on the national channels, thus giving the impression of a sudden communication blackout. The publication of polls was halted in the last two weeks, according to the dictates of the law.

From that moment, the candidates began their personal campaigning in their constituencies. Compared to the media show of the national campaign led by the leaders of the major electoral tickets, the local campaigns got very little media attention. It could not be otherwise, as the unique political atmosphere of the 1994 general election was epitomized in the mighty confrontation between the conservative forces led by Silvio Berlusconi and the progressive forces led by former Communist Achille Occhetto. The "big shots" gave so high a pitch as to almost completely drown out the search for publicity of their followers.

Nevertheless, local candidates were anything but inactive. They successfully bypassed many restrictions by devising ingenious communication tactics, mostly in line with peculiar local subcultural patterns. The result was sometimes a bizarre mix of American-like campaign hoopla and traditional Italian practices. The candidates with a more cosmopolitan outlook did resort to some marketing (leaflets, posters, gadgets, phone calls, etc.) and sought advice from public-relations and advertising experts. Some new communication technology was also tested for the first time in Italian campaign history.[5] The Berlusconi troops, as well as competing parties, established chat lines and other audiotex services to publicize their political programs and reply to the voters' queries. The money received from these sources provided partial funding for their campaign machines.

The local candidates did not abandon the old ways of getting in touch with their potential voters, like going door to door, street by street; shaking hands in the market squares; and addressing people in theaters and in staged public encounters. The local media were also involved in the candidates' campaigns. The television stations aired a singular kind of paid television propaganda, short films mixing information (according to the Guarantor's guidelines) and (nominally forbidden) advertising.

In the end, however, what seemed to count most was the local candidate's affiliation with one of the key political arrays: Most of the Berlusconi candidates won, no matter how sophisticated or poor were their campaigns; many candidates of the Progressive formations of other parties lost in spite of a very good campaign organization. In fact, the victory of the Berlusconi alliance (which included the Northern League, *Forza Italia*, and the rightist party *Alleanza Nazionale*) was obtained despite having fielded hundreds of unknown candidates, and the defeat of the opposing parties was not avoided by the popularity of many of their candidates. For this reason, commentators analyzed the election results by invoking the concept of a "Berlusconi effect" that annulled or limited the influence of other campaign factors, such as the ability of single candidates to sell their personal images.

A NEW ROLE FOR THE MEDIA

The Italian mass media played only a marginal role in the electoral dynamics of the campaigns of the First Republic. Their relationship to the political establishment prevented them from exerting a decisive influence on interparty debate or from playing the roles of "watchdogs" in the political arena or "referees" in the horse race. The public television channels were, in fact, under the control of the party system, and most of the journalists working in them were linked to one or another political faction. In contrast, in the private broadcasting domain the commercial channels quickly distinguished themselves for their lively coverage of campaign events, for creating special election broadcasts and testing new presentation formats, and, above all, for airing thousands of spot ads, a really impressive novelty in the campaigns of the 1980s. However, the role of these media in the political game was limited, because they carried very little news.

The 1994 campaign, at least in the feverish pre-campaign, was a revolution in the media system as well as the political system. The fall of the old party system brought with it the dissolution of traditional patterns of party–media interaction. The journalists, following (not leading) the popular protest against the traditional party system, broke from their traditional political allegiances and began to take on a critical outlook.

The big ideological clash between the conservatives and the progressives took place almost entirely on television screens. For the first time in its forty-year history, RAI, the public television company, stepped directly into the campaign debate by producing special election broadcasts (such as *Al voto, al voto!* and *Oltre le parole*), where the journalists' professional values were privileged over the guarantist rules (that were instead applied in the party broadcasts that, by law, had to be aired, but were not produced by RAI). In addition, some of RAI's most popular journalistic current-events programs (such as *Milano Italia*, *Il rosso e il nero*, and *Mixer*) were transformed into "electronic squares," where political leaders and the new parties' spokesmen were questioned, scrutinized, and challenged by tenacious (even if at times biased) journalists, and where they confronted, quarreled, and debated passionate members of the public. The commercial channels (owned by Berlusconi) also produced several special programs (such as *Funari News*, *O di qua o di là*, and *Elettorando*), most of which scored quite high audience ratings and distinguished themselves for their absence or near absence of pro-Berlusconi bias.

In sum, the media system as a whole gave close attention to the campaign issues, and took up an advocacy role very similar to the American one, by thoroughly informing and exciting the voters as never before. This new outlook and stance of the news media makes them co-actors in the domestic campaign contests.

DISCUSSION

Electoral reforms for the 1993 mayoral and 1994 general ballots were the key factor in the general renovation of Italy's democracy. The domestic political arena and its liturgies, such as electioneering, were deeply affected by the structural changes introduced and tested in 1993 and 1994. The new majoritarian system favors the establishment of large alliances between small political movements and parties. It rewards those with the most efficient and flexible organizational machines. And it demands strong leadership to consolidate the fragile connections of the new parties to the electorate. Successful campaigning for election in such a context requires that the allied parties and candidates emphasize their common values and mute controversial issues. This is indeed a novelty in Italian campaigns, where, in the old proportional system, the smallest parties had a good chance to win a parliamentary seat. Today, either you are big or you are out. However, if even large electoral tickets lack prestigious leadership, their chances of winning may be poor.

The ingredients required for success in the new era seemed to be exemplified by Berlusconi's entry into the arena: a leader with a strong personal image, who was able to exploit the new rules of the game to build a correspondingly strong image of himself as a political leader through shrewd use of communication tools. He launched his personal candidacy and his party *before* the regular campaign (thus circumventing the severe restrictions), and he relied heavily on the broadcast media, market research, and on professional image management.

Thus, the campaign of Berlusconi and *Forza Italia* best represents the trend toward further Americanization of Italian electioneering. Like U.S. presidential candidates and election machines, the fortunes of Berlusconi and *Forza Italia* do not rest on a mass-party structure or any particular political subculture. Their search for the voters' support is based on persuasion through the mass media. *Forza Italia* would hardly exist without the "shopping windows" provided by the communication channels, for it is a provisional party with the same task-force character seen in American PACs that exist only for electoral purposes.

The competing political forces (the centrist PPI, *Partito Popolare Italiano*, born out of the former governing party *Democrazia Cristiana*, and the leftist *Polo Progressista*, an alliance of the former Communist Party with a series of smaller parties) failed on all fronts. They did not fully exploit the communication possibilities offered by the pre-campaign period; their use of the media was too traditional; and, above all, they lacked leaders with strong images. Both the PPI leader, Mino Martinazzoli, and the leader of the Progressives, Achille Ochetto, refused to Americanize their campaigns. In doing so, they showed they did not see or did not hear the implications for political communication of the innovations imposed by the new electoral rules.

Of the many consequences of this new campaign pattern, perhaps one is most significant of all: Individual candidates, and even the parties, are overshadowed by the leader's personality. This certainly happened in 1994, because of the exceptional candidacy of Berlusconi. It was not the case with the opposing forces, however. In the former case, success consecrated the leader's primacy; in the latter case, the prestige of individual candidates did not secure party success. This is an unexpected outcome of the process of personalization that was observed by researchers in the Italian campaigns of the 1980s. There is a degree of risk in this development. Several political analysts have expressed concern about the consequences of the centrality of personal leadership in the domestic political arena. While in the American context personal leadership is an accepted condition of the Presidential system, in parliamentary Italy there is a strong aversion to all forms of strong personal leadership, for historical and other reasons. Apart from these worries, however, the evident personalization of Italian politics and campaigning fits the editors' definition (along with Duverger, 1991) of the phenomenon as "the more general, pervasive, and fundamental element in the process of change of election campaigns."

A more independent and critical journalism may offer a counterbalance to some of the dangers inherent in the new era of personalized politics based on mass persuasion. As we have seen, the new political atmosphere and the innovations introduced by the new electoral system made possible the diffusion of a new outlook among media professionals; a new awareness of the key role of journalism in the power game. The intense involvement of Italian media in the 1994 campaign on both the referential–informative and editorial–critical levels is a sign of a new trend in domestic journalism toward approaches and models that, in the collective imagery, are identified also as "American." In the recent Italian campaigns, this form of journalism showed itself to be capable of acting as the spokesman of civil society, challenging political arrogance and political rascality, and ensuring that all players in the game can make their voices heard.

The process of building a genuinely independent professional culture of journalism still has a long way to go. It could hardly be otherwise, after decades of subservience to the political logics. Nevertheless, the last campaign represented a great opportunity, swiftly exploited by the news media, to ransom themselves from a grey past. It was a clear sign of the modernization of the domestic democratic process, pointed to by the editors in terms of "mass media moving to the center stage," of their becoming an "autonomous power center," and of a dramatic change in their roles from that of "channels to that of actors." To these observations, a further one should be added: Italian politics is being increasingly recast by a strong process of mediatization. The 1994 campaign has been, by far, the most media-centered political event of the Second Republic. The point is captured by observing that Berlusconi may have not won thanks to the media, yet he could not have won without the media. All political leaders, big or small, as well as all candidates, known or unknown, had to adjust their communication and public-visibility strategies to the requirements of the mass communication process. This media dependency of political action is going to be a permanent feature of all future election campaigns in Italy.

The 1993 mayoral and 1994 general election campaigns have provided an important benchmark in the evolution toward a more democratic and participative electoral system. The third party in the election contest, the voter, has been shown to appreciate the new conduct of the news media, as well as the information and propaganda messages addressed to him or her by the competing parties. The response of Italian electors to the intensive advertising and image selling (in the pre-campaign period) by the newly founded Berlusconi party was, in fact, very positive. In terms of audience ratings, the response to the campaign-centered programs offered by the television networks was also very positive. The Italian voter of 1993–1994 was far from being a "passive" recipient of party and media-originated communication through television. Rather, the voter could fulfill the need for "surveillance" and enjoy the "contest excitement," very much like the viewers–voters observed by J. Blumler and D. McQuail in their seminal study of early electoral television (1968). This is also an indicator of modernization of the democratic process, yet not fully consistent with what the editors consider a slip from "personal involvement to spectatorship." It was, in fact, a kind of "necessary" spectatorship that was imposed by the political arena's focusing almost exclusively on the mass media. Yet, at the same time, the media-centered campaign did not prevent voters' from feeling personally involved. High voter turnout is a traditional feature of Italian elections. Although the 1994 campaign was waged primarily through mass media, it did not prompt mass desertion of the voting sites.

NOTES

1. *The Economist* of February 20, 1993, commenting on the events that brought the collapse of Italy's old political order, wrote that it was "a system which placed loyalty to party above loyalty to state, and which offered unending rule by the same cast of characters. . . . Nothing was so important as a party connection. Patronage was king. Access to jobs, pensions, hospital beds was eased by *raccomandazioni*—the favours of a local politician. Bigger jobs, bigger pensions, industrial companies, television stations—all were parcelled out by *lottizzazione*, the practice of rewarding parties according to their support at the most recent election" (p. 11).

2. The "opinion vote" parallels the "opinion party," which is significantly referred to by European observers as the "American party," because it reflects the typical voting

pattern of the U.S. political experience. An increase in voting behavior of this kind, as is now happening in Italy, is a further indication of the Americanization of the electoral arena. For an extended discussion of the opinion vote, see the editors' introductory chapter in this volume.

3. The name of the Berlusconi's party, *Forza Italia*, contains the overt message that "Italy can make it." He drew the name from the slogans used by the fans of the national soccer team in international contests.

4. The actual conduct of the national television channels, both public and commercial, was far from complying with the requirements of equal opportunity and fairness. The campaign recorded several charges and countercharges, from all sides, of flagrant bias and systematic violation of the Guarantor's guidelines.

5. The absolute first time was in the mayoral campaign of Milan (May 1993), where a couple of candidates for office used audiotex technology to inform the citizens about the campaign and the candidates' stands and to gather financial support.

REFERENCES

Blumler, J. G., & McQuail, D. (1968). *Television in politics: Its uses and influence*. London: Faber & Faber.

Duverger, M. (1991). Personalizzazione del potere o istituzionalizzazione del potere personale [Personalization of power or institutionalization of personal power]. In M. Vaudagna (Ed.), *Il partito americano e l'Europa* [The American political party and Europe] (pp. 259–268). Milan: Feltrinelli.

Giglioli, P., & Mazzoleni, G. (1991). Concentration trends in the media. In F. Sabetti & R. Catanzaro (Eds.), *Italian politics* (pp. 112–125). London: Pinter.

Mazzoleni, G. (1987). Media logic and party logic in campaign coverage: The Italian general election of 1983. *European Journal of Communication, 2*(1), 81–103.

Mazzoleni, G. (1991a). Emergence of the candidate and political marketing: Television and election campaigns in Italy in the 1980s. *Political Communication and Persuasion, 8*(1), 201–212.

Mazzoleni, G. (1991b). Media moguls in Italy. In J. Tunstall & M. Palmer (Eds.), *Media moguls* (pp. 162–183). London: Routledge.

Parisi, A. (1980). *Mobilità senza movimento* [Mobility without movement]. Bologna: Il Mulino.

Parisi, A., & Pasquino, G. (1977). Relazioni partiti-elettori e tipi di voto [Party-voters relations and types of voting]. In A. Parisi & G. Pasquino (Eds.), *Continuità e mutamento elettorale in Italia* [Electoral continuity and change in Italy] (pp. 215–250). Bologna: Il Mulino.

Chapter Eleven

Secular Politics: The Modernization of Argentine Electioneering

Silvio R. Waisbord

> Political activism doesn't exist anymore. Twenty years ago we believed in the "organized community" and we had shoot-outs with those who believed in the "socialist fatherland." But we were all militants then. Now everything has a price: wall-painting, mobilizing, intimidating or organizing.[1]
>
> Política en la Matanza, September 18, 1993

These words of an anonymous militant turned gun-for-hire encapsulate what has happened to recent Argentine election campaigning. From enthusiastic (and violent) ideological crusades to more apathetic and expensive exercises for seducing voters, electioneering activities have undergone important transformations. Similar to what has been observed about U.S. campaigns, the epigraph nicely describes the transition in Argentine politics from "militaristic" to "mercantilistic" (Jensen, 1971); from "labor-intensive" to "capital-intensive" (Ginsberg, 1986) campaigning. Political marketing and modern campaign gadgetry, commonly seen as synonymous with American election campaigns, have become widespread. Since the return of democracy in 1983, a variety of "modern" stumping styles and technologies have been extensively incorporated into the repertoire of electoral campaigning.

Argentina offers an interesting example for discussing the Americanization of contemporary campaign practices. The oft-mentioned "exceptionalism" of U.S. political and communication institutions, responsible for the uniqueness of American electioneering, is less exceptional in Argentina than in Europe. U.S.-like institutional arrangements have long existed in Argentina. Like all Latin American countries, Argentina has a presidential system, and its broadcasting structure has consistently followed commercial practices. However, it is only in recent years that Argentine electioneering dis-

plays American campaign features. If factors commonly seen as responsible
for having shaped contemporary U.S. campaigning already existed, why has
Argentine electioneering only progressively adopted U.S.-style practices
during the last decade? In other words, if a presidential system and commercially run mass media were not sufficient for spawning American campaigning, then what other developments account for the modernization of Argentine
election campaigns?

The task of this chapter is to provide an answer to these questions. Briefly
stated, my argument is that the breakdown of partisan identities, upon which
the "old political order" was based, has propelled the modernization of electoral routines in Argentina. The Argentine case, I suggest, provides evidence
for understanding that the current Americanization of worldwide electioneering is rooted, not only in the spread of U.S.-like political and communication institutions, but also is motivated by the ebb of partisan gospels and the
loosening of partisan identities.

THE RETURN OF DEMOCRACY

The last decade has been a turning point in Argentine political history. The
debacle in the 1982 Malvinas–Falklands war dealt a death blow to the authoritarian regime that overthrew Isabel Perón in 1976. Unable to revamp a
stagnated economy and beset by internal differences and embryonic democratic opposition, the regime resorted to the invasion of the long-claimed
South Atlantic islands for cementing support and gaining legitimacy. The
operation backfired, however, and resulted in a military and political fiasco.
This ill-planned gambit proved to be the swan song for a regime that was
responsible for a disastrous economic performance and the systematic violation of human rights in the "dirty war" waged against real and imagined
guerrilla movements. The regime's sudden "collapse from above" opened
the road for democracy, much sooner than anticipated before the war.

Elections were scheduled for October 1983. After more than a six-year hia-
tus, in which democratic activities were banned and persecution was widespread, political parties rapidly turned to reorganizing and preparing for the
electoral campaign. Contrary to most expectations, Raúl Alfonsín, the candidate of the middle-class, urban, centrist Radical party, conclusively defeated
Peronist Italo Luder. Amidst unbridled optimism about the future of democracy, the Radical victory represented a new development in Argentine politics: It
was the first time that Peronism lost a presidential election since its founding
in the 1940s. An arduous task awaited President Alfonsín: to guarantee the
consolidation of democracy and simultaneously to deal with the heavy political, social, and economic burden inherited from the military regime.

If high hopes dominated the general mood when Alfonsín took office, de-
spair reigned at the time of the 1989 election. By then, severe problems not
only undermined Radicals' chances for staying in power, but also threatened
the stability of Argentine democracy. The trial and sentence of the former
governing juntas and other military officers accused of human rights violations caused constant friction between the government and the Armed Forces.
Military resistance was best expressed in two rebellions staged by middle-

ranking officers in 1987 and 1988. Government plans for economic stabiliza-
tion and growth proved to be ineffective after mildly successful initial results. The Alfonsín administration was unable to control an economy which,
in the first half of 1989, showed triple-digit inflation, massive foreign debt,
stagnation, and fiscal crisis. In addition, the storming of an army garrison by
a guerrilla group and looting and riots in main urban centers amidst swell-
ing hyperinflation brought back fears of a return of authoritarianism.

All these problems, especially the critical economic situation, torpedoed
the presidential bid of Radical candidate Eduardo Angeloz. Peronist Carlos
Menem, the three-time governor of the small and impoverished northwest-
ern province of La Rioja, convincingly won the elections in May 1989. The
passing of the presidential sash from Raúl Alfonsín to Carlos Menem in July
signaled the first democratic transferral of power in almost sixty years, and
the first time since 1916 that presidents from different parties alternated in
government. Amid economic chaos and social upheaval, which led to the
inauguration's being held five months before its originally scheduled date,
Argentine democracy passed a crucial test: the peaceful rotation of opposition parties into power.

Reversing much of its electoral platform, the Menem administration carried out major, ambitious, economic and political transformations beginning
in July 1989. The government's take-no-prisoners actions to dismantle the
state-regulated economy, to weaken the power of the unions, and to realign
the country in foreign affairs are the best indicators of a new emerging economic and political scene. Such transformations also speak of unprecedented
changes in the ideology of the governing party: Peronism has virtually repu-
diated its nationalistic philosophy and programmatic goals put forth under
the leadership of Gen. Juan Perón in the post-war period. Whereas a state-
managed economy, strong unions, and nationalistic and anti-imperialistic
causes have traditionally been at the forefront of its agenda, today's Peronism
fully embraces free-market economic recipes, neoconservative policies, and
an undivided alliance with the United States. To many observers, contemporary Peronism is rapidly undoing much of what it introduced in the 1940s
and 1950s.

NEW BOTTLES, NEW WINES

These new winds blowing in Argentine politics have also affected election
campaigns. Before the 1980s, Argentine parties and politicians had few opportunities for campaigning amid a cycle of democratic and authoritarian
regimes. Thus, they were mostly unfamiliar with modern technologies and
strategies at the time of the transition to democracy. The election of 1983 was
a watershed in Argentine electioneering history, as the uses of new communication technologies during the campaign shook old-fashioned conceptions
and generated a reevaluation of the role of traditional stumping activities in
a new and dynamic political and communication scenario.

Raúl Alfonsín's 1983 campaign is credited with having substantially
changed the rules and routines of Argentine campaigning. The reliance upon
a professional advertising agency for designing campaign paraphernalia, the

incorporation of public-opinion surveys, the planning of campaign events on the basis of poll information, the growing role of television campaigning, and the emphasis on individualistic over party appeals are commonly attributed to Alfonsín's successful bid for the presidency (Borrini, 1984).

Although some practices were truly innovative by local standards, it would be an exaggeration to attribute these novelties to the Radical campaign. For example, the Radicals used track polling for following electoral tendencies and for drafting the schedule of campaign activities. Yet strategies and routines were only occasionally decided on the basis of poll information. Personal convictions and intuitive feelings about voting preferences determined much of the electoral message. Similarly, most campaign routines were not dictated by information from strategic polls. Party dynamics and the general popular effervescence during the transition to democracy deeply influenced both the calendar and characteristics of campaign activities.

By the same token, advertising was not uncommon in Argentine electioneering prior to 1983. On the basis of political and personal sympathies, advertising agencies had been collaborating with the political parties since the 1920s. What was new about the Radical campaign was the direct incorporation of a well-known advertiser in the candidate's entourage, and the modernization of designs by using techniques and styles common in consumer advertising. More than advertising per se, the novelty was the active participation of advertiser David Ratto, head of his joint venture with BBD&O in Argentina, and the high visibility and wide repercussions of some slogans, logos, and television spots.

The 1983 Radical campaign is also commonly credited with having fueled the presence of individualistic appeals over partisan elements. The decision to emphasize Alfonsín's name and personal attributes over party symbolism and tradition caused a brouhaha among the old guard of party leaders. However, the stress on individual characteristics was not new in Argentine politics. Personalism has been a constant feature of the country's political culture (Calvert & Calvert, 1989). Networks of clients, structured around local caudillos (leaders), have been historically central to all parties; individual figures unquestionably have dominated national politics. Until the death of Juan Perón in 1974, Peronism was perhaps one of the best worldwide examples of a political party strongly identified with a leader. Neither was personalism new to Radicalism: The century-old party traditionally had magnetic personalities commanding votes and partisan loyalties.

The new element was not personalism, but the use of individual appeals within the overall campaign design. Radical strategists reasoned that hammering Alfonsín's personality and rising popularity and dimming party ideology was key for seducing much needed non-Radical voters. The latter were crucial for Alfonsín's presidential aspirations for two reasons. First, a massive campaign for registering new party members was indispensable to defeat the traditional Radical top brass in the primaries (only party members are allowed to vote in primaries, and Alfonsín had lost, in 1972, against the apparatus commanded by veteran leaders). Second, the party's traditional electoral base had been insufficient for defeating Peronism, so Alfonsín's collaborators concluded it was necessary to "go outside" the party and canvass among voters traditionally wary of Radicalism. The maneuver proved to be highly effective, as Alfonsín won the primaries in a landslide supported by massive numbers of new Radical members, and later made decisive inroads among historical Peronist voters.

Finally, the remarkable influence and presence of television in contemporary Argentine electioneering is also generally seen as a byproduct of the 1983 Radical campaign. Observers and politicians have argued that Alfonsín's campaign "discovered telepolitics," made intensive use of television presentations, and produced modern visual spots (Landi, 1992). Television, however, was not a novelty. Free airtime has been consistently granted by the state to competing political parties, candidates have regularly appeared on political talk shows, and advertisements have been widely broadcast. Nor were Radicals the only party to resort to televisual politics: All parties had state-allocated time and also produced television spots. Finally, Radicals' television ads could hardly be labeled as modern. They displayed a noticeable amateur quality, far from the glossy, professional productions usually associated with modern campaign advertising. The widespread conviction that the Radical campaign introduced modern uses of television thus needs to be somewhat corrected: It was neither pioneering nor fully modern. Instead, some spots—devoid of high-wire tricks or Madison Avenue luster—had a great impact, as they resonated with public demands for democracy, freedom, and peace.

THE MODERNIZATION OF ARGENTINE CAMPAIGNING

Campaign practices changed in important ways after 1983. Party elites slowly accepted and fully incorporated new technologies and redesigned traditional stumping practices (Muraro, 1992). The widespread conviction that modern campaign technologies had been decisive in Alfonsín's victory certainly fueled the expansion of modern campaign practices.[2] Yet, as I will discuss later, this expansion is rooted in the breakdown of partisan ideologies and identities and rising electoral volatility. The most important changes can be detected in the measurement of public opinion, the characteristics of campaign street activities, the role of television, the strategic uses of individual over partisan appeals, and the presence of professional campaign consultants. In what follows, I shall review these changes in order to ultimately offer an explanation for the recent modernization of Argentine campaigning.

Testing Public Opinion

In Argentina, the typical yardsticks of public opinion have been the size of attendance at rallies, the presence of candidates and parties in the media and in urban spaces, and the informal calculations made by party bosses on "how things were looking" in their districts. Although extensively used in consumer-marketing research for many decades, opinion surveys were hardly used in campaigning. They were considered both inappropriate and unnecessary. Indeed, electoral results were believed to be predetermined, given Peronism's unchallenged electoral majority for forty years. Instead, taking the pulse of public opinion meant observing the capacity of parties and politicians to draw voters to public meetings, to be in newspaper headlines, and to deliver votes. These were understood as reliable measurements of the public pulse, unmistakable signs of trends in the public mood.

This perception has significantly changed in recent years, however. Nowadays, politicians favor polls as more reliable than the traditional, "impressionistic" methods (Mora y Araujo, 1991). Within contemporary Argentine political culture, polls have lately gained legitimate status as "scientific" instruments for fathoming the public mind. Distrusted and scarcely used until the 1983 election, polls have now become ubiquitous during campaign months. Fueled by candidates' obsession with survey results (especially horse-race numbers), the polling industry bloomed. More than thirty polling firms have opened in a decade, although they all do not enjoy the same level of esteem and respect among political circles. Several polling firms have meticulously combed voting districts and entire provinces that had never before polled. Some major newspapers have even started their own in-house surveys, and have included polls as staple information during the campaign season.

A changing perception of the uses and significance of polling results was particularly remarkable among Peronist ranks. Within Peronist culture, the power of mobilization and public display was still considered to provide an infallible x-ray of political opinions in 1983. Polls were dismissed as "foreign" and, as the 1983 presidential candidate observed, inappropriate for "a culture like ours" (Blanck, 1990). Such views changed most notably once the *Renovación*, a faction that opposed the leadership of traditional bosses and union leaders, conquered party structures in 1985. According to most observers, the educational background of the *Renovadores* (politicians who were mostly college trained in economics, literature, journalism, communications, psychology, and advertising) was crucial for the acceptance of polling and other modern campaign technologies.

Gradually, polls achieved a remarkable influence. Not only did track polling became established as a common practice, but—unthinkable until a few years before—information from polls directly influenced campaign messages and stump speeches. Furthermore, poll results were commanding references in the nomination of candidates during the 1991 party primaries. In some cases, party leaders favored candidates who were popular in opinion polls. In others, party chiefs resorted to polls to test the possibility of launching the candidacies of highly popular individuals (entertainers, athletes, journalists, and intellectuals) without previous political experience. With the rising public distrust of politicians, parties offered popular figures, with high approval ratings in opinion polls, the chance to start a political career. The successful Peronist nominations as gubernatorial candidates of Ramón Ortega, a 1960s musical idol, and Carlos Reutemann, a former international car racer, are the clearest, although by no means the only, examples of this phenomenon.

Street Activities

Historically, Argentine campaigning could almost be equated with the staging of activities in urban public spaces. These were not just occasions when candidates "went down to the people" but, above all, were central moments within party life. By mobilizing members in the party ranks to blanket districts with advertising and to organize public meetings, local bosses showed their political muscle to, and support for, national party leaders. For presidential candidates, appearances at party rallies functioned as mechanisms for weaving alliances with regional caudillos, testing party waters, blessing local candidacies, galvanizing party energies, receiving media attention, and getting out the vote. Public squares offered stages for massive congregations, streets were sites for crowded parades, and walls provided unlimited room for touting candidacies and campaign slogans. Rallies at central plazas and other public symbolic centers were sacred moments for constructing and displaying the party faith, mandatory activities for concluding a day on the campaign trail, and final ceremonies for local and national campaigns.

Much has changed in this regard. The overall structure of stumping in public spaces has suffered important transformations. The fact that party rallies could put off nonpartisan voters, or that disturbances among party factions could generate bad publicity and scare away votes, led campaign intelligentsia to reconsider the organization and design of public meetings. Increasingly aware of the potential impact of rallies on media audiences, and aiming to attract attendants beyond party militants, organizers grew concerned with the overall presentation of rallies. Consequently, they modernized public meetings by including fireworks, popular musical attractions, new audio, visual, and illumination systems, and better facilities for journalists covering the event. But, after this initial *aggiornamiento*, the basic structure of campaign rallies experienced major transformations. As voters became less willing to flock to central plazas for exalting party ideology and listening to endless stump speeches, campaign planners substantially modified the overall design of public meetings. With voters more apathetic to partisan causes and less attached to partisan identities, they reasoned, rallies needed not just facelifts, but major surgery.

The response to a changing political culture was the organization of precinct walks and, above all, *caravanas*. The latter are day-long motorcades, crisscrossing boulevards and neighborhoods showcasing national and local candidates waving to onlookers from the top of trucks and buses. Differences between these events and traditional rallies are notable. *Caravanas* do not invite people to congregate in symbolically laden central squares, but take place in everyday sites and demand minimal involvement from bystanders. They do not attract exclusively die-hard, mostly male, party members, but appeal also to families, who peek at candidates from their houses or stand along the parade route. Candidates do not harangue the masses, but wave, receive gifts, and only briefly address onlookers. The disenchantment of voters with traditional partisan credos and the growing distrust of parties and politicians has prompted campaign strategists to replace the giant campaign rally, the former sacred tradition of Argentine electioneering, with *caravanas*. Attuned to these times in which the importance of ideology has declined greatly, election rallies have been moved from symbolic sites where epic events in Argentine history had taken place to politically secular places. Itinerant rallies are a symptom of the desacralization of politics; the migration of rallies from central squares to the barrios can be considered an allegorical representation of the migration of Argentine politics from sacred to secular politics.

Adjusting campaign activities to new political moods can also be detected in the organization of street advertising. The carpeting of city walls with graffiti and affiches or campaign posters has been traditional in Argentine campaigning. It has been a mechanism for displaying party alliances, making public the presence of a party or candidate, and indicating the symbolic capturing of an electoral district. Though the goals remain similar, this conventional feature of Argentine campaigning displays new characteristics. Compared to previous campaigns in Argentine history, the "conditions of production" for painting slogans and plastering posters on city walls in recent elections are now significantly different. Once a rite of passage for party militants, street advertising is done today by hired teams working for campaign headquarters. Whereas it formerly was the disorganized product of mostly underground activities, now it is the work of "experts," toiling in broad daylight and following the instructions of campaign officials and advertising agents. Thus, more sophisticated designs and standardized messages have replaced austere layouts and inconsistent slogans. Street advertising, the former mechanism for unofficial political expressions to acquire public visibility, has been refashioned to serve the strategic goals of established candidates.

Political Screens

Television has become a staple of electoral campaigning. Overcoming earlier distrust and ignorance about the medium, candidates and parties have overwhelmingly resorted to television to go public. Recent campaigns have been planned, in the words of party strategists, as "fundamentally electronic," to reach voters through "their roofs rather than ringing their doorbell" (Hugo Haime, personal communication, July 19, 1990).

For pitching their message and image, Argentine politicians enjoy the benefits of a television system which mixes elements from the United States and traditional European models of broadcasting. Argentine television is ruled by commercial imperatives, but it has been continuously subjected to the action and influence of governments and political parties. Whether television was government or privately owned, parties had ample access to television screens. As television is essentially a private enterprise, political advertisements can be placed just like any other commercial. But unlike U.S. electioneering, there are no restrictions on the time length of political commercials in Argentina. Nor is there a legal ceiling for expenditures in television advertising: The size of campaign war chests, nourished by state finances and, primarily, by private funds, sets the only limit for buying broadcasting time.[3]

In addition, the state grants free prime-time segments on both government-owned and private stations to all competing parties during the weeks immediately preceding election day. Recently, the criteria for allocating broadcasting time have changed. Whereas formerly it was equally distributed among all forces running for the presidency, the state now allocates television airtime similar to the manner in which it distributes funds for financing party campaign activities; that is, proportionately based on performance in the most recent election. For parties, then, more votes bring a higher proportion of television airtime and campaign finances as well. These free segments commonly feature candidates talking straight to the camera and a barrage of commercials, the same ones broadcast in paid time.

Television ads and state-allocated time, however, have not been enough to satiate politicians' craving for television exposure. In addition to prime-time political talk shows, which commonly mushroom during campaign season, newscasts have featured politicians as "special commentators." However, the low ratings of the unimaginatively produced free segments, the limited audience of political talk shows (an audience mainly of politicized viewers who are less likely than other citizens to switch their votes), the high costs of paid commercials, and the belief that voters are tired of traditional political talking heads have driven campaign politics into uncharted television territory. Obsessed that their candidates might have a low level of public recognition in opinion polls, campaign headquarters have pursued almost all television genres for reaching large audiences. Hoping to shake the image of being wooden and removed from people's everyday interests, candidates have sought to be in a series of variety shows. They have starred in sitcoms as "surprise guests," have enthusiastically participated in game shows, have exchanged jokes with music-hall hosts, have danced and sung on "omnibus" shows (day-long programming during weekends), and have blushed at questions from a late-night show hostess about their sexual lives. Amid growing public distrust of officeholders, fueled by accusations of both corruption and inefficiency, entertainment shows have provided unmatched opportunities for candidates to shed their image as traditional politicians and wrap themselves in mundane, guy-next-door clothing.

Within this general pattern, it is important to recognize that the use of television has varied according to the specific situations and skills of individual candidates. As Governor Eduardo Angeloz was mostly unknown outside the province of Córdoba in 1988, his campaign advisors mainly emphasized television appearances for increasing his name recognition as the 1989 Radical presidential candidate. The result was an intense television blitz, especially through spots and the presence of the candidate in political talk shows, a terrain Angeloz felt most comfortable with. Peronist campaign planners also approached television as a central mechanism for electioneering, although they faced a different problem. Governor Carlos Menem was already a highly popular figure, but he did not perform well discussing hard politics and was prone to contradictions when interviewed in front of television cameras. The solution was an operation of "damage control," by staging sporadic tours in the city of Buenos Aires, where nationally distributed newscasts and political interview shows are produced. Campaign engineers strategized that by limiting the opportunities for television reporters (and the press in general) to have access to the candidate, television would only stress what Menem did best. Thus, the emphasis was put upon spots showing images of the candidate on the campaign trail, with little concrete references to future government plans, and on the presence of Menem on the television turf where he excelled: entertainment shows. Almost a "television personality," according to many analysts, now-President Menem has a remarkable ability, rarely found among traditional politicians, for dealing with the codes and timing of variety shows. The failed attempt to organize a televised debate between the two main presidential candidates moderated by a political talk-show host reflected how differently Peronism and Radicalism used television during the 1989 campaign. After constantly but unsuccessfully trying to corner his opponent on specific policy issues, Angeloz challenged Menem to meet in an arena he knew better: the traditional format of a television debate for discussing plans for revamping the country's ailing economy. Peronist aides discouraged Menem from appearing, not only because polls showed him to have a substantial advantage over Angeloz, but also because, given his shortcomings when discussing issues, he seemed to have little chance of winning a televised debate.

Beyond the particular preferences for television genres, recent elections have revealed that, more than just having gained a foothold in Argentine electioneering, television has provided ideal stages for addressing voters in times of breaking partisan ideologies and growing apathy about electoral activities. In this context, the nonpartisan character of entertainment shows offers a fitting backdrop for candidates to show their human side; to send signals to voters that they are not professional politicians, but regular folks with political aspirations (Sarlo, 1993).

Individual over Party Appeals

Personal loyalties, as much as ideological differences, have usually divided political parties and dominated Argentine politics. In a presidentialist system and a highly personalistic political culture, individual politicians have exercised a powerful and unique influence. However, ideological principles have historically been the basis for the organization and division of Argentine political parties, and have been at the forefront of electioneering. To consider the most obvious example, much of twentieth-century Argentine political history cannot be understood without fully comprehending the authority and legacy of Gen. Juan Perón. As no one else in Argentine history, Perón did (and still does) generate profound sympathies and animosities. His figure and aura definitely branded Peronism as the quintessential personalistic party. However, as much as Perón's charisma, a populist and ideologically eclectic platform also branded the Peronist party. These two components, individual and partisan appeals, were inextricably linked.

In contrast to other Latin American cases, such as Brazil or Colombia, Argentine parties have not been structured solely as national electoral structures, organized through an elaborate network of clientelistic relations devoid of programmatic commitments. Perhaps not as strongly ideological as their classic Chilean or Uruguayan counterparts, the organizational bases of Argentine parties have been rooted in different political *Weltanschauungen*. For example, the hemorrhaging that the Radical party suffered for many decades was mainly the consequence of irreconcilable ideological differences. The latter were also at the center of the violent disputes that rocked Peronism and Argentine society during the 1960s and 1970s. Behind common allegiance to Perón's leadership, opposing leftist and rightist Peronist factions furiously battled each other. Amid highly charged ideological disputes and strong personalities, Argentine election campaigns have historically both reflected different platforms and emphasized the personal attributes of candidates.

This situation has changed somewhat in recent years, as the personal qualities of candidates have tended to overshadow party doctrine. This certainly applies to general elections, although primaries continue to be displays of partisan folklore. As only party members are allowed to vote and internal structures are crucial for canvassing and mobilizing voters on election day, primary campaigns continue to be celebrations of the partisan faith. In contrast, pushing partisan buttons is no longer typical in general elections, as the numbers of independent voters have grown significantly and skepticism about parties and politicians runs high (Catterberg, 1989). Consequently, candidates are obliged to address common demands and focus on their individual qualifications for office.

After winning the party nomination, candidates have to disentangle themselves from their parties in order to claim to be "of all the people" (and not just Peronists or Radicals). The difference between voting publics in primary and national campaigns makes major changes indispensable. Candidates have to downplay their origin after soliciting party support. Although their political trajectories are anchored in party life, and their nominations result from intensive negotiations inside the party, candidates have to move party themes to the background and bring "universal" concerns to the forefront of the national campaign.

As discussed previously, the 1983 national Alfonsín campaign notably and successfully stressed individual over partisan appeals. Campaign strategists clearly intended to rally voters behind Alfonsín by emphasizing the candidate's presence and platform and underplaying party symbolism. Not to be neglected, ideological concerns were important to the campaign message; namely, the reestablishment and respect of civic liberties. Though inspired by Radicalism's long-time concern with democratic rights, Alfonsín's agenda and rhetoric were only tenuously related to the party tradition. Instead, the most prominent themes of the campaign ("life," "hope," "democracy") had his unmistakable signature: All these issues were conflated with Alfonsín, not the Radical party.

The Peronist campaign, in contrast, waved partisan banners, namely "the return of Peronism," together with social and anti-imperialistic themes of the traditional Peronist gospel. The fact that Italo Luder was selected to lead the presidential ticket only forty days before the election date best indicates the belief that candidate's qualities were an accessory to the campaign. Peronist ranks reasoned that dusting off the party liturgy and Perón's image would be enough to win the elections. Battling each other to inherit the late leader's mantle, party factions assumed that the election was already decided: Peronism would hold its historical majority. Believing that carrying the Peronist flag was enough for any candidate to be elected president, individual attributes were not thought to be decisive. Needless to say, the electoral loss jolted the extremely optimistic and self-confident Peronists.

Conversely, the emphasis upon individual appeals was remarkable during the 1989 general election campaign. After winning an intense primary that was saturated by party traditions and symbolism, the Menem campaign headquarters downplayed partisan themes and accentuated individual appeals for the general election campaign. The campaign presented Menem as an alternative to party politics. The subtext of the campaign was that Menem was a politician who first defeated the established Peronist apparatus and, free from partisan maneuvers, then appealed to the voters to take him to the presidential office. While the figure of Menem as a political outsider, removed from party bickering and politics as usual, was hammered, the Peronist gospel was replaced by ambiguous promises of "productive revolution" and "massive wage increases."

Emphasis on the candidate over the party was even more blatant in the 1989 Angeloz campaign. As Radicalism was widely perceived as responsible for a disastrous economic performance, the Angeloz campaign headquarters virtually eliminated all partisan references and instead heightened the governor's economic record. Angeloz strategists reasoned that there was little to vindicate from the Alfonsín administration. Nor did they resort to unearthing old Radical axioms. Their strategy was quite the opposite: Angeloz ran a campaign with a free-market economic program that directly cut against the party grain. Unlike 1983, demands for civil liberties were no longer central and, instead, economic demands dominated an electorate suffocated by hyperinflation. Trailing Menem by double-digit points, Angeloz made the economic team of the Alfonsín administration the target of his attacks. Angeloz endlessly (and somewhat successfully) tried to detach himself from the government, under the assumption that the Radical label was a dead weight on his candidacy.[4]

Personal Organizations and Political Consulting

The growth of personalized campaigning ran parallel to the rise of autonomous campaign headquarters; that is, cliques of candidate-appointed experts for masterminding activities at the margin of official party structures. No doubt, campaign staffs were not entirely detached from party hierarchies. Though candidates originally tried to deflect party influence, local and regional bosses continuously demanded the opportunity to participate and sway the course of the campaign. Notwithstanding the continuous brawls between party and campaign aides over the control of the campaign, the formation of candidates' "inner circles" for charting stumping activities is a new feature of Argentine electioneering.

Campaign headquarters are commonly staffed by personnel enrolled in the candidate's faction and with experience in different activities. The credentials of campaign aides include both personal relations with the candidate and past party militancy. For most, participation in campaign teams is more an amateur activity than a professional–client relation. In fact, only a few are paid (mostly pollsters), and many view joining campaign headquarters as another way of staying active in party politics. The modern figure of the politically independent, professional consultant with no partisan trajectory is practically unknown. In a small and centralized political market, only a few practitioners had the chance to launch independent consulting careers, as their business fortunes remained unequivocally tied to the political fortunes of individual candidates.

Amid the incorporation of different technologies and the growing scientificization of politics, candidates started looking abroad for ideas and novel campaign techniques. Having developed an interest in campaign techniques and strategies, many candidates attended seminars given by foreign experts and flew to observe in situ campaigns in developed democracies. Together with *Campaign & Elections*, a respected local polling firm has organized highly attended seminars on a vast array of subjects that are new by local standards, such as targeting, tracking, media management, and scheduling. Many innovations (e.g., television debates, direct mail, precinct walks, and motorcades) were inspired by campaign experiences in several countries, such as the United States, Spain, Italy, France, and Germany.

As campaigns are masterminded essentially by a pro-bono workforce, only outside consultants are seen as impartial professionals, as authorities in the subject who are removed from party squabbling and therefore possess the cachet to "say things straightforwardly." Although frequently invited for brief sessions, foreign consultants have been formally incorporated into campaign headquarters only occasionally. Use of these specialists was usually kept secret, mostly to avoid accusations of "foreign powers" influencing national politics.

Amid long-running nationalistic and anti-imperialistic sentiments, this issue has been particularly sensitive regarding the role of U.S. consultants. The debates surrounding the participation of the New York–based Sawyer/ Miller group in the Angeloz campaign illustrate the potential problems of hiring foreign services. In response to television spots representing Menem as dangerous for the stability of Argentine democracy, Peronists accused Radicals of following the recommendations of U.S. experts to stage an aggressive campaign (see Libro Azul y Blanco, 1989). Although U.S. consultants advised hard-hitting ads, negative advertising was not purely imported but expressed the conviction inside the Angeloz campaign headquarters that a possible Menem presidency would endanger the nascent Argentine democracy. Negative ads and themes of the 1988 Bush–Dukakis campaign, observed firsthand by numerous Argentine campaigners, were certainly influential (e.g., Dukakis's "Massachusetts miracle" inspired Angeloz's "Córdoba miracle"). But, more important, the advice of outside experts echoed fears and opinions already present in the campaign staff (as well as, according to poll surveys, in a large portion of the Argentine middle class) about a future Menem administration.

FALLEN IDOLS

This overview shows that Argentine campaigning has incorporated practices commonly labeled as typical of American electioneering. The surveying of public opinion, continuous televised presences, display of glossy advertising, emphasis on personalized appeals, formation of candidate-based campaign organizations, and rise of political consulting all are novel, but now common, practices. Unlike European or Australian elections, the establishment of U.S.-like political or media institutions in Argentina does not account for this phenomenon (see Gurevitch & Blumler, 1990; Kaase, 1992; Kaid, Gerstlé, & Sanders, 1991; O'Neil & Mills, 1986). No institutional changes, which might have encouraged the adoption of U.S. campaign features, have occurred in the last decade. As in previous elections, presidentialism remains unchallenged, primaries continue to be party affairs, and the broadcasting system still follows commercial criteria. Nor has the arrival of U.S. campaign professionals been responsible for the remodeling of Argentine electioneering. The arrival of U.S. consultants was not the cause, but the consequence of modernization. Foreign campaign handlers were not uninvited merchants and *conquistadores* colonizing the world, unloading and imposing new ideas and practices onto the natives. Rather, local elites frequently asked foreign consultants for their expertise and modern weaponry after having discovered *terra incognita*: new voters, new media, and new demands.

The reasons for the refashioning of campaign routines are found in a kind of Weberian disenchantment within Argentine politics. Social justice and civic liberties, the two partisan confessions which formerly mobilized millions and nurtured old-style electioneering, have lost much of their allure among voters. Thus, Peronism and Radicalism, which together usually gathered over 70 percent of the national vote, have slowly dropped the traditional partisan cants from their electoral promises. Those ideologies have certainly not been swept away from the Argentine political landscape. However, they survive in cultural pockets situated at the margins of the political spectrum. Currently, small leftist and rightist parties are the most vociferous carriers of the flags of social and democratic rights, historically wielded by Peronism and Radicalism, respectively.[5]

Powerful narratives that governed Argentine politics for decades have succumbed to less grandiose and more pragmatic moods. Unlike previous times, *causes célèbres* such as nationalism, anti-imperialism, social equality, or democracy no longer mobilize huge masses of voters. The 1983 election campaign, with its monumental scenes of crowded rallies and feverish canvassing, was the coda of old-style campaigning. It was the last epic crusade: The military infidels had to be thrown out of the holy site and the democratic faith had to be restored. The quest for democracy awakened popular spirits, unified partisan differences, and drew legions of foot soldiers to the campaign trenches.

But the aura of ideological faiths has disappeared and ancient idols have fallen. Argentine political culture has been secularized. Pragmatism has diluted the magic of discourses that impregnated party life and political debates. The historical core of Argentine partisan faiths was made not out of lowly pledges, but sublime aspirations: national sovereignty, liberty, and social justice. But these hopes are shuddering amid parties searching for identities and raisons d'être.[6] These days, only single-issue movements or specific events can draw people, though in significantly more modest numbers, out into the public sphere.

In recent elections, voters have demanded less celestial and more terrestrial goods: economic stability and, to a lesser extent, public honesty, better education, and safer cities. Generally, most voters do not massively flock to the streets to demand anti-inflationary measures or more ethical governments. Partisan campaign pilgrimages to central plazas and political effervescence require spellbinding utopias, not just secular public demands.

The vanishing of the charm and romanticism of old rallying cries looms behind the transformations in electioneering. Formerly strong identities have become thinner, and ideological convictions that dominated policymakers have receded in favor of pragmatic solutions. This cultural transformation has undermined the bases upon which the old campaigning order was grounded. As Western secularization brought about the modern world of rationalized economic activities and political administration, so the secularization of Argentine political life ushered in a new era of modern campaigning.

Political parties lost much of the mobilization capacity to engineer old-style campaign activities as traditional partisan appeals became less captivating. Candidates could no longer assume that historical causes were enough to win elections; voters offered only momentary support, not eternal loyalty. Facing an electorate less loyal to partisan identities and less willing to consecrate partisan folklore, parties and candidates had to restructure the design of campaign activities. Campaign headquarters had to resort to polls for reading a fickle public mind; to television studios and advertising for bridging the gap between party structures and voters; to choreographed outdoor activities for drawing media attention and spectators; to foreign missionaries for "crash courses" on modern campaign strategies and technologies; and to popular individuals, outside party limits, for counteracting the falling legitimacy of party-bred politicians and party ideologies.

If the consummation of Weberian rationalization has been the Habermasian scientificization of politics, then the disenchantment of Argentine politics has been crowned in the rise of campaign technocrats. Campaign rationality and scientificism, that is, the separation of tasks and the emergence of specialists, have lately gained ground in Argentine politics. The modern division of labor in Argentine campaigns is best incarnated in the creation of separate committees for plotting and monitoring campaign activities. In turn, campaign headquarters have been staffed with an army of local and foreign specialists on polling, political marketing, image making, staging public spectacles, and media relations. Moreover, Argentine campaign intelligentsia have successfully marketed their skills in recent elections in other Latin American democracies and in Eastern Europe.

THE "AMERICAN" FLAVOR

Argentina offers an interesting case for analyzing the Americanization of election campaigning. The causes for the latter are usually attributed to two processes. The first refers to the direct influence of U.S. institutions and practices on campaigning in other countries. Sharing common conceptual frameworks with the vast literature on cultural–media imperialism, this line of interpretation suggests that modern campaign routines become Americanized as a result of local campaigners having been exposed to (or manipulated by) U.S. ideas, and national institutions having been shaped by the pressures of U.S. interests. From this perspective, the homogenization of worldwide electioneering practices under the U.S. model is a latent possibility. Three recent developments may give support to this idea: Commercial canons have lately gained currency in European broadcasting; diplomatic envoys have championed U.S. party structures and constitutions in new democracies; and U.S. campaign wizards have extensively marketed their skills to the recent wave of democratization in various continents. From this rendition of cultural imperialism, the export and adoption of U.S.-style campaigning can be analyzed as a process that is parallel to the dissemination of commonly labeled archetypical "American values" (e.g., consumerism, individualism) and fashions in other cultures.

In contrast, a second position stresses internal rather than external factors as responsible for the rise of modern campaign styles (see Gundle, 1992). Different domestic processes have been responsible for the adoption of campaign routines and tactics pioneered in the United States. Americanization, then, is not the outgrowth of invading U.S. practices; instead, internal developments have promoted the development of campaign features commonly attributed to U.S. electioneering, such as candidate-centered organizations, personalistic rhetoric and image appeals, the centrality of the mass media at the expense of traditional forms of political communication, and the adoption of new campaign technologies (e.g., polls, commercial advertising techniques, direct mail).

In this case, U.S. campaign practices do not exert direct influence, but rather provide clues for candidates and campaign headquarters facing comparable situations, such as parties with weak structures for communication or growing electoral volatility. Americanization of electoral campaigning results from the emergence of American-like political and communication developments in other countries, and not from the injection of U.S. styles. Some characteristics formerly attributed to American exceptionalism are not unique anymore, but are present in other political contexts.

The Argentine case suggests that the Americanization of campaigning cannot be understood simply à la theories of cultural imperialism; that is, as the result of the establishment of American political and media institutions and the injection of U.S.-style stumping techniques. Neither institutional factors nor the introduction of modern techniques account for the use of American styles in Argentina. For decades, a strong presidentialist system and the high penetration of commercially operated television were not the cradle for the Americanization of electioneering. In the country's intermittent campaign history, previous attempts to inculcate Madison Avenue advertising formats, Beltway-tested strategic recipes, and polling have failed. It was only in the mid-1980s that these instruments were welcomed and refashioned campaigning. It is then necessary to address the "conditions of reception"; that is, domestic developments that have lately encouraged the incorporation of campaign practices previously used in the United States.

Prior to the 1980s, modern techniques could not make inroads in electioneering. Politicians firmly believed in the whole array of traditional routines for garnering votes. History offered enough evidence for sticking to well-rehearsed practices. Peronism, which had won every free election between 1946 and 1975, was the epitome of old-fashioned campaigning. Its capacity for mobilizing voters was both envied and abhorred by adversaries. In Argentine political culture, democratic power was equal to the capability of swamping public spaces with party followers. Empty plazas and silent streets meant the opposite: the overthrow of an electoral majority by a military regime.

Peronists were firmly convinced by the power of mass mobilization, and relegated electronic media to a secondary role. The statement often attributed to Perón, "with all the media in our hands we were thrown out [of government] in 1955, and with all the media against us we came back in 1973," best represents the former Peronist belief that mass media were thought to be an accessory, not central, for sweeping into power. Similarly, impressionistic observations were considered to be as accurate as information polls for testing political waters. Ward bosses and national candidates trusted their "gut-rationality" (Popkin, 1991); that is, observations shaped by firsthand and extensive knowledge of their electoral districts. Polls were considered to be faulty. In a country where authoritarian regimes have intensely patrolled and repressed civil society, politicians doubted that voters would honestly confess their political preferences to polling agents showing up on their doorstep.

Though much has changed in this regard as Argentine campaigns have been remodeled in the last decade, it would be mistaken to assume that the coming of modern practices has put old-style campaigning in history's dustbin. Traditional and modern electioneering need to be viewed as abstract typologies, not concrete entities. Similar to the classic sociological concepts of traditional and modern societies, these categories are "ideal types." Campaign routines are not pure incarnations of one model, nor is there a smooth passage from traditional to modern practices. In this sense, it is necessary to understand the modernization of electioneering while bearing two points in mind. First, national politics are not homogeneous, but encompass pockets of different traditions. Thus, modern campaign technologies arguably find better soil in regions where institutions and political cultures provide a more fertile terrain for modernization. In the Argentine case, electioneering outside big urban centers (the so-called "Argentina Profunda") still follows traditional practices, especially in local elections. In regions where local media production is scarcely developed, stations are firmly controlled by governing powers, party politics are basically organized around caudillo apparatuses, and traditional methods are still pivotal. In these contexts, "pumping the flesh" routines, mobilizing voting networks, and corralling voters on election day, rather than patiently addressing voters through media efforts, are still rules of thumb for winning at the ballot boxes.

Second, the remaking of local political practices does not operate by simple replacement or imposition of foreign formulas, but, rather, by selection and adaptation. In a changing political scenario, Argentine campaigners have lately borrowed tactics and technologies that best fit their needs and resonate with local campaign traditions. Not only U.S. campaigning, but also European experiences and campaign intelligentsia have been both a benchmark and source of inspiration for renovating stumping practices. Yet local strategists have remained loyal to old practices, given the particular arrangements of the Argentine political and communication geography. The centrality of party dynamics for winning the nomination and the persistence of clientelistic networks in many regions, together with impartial management of local television stations and the lack of national television networks, have pushed campaigners to follow traditional campaign routines (Waisbord, 1994). Thus, the tapestry of contemporary Argentine campaigning shows patches of old and new styles: 1920s-like whistle-stop tours and television appearances, barbe-cue fairs and precinct walks, interminable speeches to party militants, and sound-bite television commentaries.

CONCLUSION

Amid the loosening of traditional political confessionals, the modernization of Argentine campaigning has recently taken place. Partisan identities have become weaker, electoral volatility has grown, and parties have entered a still unsolved identity crisis. In this scenario, modern campaign technologies have provided candidates invaluable help for crossing the growing distance between parties and voters.

The Argentine case suggests that the global Americanization of campaign activities runs parallel not only to the spread of institutional conditions, such as commercially run media or U.S.-like political systems, but also to cultural changes: the ideological disenchantment of party politics. That is, the waning of the "electorate of belonging" (Panebianco, 1988) coupled with the abandon-ment of classic partisan precepts undermines the traditional order upon which old-style electioneering was based. The crumbling of ideological partisan frameworks that characterized both old and new democracies for much of the twentieth century acts as a major, though certainly not the only, catalyst for the ongoing worldwide process of Americanization of electoral campaigning.

NOTES

1. "Organized community" (*comunidad organizada*) and "socialist fatherland" (*patria socialista*) were respectively the rallying cries of the right and left wings of Peronism during the political violence of the late 1960s and 1970s.

2. How much the use of new technologies actually contributed to Alfonsín's vic-tory has been a matter of debate. Whereas their opponents claimed that the use of modern techniques was decisive, Radicals argued that the message, rather than the packaging, was responsible for the triumph.

3. Article 46 of Law 23298 establishes that the state provides funds for financing campaigns to political parties that gather at least 3 percent of the total vote.

4. In turn, both criticisms and attempts to separate Angeloz from the party fueled existing animosities between his campaign headquarters and the bulk of the Radical party, still dominated by pro-Alfonsín leaders.

5. The Argentine party system can be defined as an imperfect two-party system, as Perónism and Radicalism gather 70 percent of the vote, while over a dozen small political parties share the rest.

6. What Radicalism and Peronism stand for is much less clear today than ten years ago. Both have resorted to comparable diagnoses and solutions for reorganizing the country's economy and to non-party-affiliated technocrats for staffing their adminis-trations.

REFERENCES

Blanck, J. (1990, September 9). Los políticos y las encuestas: creer o no creer es la cuestión [Politicians and pollsters: To believe or not to believe, that is the ques-tion]. *Clarín*, p. 10.

Borrini, A. (1984). *Como se hace un presidente* [How to make a president]. Buenos Aires: El Cronista Comercial.

Calvert, S., & Calvert, P. (1989). *Argentina: Political culture and instability.* Pittsburgh: University of Pittsburgh Press.

Catterberg, E. (1989). *Los Argentinos frente a la política* [Argentines facing politics]. Buenos Aires: Grupo Editorial Planeta.

Ginsberg, B. (1986). *The captive public: How state power promotes mass opinion.* New York: Basic Books.

Gundle, S. (1992). Italy. In D. Butler & A. Ranney (Eds.), *Electioneering: A comparative study of continuity and change* (pp. 173–201). Oxford: Clarendon Press.

Gurevitch, M., & Blumler, J. G. (1990). Comparative research: The extending frontier. In D. L. Swanson & D. Nimmo (Eds.), *New directions in political communication* (pp. 305–325). Newbury Park, Calif.: Sage.

Jensen, R. (1971). *The winning of the midwest: Social and political conflict, 1888–1896.* Chicago: University of Chicago Press.

Kaase, M. (1992). Germany. In D. Butler & A. Ranney (Eds.), *Electioneering: A comparative study of continuity and change* (pp. 278–286). Oxford: Clarendon Press.

Kaid, L. L., Gerstlé, J., & Sanders, K. R. (Eds.). (1991). *Mediated politics in two cultures.* New York: Praeger.

Landi, O. (1992). *Devórame otra vez: Que hizo la televisión con la gente, que hace la gente con la televisión* [Devouring each other: What television does to the public, what the public does to television]. Buenos Aires: Grupo Editorial Planeta.

Libro Azul y Blanco. (1989). *2000 días de mentira Radical* [2,000 days of Radical lies]. Buenos Aires: Línea Argentina.

Mora y Araujo, M. (1991). *Ensayo y error* [Trial and error]. Buenos Aires: Grupo Editorial Planeta.

Muraro, H. (1992). *Poder y comunicación* [Power and communication]. Buenos Aires: Letra Buena.

O'Neil, H., & Mills, S. (1986). Political advertising in Australia: A dynamic force meets a resilient object. In L. L. Kaid, D. Nimmo, & K. R. Sanders (Eds.), *New perspectives on political advertising* (pp. 314–337). Carbondale: Southern Illinois University Press.

Panebianco, A. (1988). *Political parties: Organization and power.* Cambridge: Cambridge University Press.

Política en la Matanza: Como en tiempos de los conserva [The politics of shoot-outs: Like old times]. (1993, September 18). *Página 12*, p. 3.

Popkin, S. (1991). *The reasoning voter: Communication and persuasion in presidential campaigns.* Chicago: University of Chicago Press.

Sarlo, B. (1993, November 2). Zapatero, a tus zapatos [Stick to your own business]. *Clarín*, p. 17.

Waisbord, S. (1994). New (air)waves: Television and election campaigns in contemporary Argentina. *Journal of Communication, 44*(2), 123–135.

Chapter Twelve

Politics, Media, and Modern Democracy: The Case of Venezuela

José Antonio Mayobre

For the past thirty-five years or so, Venezuela has stood out in Latin America as a model of formal democratic processes. Since 1958, the country has held universal, free, and democratic elections with, on four occasions now, the opposition winning and peacefully assuming the government without any major upheavals.

With all its faults, readily recognized even by its most ardent defenders, it seemed, until recently, that Venezuelan democracy was here to stay as a permanent fact of life. The era of military dictatorships and violent takeovers of government appeared to belong to a relatively distant past that would never return.

By and large, freedom of the press and of opinion have been respected and defended, even by the authorities. Their violation, like the lamentably frequent violations of human rights, are more a product of other elements of national history and culture than of any antidemocratic attitudes on the part of the political establishment.

But in 1989—to national shock and surprise—violent and massive rioting erupted all over the country. While it was rapidly (if bloodily) controlled, the extent and anger of the demonstrations, as well as the brutality used in their suppression, shook Venezuelan society to the core. Three years later, amidst a welter of charges of corruption and criminal behavior against all sorts of political leaders including the President, the military attempted two coups d'état, one in February and the other in November. Both attempts failed, simply because of the incompetence of the plotters, not because of any support for democracy from the majority of the population.

During the course of 1993, Venezuelans also saw the elected constitutional President, Carlos Andrés Pérez, accused of corruption. After a strict application of the prescribed legal procedures, Pérez was impeached and replaced

by a member of the Senate, Ramón J. Velásquez, in what was described as a
bloodless and "legalistic" or "dry" coup.

To some—perhaps most—Venezuelans, this Presidential impeachment was
the final demonstration of the strength and vitality of the national democratic processes and institutions. Others saw the impeachment as an aberra-
tion in the system through which, by legalistic means involving an overly
creative interpretation of the law in a highly charged political context, a President who had been elected by a large majority only a few years before could
be removed from office simply because he had attempted to implement a
tough and undoubtedly painful economic policy that he and his advisors
deemed the only possible cure for the nation's difficulties. The latter group
claimed, in other words, that a coup by any other name or means is still a
coup, and that the removal of Pérez from the Presidency, although perhaps
legal and constitutional in a very generous interpretation, meant the end of
democracy and respect for the will of the people.

Whatever the merits of the arguments presented by the defenders of the
deposed President, it was evident that his lack of popularity at the time of
his removal was comparable to the magnitude of his popular approval when
he was elected, and that his continuing in office could only be increasingly dis-
ruptive to the political, economic, and even the everyday life of the country.

But the problem was not just the personality of President Carlos Andrés
Pérez, his honesty, or that of his entourage. Venezuelan democracy seemed
to many to be crumbling after three and a half decades of unparalleled and
supposedly exemplary development. It seemed at least paradoxical, but perhaps typical of the country's contrariness, that democracy would begin to disappear just when it was beginning to reappear in the rest of the continent,
where the successful Venezuelan example was constantly cited.

How did the country get from there—glorious 1958—to here, miserable
1993? Some blame the politicians, others blame the media, and still others
blame both. In a feast of self-hatred, all too many blame national character,
history, Spanish ancestry, oil wealth, "gringos," communists, the World Bank
and the International Monetary Fund, or all of the above. It is not irrelevant
to note that, during the past three decades, the country's economy followed
a steadily rising curve, in most respects, until sometime in the mid-1970s. At
that point, the economy began falling, at first gradually and then precipi-
tously over the past five years.

Perhaps the overriding questions in the country as the 1993 presidential
elections approached were whether democracy would survive and, more
worrisome, whether it was really worth saving. The first answers are in by
now and, although generally favorable to democracy, the evidence is still
inconclusive. Democracy and the democratic process seem to have been
granted a highly conditional reprieve by Venezuelans. Even at this stage, however, what the future holds is still very much up in the air.

THE AMERICANIZATION OF VENEZUELAN POLITICS

Venezuelan political activities over the past thirty-five years have also shown
a pattern of development toward what has been termed "Americanization"
and "modernization." This pattern can be seen in electoral campaign styles

and techniques, party organizational procedures and reforms, the absence of ideology from the candidates' programs and appeals to voters, growing use of the media (especially television), and professionalization of political advisors and techniques. Media, most notably television, have acquired a major and active role in national political processes, without regard to even the few possible legal constraints and limits on their participation.

The Constitution and the democratic institutions of the nation were designed by men and women whose political culture and training were grounded in the romantic notions of nineteenth-century thought. They had little if any understanding, knowledge, or even real interest in the new phenomena of mass media and technology. Accordingly, they were at a major disadvantage when the media became major factors in political life and even came to substitute themselves for the traditional, but now weakened, social and political institutions.

The attitude that all politicians are corrupt, incompetent, or both; that political parties are unrepresentative, useless, and dominated by small cliques of power-hungry shady figures; and that the organizations and institutions of democracy are inoperative or simply inefficient may become predominant when the media present themselves as the only legitimate sources of information and defense of the citizen. In turn, in such an environment, it is the media which decide what public figures or citizen's organizations are legitimate and useful to the public purpose. Individuals and groups that desire to be legitimated by the media will do anything but confront or criticize the media, for doing so risks of being demolished in the arena of public opinion. Yet, despite what one might expect, given the rise of media power in the political arena, recent studies show that the self-esteem of Venezuelan journalists tends to be very low and that the public has a very low opinion of journalists while giving credibility to the abstract entity of the media.

Before going deeper into this subject, it is helpful to first examine some important aspects of Venezuela's political background. Roughly speaking, the relatively short history of Venezuela's modern democracy can be divided into three clearly marked periods. The first period, from 1958 to 1973, saw the establishment of formal democracy in the country and the creation and strengthening of its political institutions, but within a framework provided by a leadership and organizations which responded in many ways to the myths of the past. The second era, from 1973 to 1992, saw a new, younger leadership assume power in the midst of unimaginable wealth. This wealth brought with it some difficulties and negative aspects that the leadership turned out not to be able to handle adequately. The current period began in February 1992. It can perhaps best be described as transitional, although it is impossible to know at present where the transition may be leading.

It is in the second stage, from 1973 onward, that the processes of Americanization and modernization clearly emerged in Venezuela. Their appearance was closely intertwined with other important developments, such as the fact that, at the same time, Venezuela became truly and fabulously oil rich. The overall disruptions that the sudden infusion of massive amounts of money produced in the national economy and the national psyche were so strong and marked that it is difficult to disentangle them from the separate (at least in principle) effects of the modernization process. Rather, these two sources of change are inextricably intertwined in the Venezuelan case. At the same time, Venezuela has long been in the process of Americanizing itself, culturally and politically, although, of course, it has lagged far behind the American model at each point. To understand how the process has evolved and what can be gleaned from it in terms of comparative analysis, it is useful to look back briefly at Venezuela's democratic history.

The Historical Background, 1936–1958

Venezuelan democracy, however loosely the term is understood, has a relatively short history. It can be said to have begun in 1936 with the death of the dictator Juan Vicente Gomez, or in 1942 with the ascension to the Presidency of General Isaias Medina Angarita. Others may prefer to date its starting point with the year 1945, when Medina was toppled by a revolutionary coup which launched the political process that was to culminate, in 1948, in the first free and universal presidential elections. Because the origins of democratic processes rarely spring from a single date or event, it is probably safest to accept the earliest date and to suggest that the democratic process began its difficult gestation with the coming to power in 1936 of General Eleazar Lopez Contreras, the former War Minister of the Gomez dictatorship.

Gomez had ruled the country with an iron fist for twenty-eight years and, during that time, put an end to the various political and regional chieftains that had kept the nation in a virtually constant state of civil war, almost since independence. His regime survived and thrived based on the General's legendary cunning and knowledge of the national mind. The longevity of his rule was assisted as well by, on one hand, his having brought at least a modicum of peace and a very modest level prosperity to Venezuelans and, on the other hand, a mixture of bribery, paternalism, a general acceptance of some controlled corruption, and a fiercely repressive regime. During Gomez's rule, there was no question of democracy, free speech, freedom of the press, or similar principles. The guiding lines of the regime were fixed by its brilliant intellectual mentor, Laureano Vallenilla Lanz, who propagated the thesis of the "necessary policeman."

After the death of Gomez on December 17, 1935,[1] and a short but fierce struggle for the succession, the Presidency—with its absolute power—was taken over by Eleazar Lopez Contreras. Lopez proceeded with a cautious, sustained, and ultimately successful program for national reconciliation, freeing political prisoners and gradually opening up the country to civil freedoms.

Lopez was succeeded, in turn, by his own War Minister, General Isaias Medina Angarita, who was elected according to the laws of the time by the National Congress. Medina proved to be a highly democratic figure. During his government, political parties were legalized and freedom of speech and of the press were almost total.

Nonetheless, his government was overthrown by a military coup and the new government—a civilian–military junta presided over by a thirty-five-year-old professional politician, Romulo Betancourt—proceeded immediately to announce a series of measures which attempted to eradicate corruption as well as modernize and democratize the country. The junta period was marked by the youthful arrogance of its leaders and of the governing party, *Acción Democrática*, which propagated a radical change in the heretofore conservative Venezuelan social structure and was bent on forcing important reforms.

In 1947, the first universal, popular, and free elections were held in Venezuela, resulting in an overwhelming victory for the forces of *Acción Democrática*. Its candidate, the prominent novelist and educator Romulo Gallegos, obtained almost 900,000 votes (74% of the total), against 262,000 for the conservative Christian Democratic candidate, Rafael Caldera, and just over 36,000 votes for Gustavo Machado, the candidate of the Venezuelan Communist Party. In a matter of a few months, however, Gallegos was overthrown by a military coup led by the three most senior officers in the army, Lieutenant Colonels Carlos Delgado Chalbaud, Marcos Pérez Jiménez, and Luis Felipe Llovera Paez.

During the following years, two electoral processes took place. In 1952, the junta, by now composed of a civilian, Germán Suarez Flamerich, along with Llovera Paez and Pérez Jiménez,[2] called elections to form a Constitutional Assembly. The results heavily favored the opposition, so Pérez Jiménez exiled the major opposition leaders, proclaimed himself the winner, disbanded the junta, and installed himself as President.

In 1957, besieged by growing discontent and in need of legitimacy, Pérez Jiménez called for a plebiscite where the only question posed to voters was whether they wanted Pérez to continue as President. Voters were provided with two color-coded cards, one for yes and the other for no. Less than two months after the plebiscite, on January 23, 1958, after surviving an attempted coup on New Year's Day and following desperate attempts to remain in power, Pérez Jiménez was forced to flee into exile. The departed dictator was replaced by a civilian–military junta which promised to hold free elections within the year, freed all political prisoners, allowed the return of exiles, and lifted all restrictions on civil and political freedoms.

Throughout these periods, the media played a relatively small role. Until the early 1940s, newspapers tended to be cautiously conservative, as it was deemed dangerous to express any criticism of the government. However, at various times in Venezuelan history, different political leaders and parties had published highly polemic and, at times, virulent newspapers, which were used openly to further the sponsor's interests and to defame the sponsor's personal and political opponents through insult, humor, or both. Along with other expressions of political freedom, Gomez ended this style of publishing and, for the next twenty-eight years, the press was simply a docile instrument which did not involve itself in politics except to sing the glories of the President.

In 1942, a group of young leftist intellectuals started a new and very modern newspaper, *El Nacional*, which rapidly attracted the intellectual and political elite of the country, both as its readers and as its writers. A humorous magazine published by almost the same group of journalists, *El Morrocoy Azul*, became highly popular with a constantly satirical view of politics.

Radio, which first appeared in the late 1920s, was still very much in its infancy and mostly was a vehicle for music and cultural programs, although it occasionally broadcast official presidential speeches and, during a brief period from 1942 to 1948, speeches of candidates during political rallies. In

1948, however, radio appears to have played an important role, according to some observers, when parliamentary debates were broadcast daily as an experiment in democracy. However, the vicious and controversial nature of the debates in a highly politicized country still unversed in democratic give and take seems to have contributed greatly to the antagonistic atmosphere that eventually helped lead to the coup.

In 1952, General Pérez Jiménez started television in Venezuela, shortly before elections were due to take place. The available evidence indicates that the new medium was used not for political means per se but, rather, to demonstrate how the military dictatorship was bringing modern technologies to the country.

The Democratic Periods, 1959–1993

The toppling of the Pérez Jiménez regime was, in great part, the result of a spontaneous popular movement led basically by previously unknown political leaders, students, and workers. Individual journalists also played an important activist role in toppling the regime. Furthermore, many of the political leaders returning from exile had survived by working as journalists abroad and had managed, thanks to the cooperation of some editors within the country, to even publish as columnists with some frequency inside Venezuela itself, although always under a pen name. So it is not surprising that the 1958 "revolution" was glorified and mythologized, both by the media and by political leaders, as a great revolutionary event. In turn, the myth of the democratic revolution engendered in Venezuelans a proprietary feeling toward democracy. This attitude was made patent throughout the years 1958 to 1960, when various attempts by military factions to overthrow the governments of, first, the junta and, later, Betancourt, were unsuccessful, in great part because of massive, spontaneous street demonstrations of strong support for the Democratically elected governments.

In December 1958, elections were held for both the Presidency and the legislative chambers. The candidates were Romulo Betancourt, leader of the social democratic Democratic Action Party (AD); Rafael Caldera, the undisputed chief of the Social Christian Party (COPEI);[3] and Rear Admiral Wolfgang Larrazabal, former head of the junta which succeeded Pérez Jiménez and a greatly popular and populist figure who was the candidate of a coalition led by the Communist Party of Venezuela (PCV) and the Democratic Republican Union (URD), another social democratic group. Just over 93 percent of the voters cast ballots in the election, which was won by the forceful and talented political leader Betancourt with 49.18 percent of the vote, despite dire threats against him from both left and right. Larrazabal received 34.59 percent of the vote, with 16.19 percent for Caldera.

The new President immediately reached an agreement to form a coalition government with both COPEI and URD, the *Pacto de Punto Fijo*, but pointedly excluded the PCV in order to ensure the survival of democratic processes in Venezuela, which he believed to be the major task before him. In January 1961, the Congress of the Republic approved a new democratic Constitution.

The Betancourt government was rapidly faced with opposition from extreme right-wing elements both within the national civilian structure and within the military, with clear assistance from foreign dictatorial governments, such as that of Rafael Leonidas Trujillo of the Dominican Republic, who went so far as to finance the preparation and execution of an elaborate and nearly successful plot against the President's life. At the same time, the triumph of Fidel Castro in Cuba and his accession to power at almost the same time as Betancourt provided the new President with another and stronger source of violent opposition from the left.

Within Betancourt's own party, an important segment felt that Betancourt was abandoning the progressive principles and goals of a socialist party. These groups, which included almost all registered members of the youth movement of AD, left the party to form the Revolutionary Movement of the Left (MIR) and, stimulated by Castro's recent example and later by his political, economic, and military support, began calling for a popular guerrilla movement to create a revolutionary government similar to that already installed in Cuba.

The next elections proved to be, in many ways, a victory for Betancourt and his party, even if the newly elected President was not in fact the outgoing leader's first choice. In 1963, Raul Leoni, also from AD and the former Chairman of the Senate, was elected President with 32.8 percent of the vote. Rafael Caldera, of COPEI, came in second with 20.18 percent, and Jovito Villalba of URD obtained the third place with 18.87 percent. Turnout at the polls was nearly 92 percent of the voters.

Where Betancourt had a pugnacious and aggressive style of government, Leoni proved to be a quiet, paternal figure more bent on reconciliation than on political infighting. His was a low-key government which devoted itself to consolidating the institutional achievements of the Betancourt era, while developing the economy and attempting to reach peace with the guerrillas or, barring that, to defeat them.

When the next elections came, the AD party found itself seriously divided between two important candidates: Gonzalo Barrios, a respected but somewhat gray figure, and Luis Beltrán Prieto, a forceful and popular leader now on the left of a party that had been obviously moving to the right over the past years. Thus, in 1968, and after three failed previous attempts, Rafael Caldera was elected President with 29.13 percent of the vote against 28.24 percent for Gonzalo Barrios of AD, 22.2 percent for Miguel Angel Burelli of an opposition coalition, and 19.3 percent for Prieto. Turnout was the highest ever, at almost 97 percent.

Caldera led a relatively quiet government, marked mainly by his constant difficulty with an obstructionist, opposition-controlled parliament. Perhaps the major achievement of his government was the culmination of the process of "pacification," whereby the guerrillas were allowed to come down from the hills and reintegrate themselves into civilian life and, later on, into national democratic politics.

The year 1973 brought with it the landslide victory of Carlos Andrés Pérez, the charismatic and dynamic candidate of *Acción Democrática*, and marked the first major and radical change in Venezuelan electoral politics. Pérez obtained 48.7 percent of the vote, against 36.7 percent for the official government and COPEI candidate, Lorenzo Fernandez, with none of the other three supposedly major candidates obtaining more than 5.5 percent percent of the vote. Abstention was at the 3.4 percent level. The 1973 election marked perhaps the first important use and abuse of the media and of mass communication consultants by the candidates, particularly by the winning candidate, as we shall discuss in detail.

The Pérez government was characterized by three major elements. Pérez's accession to power coincided with the beginning of the great oil boom, so prosperity became a fact of life for Venezuelans and the new income allowed the government to spend wildly, if not always wisely. Second, Pérez, a forceful personality, rapidly made himself an important and influential figure on the international scene while, at home, he brought to reality some of the most grandiose development schemes he or his advisers—local and foreign—could dream of to take advantage of the seemingly unending and ever-increasing flow of oil money. Third—and inevitably, at least in retrospect—the combination of a strong, charismatic, and powerful leader with an apparently inexhaustible supply of funds led, after a short period of time, to new heights of waste and inefficiency, to exponential growth in the size of the bureaucracy, and, especially, to corruption on levels and in amounts never seen before.

The trend at this time appeared to be toward a strong two-party system, dominated by two moderate centrist groups which would continue to alternate in power without pursing policies that differed radically from each other. *Acción Democrática* represented the moderate left-of-center social democrats, while COPEI was the moderate right-of-center social Christians or Christian democrats. The Movement Toward Socialism (MAS), ideologically to the left, seemed destined to play the role of the third party that would always be in opposition. Furthermore, Venezuelan democracy had achieved an important state of social peace through the incorporation of the CTV, the National Workers Union, into the processes of decision making at the highest levels and also, and especially, due to the oil boom then developing in the world—thanks in good part to the political ability and foresight of Juan Pablo Pérez Alfonzo, a Venezuelan who is generally credited as one of the two founding forces of the Organization of Petroleum Exporting Countries (OPEC).[4] OPEC not only made the country very rich but, no doubt also helped to give Venezuela an important and potentially prominent leading role in world affairs.

Nevertheless, despite the initial good intentions, things eventually began to unravel. Excess wealth ended up producing not prosperity, but economic indigestion and, more important, galloping corruption on a scale heretofore unknown in Venezuela. The Pérez government ended in defeat when the dour and non-mediagenic AD candidate, Luis Piñerua Ordaz, lost to the COPEI candidate, Luis Herrera Campins, by the small margin of 43.41 percent to 46.64 percent. Herrera's government was characterized by the folksiness of the President and by more of the same large-scale waste, inefficiency, and corruption until, in 1982, the fall of oil prices and the debt crisis forced the government to devalue the national currency, the bólivar. Devaluation was a blow to national pride[5] and a very costly electoral move for the President's party.

In the 1983 elections, AD once more came to power, riding on the image of Dr. Jaime Lusinchi, a chubby, charming, and apparently inoffensive pediatrician and long-time professional politician and parliamentarian who was also one of the major "old guard" figures of the party. In the elections, Lusinchi outpaced even the first Pérez landslide to obtain 56.74 percent of the vote against COPEI's Rafael Caldera (again), who obtained 34.54 percent. Lusinchi's government, mired in the economic and debt crisis, constantly falling oil prices, permanent attacks of the now-strong neoliberal right, and a crumbling national infrastructure which had not been maintained over the past ten or fifteen years, compounded its problems by allowing corruption to continue to flourish, almost openly. Still, the opinion polls were generally favorable to Lusinchi and his government, even through the first months of the government of his elected successor, once again Carlos Andrés Pérez, also of *Acción Democrática* and the protagonist of a comeback story equivalent only to that of Richard Nixon in the United States.

In fact, Pérez, after surviving a congressional investigation of corruption charges relating to his first presidency and finding himself execrated by many within his own party, had staged an amazing comeback and, in 1988, won the national elections with 52.9 percent of the vote against 40.3 percent for COPEI's Eduardo Fernandez. During the second Pérez government, the corruption, by now almost normal, turned into rapacity, an element which grated upon Venezuela. A first warning of what was to come arrived in the very first days of the Pérez government, when the first major increase in the price of public-transport fares led to a major popular uprising in Caracas and several other cities. These events initially received wide television coverage, and debate still continues on whether or how much the conflagration was aided by such coverage.

The government's response, through the army, was extremely brutal. But given the imposition of television censorship after the initial events, even today it is impossible to know exactly how many people were killed during the repression of the February 1989 protests. However, it is clear that the number was extremely high and that the phenomenon of a spontaneous popular uprising with evident class undertones created a tremendous amount of fear among many Venezuelans.

All these elements, combined with the large number of important and persistent personal and political enemies Pérez had gathered throughout his political life and the discontent generated by the contrast between the harshness of his economic policies and the opulence visible in certain elite circles of the country, led to the two attempted military coups d'état, something which Venezuelans believed had been left in the past, and later to the formal impeachment and removal from office of Pérez and his replacement by a Senate-appointed President, the historian and journalist Ramón J. Velásquez, who it was hoped would finish the presidential term prescribed by the Constitution.

The 1993 Presidential Elections

On December 5, 1993, close to 6 million Venezuelans went to the polls to elect a new President of the Republic and all the members of the Senate, the House of Deputies, and the State Legislative Assemblies, as well as one State Governor and a couple of mayors. For Venezuelans, the holding of an election was extraordinary, since even as the voting went on there were still doubts and fears about whether the national armed forces might not step in and cancel the whole process, taking power through another coup d'état.

As has been seen, the elections themselves were the culmination of a tense and difficult two years for the Venezuelan democratic system, which had seen a constitutional President legally impeached and removed from office, a new President installed, two attempted coups d'état, a constant and apparently unending process of denunciation in the media of corruption at all levels of government, and the steady worsening of the most severe economic crisis that the country had suffered in its recent history. For at least the past twelve months, rumors had abounded about when the coup would take place and who would lead it. It had become almost routine for Venezuelan housewives to stand in long lines at the supermarkets to ensure that their families would have ample food supplies when the crisis came.

Furthermore, variations on the electoral system had been introduced, with a certain percentage of the candidates for congress and the state legislatures being elected "uninominally," that is to say, on a personal basis, and another group to be elected following the traditional lists prepared by the parties. The system was not totally organized by the authorities when the elections came around, and some believe that this was done on purpose, since it would eventually benefit the traditional parties and politicians—as it appears in fact to have done.

The 1993 Presidential Elections: The Issues According to most surveys taken at the time, the major issues in the 1993 elections could be summarized as follows: first, personal security (crime); second, the economy, with a major ideological debate between proponents of a neoliberal free market versus the traditional populism of Venezuelan politics; and third, corruption and the general disgust of the electors with the dishonesty of politicians. These and other issues were undoubtedly part of every candidate's campaign discourse and figured prominently in their speeches and proposed programs. But underlying the issues were two major questions: How far and how deeply had discontent and disillusionment with the traditional political parties and leadership permeated the attitudes of Venezuelans, and how important was personal honesty as a factor in the election of the next government? Subero (1994) has pointed out how, according to a prominent and perceptive foreign observer, there was an opinion climate which attributed the very real problems faced by the voters to excessively simple concepts such as "politicians," "corrupt persons," or "wastrels," which touched all leaders and all traditional parties, with or without justification.

The 1993 Presidential Elections: The Process In this tense atmosphere, with seventeen candidates in the running for President and at least four of them—according to most polls—running very closely and with very good chances of winning, there appeared to be great risk of the situation running out of control, even as the election took place peacefully. The highest electoral authority in the country, the autonomous and independent Supreme Electoral Council (CSE), promised publicly and repeatedly that it would ensure the honesty and impartiality of the process and warned that, to avoid early victory pronouncements and the concurrent danger of street eruptions from various factions, no results could be made public by anyone but the Council itself. Those results, the CSE promised, would be available in a relatively short time after the closing of the polls, thanks to the use of new and efficient computerized counting systems that had been installed expressly for this purpose.

In particular, the Council had strongly requested all political parties, their candidates, and their electoral staffs to refrain from making any public announcements regarding the results until the final tally was announced by the electoral authorities. A similar request was made of the media, in particular the two major television networks, which were setting in motion large electoral coverage operations with modern and sophisticated computer equipment to ensure that they could scoop each other with the results. This competition between the two networks, Radio Caracas TV (Channel 2) and Venevisión (Channel 4), dated back at least two previous presidential elections and was, of course, closely tied in with ratings and commercial prestige as well as with the electoral affinities and alliances of the respective owners.

The logic behind the CSE's policy was impeccable: In such a close race, with emotions running high, any early and nonofficial announcements which might later clash with the formal figures provided by the authorities carried a large risk of promoting violence and of creating doubts as to the legitimacy of the results.

The election took place on a Sunday, with the polls closing at five o'clock in the afternoon but staying open until the last of the voters in line had a chance to cast his or her ballot. According to the CSE, results could be expected by sometime in the evening of that same Sunday or, at the latest, by the morning of Monday, December 6.

This was not to be. It soon became evident that the Council's facilities were not up to the task. Meanwhile, the television networks were chafing at the bit, hinting broadly over the air that by noon Sunday they already knew who the winner was, thanks to their projections. In fact, by early Sunday afternoon the networks had shared their information with foreign correspondents covering the election, and both CBS and CNN were apparently already broadcasting the projected results of the voting abroad. The news was, of course, picked up easily by the thousands of upper- and upper-middle-class Venezuelans with satellite TV dishes in their homes and rapidly relayed by word of mouth. So, even if the media and the candidates abstained, in a commendably disciplined fashion, from providing anything but broad hints and winks about the electoral results, and the Electoral Council meanwhile insisted that only they knew what was going on but were not telling, rumors proclaiming the winners were already flying all over.

In this situation, the pressure on the Council, desperately struggling with its own terminal incompetence, from the television networks, from at least some of the candidates, and perhaps from even the government itself, proved to be too much. The CSE finally agreed to allow the television stations to air their projections. This they proceeded to do with alacrity, and Channel 4, which had arrayed an impressive operation for the election, immediately made their figures public. As could perhaps have been expected, and in a highly symbolic if unplanned action, these results were announced over Channel 4, not by a journalist or a professional political analyst, but by the highly popular television show host who every year also announces, using the same style, the Miss Venezuela contest. What he said, with his trademark breathless smile and charming manner, was, "Here he is . . . the new Mr. Venezuela . . . and the winner is . . . Rafael Caldera, of the Convergencia electoral group." The announcement, of course, was interspersed all too frequently with self-promotional comments on how Channel 4 (and Pepsi Cola, which in Venezuela are owned by the same group and which had provided the computerized facilities) had once again beaten the competition to be the first with the news in your home. The final projected results, according to Venevisión, based on their impressive tabulating operation and a large number of exit polls were as follows: Rafael Caldera of Convergencia in first place; Claudio Fermín of the government's *Acción Democrática* in second; Andrés Velasquez of the leftist Radical Cause Party (Causa R) in third; and Oswaldo Alvarez Paz of the opposition Social Christian party, fourth.

In a few short hours after the Channel 4 announcement—which was rapidly followed by announcements from the other stations—and while the CSE was still unable to provide even one official bulletin, candidate Fermín, who had projected the electoral image of a serious, responsible, well-behaved, and gentlemanly young man, conceded publicly and congratulated Caldera on his election. The winner, in turn, graciously expressed his appreciation for Fermín's sporting spirit and democratic sense of fair play, while blasting the other two major candidates, Alvarez and Velasquez, who had indicated that they could not concede on the basis of unofficial results coming from a private television network, for being "spoiled brats." The latter two candidates were quickly branded by many media and public figures as "sore losers" and "bad sports." Fortunately for everyone concerned, public-opinion polls in the days before the elections had generally pointed to the results finally obtained.[6]

Electoral-History Analysis

This narrative of these recent election processes provides some useful information which can help in drawing conclusions about recent Venezuelan political history. A first conclusion is that, whatever its merits, there is no doubt that the social democratic *Acción Democrática* has been, by far, the dominant party in the country throughout its democratic history. Of the nine democratic elections held in the nation, AD has won six, generally by a wide margin. In the first election it lost, 1968, the defeat was due basically to the third and most important division of the party, which went into the elections with two candidates.[7] The total of the votes obtained by the two "adeco" candidates comes close to what would have been the final vote for a single candidate for the party, and would have resulted in victory over Rafael Caldera. It is also interesting to note that, in all elections they won (except the 1963 election, where the guerrilla movement was still an important factor), the AD candidates always obtained either close to or above 50 percent of the vote, while in the cases where COPEI won, their margin of victory was much lower.

Another salient fact is that, until the 1993 elections, the rate of abstentions was extremely low; even in 1988, when it rose to 18.1 percent of the voters. The obligatory nature of the vote in Venezuela is not really an explanation, or at least not a sufficient one, since penalties for violation of this norm have never really been enforced.

Perhaps the more likely reason is that Venezuelans are a highly politicized society and that, whatever its faults, the formal democratic regime seemed to be working well and the alternatives offered were not deemed particularly attractive. Until very recently, politics was rivaled only by the national sport, baseball, or the national pastimes, dominoes and horse racing, as the number-one conversation topic of Venezuelans.

At the same time, the astounding (even if expected) increase in abstentions, rising to nearly 40 percent in the 1993 elections, would indicate a general and growing discontent with the recent regimes, discontent which also manifested itself in violent forms such as the February 1989 riots or the two attempted coups.

American pollster George Gaither, a veteran adviser and observer in Venezuelan politics, has noted that, "Democracy in Venezuela began with great expectations—maybe exaggerated ones . . . [and] enormous expectations caused an equally enormous deception" (quoted in Subero, 1994). He indicates that the first thing that polls in the 1960s showed was an uncontrolled optimism that has now turned into "uncontrolled pessimism."

MEDIA, POLITICS, AND ELECTORAL CAMPAIGNS IN VENEZUELA

The subject of the symbiotic relationship between media and politics and, in particular, between media and electoral processes, has been and will probably continue to be a complex and unresolved one. Every journalist has good arguments for why a free press is essential to democracy, while every politician or government official, among others, has equally abundant and persuasive evidence that the media exaggerate, distort, and, finally, harm the possibilities of government to act. It would appear that there is an inherent, or at least still unresolved, tension—perhaps even a contradiction—between the interests of the media and the best interests of the democratic process.

One cannot speak of "the media" as a disembodied abstract entity, all knowing and all just, which dispenses wisdom in the name of another mythical element—public opinion—and which represents the best interests of all citizens in their permanent fight against a corrupt caste, the "politicians." Media professionals, according to the myth they themselves created and perpetuate, are the quixotic defenders of truth in a venal world dominated by corrupt pols and a naïve, defenseless public. It is perhaps no accident that, in their far stronger personas, Superman turns himself into Clark Kent, fearless reporter, while Captain Marvel became Billy Batson, radio personality. But media institutions, as well as media professionals, cannot be seen outside their context, and they are part of a much larger and complex world where personalities, economic interests, and cultural perceptions are very much part of the whole.

So it is in Venezuela as everywhere else. As was indicated earlier, the truly important use of media as an instrument in Venezuelan electoral politics does not begin until the 1973 campaign. Agudelo states that

In Venezuela, the tendency to introduce advertising mechanisms in electoral contests is relatively recent. It starts basically during the 1968 election won by a scant majority by Dr. Rafael Caldera, the Christian democratic candidate. . . . It is said that he [Caldera] was the first Venezuelan candidate to accept image advisory services from US experts . . .

but political advertising really begins to grow in Venezuela from 1973 when the Democratic Action party also decided to invest an important part of its campaign resources in the hiring of an American image consultant, Joe Napolitan. (Agudelo, 1993, pp. 23–24)

While Napolitan was consulting for the Social Democrats, the Christian Democrats were availing themselves of the services of another image guru, David Garth. Other sources indicate that the first foreign political-media adviser to come to Venezuela was the German, Gerhard Elschner, who was sent by the German Christian Democrats, with the support of Konrad Adenauer, to assist the 1963 campaign of Caldera.

Obviously, this does not mean that mass media had not been used as a political tool prior to the arrival of foreign political consultants. Print media have a long and, at times, honorable tradition of involvement in the political life of the country. Modern Venezuelan newspapers do not have a tradition of expressing their opinions in editorials, but they have made clear their presidential preferences over the past years in their selection of columnists for their Op Ed pages and even in their selection of straight news items. In particular, the print media entered into electoral agreements with parties, which resulted in having members of particular newspapers presented in the lists of candidates for Congress.

Personal affinities and long-standing enmities were an important factor in the forging of these alliances, although at times some astounding agreements were reached and the covenants were not always respected. Miguel Angel Capriles, for example, owner of the influential Capriles chain of newspapers and magazines, was elected to Congress on the lists of Rafael Caldera's COPEI. But Capriles had a falling out with Caldera once he was elected President, and the virulent dispute ended with his exile for a short time.

A long-standing personal feud based on business differences—they were once partners—has separated Capriles and his major competitor, Armando de Armas, owner of the Bloque de Armas, which also controls newspapers and magazines. As a result, when one of these newspaper owners deals with a candidate, the other will deal with his rival, but, in reality, this conflict has produced somewhat feeble alliances. Nonetheless, both Capriles and de Armas have their own group of representatives in the House of Deputies.

Television arrived in Venezuela in 1952 (the ninth country in the world to have television, according to media historians), but it did not really take off until the mid-1960s. In 1963, only 25 percent of all Venezuelan homes had television, but this figure had risen to 45 percent by 1969 and to 85 percent by 1982. Currently, about 90 percent of Venezuelan homes have at least one television set and an average of about 33 percent have multiple sets (roughly 63% of upper- and upper-middle-class homes have multiple sets). As of 1990, the national average was 1.5 sets per home. Until recently, no transmissions were allowed on UHF, and there were only three major networks permitted, two privately owned and one owned by the government. Meanwhile, radio lost ground because, with the single exception of one cultural station, legal restrictions did not permit broadcasting on the FM frequency until just a few years ago.

Individual examples of the various ways in which media participated in the various elections and in the political process as a whole are not easy to find. Open and declared hostility from the media toward a particular candi-

date or political party or figure has been relatively rare and difficult to docu-
ment. But one often finds cases of "boycotts," where media owners, or even
journalists themselves, decreed that a particular person would not appear
anymore—or for a given period of time—in the papers or on TV. However,
this was always an undeclared war, with no evidence left behind save for the
off-the-record or not-attributed comments among colleagues, always denied
if made public. Officially, the media remain neutral, and all parties create
special committees to monitor and survey news programs in order to identify and denounce—if necessary—any unbalanced or biased reporting. During and after every election, allegations are made about the antipathy of a
given medium towards a particular candidate; they are also routinely denied
and never really proven or fully documented.

Pacts and allegiances change, and the media's loyalties can be fickle, so
that it is not convenient for anyone to be aggressively hostile toward anybody. Yet there are, of course, subtle ways of doing things. A veteran and
highly respected local journalist expressed to the author that, while he was
news editor of a major television network, he had daily evidence of how
unpopular the government was at the time of the election and how this was
hurting the official party's candidate. What he would do, he said, was to
provide equally "neutral" material during the newscasts and, in fact, always
give slightly more airtime to the government's candidate than the major opposition leader. He would, however, usually open with a "negative" news
report on government and presidential activities, followed by other general
news, some international news, and only then clips on the major opposition
candidate. This news report would be followed, in turn, by some more general
news and then by more news about government or presidential activities
that he knew would not be well received. He would then close with ample
airtime given to the official candidate and hope that viewers would connect the
various stories and be left with a negative feeling toward the government.

Whether this journalist's strategy was successful or not is difficult to tell.
The journalist believes it had an important effect. In any case, the government
lost the elections. The government and its candidate could not accuse the
television network or its news editor of bias, since they had, in fact, received
more time than anybody else. Only very careful and detailed semiologic analysis of each news item could have shown bias and, even then, the ruling party and
its candidate would have had to admit that the emphasis on the government's
own unpopularity was the major factor in the unbalanced reporting.

Similar strictures apply to print and radio. There is a cumulative effect
that results when the audience gets the truth and nothing but the truth; but
never, of course, the whole truth, and, normally, either out of context or in
such a context as to become false. This, of course, is a problem that tran-
scends political coverage and extends to much of the way in which journalism works at present.

BY WAY OF TENTATIVE CONCLUSIONS

Most definitely, the formal manifestations of Venezuelan democracy have
become highly Americanized throughout the history of that democracy. The
use of political commercials, the search for telegenic candidates or, failing

that, the effort to make candidates project an appealing image on television, the use of technical experts to provide advice on campaigns, and the constantly growing importance of the media—in particular television—in the electoral process are all present and clear. As in other parts of the world, there has also been a tendency toward compressing the political arena into a two-party system, and a loss of ideology in favor of a pragmatic, pluralistic approach in which the parties tend to become more machineries for winning elections than instruments designed to obtain power in order to change the world or move it in a given direction.

At the same time, there is no doubt that both Venezuelan democracy and the national quality of life have deteriorated over the past twenty years, and that there is at least a chronological parallel in the development of the Americanization process of politics and the impoverishment of Venezuela's lifestyle. However, there is no evidence, beyond the fortuitous and anecdotal, to indicate that there is more than a casual relationship between Americanization of the electoral arena and the deteriorating quality of Venezuelan life, at least for now and pending much further study. Thus, it would be adventurous to assert any relationship of cause or consequence between Americanization and the recent travails of Venezuelan democracy. One can hazard some guesses, but the available data do not support any clear conclusions.

One does find an evident friction and contradiction between the discourse of the media and of the candidates concerning the best and most democratic ways of conducting elections and of portraying and understanding the actions of both media and politicians. Media clamor the need for journalistic independence and proclaim their purity, while media owners are negotiating places in the lists of candidates for themselves, their relatives, or their employees. Candidates proclaim fiercely that they care only about principle and the best interests of the people. They publicly disdain the efforts of the media to turn them into pretty personalities, while at the same time making sure that they are looking at the right camera and unctuously paying frequent courtesy visits to media owners or to influential columnists and reporters. Every political figure insists that polls are totally unreliable, except for a few which coincidentally happen to favor their candidate; the media do the same.

Although it is difficult to reach any definite conclusions, perhaps one can point toward some interesting trends to observe. There is no doubt that the prevalence of television as the most cost-effective instrument for electoral campaigning has altered the very way in which electoral campaigns are designed and implemented. Because it reaches an undifferentiated audience that is normally larger than any to which a politician could aspire through traditional means, television leads to candidates changing their objectives; from rallying voters behind their cause and making them enthusiastic about a given objective or ideology, to having not offending anybody as their supreme objective. Essentially, this means that the preferred candidate is a bland one who can speak in sound bites, provide good photo opportunities, and look like a "movie" politician. More and more, political candidates have the same "genuine" look as sexy starlets or television anchorpersons. In this respect, one can imagine the day in the very near future when the selection of candidates will formally be taken out of the hands of "unscientific" methods such as conventions, primaries, or smoke-filled back rooms and be placed instead in the care of professional casting directors.

At the same time, Venezuelan media appear to have lost credibility through excess in their presentation of violence and gore, both in their fictional programming and in their newscasts, and there is already the possibility of a negative reaction against them. These same media have engaged in fierce internecine battles, network against network and family against family, which would appear to have contributed to the rapid deterioration of their public image, although there have been no studies on the subject and none are expected in the future.

The Venezuelan political, economic, and social situation, at present and in the foreseeable future, is particularly complex and difficult to assess. As was the case in the United States, according to Jimmy Carter's diagnosis, a "malaise" is prevalent in the country, which evidently affects the media and is at the same time nurtured and reinforced by them.

Finally, the idea of covering elections as horse races, beauty pageants, blow-by-blow fight accounts, or holier-than-anybody-but-the-media disclosures of real, perceived, or merely vaguely denounced sins of all sorts seems to have gone haywire and is damaging not only democratic processes and institutions but, more important, responsible journalism itself.

NOTES

1. Even this date is disputed. Some historians believe that Gomez may have died some days earlier, but that his potential successors kept the event quiet for two reasons: to ensure that they could keep the country under control and prevent any popular explosions on learning of the dictator's death, and to assist this first objective by contributing to the myth which established a parallel between the life of Gomez and that of the revered Liberator of Venezuela, Simon Bolivar. In effect, it was held that Gomez had been born on July 24, the same birthdate of Bolivar, and so his death on the same date as that of the Liberator's demise would neatly close the circle and emphasize the parallel. Whatever the truth, it seems to have at least partially worked. Venezuelans who remember the date have indicated that when rumors of the death of Gomez began to circulate, many feared it was a trap and that anyone who expressed the least rejoicing about the news would be immediately arrested.

2. In 1950, Commander Delgado Chalbaud was kidnapped and murdered in a still murky incident for which some place responsibility, if not the intellectual authorship, on his fellow junta member, Marcos Pérez Jiménez.

3. The name of COPEI merits an explanation, since it has become one of the two major identifying forces in Venezuelan politics. It is an acronym for *Comite Organizador Pro Elecciones Independientes,* or Independent Organizing Committee for the Elections, formed by a group of young conservative professionals, led by former student leader Rafael Caldera, to ensure that in the 1947 elections the *Acción Democrática* government did not commit fraud.

4. The other founding father of OPEC was Sheik Abdullah Tariki of Saudi Arabia, who had fallen out of favor when some of his ideas collided with the interests of the absolutist Saudi monarchy.

5. In fact, one of the major sources of national pride in Venezuela was the strength and solidity of the national currency. Named after the Liberator, as all major icons in the country seem to be, it had been pegged at 3.35 per U.S. dollar until devalued to 4.50 during the Betancourt government in 1959, and later brought to 4.30 under Caldera.

Ian Fleming, in one of his James Bond sagas, had financial wizard Goldfinger keeping all money in either Swiss francs or Venezuelan bólivars, which he considered the two safest and most solid currencies in the world. In fact, according to many economists, it was the delay of more than a year in devaluing the bolivar during the Herrera government, caused by fear of the political consequences of such a move, which helped turn what could have been an important but manageable crisis into the major economic disaster which is still part of the national landscape. Then again, in the interest of historical fairness, one must remember that economists tend not to be the best judges of economic reality in the world.

6. By law, in Venezuela, neither media nor political parties or their campaign machines are allowed to make public any public-opinion polls or to conduct any electoral activities, beginning a week before the date of the election. Of course, this does not prevent anyone from having friends who claim access to the various polls and then spreading the word. In general, the poll figures during the week before the election indicated that Caldera was leading with Alvarez closely behind, Velasquez rapidly moving into a possible second place by displacing Alvarez, and Fermín a distant fourth.

7. *Acción Democrática* first divided in 1960, when the more left-wing-oriented youth section of the party felt that Betancourt had betrayed the social democratic principles and left, or rather were thrown out, of the organization and created the MIR, which became the initial center of the guerrilla movement. It then divided itself once more in the early 1960s, with an important part of the party's leadership leaving to create the PRIN. In the 1968 elections, a primary election chose Dr. Luis Beltran Prieto Figueroa, a highly respected educator, former Minister of Education, and one of the founding figures of the party, as the AD candidate. Betancourt and the more conservative or pragmatic faction of *Acción Democrática* considered Prieto as too far left and maneuvered to have Dr. Gonzalo Barrios, another important and respected founding figure, finally nominated. This resulted in Prieto and a large group of his followers leaving the party to run on their own under a new political label, MEP (Popular Electoral Movement), against the AD candidate.

REFERENCES

Agudelo Caceres, L. (1993). *Imagen y poder—La caída electoral de los grandes partidos* [Image and power: The fall of the major political parties]. Caracas: Eduven.
Subero, C. (1994, January 15). Dudo que los partidos tradicionales desaparezcan del escenario [I doubt that the traditional parties will disappear from the scene] (Interview with G. Gaither). *El Universal*, sec. 1, p. 12.

FURTHER READING

Agudo Freites, R. (1976). *La reglamentación legal de la comunicación en Venezuela* [Legal regulation of communication in Venezuela]. Caracas: Ediciones de la Facultad de Humanidades y Educación, UCV.
Breton, P., & Proulx, S. (1990). La nouvelle télévision traversée par l'idéologie de la communication [The ideology of communication and television news]. In F. Casetti & R. Odin (Eds.), *Télévisions/mutations* [Televisions/changes], *Communications Magazine*, No. 51. Paris: Editions du Seuil.
Consejo Supremo Electoral. (1985). *Los partidos políticos y sus estadísticas electorales 1946–1984* [Voting statistics of the political parties] (Vol. 2). Caracas: CSE, División de Estadísticas.
Cotteret, J. M. (1977). *La comunicación política* [Political communication]. Buenos Aires: El Ateneo.

Davila de Vela, G. (Ed.). (1993). *Inventario de medios de comunicación en América Latina* [Almanac of communication media in Latin America]. Quito, Ecuador: Ciespal.

Esteinou, J. (Ed.). (1992). *Comunicación y democracia* [Communication and democracy]. Mexico City: Opción.

Estrella, M. (1993). *Programación televisiva y radiofónica—Análisis de lo que se difunde en América Latina y el Caribe* [Television and radio programming: An analysis of what is broadcast in Latin America and the Caribbean]. Quito, Ecuador: Ciespal.

Grases, P. (Ed.). (1989). *Venezuela contemporanea 1974–1989* [Modern Venezuela, 1974–1989]. Caracas: Fundación Eugenio Mendoza.

Guzman, F. (1992). *Manual de campañas electorales* [Manual of election campaigns]. Caracas: Fundación CSE.

Keller, A. (Ed.). (1985). Comunicación política [Political communication]. *Conciencia, 21.*

Levine, D. H. (1977). Venezuelan politics: Past and future. In R. D. Bond (Ed.), *Contemporary Venezuela and its role in international affairs.* New York: Council on Foreign Relations, New York University Press.

Linares Aleman, M. (1975). *El nacional y las elecciones presidenciales Venezolanas (1947–1973)* [Venezuelan national presidential elections, 1947–1973]. Caracas: UCV.

Lubrano, A., & Sanchez, R. H. (1987). *Del hombre completo a Jaime es como tu—Recuento de un proceso electoral venezolano* [From "renaissance man" to "ordinary Joe": An account of a Venezuelan political campaign]. Caracas: Vadell Hermanos Editores.

Martinez, T. E. (1984). Radio, prensa y televisión: entre el equilibrio y el estancamiento [Radio, the press, and television: Between development and stagnation]. In M. Naim & R. Piñango (Eds.), *El Caso Venezuela—una ilusión de armonía* [The case of Venezuela: An illusion of harmony] (pp. 310–325). Caracas: Ediciones IESA.

Montero, M. (Ed.). (1987). *Psicología política Latinoamericana* [Latin American political psychology]. Caracas: Editorial Panapo.

Naim, M., & Piñango, R. (Eds.). (1984). *El Caso Venezuela—una ilusión de armonía* [The case of Venezuela: An illusion of harmony]. Caracas: Ediciones IESA.

Nimmo, D. D., & Sanders, K. R. (Eds.). (1981). *Handbook of political communication.* London: Sage.

Paletz, D. L., & Entman, R. M. (1981). *Media, power, politics.* New York: Free Press.

Proaño, L. E. (1989). *Comunicación y política* [Communication and politics]. Quito, Ecuador: Colección Intiyan, Ciespal.

Quevedo, L. A. (1992). *La política bajo el formato televisivo* [Politics made for television]. In H. Schmucler & M. C. Mata (Eds.), *Política y comunicación* [Politics and communication]. Cordoba, Argentina: Universidad Nacional de Cordoba.

Ramos Jiménez, A. (Ed.). *Venezuela—Un sistema político en crisis* [Venezuela: A political system in crisis]. Merida: Kappa Editores.

Rivadeneira Prada, R. (1989). *Agresión política* [Attack politics]. La Paz, Bolivia: Editorial Juventud.

Schmucler, H., & Mata, M. C. (Eds.). *Política y Comunicación* [Politics and communication]. Cordoba, Argentina: Universidad Nacional de Cordoba.

Urbaneja, D. B. (1984). El sistema político o como funciona la máquina de procesar decisiones [The political system, or how the decision-making process works]. In M. Naim & R. Piñango (Eds.), *El caso Venezuela—Una ilusión de armonía* [The case of Venezuela: An illusion of harmony] (pp. 228–257). Caracas: Ediciones IESA.

Velásquez, R. J. (1976). Aspectos de la evolución política de Venezuela en el último medio siglo [Aspects of the political evolution of Venezuela in the last half-century]. In *Venezuela moderna—Medio siglo de historia, 1926–1976* [Modern Venezuela: A half-century of history, 1926–1976]. Caracas: Fundación Eugenio Mendoza.

Woldenberg, J., et al. (1990). *Medios, democracia, fines* [Media, democracy, outcomes]. Mexico City: UNAM.

Chapter Thirteen

Patterns of Modern Electoral Campaigning and Their Consequences

David L. Swanson and Paolo Mancini

The rituals and protocols by which aspirants to public office seek support and people select their leaders are part of the essential character of a democracy. Electoral practices are one of the fundamental forms through which democratic societies constitute and express their nature, and they are connected reciprocally to the civil, moral, economic, mythic, and other forms that create the public and private faces of every culture. To be sure, many important aspects of society have nothing to do with electoral campaigns, but in a democracy's electoral practices are found the influence and imprint of much that makes a culture as it is. Thus, electoral campaigns speak beyond themselves, and it is for this reason that significant changes in a democracy's electoral processes may reflect and portend related transformations in some of the institutions and relationships that shape nations.

Electoral practices are, of course, dynamic. Change is more or less constant in the customs and practices of seeking office and, in any given country, no election campaign is precisely like any other. But in recent years we have seen the emergence of an at least superficially common pattern in the kinds of innovations in campaigning that have surfaced at an accelerating pace within democracies of all kinds—established democracies with stable political cultures, newly created or restored democracies, and democracies that labor under powerful and potentially destabilizing internal and external tensions. This pattern consists of the appearance, in various guises and locally adapted forms, of many of the elements that are associated with the now-familiar concept of modern media-centered (or as some would have it, media-dominated) democracy. As practiced in one of its most extreme forms in the United States, media-centered democracy has been characterized by some analysts as corrosive to the very political institutions and vibrant public sphere of civic discourse that are integral to the liberal democratic idea (e.g., Bennett, 1992a, 1992b; Jamieson, 1992; Patterson, 1993; Swanson, 1992). Similar concerns have surfaced in other countries where mass media, especially television, have come to dominate political and electoral processes (e.g., Butler & Ranney, 1992; Franklin, 1994).

The emergence of an apparently common pattern in dissimilar national settings invites us to consider how the variations and forms of democracy are evolving in the late twentieth century and where their present tendencies may lead. To explore these questions, scholars in a number of countries joined in an effort to understand the character, significance, and implications of changing electoral campaign practices in democracies of various kinds. Contributors were encouraged to provide detailed analyses of the causes, nature, and effects of campaign innovations in their own countries, attending especially to the ways in which the recent experience of each nation reflects its unique culture, history, and institutions.

In order to provide a common frame of reference and foil against which to develop their own analyses, contributors were provided with the general theoretical framework that is outlined in the introductory chapter to this volume. That framework proposes, as a working hypothesis, that "Americanization" is a suitable description of the campaign innovations that have emerged and are continuing to surface in so many democracies around the world. The term was chosen not to suggest that campaign practices in the United States are by any means an ideal toward which others should strive, but rather to indicate that, for the most part, as others have noted (e.g., Butler & Ranney, 1992), many of the electoral changes seen nearly everywhere have been inspired by or are variations on techniques that emerged first in the United States. The framework also proposes that these changes in electoral practices are an outgrowth of an underlying process we call "modernization," in which the functions and hold on citizens of traditional institutions declines and is replaced by a profusion of more specialized groups and fragmented identities that create the conditions which lead to campaigns based on the essential role of mediation played by mass media systems. Finally, our introductory framework proposes that, in each democracy, the particular forms and influence of campaign innovations are shaped by such local contextual factors as the nature of the electoral system, structure of party competition, regulation of campaign activities, national political culture, and national media system. The task we set for contributors was not to validate the proposed framework, but rather to test it against the recent experience of their own countries.

The purposes of this concluding chapter are to assess the merit of the general framework based on the findings offered by our contributors, to identify the framework's shortcomings and suggest modifications that are needed, and to consider what our results imply for larger questions about the practices and futures of democracies at the turn of the century. Before doing so, however, it is important to acknowledge again the particular strengths and limitations of comparative analysis (see Blumler, McLeod, & Rosengren, 1992, for a discussion of these issues). Every country's electoral practices are a singular expression of particular national institutions, history, culture, leadership, mythology, and the like. The effort to compare practices across countries requires that we shift our focus to a level of abstraction at which many of the unique details of each country's experience become obscured or lost to view altogether. On the other hand, preoccupation with the uniqueness of each country's experience leaves us unable to notice similarities across countries that may reveal transnational trends. The challenge of comparative analysis is to identify similarities and patterns, if they exist, while keeping in mind, insofar as possible, the unique national circumstances out of which they arise. This is what we endeavor to do in the following discussion.

THE THEORETICAL FRAMEWORK REVISITED

The detailed analyses of campaign innovations in the eleven democracies treated in this volume provide much support for our proposed general framework, though not without important qualifications and reservations. As so often turns out to be the case, things are more complicated and variable than our framework contemplated. In this section, we note those aspects of the framework that have received strongest support and suggest qualifications and revisions that appear to be needed based on the findings of our contributors.

The Modern Model of Campaigning

It is clear from the reports of our contributors that there are no disagreements about what constitutes the modern model of campaigning. Its key attributes—including personalization of politics, expanding reliance on technical experts and professional advisers, growing detachment of political parties from citizens, development of autonomous structures of communication, and casting citizens in the role of spectator—figure in one way or another in nearly every chapter in this volume. There is disagreement, however, about whether the term Americanization is the most appropriate label for these campaign innovations. Some readers may take the term as implying that adoption of modern campaign methods necessarily results from a desire to emulate U.S. practices, perhaps with overtones of U.S. superiority and power. As Waisbord, Caspi, Asp, and Esaiasson; Blumler, Kavanagh, and Nossiter; and others in this volume point out, elements of the modern campaign model have emerged in various countries in response to internal developments in those countries, not out of desire to imitate the United States, which, after all, conducts its political campaigns in ways that more often elicit opprobrium than approval within the United States and around the world.

A number of countries including Germany, France, and the United Kingdom are now "exporters" of consultants and technical experts who provide advice about modern campaign methods. The result is reciprocal influence, as seen in instances such as that described in this volume by Blumler, Kavanagh, and Nossiter, where consultants from other countries have provided advice to U.S. campaigners. More generally, as Caspi points out, we have entered an era in which routine exchanges between countries, at many levels, lead naturally to cross fertilization in the political and other domains. Thus, perhaps the best description of the present situation is an international network of connections through which knowledge about new campaign practices and their uses is disseminated constantly across national borders by independent consultants for economic reasons, by ideologically kindred political parties for political reasons, and by mass media to aspiring political candidates and interested members of the public worldwide.

While we acknowledge that the term Americanization refers more to the origins of most of the campaigning techniques we are interested in than to the present system for exchanging technical knowledge about them, it is important not to overlook the fact that each new development in U.S. campaigns is studied with special care by political parties and candidates around the world. As Blumler, Kavanagh, and Nossiter observe in this volume, the United States continues to be "perceived as on the cutting edge of election-eering innovation." Nevertheless, to best represent the current international network of reciprocal exchange, we shall refer to the "modern model of campaigning" rather than to the Americanized model.

Comparing the experiences of the countries that have been examined, we are struck by two themes that most often are cited by our contributors as the direct and immediate causes of electoral innovations. One theme is a fundamental transformation in the relationship of political parties to their constituents. In the established democracies, we are hard pressed today to find successful, competitive political parties that retain the traditional organic relationship with constituents that is cemented and perpetuated by well-defined, stable commitments to class and group interests. Instead, the parties' links to particular groups and institutions generally have weakened, while at the same time these groups and institutions have lost much of their former ability to influence members' voting choices (such as trade unions and farmers' organizations in Sweden, religion and social class in Germany, and religious affiliations and traditional subcultures in Italy). The point is perhaps put best in this volume by Waisbord, who describes the transformation of parties in Argentine politics from "sacred" to "secular." In many democracies, voting seems to have been transformed from an expression of solidarity with one's group and its institutions to, today, an expression of one's opinions. Moreover, the opinions which are cited most often as shaping persons' voting choices—such as opinions about the performance of government, the appropriate ideological and pragmatic bases for public policy, and the appeal of a party's leader and other visible spokespersons—cut across class lines and other traditional social cleavages, so that a sharp decline in the relationship between social class and voting has been observed nearly everywhere. In this volume, examples of the decline of partisan allegiances and the rise of the opinion-based party include Argentina, Venezuela, Italy, Israel, Sweden, the United Kingdom, and Germany.

No longer able to rely on a secure base of party loyalists, the most competitive political parties in many countries have taken on attributes of "catch-all" confederations that exist more to win elections by appealing to a broad range of voters' opinions than to implementing defined programs, and their electoral fortunes wax and wane with voters' pragmatic assessments of their leaders and the performance of the current government. The evolution to catch-all parties and the adoption of various media-centered campaign techniques often relegate specific ideological commitments to the background of campaigns and blur programmatic differences between parties, except on a few issues where a party believes it holds the more popular view.

A second theme that stands out in nearly every chapter is that when the fortunes of political parties rest on opinion rather than membership and historical allegiances, the means for cultivating and shaping public opinion become crucial to electoral success. In modern society, these means are, of course, the mass media of communication, which have proliferated especially as commercial enterprises while government and party influence over media has generally declined. The media have become the dominant source of information and entertainment in nearly every society and, in many countries, have assumed a new level of independence from which to interject their own voice into the political dialogue. Among other things, the independent voice of mass media in politics reflects the development and spread of an ideology of journalism as a profession in its own right with an autonomous role to play in the political process. Increasingly, this professional ideology has become evident both in public-service broadcasting systems (as in Germany and Italy) and in nations where a party press still exists but generally excises partisanship from its news columns in favor of professional news values (as in Sweden). Media independence is more problematic in the newer democracies we have examined, such as Russia, which has experimented with a different role and voice for television in each election; Poland, where television has been reluctant to assert a viewpoint of its own; and Spain, where the government-controlled, sharply partisan public television service faces growing competition from commercial, politically independent media.

It seems to be the case nearly everywhere that mass media have developed their own "media logic" for covering political campaigns, with news values and interpretive frames that are thought to best serve the need to attract and hold an audience in a competitive media environment (see Altheide & Snow, 1979; Mazzoleni, 1987). Among other consequences, this logic leads to a style of political reporting that prefers personalities to ideas, simplicity to complexity, confrontation to compromise, and heavy emphasis on the "horse race" in electoral campaigns. These frames of political journalism have been observed in most of the democracies examined in this volume, including the United States, the United Kingdom, Italy, Sweden, Spain, and Venezuela.

Recognition of their dependence on mass media has shaped the activities and decision-making processes of political parties in various ways. Many parties have, to greater or lesser degrees, incorporated into their strategies a "marketing" approach to campaigning, relying on experts in public relations, opinion polling, and communications for advice about how to craft an appealing message tailored to the voters' opinions and concerns. The centerpiece of this approach typically consists of focusing attention on the personalities of party leaders, for appealing personalities are currency of high denomination in media logic.

Television appears to be the mass medium of greatest importance to the political process, because of its strategic position as the dominant source of news and entertainment and its ability to reach the mass audience, not just those who have particular interests in politics. Television news and election programs are almost universally regarded as having great influence on the success of candidates and parties. Even in countries where political parties are provided free airtime for political programs (such as Russia, the United Kingdom, Spain, Israel, Italy, and Argentina) or may purchase or receive free airtime for broadcasting political advertisements on television (such as Germany, Italy, Argentina, Russia, and the United States), frequent and favorable coverage in television news is believed by many to be critical to electoral success.

In many countries, the presumed importance of mass media, especially television news, as a conduit to citizens whose voting decisions reflect momentary opinions rather than historical allegiances has led to a struggle between politicians and a more or less independent media establishment over who shall control the agendas of campaigns. For their part, politicians everywhere seem to have become embroiled in what Blumler (1990) has aptly described as "the modern publicity process": tailoring more of their activities and decisions to the demands of media logic, engaging in highly visual events staged for television, scheduling activities to meet media deadlines, pushing telegenic candidates and spokespersons to the forefront, polishing their ability to produce "sound bites," and so on. On the other side, journalists often have sought to assert their neutrality and independence from politicians' manipulation, by such means as concentrating on the campaign horse race rather than candidates' statements, reporting candidates' strategic blunders, adopting a "disdaining" style of reporting that exposes the manipulative intention behind staged campaign events (see Gurevitch & Blumler, 1993; Semetko, Blumler, Gurevitch, & Weaver, 1991), and producing independent coverage of issues to prod the parties to address pressing national concerns (as in the case of the BBC; see Gurevitch & Blumler, 1993). In turn, politicians have responded by becoming even more sophisticated in manipulating journalists and, in the 1992 U.S. presidential campaign, by going around journalists to reach the public directly through "the new news"—popular interview programs, unorthodox venues such as appearances on music television cable channels, and the like (see Rosen & Taylor, 1992). This struggle between journalists and politicians has often been cited as leading to a greater amount of campaign coverage that is negative in tone, reflecting poorly on politicians and occasionally undermining the public standing of the mass media. In the countries we have examined, concerns about rising negativity of campaign coverage have been voiced in the United States, the United Kingdom, Israel, Sweden, Venezuela, and elsewhere.

In sum, the experience of the democracies considered in this volume provides support for the description of the modern media-centered model of campaigning outlined in our general theoretical framework. The defining elements of that model—including personalization of politics; adapting campaign practices to media logic and priorities; and employing technical experts to advise parties on public relations, opinion polling, and marketing strategies—have emerged to a greater or lesser extent in every country we examined. Most often, these innovations are linked to two related developments: weakening of political parties and the proliferation of an increasingly independent mass media system that pursues an autonomous agenda.

Modernization as the Origin of Campaign Innovations

In proposing the term *modernization* to describe a wide-ranging ensemble of social and institutional changes that lead to the innovations of modern electoral campaigning, we sought to employ a usage that is fairly conventional and readily understood. For some readers, however, modernization suggests a linear pattern of development among related institutions and processes that moves inexorably in the same way in every country toward a foreordained conclusion. The term might be taken, as well, as expressing a value-laden preference for modernization over other patterns of social and institutional development. We attempted in the introductory chapter to explain our understanding of the term in a way that would forestall such readings. To the extent that modernization undermines the organic relationship between citizens and political parties that, in the traditional view, constitutes the basis of effective democracy, it would be difficult to view modernization's political and electoral consequences with unqualified approval. We shall continue to use the term for convenience and consistency and because the term captures our subject more adequately than other descriptions, and we shall hope that readers take care to understand it in the sense in which it is meant in the present context.

Without repeating the discussion of this subject offered in the introductory chapter, we may highlight here some of the more important elements of the modernization process. Following Giddens (1990), Murdock (1993), and Tomlinson (1994), we hypothesize that increasing functional differentiation within society leads to growing numbers of subsystems of all kinds that develop to satisfy the specialized demands of particular groups and social sectors. The rise of these subsystems undermines the traditional aggregative structures of socialization, authority, community, and consensus, producing social fragmentation and exclusion. In the political process, more and more specialized groups compete for public resources and social capital, as citizens deputize these groups to act as intermediaries between themselves and traditional political institutions. In turn, political parties tend to become segmented, pluralistic, catch-all confederations with weak or inconsistent ideological bases, whose links to voters are fragile and inherently unstable. In such a political context, individual political figures who can aggregate support around their personal appeal become empowered at the expense of the traditional authority of political parties. The result of these developments coming together is a form of democracy that Dahl (1956, 1971) has described as "polyarchy."

Among the cases that best fit our expectations about how modernization leads to campaign innovations are the experiences of the United States, where the proliferation of Political Action Committees and narrowly focused advocacy groups has been well publicized; the rise of single-issue movements in Argentina; the increasing struggle of business groups and organizations for media and political attention in Sweden; and the rise of one-issue groups and the growing appeal of third parties in the United Kingdom. Some of the consequences of modernization that we postulated, such as the surrender by political parties, to the media and other institutions, of the parties' tradi-

tional functions of political socialization and informing the public about political affairs, also seem to be widespread in the countries we have examined.

Across all the democracies considered in this volume, there is evidence
that elements of the modern campaigning model are being adopted and widely
diffused, but it is clear that these developments bear a complex and variable
relationship to the process of modernization. In a number of cases, components of the marketing approach to media-centered political campaigning
have been adopted for reasons that initially seem to have little to do with the
advance of modernization. For example, Caspi attributes early adoption of
some campaign innovations in Israel to the influence of independent political consultants who, inspired by new practices in the United States and elsewhere, sought to market their services to the political parties in order to
establish a political consulting industry in Israel. Waisbord describes a similar circumstance in Argentina, where seminars on campaign methods given
by foreign experts and observation of new practices in other countries led to
the adoption of many foreign-inspired innovations. In both of these cases,
the new methods were urged and adopted for economic and competitive
motives that have little to do with modernization. But it is important to notice that, in each case, the new methods ultimately won acceptance because
of the two developments described in the preceding section as the immediate
causes of campaign innovation: weakened political parties and emergence of
the mass media as the essential conduit between the public and political actors and as an autonomous power center in the political process.

Campaign innovations have also come about as perhaps unforeseen results of political reforms that were undertaken for reasons that have no obvious connection to modernization. Mazzoleni singles out a reform that
provided for direct election of mayors as an early stage in movement toward
the modern campaign model in Italy, although the reform was prompted simply by a desire to produce more efficient city administrations. Caspi argues,
in this volume, that one of the causes of the emergence in Israel of innovative, especially personalized, campaign methods was a set of reforms that
provided for direct election of mayors and the introduction of party primary
elections to select candidates to appear on party lists. In the same way, we
might point, with Nimmo, to the proliferation of primary elections in U.S.
presidential campaigns as contributing to the decline of party authority and
helping to pave the way for candidate-centered campaign organizations. In
each of these cases, the explicit goal of reform was not to move to a different
model of campaigning, but that has been one of the ultimate results because
of the modernization process taking place at the same time.

The new and recently restored democracies provide additional variations
on the relationship between modernization and campaign innovations. In
Russia, Poland, and Spain—nations which made sudden transitions to democracy—new-style campaigning seems to have been adopted as part of an
effort to stimulate and accelerate modernization processes. In each case, democracy was desired not just as an end in itself, but also as a means of achieving other desired changes, such as rising prosperity through development of
a market economy or fuller integration into the economic life of Western Europe. Campaigning and elections began before democratic political institutions were fully established, and popular support of elections was regarded

as key to the ability to achieve more general modernization. In all three cases, but especially in Spain, the approach to campaigns and elections that was adopted was thoroughly contemporary. Indeed, Russia and Spain offer examples of media-centered campaigning that are as "pure" as those found anywhere. These new democracies thus present evidence of a connection between modernization and methods of campaigning, but they reverse the order of occurrence and causation that was contemplated in our theoretical framework.

Based on the foregoing discussion, it seems appropriate to define the role of modernization in changing campaign practices in this way: Modernization leads to a weakening of political parties and emergence of a powerful role for mass media. These conditions seem to be the immediate causes of changes in electoral practices, and thus mediate between modernization on the one hand and the modern model of campaigning on the other. To this view of underlying causes (modernization), intermediate facilitating conditions (weakened parties and powerful autonomous media), and results (modern campaign practices) should be added three variations. Sometimes, an additional intermediate condition is present in pragmatic political reforms that also may grow out of the pressures of modernization (such as desire for more efficient civil administrations) and lead to further weakening political parties and ensuing adoption of modern electoral practices. At other times, professional consultants endeavor to persuade candidates and parties to adopt innovative campaigning techniques before the conditions that favor them are in place. In these cases, the techniques are not likely to be widely practiced until the appropriate political and media environment has developed, at which point the new techniques move to center stage in the political process, as in Argentina. Finally, in the case of new democracies, the modern model of electoral practices may be adopted in order to stimulate more general modernization processes, rather than as an outgrowth of them. Modernization plays a critical role in the emergence of campaigning innovations in all these cases, but the path that leads from the former to the latter can take several different turns that represent important variations.

Contextualization of the Modern Model of Campaigning

As we have seen, the precise forms and influence of the modern model of campaigning are shaped in each country by a number of contextual factors. It is important to recognize that these contextual factors are closely interlinked and act jointly, not independently, to shape campaign practices. Consequently, it is at best difficult and at worst misleading to attempt to isolate the unique influence of each factor. As long as we take care to keep these difficulties in mind, however, the analyses offered in this volume allow us to elaborate more fully how contextual factors relate to the scope and consequences of campaign innovations.

The Electoral System   In the introductory chapter, we proposed that the key attribute of electoral systems which influences the adoption and impact of modern campaigning was whether voters cast their ballots directly for individual candidates, with the candidate who receives the most votes being elected (majority or plurality voting systems), or whether voters cast ballots for lists of candidates chosen by each party, with seats being divided in proportion to the share of votes received by each party (proportional voting systems). Majority and plurality voting systems, we hypothesized, favor the personalization of politics, which is such an integral part of the modern model of campaigning, while proportional voting systems may limit personalization.

The democracies we have examined provide evidence of the expected consequences of direct voting for individual candidates. In many of the cases we have considered in which candidates run as individuals—such as the 1989 Soviet elections, Italian and Israeli mayoral campaigns, the 1994 Italian election in which 75 percent of the seats in the parliament were filled by majority voting, and Argentine parliamentary elections—direct election has been cited as fostering personalization of the electoral contest. In some instances, direct election has led candidates to create their own campaign organizations and attempt to create a highly personalized relationship to their constituency, as in the cases of elections to the national legislatures of the United States, Argentina, and Italy.

At the same time, we have found personalization to be a theme of recent campaigns in virtually every democracy examined, whether presidential or parliamentary, whether practicing direct or proportional voting. The difference between these systems seems to be in the degree to which they foster personalization in a context in which personalization of politics is becoming ubiquitous. In proportional and parliamentary systems, personalization tends to focus on party leaders; in direct and presidential systems, personalization tends to focus on individual candidates as well as party leaders.

Within all electoral systems, the question of who selects the candidates to run for office seems to be key. The authority of the central leadership of a political party is undermined by use of primary elections to decide which candidates shall run in the general election. Primary elections pit aspiring candidates against others within the same political party and thus not only heighten the importance of personal considerations to the voting decision, but also take the selection of candidates out of the hands of party leaders. Primary elections are most common in presidential electoral systems, such as those found in the United States and Latin American countries, but they have also been used by some political parties in recent elections within parliamentary systems, such as Germany and Israel.

Another attribute of electoral systems that influences their hospitality to the modern model of campaigning is the frequency and timing of elections. A political system such as the United States, in which election campaigns are going on almost continuously, makes possible the development of an industry devoted to professional political consulting and campaign management. In a different context, the frequency with which elections have been held in the restored Spanish democracy has generated efforts to establish professional firms devoted exclusively to political consulting. Where elections are less frequent, political consulting is relegated to a seasonal sideline of advertising and public-relations firms. As Nimmo, Caspi, and others have noted in this volume, one of the many influences that contribute to adoption of the modern model is the development of a consulting industry having an economic stake in adoption of new campaign techniques requiring professional expertise.

The Structure of Party Competition   Our framework proposes that the speed and comprehensiveness with which the elements of modern campaigning are adopted is affected by the structure of party competition. A system of bipartisan competition dominated by two or three competitive parties encourages party appeals of the catch-all sort and favors the use of sophisticated communication strategies to create temporary aggregations of widely differing interests in order to win elections. In contrast, multiparty systems in which there are many competitive parties require that each party differentiate itself from others on distinctive ideological and programmatic grounds, creating the basis for more stable political representation that is perhaps less dependent on the modern model of campaigning for its success.

Recent experience of the eleven democracies we have examined suggests that the degree to which the structure of party competition influences adoption of new campaign practices may vary. Elements of the modern model are found nearly everywhere, from the United States' two-party system (with an unusual third party effort in the 1992 presidential campaign) to Russia's current array of thirteen political parties and Poland's profusion of 250 parties and party-like organizations. Moreover, as we have seen, traditional multiparty systems are becoming an endangered species as voting is transformed from an expression of solidarity with one's group and its allied ideology, institutions, and political party to an expression of opinion. Instead, we find catch-all tendencies in successful parties in most democracies, with their great dependence on sophisticated campaigning and communications techniques.

Among the countries we have considered, Sweden offers perhaps the best example of a traditional, competitive multiparty system, with a stable group of parties arrayed in a clear left-right pattern joined in recent years by populist and centrist parties that cut across traditional voting cleavages. Sweden also seems to be one of the countries in which the influence of modern campaign methods has been less pronounced, though even Swedish politics have become more personalized in Sweden's "mediarchy." On the analysis of Blumler, Kavanagh, and Nossiter, the United Kingdom also exhibits some of the restraints on the modern model that we expected to find in multiparty systems, although the United Kingdom has an essentially bipartisan party system and the modern publicity process is rather far advanced. Candidates' images and personal qualities are described as becoming steadily more important in elections in Germany and Israel, and as dominating elections in Spain, Italy, Argentina, Venezuela, Russia, and the United States, where we find centrist opinion parties endeavoring to attract support from across the political spectrum. Of course, the catch-all party that relies primarily on the personal appeal of its leaders is especially dependent on sophisticated communication strategies if it is to succeed in the modern political environment.

It seems prudent to conclude, then, that the structure of party competition makes less difference to the spread of campaign innovation than one might suppose, because the conditions that formerly supported ideologically and programmatically diverse multiparty systems of the traditional sort are themselves fading in many countries.

Regulation of Campaigning   Regulation of such matters as campaign finance and expenditures or political uses of mass media are not likely to forestall transition to the new-style model of campaigning, but they may well limit the particular forms and adaptations of modern methods that can be used effectively in any given country. Our contributors' reports indicate that several different regulatory approaches are being taken, generally for the purpose of limiting or avoiding altogether some of the worrisome features of contemporary media-centered campaigning. However, it turns out that the most typical forms of regulation have produced only mixed results in shaping campaign practices.

One regulatory approach is to control campaign expenditures and financing. The modern model of campaigning is expensive. It requires that parties or candidates assume substantial financial burdens in order to purchase technical expertise, fund the gathering and analysis of information about voters' concerns and sentiments, pay for the production of sophisticated campaign propaganda, purchase airtime and newspaper or magazine space for advertising, and so on. Limitations on campaigns' financial resources or expenditures thus attempt to control the extent to which the full array of new-style techniques can be deployed and the dependence of parties on financial contributors. In the United States, however, legal restrictions on private contributions to campaigns and on campaign expenditures have not succeeded in limiting the constant growth of campaign spending and development of innovations. Indeed, as Nimmo points out, election law has become a booming new legal specialty, in part to provide advice on how campaigns can pay for innovative techniques without violating legal requirements. Limits on campaign spending in Italy have been similarly ineffective, mostly because the limits only apply during the thirty-day "official" campaign period. The effect has been to shift expenditures to the unregulated period that precedes the official campaign. But the United Kingdom provides a contrary example, where tight limits on how much money can be spent in the constituencies, coupled with other regulations, have effectively controlled the scope of campaign activities.

Public financing of parties and campaigns has also yielded inconclusive results, as is illustrated by the contrast between Spain and Sweden. Parties rely on public financing for campaign expenses in both countries, yet Rospir suggests that Spanish campaigns have assimilated the modern model in its entirety, while Asp and Esaiasson maintain that new-style techniques have had somewhat less effect in Sweden than in other countries. In the Swedish case, in fact, public financing has provided resources that have allowed the largest parties to purchase technical expertise and other components of the modern model despite declining party membership. A mixture of public and private financing of campaigns is found in the United States and Argentina, both of which have embraced the media-centered model.

A more direct approach to regulating media-centered campaigning is to control campaigns' use of advertising. The most common approach is to prohibit or regulate in some way television advertising—which many view as the core of sophisticated media-centered campaigning—while allowing political advertising in other media and providing free television time for longer party broadcasts during campaigns. This approach has been followed in the United Kingdom, apparently with some success, as Blumler, Kavanagh, and Nossiter credit it in part with ensuring that "the heart of campaign communication is lodged in news and discussion programs." The most severe restriction on using television among the countries we have examined is found in Sweden, where campaigns are neither allowed to advertise nor provided time for party broadcasts. Although they write of the emergence of a "mediarchy" that dominates Sweden's political processes, our analysts maintain that Swedish campaigns are less consumed by some of the excesses of modern campaigning that are found elsewhere.

Germany follows a middle road, providing free time for a limited number of political commercials on the public television services that attract large audiences, while the parties may purchase commercial time on the private channels that reach smaller audiences. Despite the degree to which personalization dominated political advertising and news coverage in both print and broadcast media in 1990, during the first all-Germany campaign since World War II, Schoenbach found that voters remained more interested in the issues of the campaign than in the personalities of the party leaders.

In the democracies we examined, Israel offers a unique example of detailed regulations governing print advertising. The most recent (eighth) amendment to the election law controls the size of print ads, the number of colors that may be used, the number of ads a party list can run each day, and the total amount of print advertising that a party list can run during the three months preceding election day. Such finely detailed regulation of print advertising is the exception, however, to the main concern in most countries with television advertising.

What can be concluded about the effects of regulating television advertising on the character of campaigning? Limiting or prohibiting altogether the use of television advertising does seem to contain the reach, if not necessarily the character, of campaigns. The value of television advertising is that it provides access to the mass audience without journalists' mediation of the content of electoral propaganda. If campaigns cannot use extensive television advertising to reach voters who are less interested in politics and less inclined to watch longer party broadcasts, then campaigns must rely more on television news to get their message to the voters. Television news is regarded as a critical means of communicating with voters in every country we have considered, but perhaps controls on television advertising make news coverage even more important to campaigns. Ironically, as news becomes more important, politicians have greater incentive to try to manipulate journalists in order to win frequent and favorable coverage of their campaigns. Such manipulation involves staging events to appeal to the visual and dramatic preferences of television, reducing complicated issues to simple sound bites, pushing the most appealing personalities into the spotlight, and other techniques that have often been condemned for lowering the quality of political discourse found in modern campaigns. As we have seen, these manipulation techniques are practiced virtually everywhere, not just in countries where campaigns are prohibited or limited in their use of television advertising, and they lead to the struggle between politicians and journalists for control of the agenda that is a defining component of modern campaigning. The point to be made, then, is that control of advertising may well contain some of the elements of the contemporary model of campaigning while intensifying others.

A final common approach to regulating campaigns involves defining an "official" campaign period, during which electioneering practices are controlled or limited in some way. These official periods typically are of about one month's duration. As Mazzoleni explains, the rationale for declaring an official campaign period in Italy was that "a one-month period of time was thought to be too short for the feared excesses of the new politics to emerge." In countries that have taken this approach, the effect seems to have been to lengthen the actual campaign. That is, campaign activities are initiated earlier, so that desired techniques can be employed in the unregulated period before the official campaign begins. In the 1994 Italian campaign, the sophisticated media effort that made Berlusconi the leading candidate took place primarily during the two-month "pre-campaign" that preceded the official campaign. The three-and-a-half-week official 1992 British campaign was preceded an intensive period of campaigning that lasted two-and-a-half months. In Spain, as Rospir reports, the parties routinely begin campaigning long in advance of the official campaign. Thus, the strategy of defining an official period for campaigning does not seem to have succeeded, either in actually containing the duration of campaigns or in doing much to circumscribe their content and character.

Overall, there is evidence that regulation of campaigning has affected the contextualization of modern electioneering practices, although in the democracies we examined that effect is consistently pronounced only in the case of controls on television advertising. Regulations concerning campaign finance and expenditures and declarations of official campaign periods have had less impact on development of the media-centered campaign model. Indeed, the elements that comprise the contemporary model of campaigning are so tightly interwoven that a regulatory approach may limit the use of some elements by heightening the weight given to other elements of the model, or may succeed only in shifting the time when campaigning begins to an earlier point in the electoral process. We have not encountered an instance in which, by itself, regulation seems to have altered the essential character of contemporary campaigning.

National Political Culture   To political scientists, the term *political culture* refers to a particular research tradition that was launched by Almond and Verba's pioneering work, *The Civic Culture* (1963), lost popularity after a decade or so, and currently is enjoying a small revival of interest due to some recent reformulations (see Laitin, 1995). That tradition focused on the attitudes of persons living in a community or nation as constituting political culture. As explained in the introductory chapter, our framework conceives of political culture in a more sociological sense, and emphasizes structures of social aggregation and the development of consensus, mechanisms of political socialization and participation, and the roles and functions of primary and secondary groups and the effectiveness of their channels of communication as especially important components of political culture. Our view is similar in some respects to Wildavsky's conception of culture as "shared values indissolubly connected to social practices [institutions]," so that "comparing cultures means . . . *comparing cultures as totalities with values and practices joined*" (1987, p. 10). Wildavsky's perspective is quite different from our own, but both views regard political culture as the convergence of social relationships, values, and institutions in society that shape people's expectations about and behavior toward politics.

Understood in this rather expansive way, political culture encompasses a broader terrain and more of what makes a society what it is than does a nation's electoral system, structure of party competition, or regulation of campaign activities. Indeed, the latter three contextual factors might be regarded as growing out of and expressing various aspects of a nation's political culture. It is not surprising, then, that, in the countries examined by our analysts, political culture shapes in important ways how modern campaign practices are contextualized in each country.

We focus here on general patterns that emerge from the relationships between political culture and campaign practices in the eleven democracies we have examined. For purposes of this discussion, we group the countries according to the same principle that dictated the organization of this volume—more established democracies with stable political cultures, new and recently restored democracies, and democracies facing current or recent pressures that are potentially destabilizing—on the working assumption that the political cultures within each group of countries are likely to share some important structural and functional attributes which distinguish them from political cultures of countries in the other groups. That is, we assume that, among other things, a country's political culture reflects and is related to the history and present standing of political institutions and processes in that country.

The political cultures of the various nations examined in this volume are strikingly diverse. Nevertheless, the standing and functions of political parties are similar. Analysts in every country write of the weak condition of political parties, their inability to inspire partisan loyalty, and their resort to personalized appeals as a survival strategy in the face of their ineffectiveness as agents of political socialization, grassroots organization, and interest aggregation along traditional lines. Also, in every country, few have resisted the modern campaign model's allure and promise of making electoral efforts compelling when parties no longer elicit allegiance from stable constituencies. The weak state of political parties and the use of innovative campaign techniques are constants that cut across the particulars of national political cultures. This does not mean that political culture is irrelevant to the local contextualization of modern campaigning, however. As we will suggest, the political cultures of our eleven cases seem to have influenced, in patterned ways, how and why these two constants have emerged and the comprehensiveness and style with which the modern model of campaigning has been adopted.

At a general level, and notwithstanding their obvious differences, the political cultures of the four countries we characterized as having established and stable democracies—the United States, the United Kingdom, Sweden, and Germany—share several attributes. In each, support for democracy is strong and deep, although the public is less supportive and somewhat more cynical about political parties, political leaders, and the effectiveness of government than in the past. The role of broad-based traditional structures, such as religious institutions and trade unions, in aggregating interests, socializing members to the community, and vote guidance has declined. In their place have arisen more narrowly constituted microaggregations, such as one-issue advocacy groups, that compete to represent segmented interests in a more fragmented political culture. Mass media, especially television, have emerged as important agents of socialization and are widely regarded as main sources of information that shapes political opinions. The political parties' individual programs are formulated within a broad framework of consensual social values and goals.

The comprehensiveness and style with which the modern model of campaigning has been adopted in countries with established and stable political cultures have varied in ways that reflect more specific features of the political culture of each country. Despite the declining standing of politicians and political parties in all four countries, the political cultures of the United Kingdom, Sweden, and Germany retain somewhat greater respect for political actors than is found in the United States and expect political activity to be dignified and principled. Thus, candidates for office in the United States are somewhat more likely to style themselves as "outsiders" who oppose traditional political institutions and practices. The American approach to campaigning is widely disdained in these countries as undignified, Madison Avenue–dominated, unprincipled, and inappropriate to serious matters, even though various elements of U.S. campaigning are also practiced in the United Kingdom, Sweden, and Germany, as we have seen. Thus, expressions of disdain have to do more with style and the Europeans' more traditional conception of political leaders and activity than with strategies and campaign practices. Politics is personalized in each country, but the qualities of political leaders that engender favorable evaluations differ according to the respective political cultures. Adroit rhetorical skills and keen intelligence displayed in the House of Commons earn approval for British politicians, for example, whereas demonstrating that they share voters' feelings has stood candidates in good stead in recent U.S. campaigns.

The version of the modern model of campaigning practiced in the United States is more openly and unrestrainedly commercial, which Blumler, Kavanagh, and Nossiter attribute to U.S. culture being more accepting of commercialism, while the other three countries have formulated somewhat more conservative versions to suit their own political cultures. The U.S. model is also more comprehensive, as American campaigns pour more financial resources into more technologies and innovations in each election than do parties in the other three countries. With the withering of traditional grassroots organizations and the need to become sophisticated in using mass media, campaigns in each country necessarily rely on technical experts and professional advisers. In all four countries, there is tension between the traditional forms of political intelligence and principled programs preferred by political leaders and the marketing approach to audience research and decision making advocated by campaign experts. The stronger structural position of the parliamentary parties in the United Kingdom, Sweden, and Germany may restrain the professional advisers' influence more than in the United States, where candidate-run campaigns may grant the professionals more voice in decision making. But in every country, political leaders emphasize that they, not the marketing professionals, remain in charge, and stress that their motivations and goals are programmatic, not merely electoral.

The political cultures of the new and restored democracies we examined—Russia, Poland, and Spain—are similar in some general respects that distinguish them from the more established, stable political cultures. Each began life as a democracy without any democratic political institutions. As the tangible expression of democracy, election campaigns took on particular significance. Support for democracy is generally strong, but the political cultures of Poland and Russia are rent by fundamental disagreements about what forms of political and economic organization of the state ought to be preferred, and public approval of democratic and market reforms is conditional and contingent in important sectors of society. The latter two countries have not yet developed an effective system of political parties and, lacking structures for aggregating and representing interests, the bases of popular support are even more personalized than elsewhere. Enclaves of traditional subcultures and institutions, such as the Catholic Church in Poland and Spain, and their networks of interpersonal communication and influence retain more authority and influence over voting than is typical of established democracies.

Confusion and collapse within the newspaper industries in Russia and Poland, and the comparatively low levels of newspaper readership in Spain, made television the natural focus of campaigning. Highly personalized, media-centered campaigns were made necessary by the lack of any party history, and new-style techniques encountered somewhat less resistance than has been the case where change evolved more gradually as a result of processes of modernization. Nevertheless, some (largely unsuccessful) campaigns have styled themselves "against" the modern model, as when the Russian Communist Party eschewed modern campaign techniques in order to demonstrate its opposition to "foreign" models and influences in the 1993 parliamentary campaign, and the 1989 campaign of Poland's ruling Communist Party offered multiple candidates presenting personalized, candidate-centered messages in an effort to communicate that it had broken with the past and embraced democracy.

Successful candidates and parties in the newer democracies have generally practiced modern campaigning because they face even more extreme forms of the political conditions that, in more established political cultures, have resulted from gradual processes of modernization, such as the absence of political parties. Moreover, a model of political campaigning has been adopted as a de facto substitute for a democratic political culture in the new democracies. In Spain, Rospir suggests, the media-centered campaign model has been generalized to a model of government which is unsuited to an effective parliamentary democracy. In Russia, Mickiewicz and Richter worry that politicians' reliance on television for intensely personalized campaigns "could well retard the development of the very political parties that render the system efficacious."

Political parties and candidates have come to modern campaign practices by yet a different route in the four political cultures that have recently or are now facing strong, potentially destabilizing tensions—Israel, Italy, Argentina, and Venezuela. Despite their quite different political histories and present circumstances, rapid changes and daunting pressures have challenged the traditional political culture of each country. Israeli political culture has faced the formidable tasks of managing tensions and fundamental differences in outlook between traditional and modern and between sacred and secular cultures, while absorbing a tide of immigrants and effecting transition to a new generation of political leaders, all within the context of continuing struggle for a lasting and secure peace. The stable political culture of post-war Italy, which had been eroded by the gradual and corrosive effects of modernization on its traditional political institutions, was plunged into crisis by public outrage over widespread, systemic corruption which set the stage for Berlusconi's victory in the 1994 election. In Argentina and Venezuela, pessimism about political parties and politicians runs deep and wide, leading to rejection of the parties by growing numbers of independent voters in the former, and withdrawal from the political process by rising numbers of nonvoters in the latter.

The political cultures of these countries also encompass, to differing degrees, internal tensions between the traditional and the modern. As Caspi points out, strong enclaves of traditional subcultures continue to exist within the modern State of Israel. Traditional modes of social organization have survived, especially in the rural countryside, although perhaps with diminished effectiveness, amid rapid modernization and change in Argentina's return to democracy and Venezuela's dazzling economic boom and bust. Italy is, of course, the most thoroughly modernized of the four, where formerly powerful institutions, such as the church, have lost much of their traditional political influence.

The emergence and success of new-style approaches to political campaigning have been shaped by tensions and fissures within the political cultures and circumstances of each of these countries. Modern campaign practices have been embraced perhaps most fully and with greatest success in Italy, where the collapse of the post–World War II political establishment accelerated the adoption of new-style electoral practices, culminating in a "flash" party that succeeded in mobilizing widespread support by media-centered propaganda based on sophisticated market research. Campaign innovations have also permeated Venezuelan campaigns, where, in the face of intractable economic difficulties and sharply negative political journalism, they have had little success in reversing the public's discontent and pessimism about politics and government. Argentine campaigning mixes contemporary and traditional approaches, with the latter still flourishing, especially in rural areas where modernization has had less effect. This blend of the old and new reflects Argentina's complex political culture; a thoroughly modern theme— candidates try to shed the image of the discredited traditional politician and style themselves instead as embodying the concerns and desires of ordinary citizens—is developed by means which suit the particular mixture of modern and traditional cultures across the country. Israel's political culture, in which the secular and modern exist alongside enclaves of strong traditional subcultures, might be expected to give rise to a blend of campaign practices similar to what is seen in Argentina. However, as Caspi reports, Israeli campaigns have taken up most of the elements of the modern model. The lack of fit between modern campaign practices and traditional sectors of society leaves modern campaigners who fail to mobilize fully the secular and modernized electorate vulnerable to defeat by traditional groups which mobilize their members by traditional means to advance their group interests. Thus, in political cultures facing crises of confidence and conflict, politicians have adopted many elements of the modern model. In some cases, they have done so to the exclusion of traditional political activities, even though enclaves of traditional culture remain strong in their countries. In other cases, traditional electoral activities have been preserved or transformed to take on new functions within a modernized overall approach to campaigning.

Overall, a comparison of campaign methods and political cultures in the eleven democracies we have singled out for examination brings to light several different paths by which politicians have come to adopt modern campaign approaches. In the four established, stable political cultures, new-style electoral campaigning has emerged through a developmental process that reflects the gradual impact of modernization on political culture and political institutions. Some of modernization's effects on established political cultures and institutions are also seen in the newest democracies, where they are instead consequences of the absence of effective democratic institutions and political culture. Lacking effectual political parties, campaigners in the new democracies generally have seized upon media-centered campaigning as their only possibility for attracting political support. Most of the democracies we have examined which face crises of confidence and conflict also are societies that blend elements of the traditional and the modern. Argentina seems to have developed a mixture of campaign practices that reflect its culture, while Israel and Venezuela have moved to new-style electoral approaches that are mismatched to the traditional elements within their societies.

The Media System   Our framework proposed that, in any given country, contextualization of the modern model of electoral campaigning is influenced by two attributes of the local media system: ownership and degree of technological advancement. Our concern with ownership referred to television systems, where commercial ownership would favor the personalization of politics and undermine the authority of political parties by offering individual candidates the possibility of reaching voters through advertising. In public-service television systems, we thought, the practice of providing free airtime to political parties would keep the focus more on the parties than on individual candidates, and thus limit personalization. Our interest in the degree to which a national media system is technologically advanced focused on whether television had emerged as the most important medium reaching the largest and most heterogenous audience. The centrality of television, we speculated, favors adoption of new-style methods of campaigning.

It turned out that television is the central medium and core of campaign communication in each of the countries we examined (in order to obtain much variation in the centrality of television, we would have had to include in our sample one of the relatively few countries in which television is not a pervasive medium, such as India, where estimates of the television audience are as low as 25% of the population, according to Chen and Chaudhary, 1991). The more relevant technological difference affecting the status of television in these countries concerns proliferation of alternative television services and corresponding fragmentation of the television audience. On this dimension, the United States exemplifies an increasingly fragmented television audience, while Israeli television exemplifies the other extreme, with its broadcasting monopoly (although, even in Israel, the viewing audience is fragmented to some degree by access to television services of neighboring countries, such as Jordan, and introduction of cable television). Thus, in the democracies we examined, the appropriate technological issue is not whether television occupies the central position linking politicians to the public, but rather the extent to which the television audience is fragmented among many services and channels. The more fragmented the audience, the more difficult is the politicians' task of manipulating multiple television news services to their advantage and the greater the possibility that viewers can avoid exposure to political programs and advertisements carried on only one or two channels. Fragmentation, in turn, results from the commercialization of media ownership and the ensuing competition for audiences.

Policies concerning political advertising and free time for party political broadcasts on television do not map simply onto commercial versus public media ownership. Instead, availability of paid and unpaid television time has to do more with regulatory policies, which vary widely. Political advertising is allowed under various regulatory arrangements on public-service television in countries such as Germany and Russia. Free airtime is provided to political parties for election broadcasts on some privately owned television services, such as in Argentina. Sweden's public television both bans political advertising and provides no time to parties for political broadcasts. Regardless of television ownership and policies concerning advertising and free time for political broadcasts, frequent and favorable exposure on television news seems to be the primary goal of campaigners virtually everywhere. Politicians' devotion to strategies intended to win news coverage of their campaigns is documented in detail by our analysts in the United States, the United Kingdom, Sweden, Germany, Russia, Spain, Poland, Israel, Argentina, and elsewhere.

The factor which seems to determine television's influence in campaigns more than ownership or audience size is the degree of journalistic autonomy that television services exercise in electoral reportage. The countries we have considered illustrate three different approaches with respect to journalistic autonomy, reflecting primarily such matters as state control or influence over television and the presence or lack of a tradition of media autonomy. One role television can play is that of a passive conduit through which information passes from politicians to the public without significant mediation or interpretation by journalists. This passive role was seen in Russian television during the 1993 Russian parliamentary campaign, in Polish television, which gives comparatively little coverage to campaigns and is subject to more political pressure now than under the Communist regime, and German public-service television, where regulations to ensure impartiality have produced withdrawal from any independent viewpoint. At the other extreme is the case where television takes a blatantly partisan role, urging preference for one or another party or candidate. Television services have acted as propagandists for parties in Spain, where state-controlled public television is notoriously and consistently partisan in favor of the government party, in Russian television during the 1993 campaign for the Russian Federation referendum, and in the uncharacteristic "dirty tricks" campaign that Jakubowicz describes

Polish television playing during the second ballot campaign of the 1990 presidential election.

The third and most common role for television in the countries we examined is also the role most associated with the modern model of campaigning, namely, as an independent voice and co-actor in the electoral process. Here, television journalists offer their own viewpoint, based not in partisanship, but in a professional ideology of journalism that is widely shared in many countries. Their task, as journalists see it, is not to be a mere conduit for what politicians say and do, but rather to assess for viewers the accuracy and likely consequences of politicians' statements and proposals, and perhaps to provide independent commentary on the issues facing the nation. This role, as Mazzoleni explains, was newly taken on by Italian public television in the 1994 parliamentary campaign, is a goal of BBC political journalists who struggle to find a constructive role for themselves in the face of increasingly sophisticated manipulation by politicians, and is familiar in the United States, with such practices as "ad watch" stories that assess the truthfulness of political advertising. Carried to extremes, television journalists may devote themselves zealously to undermining the credibility of all politicians, as in the case of Venezuela. Despite the differences between the three roles that television services play in politics, politicians everywhere seem to devote enormous energy to manipulating media to their own ends and complain about a negative tone in much campaign coverage that, they claim, undermines public support of the political system itself.

We end this discussion of factors that influence how modern techniques are contextualized in each country by returning to the theme with which we began: The particular forms and adaptions of modern campaigning that are practiced are shaped by the full range of contextual factors acting in concert. For example, in Britain, the combination of a rather conservative political culture, party selection of candidates, prohibition of television advertising, tight limits on spending in the parliamentary constituencies, and television journalists who take an active role in providing comparatively extensive news coverage of campaigns in regularly scheduled and special election programs has produced an approach to modern campaigning that places special stress on politicians' sophistication in attracting news coverage of their activities and programs and in presenting themselves to advantage in interview programs and daily morning press conferences throughout the brief campaign period. In Italy, by contrast, the convergence of cynicism about the political establishment, access to the public through television advertising as well as party broadcasts, the possibility of candidates mounting media campaigns against opponents within their own political party, and a lengthy pre-campaign in which limits on campaign activities do not apply, invites a fuller, less selective instantiation of the modern model of electioneering. Alternatively, we have seen cases, such as Israel, where modern media-centered strategies have been adopted in spite of some important contextual factors, leading to contradictions between campaign practices and enclaves of traditional cultures. Politicians' decisions about whether and which campaign practices to adopt, and in what form, are not in every case appropriate to the context, but their motives in selecting strategies and the likelihood of modern methods succeeding are determined to a significant extent by local contextual factors.

CONCLUSION: ISSUES AND IMPLICATIONS

On the strength of our contributors' analyses of the experiences of eleven quite different democracies, it seems clear that the causes, forms, and consequences of modern campaign techniques are complex and variable. At the same time, comparison of developments in the countries we have examined makes it clear that, in its general contours, our framework for understanding the subject is close to the mark. What we have called the modern model of campaigning is real, the strategies and priorities that define it have emerged in numerous otherwise dissimilar democracies and are continuing to spread at a rapid rate, and it is contextualized in various ways but leads to roughly similar consequences wherever it is found. We attempt to capture some of the complexity, variability, and commonalities as we conclude by addressing the model's archetypal character and some issues concerning the consequences of modern campaign practices.

Model or Archetype?

One issue that figures in most of the chapters within this volume concerns the possibilities for adopting the modern model of campaigning selectively—that is, adopting some elements of the model but not others—and adapting modern practices to local contexts. This issue might be formulated as asking whether modern campaigning practices are best understood as a *model* or an *archetype*. As we use the term here, a model is an example for imitation, such that every instance of the model is precisely like every other instance. If modern campaigning constitutes a model in this sense, then we would expect contemporary practices to comprise an indivisible unity which admits very little variation and takes the same forms wherever it is found. On the other hand, an archetype, as we use the term here, is an original pattern on which subsequent constructions of the same type are based. The archetype consists of some general principles or attributes which may be expressed in various ways, leading to considerable differences between instances. If modern campaign practices are best understood as reflecting a common archetype, then we would expect to find significant variation between electoral practices in different countries and ample possibilities for local adaptation. Despite the differences, however, we should be able to observe some common underlying principles at play in each country (namely, the principles which define the archetype).

On balance, the experiences of the democracies we have considered suggest that, for purposes of this discussion, the suite of modern campaign methods is closer to an archetype than model (although, to be consistent with usage throughout this volume, we shall continue to refer to the "modern model"). Not all of the methods are found in every instance. Television advertising is fundamental to modern campaigning in the United States and some other countries, but is prohibited altogether in many other countries where modern campaigning is found. Political parties remain firmly in charge of campaigns in most countries where modern methods are employed, but campaigns are more candidate centered than party centered in some countries, as we have seen. Despite such variations, it would be wrong to conclude that campaign practices in each country have followed paths which are completely unique. On the contrary, we have found, in each country, campaign practices based on the underlying principles that define the modern model as an archetype: heavy emphasis on personalization, extensive reliance on mass media for campaign propaganda, incorporation of professional expertise, adapting campaign activities and strategies to media requirements, and so on.

Because the modern model is an archetype, it need not drive out completely traditional forms of electioneering activity where they are appropriate, although adoption of modern practices is likely to transform some of the functions of traditional activities or to develop new forms for accomplishing traditional functions (such as replacement of grand meetings of the faithful in public spaces with *caravanas* in Argentine campaigns). The archetype concept also suggests that modern practices are dynamic, developing and elaborating new forms to more fully realize the archetype's underlying principles as local circumstances change over time.

Even though the modern model permits its underlying principles to be expressed in varying ways according to local conditions, it is important to also recognize that there is a certain synergy among modern campaigning practices. That is, each of the major elements of the model implies or leads to the other elements: Political parties that cannot win elections by relying on loyal, traditional supporters inevitably focus their efforts on mass media to reach the public; in media systems that enjoy journalistic autonomy, politicians' attempts to exploit the media tend to elicit responses from journalists in the form of disdaining reporting that exposes the intended manipulation; media-focused campaigns tend to be highly personalized campaigns; personalized campaigns tend to simplify and dramatize issues; and so forth. Thus, we can acknowledge that the modern model of campaigning allows some local adaptation and selection of what methods in which forms will be adopted, while at the same time we recognize, at a general level, that modern methods are intertwined as a coherent expression of the modern conditions of politics and communications. This recognition is important, because it reminds us that modern campaigning is not only a reflection of conditions within a given country, but can also shape those conditions along certain lines.

Consequences of Modern Campaigning

We suspect most readers would agree with Nimmo's observation in this volume that the various methods and practices employed in political campaigns by politicians and journalists are so closely intertwined that "any shift in one or more aspects and/or phases [of campaigning] yields consequences not only for general campaign processes, but for the workings of all politics as well." Yet it is no simple matter to isolate the individual consequences of modern campaigning because, as we have seen, modern campaign methods are both cause and effect of the modern condition of politics and communications and are also rooted in the underlying process of modernization from which those modern conditions emerge. As McQuail observes about the difficulties of identifying how mass media have changed political and other institutions, "Because this is a slow process, occurring along with other kinds of social change, the specific contribution of the mass media cannot be accounted for with any certainty. . . . As always, it is hard to separate out the effects of media change from broad changes in society working both on the media and on political institutions and there is much room for dispute about what is the real cause of a given effect" (1987, pp. 289–291).

The above reservations notwithstanding, it is possible to identify some general consequences that seem to be strongly associated with modern campaign approaches virtually everywhere they are practiced. And it is important to do so because, as modern techniques continue to spread and to become the dominant way in which political institutions interact with the media and the public, present consequences of the modern model can reveal something about what the future of democratic politics may be like. We will identify several issues that, across countries and circumstances, seem to be most strongly associated with contemporary campaign practices.

Toward "Virtual Politics" Certainly, the most worrisome aspect of new-style electoral politics is its potential for diverting attention from political realities to a fabricated world of "virtual politics." Some characterize media-centered modern politics as an exercise in manipulating the appearance of things under conditions where the public has few if any alternative sources against which to test media representations. Can continuing to follow this path lead us to a point where appearances are all that matters? In the United States, according to Nimmo's analysis, campaigns package information in ahistorical and nonhistorical ways as ever-shrinking sound bites and "factoids," and assertions, treated as true though not supported by evidence, come to replace the facts themselves. "Symbolic inflation," in which voters are inundated by a proliferation of symbols inflated by hype, redundancy, euphemisms, and jargon, raises the specter of "the discarnate voter" who loses touch with identity, geographical location, and social function. In short, political opinions formed in a virtual world created by politicians and media may have little to do with reality. Some recent events in the United States seem to confirm Nimmo's diagnosis. President George Bush, who lost his bid for reelection to Bill Clinton in 1992, insisted during the campaign that the American economy was much more robust than it was portrayed by Clinton and by consensus of the media; Bush was proved to be correct by an economic upturn that began right after the election and before Clinton took office. Similarly, the Clinton administration galvanized national attention by proclaiming a crisis in health care for which the administration ultimately proposed sweeping reforms. The debate later subsided when, looking at the same set of facts, Clinton's opponents successfully proclaimed that there was no crisis after all.

Admittedly, the United States may be an extreme case of politics dominated by media-created, politician-manipulated reality. But concerns about virtual politics are by no means limited to the United States. In this volume,

Blumler, Kavanagh, and Nossiter worry about the possibility of politics becoming a virtual reality "in which mass perceptions of politics are all that matter." The subtext of media-created political reality is also present in more restrained terms in Asp and Esaiasson's description of "mediarchy" in Sweden, and in Polish Television's construction of a story purporting to show that 1990 Presidential candidate Stanislaw Tyminski treated his wife and children cruelly by refusing to provide them with living expenses. Echoes of manufactured realities can be seen as well in the blatant pro-government partisanship of Spanish public television, and in Caspi's worry that new-style Israeli political campaigns strive to create perceptions of general support and undoubted victory, and may divert attention from real issues and narcotize large segments of the electorate. In the same vein, Mayobre observes that, in Venezuela, "television leads to candidates changing their objectives, from rallying voters behind their cause and making them enthusiastic about a given objective ideology, to having as their supreme objective not offending anybody. . . . The preferred candidate is a bland one who can speak in sound bites, provide good photo opportunities, and look like a 'movie' politician."

Jakubowicz provides the counterweight to concerns about democratic politics becoming a politician-manipulated, media-created fiction, fabricated to interest a skeptical and bored audience. The recent experience of Poland leads Jakubowicz to claim, in this volume, that "the media's influence on election results is in inverse proportion to the gravity of issues facing the voters, the stakes involved for them personally in the election result, and the extent of their political commitment." Jakubowicz is correct that when issues such as whether to adopt a new form of government and economic system are at stake, voters may have sources other than television news on which to base their opinions. The somewhat analogous circumstance in the stable democracies is what are called "obtrusive issues" in agenda-setting research, as in the case of the unemployed worker who need not turn to television news to discover whether unemployment is a serious problem (see Weaver, Graber, McCombs, & Eyal, 1981).

Most campaign issues in most democracies most of the time are neither obtrusive, as in the case of the unemployed worker, nor calls for transforming political and economic systems, as in the case of the early Polish elections. Often, the issues featured in a campaign are not real political issues at all, in the sense of being the most pressing problems facing the country. Instead, political parties tend to manufacture or emphasize carefully selected issues on which they believe they hold the more popular position. The practice of choosing campaign issues for strategic purposes leads Blumler, Kavanagh, and Nossiter to complain that campaigns are becoming less relevant to "the post-election tasks of government." Caspi complains that "real" issues are avoided in new-style Israeli campaigns, as Rospir laments that the pressing problems facing Spanish democracy are overlooked or relegated to the background in personality-centered campaigns.

It is easy when writing about this subject to imagine some earlier golden era when politicians addressed real issues without thought to strategic advantage and when political campaigns were exercises in mass civic education within a vibrant public sphere of political discourse. Such imaginings are romantic myths, for the most part. What the combination of modern campaign-marketing methods, pervasive mass media, and the weakening of traditional institutions that formerly provided alternative information and opinions has done is to make it easier for political campaigns to take us even farther from reality. This possibility has been noted in most of the countries examined in this volume.

Undermining Political Parties   In traditional democratic theory, political parties are regarded as the essential mechanism for aggregating, balancing, and representing interests in the orderly functioning of government. As we have seen, some of the attributes of modern campaign practices tend to weaken, not strengthen, political parties. The modern campaign strategy which dominates all others and best fits media logic is personalization, concentrating on telegenic leaders while programs and policy proposals remain in the background. Personalization has been identified as a key strategy being practiced in every democracy we have examined in this volume.

Personalization undermines political parties because it engenders support for an appealing leader, not for the ideas and programs of the party as an institution. Indeed, we have seen case after case where the appeal of the leader is judged to have overshadowed the ideas of the party. As the basis of political support, personalization is transitory and fragile. Massive shifts in support occur when leaders change or lose their novelty or reveal previously unpublicized qualities. Personalization of political appeal is especially unsuited to the new democracies because it may prevent political parties per se from ever establishing themselves in the public's confidence as anything more than the platform of a popular leader. Mickiewicz and Richter are well justified in their concern that, because of its intense personalization of the political dispute in Russia, "television . . . could well retard the development of the very political parties that render the electoral system efficacious."

Democratic politics has always and everywhere been personalized to a greater or lesser degree. But some of the mechanisms that formerly held personalization in check are receding in the face of the modern condition of politics and communications. As we have seen, there are marginal differences in the degree to which different sorts of electoral and government systems have been affected by personalization. Structural arrangements, such as proportional voting systems and mechanisms that enforce strong party discipline, can maintain party effectiveness in the legislative process. But it is clear that, because of the erosion of partisan allegiances and the need to adapt to media logic, political parties everywhere are pursuing and experiencing the consequences of the strategy of personalization. Ironically, the strategy which has been adopted in part because of the weakened condition of political parties does not strengthen the position of parties. Instead, personalization allows parties with telegenic, appealing leaders and top candidates to attempt to attract momentary, opinion-based support in the fragmented, disaggregated modern electorate, support that does not create loyalty to the party and can be lost as quickly as it was won.

Growing Skepticism about Politics and Politicians   Erosion of public respect and support for politicians and the political establishment is a common phenomenon in most of the democracies we have examined. The Italian experience, where, in 1994, full implementation of modern campaigning methods occurred alongside renewal of public support for the political process stands out as the exception to the general rule. In most of the countries considered, concerns have been expressed about increasingly negative press coverage of politics as contributing to new levels of public skepticism and even cynicism. What has been described as negative coverage, in turn, often reflects the circumstance of journalists who seek a constructive role to play in the political process that is consistent with their professional ideology and who are subject to increasingly sophisticated efforts by politicians to manipulate the press. In this respect, modern campaign practices can be conceived as enmeshed in a struggle between politicians and journalists to control the campaign agenda. This struggle is perhaps most advanced and explicit in the established democracies with stable political cultures, where journalists commonly establish and display their journalistic independence by focusing coverage on poll results, campaign horse races, and campaign strategies and blunders rather than candidates' statements, and report staged political events and actions in a disdaining manner that exposes the manipulative intent behind them. In a spiraling fashion, politicians adapt their conduct to the requirements of media, which respond by unmasking politicians' strategies, which in turn leads politicians to develop even more compelling and sophisticated media strategies, which prompts further reaction from journalists, and so on. In the process, politicians and journalists may become preoccupied with their escalating struggle within a closed circuit of discourse where voters' concerns receive less attention. The political reporting that emerges from this context often offers negative characterizations of politicians and the political process as manipulative and concerned more with appearances than reality.

On the other side of the equation, practitioners of new-style campaigning further contribute to erosion of the standing of politicians by characterizing themselves as "outsiders" who are not sullied by the moral defects of typical politicians; by resorting to negative campaigning, which is thought by many to be effective in the media-centered, modern campaign environment; and by avoiding intractable problems in favor of real or constructed campaign issues with which they can advance their popularity. Variations of these practices have been noted in the United States, the United Kingdom, Sweden, Spain, Israel, Argentina, and Venezuela.

Of course, the growth of political cynicism also, and more important, reflects matters that have little to do with political campaigning, such as the actual performance of elected leaders and political parties, and the perceived effectiveness of government in addressing pressing problems. But evidence from a number of countries suggests that modern campaign practices contribute to public doubts about politicians and the political process.

Providing More Information to Less Interested Voters On the credit side of the accounting ledger, there is ample evidence from the United States, Germany, Britain, Italy, and elsewhere that the move to media-centered campaigning has resulted in voters with less interest in politics being exposed to more information about campaigns. Such information is acquired as a consequence of general media exposure, where voters need not seek out but rather happen across political information in news and public affairs programs, party broadcasts, and, where permitted, political advertising. The quality of the information provided may be uneven, as Nimmo notes in the case of the United States, but the effectiveness of modern campaigning in delivering information to a broader segment of the public is well documented in many countries and should be regarded as a positive contribution.

Looking to the Future

The reader will have noted that many of the consequences of modern campaigning we have identified are worrisome. It is perhaps ironic that the campaign innovations which have been touted so loudly by professional campaign experts and seized upon so eagerly by ambitious candidates and political parties may undermine democratic political institutions over the long term, rather than strengthen them. Certainly, the new methods have not proven to be an effective antidote for rising public cynicism and disenchantment with politics and government in many countries. Moreover, as we have seen, legislative intervention has not been very successful in preventing modernization from affecting the political process. Even prohibitions of political advertising on television and limits on campaign expenditures have not been sufficient to forestall the modernization of political communication.

Does the spread, by whatever route is taken in each country, of modern campaigning methods signal a troubled future for democracies? Certainly, there are ample causes for concern in the weakening of political parties, the declining standing of politicians, the difficulties of journalists in finding constructive roles to play in the political process, and the advance of political marketing over political representation. All of these trends make it more difficult for democracy to work in the way we have traditionally expected democratic institutions to operate. But while modern campaigning offers plenty of reasons for concern, it also gives reason for optimism by increasing the exposure to political information of historically less interested and less informed segments of the population. Moreover, traditional political forms and activities are not in every case abandoned when new methods are adopted; on the contrary, they survive where locally appropriate, sometimes with transformed functions. And the case of Italy, where the move to modern campaign methods was associated with a renaissance of support for the democratic process, reminds us that not all the outcomes of modern methods, however contextualized, are undesirable.

We are witnessing a transformation of how democracies work. Media logic, publicity strategies, and a fragmented electorate that lacks partisan allegiances are forcing political parties to take on new roles, new faces, new activities, and turn traditional activities to new purposes. The power of autonomous mass media is creating new rules for democratic practice. The pace of change has outrun democratic theory, however. Our traditional view of political parties and democratic institutions is rooted in a time when representation was anchored in stable cleavages of class and interest. Those cleavages have dissolved, leading to the modern condition of politics.

Without minimizing legitimate, well-founded concerns, it is fair to say that most of the consequences of modern campaigning that have been identified in this volume and might be read as offering a pessimistic prospect for the future of democracy are, at base, different ways of saying that political parties and democratic political processes no longer work in the way they used to. This is hardly surprising, since the conditions on which our traditional view of political parties was founded no longer exist. Ultimately, it is difficult to know what to make of the changes that are occurring so rapidly, because we have not yet developed a modern conception of democracy to match modern conditions. It is hoped that this volume has helped to clarify and explain some of the trends and sources of national variation in how elections, the most visible expression of democracy, are developing. The daunting task for the future is envisioning how, given the modern condition of politics and communications, democracy can function most effectively with transformed institutions fit to the new environment. That task must await the accumulation of more experience with the new environment and the application of greater wisdom than we are able to bring to the effort.

REFERENCES

Almond, G. A., & Verba, S. (1963). *The civic culture.* Princeton: Princeton University Press.

Altheide, D. L., & Snow, R. P. (1979). *Media logic.* Beverly Hills, Calif.: Sage.

Bennett, W. L. (1992a). *The governing crisis: Media, money, and marketing in American elections.* New York: St. Martin's Press.

Bennett, W. L. (1992b). White noise: The perils of mass mediated democracy. *Communication Monographs, 59,* 401–406.

Blumler, J. G. (1990). Elections, the media and the modern publicity process. In M. Ferguson (Ed.), *Public communication: The new imperatives* (pp. 101–113). London: Sage.

Blumler, J. G., McLeod, J. M., & Rosengren, K. E. (1992). An introduction to comparative communication research. In J. G. Blumler, J. M. McLeod, & K. E. Rosengren (Eds.), *Comparatively speaking: Communication and culture across space and time* (pp. 3–18). Newbury Park, Calif.: Sage.

Butler, D., & Ranney, A. (1992). Conclusion. In D. Butler & A. Ranney (Eds.), *Electioneering: A comparative study of continuity and change* (pp. 278–286). Oxford: Clarendon Press.

Chen, A. C., & Chaudhary, A. G. (1991). Asia and the Pacific. In J. G. Merrill (Ed.), *Global journalism: Survey of international communication* (2nd ed., pp. 205–266). New York: Longman.

Dahl, R. A. (1956). *A preface to democratic theory.* Chicago: University of Chicago Press.

Dahl, R. A. (1971). *Polyarchy: Participation and opposition.* New Haven: Yale University Press.

Franklin, B. (1994). *Packaging politics: Political communications in Britain's media democracy.* London: Edward Arnold.

Giddens, A. (1990). *The consequences of modernity.* Cambridge: Polity Press.

Gurevitch, M., & Blumler, J. G. (1993). Longitudinal analysis of an election communication system: Newsroom observation at the BBC 1966–1992. *Osterreichische Zeitschrift fur Politikwissenschaft* [Austrian Journal of Political Science], 22(4), 427–444.

Jamieson, K. H. (1992). *Dirty politics: Deception, distraction, and democracy.* New York: Oxford University Press.

Laitin, D. D. (1995). The civic culture at 30 [Review essay]. *American Political Science Review, 89,* 168–173.

Mazzoleni, G. (1987). Media logic and party logic in campaign coverage: The Italian General Election of 1983. *European Journal of Communication, 2*(1), 81–103.

McQuail, D. (1987). *Mass communication theory* (2nd ed.). London: Sage.

Murdock, G. (1993). Communications and the constitution of modernity. *Media, Culture and Society, 15,* 521–539.

Patterson, T. E. (1993). *Out of order.* New York: Knopf.

Rosen, J., & Taylor, P. (1992). *The new news v. the old news: The press and politics in the 1990s.* New York: Twentieth Century Fund.

Semetko, H. A., Blumler, J. G., Gurevitch, M., & Weaver, D. H., with Barkin, S., & Wilhoit, G. C. (1991). *The formation of campaign agendas: A comparative analysis of party and media roles in recent American and British elections.* Hillsdale, N.J.: Erlbaum.

Swanson, D. L. (1992). The political-media complex. *Communication Monographs, 59,* 397–400.

Tomlinson, J. (1994). A phenomenology of globalization? Giddens on global modernity. *European Journal of Communication, 9,* 149–173.

Weaver, D. H., Graber, D. A., McCombs, M. E., & Eyal, C. H. (1981). *Media agenda-setting in a presidential election.* New York: Praeger.

Wildavsky, A. (1987). Choosing preferences by constructing institutions: A cultural theory of preference formation. *American Political Science Review, 81,* 3–21.

[] • [] • [] • [] • []

Selected Bibliography

Agudelo Caceres, L. (1993). *Imagen y poder—La caída electoral de los grandes partidos* [Image and power: The fall of the major political parties]. Caracas: Eduven.

Asp, K. (1990). Medialization, media logic and mediarchy. *The Nordicom Review of Nordic Mass Communication Research*, No. 2, 47–50.

Benn, D. W. (1989). *Persuasion and Soviet politics*. Oxford: Basil Blackwell.

Bennett, W. L. (1992). *The governing crisis: Media, money, and marketing in American elections*. New York: St. Martin's Press.

Blumler, J. G. (1990). Elections, the media, and the modern publicity process. In M. Ferguson (Ed.), *Public communication—The new imperatives: Future directions for media research* (pp. 101–113). London: Sage.

Butler, D., & Kavanagh, D. (1992). *The British general election of 1992*. London: Macmillan.

Butler, D., & Ranney, A. (Eds.). (1992). *Electioneering: A comparative study of continuity and change*. Oxford: Clarendon Press.

Calvert, S., & Calvert, P. (1989). *Argentina: Political culture and instability*. Pittsburgh: University of Pittsburgh Press.

DiPalma, G. (1990). *To craft democracies: An essay on democratic transitions*. Berkeley: University of California Press.

Elazar, D., & Sandler, S. (Eds). (1992). *Who's the boss in Israel? Israel at the Polls: 1988–89*. Detroit: Wayne State University Press.

Esteinou, J. (Ed.). (1992). *Comunicación y democracia* [Communication and democracy]. Mexico City: Opción.

Franklin, B. (1994). *Packaging politics: Political communications in Britain's media democracy*. London: Edward Arnold.

Furtak, R. K. (Ed.). (1990). *Elections in socialist states*. New York: St. Martin's Press.

Giddens, A. (1990). *The consequences of modernity*. Cambridge: Polity Press.

Jamieson, K. H. (1992). *Dirty politics: Deception, distraction, and democracy*. New York: Oxford University Press.

Landi, O. (1992). *Devórame otra vez: Que hizo la televisión con la gente, que hace la gente con la televisión* [Devouring each other: What television does to the public, what the public does to television]. Buenos Aires: Grupo Editorial Planeta.

Lubrano, A., & Sanchez, R. H. (1987). *Del hombre completo a Jaime es como tu—Recuento de un proceso electoral venezolano* [From "renaissance man" to "ordinary Joe": An account of a Venezuelan political campaign]. Caracas: Vadell Hermanos Editores.

Mickiewicz, E. (1988). *Split signals: Television and politics in the Soviet Union*. New York: Oxford University Press.

Paletz, D., Jakubowicz, K., & Novosel, P. (Eds.). (In press). *Glasnost and after: Media and change in East and Central Europe.* Cresskill, N.J.: Hampton Press.

Panebianco, A. (1988). *Political parties: Organization and power.* Cambridge: Cambridge University Press.

Patterson, T. E. (1980). *The mass media election: How Americans choose their president.* New York: Praeger.

Patterson, T. E. (1993). *Out of order.* New York: Alfred A. Knopf.

Petersson, O. (1994). *The government and politics of the Nordic countries.* Stockholm: Fritzes.

Popkin, S. (1991). *The reasoning voter: Communication and persuasion in presidential campaigns.* Chicago: University of Chicago Press.

Schoenbach, K. (1992). Mass media and election campaigns in Germany. In F. J. Fletcher (Ed.), *Media, elections and democracy* (pp. 63–86). Toronto: Dundurn Press.

Semetko, H. A., Blumler, J. G., Gurevitch, M., & Weaver, D. H., with Barkin, S., & Wilhoit, G. C. (1991). *The formation of campaign agendas: A comparative analysis of party and media roles in recent American and British elections.* Hillsdale, N.J.: Erlbaum.

Semetko, H. A., & Schoenbach, K. (1994). *Germany's "unity election": Voters and the media.* Cresskill, N.J.: Hampton Press.

Vaudagna, M. (Ed.). (1991). *Il partito americano e l'Europa* [The American political party and Europe]. Milan: Feltrinelli.

Wattenberg, M. J. (1990). *The decline of American political parties.* Cambridge: Cambridge University Press.

Wattenberg, M. J. (1992). *The rise of candidate-centered politics.* Cambridge, Mass.: Harvard University Press.

Wiatr, J. J. (Ed.). *The politics of democratic transformation: Poland after 1989.* Warsaw: Scholar Agency.

[] • [] • [] • [] • []

Index

[] • [] • [] • [] • []

About the Editors
and Contributors

KENT ASP holds a Chair in Journalism in the Department of Journalism and Mass Communication at Göteborg University (Sweden). His research and interests concern journalism and politics, media power, and democracy. Professor Asp is also Director of the Swedish Media Election Studies.

JAY G. BLUMLER is Emeritus Professor at the University of Leeds (England), where he directed the Centre for Television Research until his retirement in 1989. From 1983 to 1995, he was also Professor of Journalism at the University of Maryland (USA). A Past President and Fellow of the International Communication Association, he is the International Editor of the *Journal of Communication*, a Founding Co-Editor of the *European Journal of Communication*, and a Research Consultant to the U.K. Broadcasting Standards Council. His principal books concerned with political communication include the following: *Television in Politics: Its Uses and Influence* (with D. McQuail, 1968), *The Challenge of Election Broadcasting* (with M. Gurevitch and J. Ives, 1977), *Communicating to Voters: Television in the First European Parliamentary Elections* (1983), *The Formation of Campaign Agendas* (with H. Semetko, M. Gurevitch, and D. Weaver, 1991), and *The Crisis of Public Communication* (with M. Gurevitch, 1995).

DAN CASPI is Senior Lecturer and Head of Communication Studies at the Open University of Israel. His research concerns Israeli communication institutions and political communications. He is Chairperson of the Israel Communication Association and has served as consultant to the Israeli Ministry of Education and Israeli Educational Television for educational programs on communications. Among his major publications are: *The Mediators: The Mass Media in Israel 1948–1990* (Hebrew, with Y. Limor, 1992), *Media Decentralization: The Case of Israel's Local Newspapers* (1986), and *The Roots of Begin's Success: The 1981 Elections* (with A. Diskin and E. Gutman, 1984).

PETER ESAIASSON is Associate Professor of Political Science at Göteborg University (Sweden). Formerly, he was a Visiting Scholar at Arizona State University (USA). His research interests concern election campaigns, legislative behavior, political leadership, and representative democracy.

KAROL JAKUBOWICZ is a Lecturer at the Institute of Journalism, University of Warsaw (Poland). He is also Chief Expert, the National Broadcasting Council of Poland, and holds the position of Deputy Chairman, Board of Directors, Polish Television Ltd. Dr. Jakubowicz's research interests concern media and especially broadcasting policy, comparative broadcasting systems, transformation of broadcasting systems, and media and change in Central and Eastern Europe. He has published extensively on these subjects in scholarly books and journals in Poland and internationally.

DENNIS KAVANAGH is Professor in the Department of Politics and Communications at the University of Liverpool (England). He is author of *Thatcherism and British Politics: The End of Consensus* (2nd ed., 1990) and co-author (with D. Butler) of *The British General Election of 1992*, as well as co-editor of *The Major Effect* (1994). His latest work is *Election Campaigning: The New Marketing of Politics* (1995).

PAOLO MANCINI is Professor of Sociology of Communication and Academic Director of the School of Broadcast Journalism at the Universitá di Perugia (Italy). He has published several books in Italy: *Videopolitica* (1985), *Come Vincere le Elezioni* (1989), *Guardando il Telegiornale* (1991), *Il Giornalismo e le Sue Regole* (1992). A number of his papers have been published in such international journals as *Theory and Society, European Journal of Communication,* and *Journal of Communication.* His research concerns primarily political communication and comparative analysis of mass media systems.

JOSÉ ANTONIO MAYOBRE is Director of the National Audiovisual Archives of Venezuela, a major program within the Venezuelan National Library Institute, and Professor of Mass Communication at the "Andres Bello" Catholic University of Caracas. His teaching and research concern the relationship between international communications, diplomacy, and new communication technologies, as well as communication theory and communication and development. He was formerly Executive Director of the International Center for the Study of Communication and Development (CIEDESCO) in Caracas, from which he is on leave at present. Previously, he was Director of the Foreign Affairs Institute at the Venezuelan Ministry of Foreign Affairs and a member of the UNESCO Secretariat in Paris. He headed the Venezuelan delegation to UNESCO's International Programme for the Development of Communication from 1984 to 1994, and served as the Programme's Vice-Chairman for Latin America and the Caribbean. His major works include the following: *Informacion, Dependencia y Desarrollo* (1978) and *La Labor de SSIFO: Los Intentos por Reforma la Television en Venezuela* (1993).

GIANPIETRO MAZZOLENI is Associate Professor of Sociology of Communication at the Universitá di Salerno (Italy). He is author of a number of research studies and publications in the field of political communication. He is a member of the Euromedia Research Group and corresponding editor of the *Journal of Communication*.

ELLEN MICKIEWICZ is James R. Shepley Professor of Public Policy Studies, Professor of Political Science, and Director of the DeWitt Wallace Center for Communications and Journalism of the Terry Sanford Institute of Public Policy, Duke University (USA). Also, she is Director of the Commission on Radio and Television Policy of Duke University and the Carter Center of Emory University, and a Fellow of the Carter Center. Her book, *Split Signals: Television and Politics in the Soviet Union* (Oxford), received the Electronic Media Book of the Year Award from the National Association of Broadcasters and the Broadcast Education Association. She is author or editor of five other books, and her articles have appeared in such journals as *American Political Science Review, Public Opinion Quarterly, Slavic Review,* and *Journal of Communication,* and newspapers such as *The New York Times* and *Corriere della Sera.* She has served as adviser to the Council for International Exchange of Scholars and the Kennan Institute of the Woodrow Wilson Center. She is a member of the Council on Foreign Relations and a former President of the American Association for the Advancement of Slavic Studies. Currently, she is writing a book on television and democratization in Russia to be published by Oxford University Press. Her research has been supported by Guggenheim and Ford Fellowships and grants from the Eurasia Foundation, Ford Foundation, John and Mary R. Markle Foundation, Rockefeller Foundation, and W. Alton Jones Foundation.

DAN NIMMO is a Visiting Scholar in Political Science at Baylor University (USA). He has served on the faculties of the Universities of Houston, Missouri, Oklahoma, and Tennessee. Author and editor of numerous volumes in political communication, his most recent books are the following: *The Political Pundits* (1992), *The New Propaganda* (1992), and *Comedy and Democracy* (in press).

T. J. NOSSITER is Visiting Professor in Politics at the University of Leeds (England). Prior to his retirement, he served for twenty-two years as, variously, Professor of Government, Dean of the Graduate School, and an Academic Governor at the London School of Economics and Political Science. His research has focused on Indian politics and on television and politics in Britain. Currently, he is studying the political context of economic reform in India. His major publications are the following: *Imagination and Precision in the Social Sciences* (1971), *Influence, Opinion, and Political Idioms in Reformed England, 1973–74* (1975), *Communism in Kerala* (1982), *Marxist State Governments in India* (1987), and *Range and Quality of Broadcasting Services* (1986).

ANDREI RICHTER is a member of the faculty of the School of Journalism at Moscow State University (Russia). His prime teaching and research areas concern mass media regulation and international journalism. Dr. Richter is the editor of *Zakonodatelstvo I praktika sredstv massovio informatsii* (Law and Practice of Mass Media), a monthly bulletin published in Russia, and an Associate Editor of the New York–based *Post-Soviet Media Law and Policy Newsletter.* He is author or editor of about forty articles, chapters, and books, the most recent being an extensive report on "Journalism and War," which concerns Russian mass media coverage of the military actions in Chechnya.

JUAN I. ROSPIR is Professor of Public Opinion in the Faculty of Information Science at the Universidad Complutense de Madrid (Spain). His research interests include electoral campaigns, political communication, and the history of public opinion, and he was one of the organizers of the first international meetings concerned with political communication to be held in Spain (in 1992 and 1993). His major publications in political communication are *Opinión Pública y Comunicación Política* (co-author, 1990) and *Comunicación Política* (co-editor, 1995).

KLAUS SCHOENBACH is Professor of Journalism and Communication Research and Director of the Department of Journalism and Communication Research at the University of Music and Theatre, Hannover (Germany). Formerly, he was Director of the Content Analysis Department of ZUMA in Mannheim (Germany), a member of the faculties of the universities of Muenster and Munich (Germany), and visiting professor at Cleveland State University, Indiana University, and San Jose State University (USA). His major teaching and research interests concern mass media and elections, and audience and media effects research. His major publications on these subjects include *Audience Responses to Media Diversification: Coping with Plenty* (with L. Becker) and *Germany's "Unity Election": Voters and the Media in 1990* (with H. Semetko).

DAVID L. SWANSON is Professor and Head of the Department of Speech Communication, University of Illinois at Urbana–Champaign (USA). His research concerns the social effects of mass communication, with particular attention to the role of media in politics. His scholarly work on these subjects has appeared in various journals and volumes in the United States, Europe, and Asia, and includes *The Uses and Gratifications Approach to Mass Communication* (in press), *New Directions in Political Communication* (with D. Nimmo), and *The Nature of Human Communication* (with J. Delia).

SILVIO R. WAISBORD is Assistant Professor of Communication at Rutgers University (USA). His research interests are international broadcasting, global media and cultures, and press and democracy in Latin America. He is author of *El Gran Desfile: Campañas Electorales y Medios de Communicacion* (1995), and has published articles on media and politics in Latin America in the *Journal of Communication* and *Political Communication*.

ISBN 0-275-95182-0

90000>

EAN

9 780275 951825

HARDCOVER BAR CODE